THE BEST PLACES FOR EVERYTHING

PETER GREENBERG

The Ultimate Insider's Guide to the Greatest Experiences Around the World

RODALE.

Rodale books may be purchased for business or promotional use or for special sales.
For information, please write to:
Special Markets Department, Rodale Inc., 733 Third Avenue, New York, NY 10017.

Printed in the United States of America
Rodale Inc. makes every effort to use acid-free ♾, recycled paper ♻.

Book design by Mark Michaelson
Cover illustrations by John Pirman

**Library of Congress Cataloging-in-Publication Data is on file with the
publisher.**

ISBN-13: 978–1–60961–829–2   paperback

Distributed to the trade by Macmillan
2   4   6   8   10   9   7   5   3   1   paperback

We inspire and enable people to improve their lives and the world around them.
www.rodaleboooks.com

To my mother,
who inspired me to travel,
then encouraged it,
and then worried that
I couldn't afford it.

CONTENTS

GREAT FOODS AND DRINKS
OF THE WORLD

EDUCATIONAL TRAVEL

SHOPPING

AND EVERYTHING ELSE...

INTRODUCTION

I have been traveling the world since I was 6 months old and actually have the documentation to prove it. In fact, I flew so much as a baby that one airline—American Airlines—presented my parents with a framed certificate inducting me as the first member of its "Sky Cradle Club."

I was a million miler many times over before I was 26. And if you add up just the official flight miles I've earned since the frequent-flier programs were started in 1981, I'm well north of 24 million.

Through my years as a college journalist from Wisconsin (covering the wars in the Middle East and never letting school interfere with my education) and then as a correspondent for *Newsweek*, I traveled to 151 countries.

Currently, I spend about 300 days a year traveling the world, either for my nationally syndicated radio show (broadcast from a different location around the world each week) or on assignment as the travel editor for CBS News.

I've seen astounding beauty and staggering poverty and tragedy. I've seen the worst and, in my admittedly charmed life, I've also seen the best: from the favelas outside Rio to the guarded mansions of Cairo, from the backroads of Calcutta to the precious Côte d'Azur; from the top of the Jungfrau to deep caves in Australia; from the barren Chukchi Sea above Alaska to the intense heat of the Wadi Rum in Jordan. If the list seems endless . . . that's because it is.

But this book is not about how to collect frequent-flier miles. It's not even about destinations as a primary focus. Instead, the destinations in this book are the enablers to the best experiences. If you define "travel" as one of the great experiences of life that are meant to be shared, then I am happy to share my experiences with you. I don't have a personal bucket list. I'd like to think—as self-serving as this sounds—that I *am* a living bucket list.

Not surprisingly, I am constantly being asked by just about everyone to name my choices for best, and the travel categories are almost endless. After resisting for many years (partly because I didn't think I could give it the completeness it needed), I've now been able to compile *The Best Places for Everything*. It's based on my personal travel history of comparison and constant points of reference, relevance, and long-term value. In this book, I answer the question of "best" with a caveat: It's not done in an arbitrary way, but by personal experience, measured by relative terms, not absolute or impossible ones.

This book is not about where to go or how to get there. It's about how to get the best experience when you get there. It's about accessibility—to be able to do things when you're there that no one else knows about or think they can't experience. Things like:

- Circumventing the tourist-filled tango shows of Buenos Aires in favor of dancing with the locals in a tucked-away *milonga*
- Getting access to one of the most coveted private golf course in America AND finding the affordable public golf courses that are, well, on par with the iconic spots
- Finding the exact whitewater rapids, mountain biking trails, and ski slopes to suit your level of expertise
- Tasting—and then learning the secrets of how to make—your favorite dishes, from Mexico to Italy to China
- Discovering the best place to shop for specialty items, whether you're in the market for perfume in Paris or custom-made suits in Hong Kong

Believe it or not, I hate top 10 lists and words that end in "st." You know these words: *most, greatest, loveliest, coolest,* and yes, of course . . . *best.* Words that end with "st" are the tyranny perpetrated—often with the best of intentions—by the travel industry. These are red flags that concern me as a journalist and as a consumer. They are often confusing, if not intentionally misleading, and in a world already overrun with hyperbole and absolute terms, they should bother you as well. They perpetuate a brochure language that, in the long run, angers just about everyone already conditioned to live in a world of unrealistic expectations.

There are some hotels out there that claim they've been awarded six and seven "stars" and are thus categorized as the best in the world. Well, technically. A little research quickly reveals that the "stars" were awarded to the hotel, *by* the hotel. Or in some countries, the stars are nothing more than a government indication of the rates they charge. The "best"? Hardly. But easily the most expensive.

The Best Places for Everything was a research-intensive project that was assembled with a 24/7 global clock by my team of great researchers and assistants, who sourced and fact-checked tirelessly. This book is, by definition, subjective, but fair and with portfolio.

Please feel free to agree or disagree with my choices. After all, in a world where permanence and consistency of quality are often short-lived, where experiential one-upsmanship has become the name of the travel game, I am, of course, prepared to be . . . bested!

OUTDOOR ADVENTURES

Best Places to Do

BIRD-WATCHING

As I travel around the world, I meet more and more birders. They are passionate, they get excited—in their own quiet way—about their discoveries of a species or a behavior of one, and they are the first to explain when nature is in sync and when it isn't. If you want to see the natural world in a new light, ask a birder. Or become one yourself!

Bird-watching, or "birding," can be done on nearly every continent and in both urban and wilderness environments. Picking the best place to see birds depends on what kind you want to see and in what volume.

NORTH AMERICA

The area around **Utah**'s Great Salt Lake offers some of the most celebrated birding in western North America. Millions of shorebirds, ducks, and other waterbirds live in the region, including more than 250 species that nest and feed on Antelope Island. You can spot gulls, egrets, and chukars year-round, but the big attraction is the bald eagle, which appears between January and March.

The 760-acre Bentsen–Rio Grande Valley State Park in the Lower Rio Grande Valley of **Texas,** just north of the Mexican border, is one of the top birding destinations in the United States, for good reason. The park, plus an additional 1,700 acres of adjoining US Fish and Wildlife refuge land, has a rich population of birds that aren't found anywhere else in the country, and it's home to the renowned World Birding Center. Birders come here year-round to spot everything from green jays, ferruginous pygmy-owls, gray hawks, and more. Every spring and fall, Swainson's and broad-winged hawks migrate in such large droves that they've been likened to a flying cloud.

The area around **Tucson,** the gateway city to southeastern Arizona, is one of the best places in North America for year-round bird-watching. It has a surprisingly varied terrain—including grasslands, wetlands, forests, and narrow canyons with creeks—which attracts a host of wildlife. The region is home to Tucson Mountain Park, Saguaro National Park, Agua Caliente Park, Tohono Chul Park, Coronado National Forest, the San Pedro Riparian National Conservation Area, and the Buenos Aires National Wildlife Refuge. In these spaces, you'll find hundreds of desert and water species, including at least five types of hummingbirds, cactus wrens, and the pygmy nuthatch.

You don't even need to leave Tucson city limits to see a variety of typical desert birds. Meander through the city's parks, washes, and undeveloped lots to catch a glimpse of what the area has to offer. Tucson Audubon Society has a nature shop inside Saguaro National Park that conducts bird walks on a regular basis. The Arizona-Sonora Desert Museum, located just west of the city, is also a good place to learn about the native birds and their habitats. And don't forget the Southeastern Arizona Bird Observatory in Bisbee (about 50 miles southeast of Tucson), where you can take guided bird walks, go on tours, and attend educational workshops at local birding hot spots.

Florida in general is ripe for birding—in fact, the state boasts the Great Florida Birding and Wildlife Trail, a 2,000-mile, self-guided nature highway. But if you have to choose one spot in the state to focus on, hone in on the south-central region. Its diverse habitat and areas of both temperate and subtropical climate draw more than 250 species of birds, including bald eagles, cerulean warblers, sandhill cranes, bobwhite quail, and grasshopper sparrows.

Also in Florida, the Merritt Island National Wildlife Refuge/Canaveral National Seashore, the J. N. "Ding" Darling National Wildlife Refuge, Everglades National Park, the St. Marks Wildlife Refuge, and Paynes Prairie Preserve State Park are just a few more places you can spot birds. In addition, the area has several sanctuaries and conservation operations, including the Suncoast Seabird Sanctuary in Indian Shores, the Conservancy of Southwest Florida in Naples, and Busch Gardens in Tampa. During the last weekend of January, Brevard County hosts the Space Coast Birding and Wildlife Festival, a 6-day annual event that is one of the most popular in the United States and features field trips, classes, and workshops.

Georgia's Colonial Coast Birding Trail includes a number of islands with prime birding opportunities. One of the best is on Jekyll Island where, by law, 65 percent of the island has to remain in its natural state. The North End Beach is a mix of beach, forest, and saltwater habitats that provide a range of birds including red-throated loons, least terns, scoters, and scaup. Just next door is Cumberland Island, Georgia's southernmost barrier island and a national seashore, where more than 335 species of birds have been recorded, including bald eagles and falcons.

To the north, more than 420 bird species can be spotted throughout the year in **Minnesota.** Because of its location on the Mississippi Flyway, a bird migration route that generally falls along the Mississippi River, you can see Canada geese and trumpeter swans migrating south for the winter. Duluth is home to Hawk Ridge Nature Reserve and the Hawk Ridge Bird Observatory, where at least 20 species of raptors and vultures fly down from Canada and northern Minnesota along the shores of Lake Superior. Peak migration takes place from mid-September to late October, with more than 1,000 raptors passing through Hawk Ridge each fall.

INTERNATIONAL

Veracruz in eastern **Mexico** is a favorite of experienced birders, as it hosts an unbelievable 650,000 migratory birds a week during the fall-winter season, plus more than 500 species that are either native or transient to the area. The sheer volume of birds derives from a variety of habitats that range from mountains to tropical rain forests to highland grasslands. Cardel is the place to go in October to see the "river of raptors," the incredible autumn migration when more than a million Swainson's and broad-winged hawks can pass overhead in a single day. Chichicaxtle, the San Julian Lagoon, the La Mancha ecological reserve, the Alvarado Wetlands, the Selva Zoque tropical rain forest, and the Sierra de los Tuxtlas range are great (and generally easily accessible) places to see migrating raptors, warblers, orioles, falcons, hummingbirds, parakeets, spoonbills, terns, kingfishers, and hundreds of other species.

A variety of different ecosystems, from rain forests to wetlands and coastal zones, allow for prime birding in the country of **Belize.** The Belize Audubon Society offers customized bird-watching tours in protected areas like Cockscomb Basin Wildlife Sanctuary, Crooked Tree Wildlife Sanctuary, Aguacaliente Wildlife Sanctuary, Mountain Pine Ridge Forest Reserve, Ambergris Caye, Caye Caulker, Half Moon Caye Natural Monument, and Red Bank Village. If you have to choose one, opt for the Crooked Tree Wildlife Sanctuary, which is packed with endemic species, meaning they are unique to that region. In fact, between October and January alone, you can catch sight of at least 120 bird species. Of course, you can go any time of year and get a great view.

You might expect the nearby Galapagos Islands to win out, but as far as overseas birding destinations go, **Ecuador** is a top pick—not only because of its variety of birds, but also its user-friendliness. The government and private enterprise have done a great job making trails accessible, encouraging the building of ecolodges, and promoting the country's mountains and cloud forests, which is where most of the birds are found. The Santa Lucia Cloud Forest Reserve is home to more than 394 different species of birds, including the rare white-faced nunbird, the wattled guan, the long-wattled umbrella bird, and more. Mindo is another area popular with birders. Located on the western slope of the Andes, it's the winter home of many temperate species and has one of the highest bird counts in the world. Favorite trails in the area include the Flat Loop Trail, the Rio Mindo Dirt Road, and the trail that runs along the Cordillera San Lorenzo.

Few places in the world compare to **Brazil** when it comes to birding. The bird population of Brazil is so abundant and diverse that enthusiasts will often return over and over to different parts of the country. The Pantanal wetlands is a massive wilderness paradise and is home to as many as 650 species of birds. We're talking mega-size, brilliantly colored birds like the hyacinth macaws and the turquoise-fronted parrot toucans, the rare helmeted woodpecker, and nocturnal creatures such as pygmy-owls. Alternately, in southeastern Brazil, Itatiaia National Park, the oldest national park in

A Bird's-Eye View in Belize

Headed to Belize on a cruise? Arrange your own independent shore excursion instead of following the rest of the cruise-ship crowds. The Belize Audubon Society can help point you in the right direction, like the Bird's Eye View Lodge and Tours that lies within a protected area and employs especially knowledgeable guides. www.birdseyeviewbelize.com

the country (established in 1937), is home to at least 250 species, about 50 of which are endemic. There are plenty of paths around the hotels that are easily explored on foot, including the Três Picos trail, or head to higher mountain elevations of Pico das Agulhas Negras.

With its diverse habitat and unique ecosystem, the Cape of Good Hope in **South Africa** is home to at least 250 species of birds. Located just a short drive south of Cape Town, the area's terrain ranges from rocky mountaintops to beaches and is home to birds such as the South African black-footed penguin, bush birds, curlew sandpipers, and ostriches. The Cape of Good Hope Nature Preserve and Cape Peninsula National Park are good places to explore, while Boulder's Beach, Kirstenbosch National Botanic Garden, and the Rondevlei Nature Reserve also offer prime viewing opportunities. Solo excursions are perfectly safe, but if you prefer not to go it alone, there are plenty of private small-group trips led by experienced local operators such as Lawson's Birding, Wildlife, and Custom Safaris. www.lawsons-africa.co.za

The island of **Madagascar** isn't so much known for its volume of bird species but its individuality. Out of about 285 species of birds, 100 are endemic. One of the easiest places to see a wide variety is the wetlands Lake Alarobia. This privately owned park is within a few miles of the capital city of Antananarivo, and it's filled with brilliantly plumed birds. From the Madagascar pond heron to the Madagascar kingfisher, you're sure to spot feathered creatures that you can't see anywhere else in the world. However, if you want go beyond the touristy areas, go about 3 hours east of the capital to the Perinet Special Reserve (also known as the Indri Special Reserve), a rain forest inside the Andasibe-Mantadia National Park. It's teeming with endemic birds as well as a thriving lemur population.

If there's one thing on your birding bucket list, it should be the tiny fairy penguins of **Australia,** which are known as little blue penguins in New Zealand. These are the smallest of the penguin species, and to watch them parading back from the sea at dusk is a sight you'll remember. Though touristy, the best place to see them in action is Phillip Island outside of Melbourne, which is home to one of the largest colonies in the world. Every day at sunset, you can sit on the beach and wait for the wild penguins to return from their day of feeding and waddle across the beach back to their burrows for the night. Well-enforced rules prohibit anyone from getting too close or taking photographs, and the walkways make it possible to see these little guys from all angles without disturbing them. In **New Zealand,** the penguins live all along the coastline, but they're easily spotted (along with the equally cute yellow-eyed penguins) at Penguin Place on the South Island's Otago Peninsula, near Dunedin.

Of 17 species of penguins, only a few inhabit **Antarctica,** but they're worth the trip. Whether it's the mighty emperor penguins (think *March of the Penguins*) or the chinstrap penguins (named for the thin black line under their chins), these creatures are best seen on an expedition cruise. The benefit of a guided cruise is that you can reach otherwise inaccessible areas. Lindblad Expeditions has partnered with *National Geographic* experts on the *National Geographic Explorer*, where you'll travel with naturalists who really know their stuff, whether you're cruising on the Zodiac, kayaking between ice floes, or hiking through the wild where penguins roam freely.

National Wildlife Refuges

Surround yourself with enthusiasts at a national wildlife refuge (www.fws. gov/refuges). These attract large numbers of birds and are the sites of bird festivals all around the country during spring and fall migrations. Catch sight of green jays and Altamira orioles during the Rio Grande Valley Birding Festival in Harlingen, **Texas,** which includes field trips to several area refuges. The majestic Festival of the Cranes takes place every November at the Bosque del Apache National Wildlife Refuge in **New Mexico,** where sandhill cranes and snow geese take to the skies at dawn and dusk. Search for bald and golden eagles at Wichita Mountains National Wildlife Refuge in **Oklahoma,** and see the unique scrub jays in **Florida**'s Hobe Sound, Lake Wales Ridge, and Merritt Island National Wildlife Refuges. If you really know your stuff, the Cache River Birding Blitz in **Illinois** involves teams competing to see who can identify the most species of birds in 24 hours in areas like the Cypress Creek National Wildlife Refuge and Crab Orchard National Wildlife Refuge.

BOATING

As someone who grew up on boats, I find that trying to write about the best places for boating is somewhat contradictory, because in my experience, any time I can get out on the water immediately qualifies as the best place for boating! Simple as that. Well, not so simple, because in the end, it gets down to your definition of boating. Are you going to physically operate the boat or passively enjoy your experience as a passenger? Sail or power? Ocean, bay, river, or lake? Rough water or calm? Beginner or perfect storm boating? You get the picture.

MOTORBOATS

The British Virgin Islands are known as the sailing capital of the world for a number of reasons: steady breezes, easy line-of-sight navigation, comfortable anchorages, and great yacht availability (not to mention it's an easy destination for Americans to reach, the language is English, and the currency is the US dollar). Adding to its appeal is the diversity of possibilities for water-based exploration and the abundance of onshore activities. Many of the best snorkeling, diving, and fishing spots in the area are only accessible by boat: the caves of Norman Island, the extensive reefs off Eustacia Island, and the famous wreck of the HMS *Rhone*. You're best off sailing December through May, outside of hurricane season, though the best game fishing tends to be in summer.

Spain's Balearic Islands—Majorca, Minorca, Ibiza, and Formentera—are well known to land-based vacationers, who come from all over Europe between April and November. But this is also a sailor's paradise. The sailing is varied but relatively calm, and there are dozens of marinas and anchorages. Add to that the fact that almost every make and model of boat imaginable are available to charter. You can hop from island to island or spend a week just circling one, stopping in a different port every night. At sea you can jump off the boat and go snorkeling at any of the dozens of reefs surrounding the

Iceboats

Surprisingly, sailing during winter is a popular sport—not on water but on ice. Wind powered and capable of speeds up to 100 mph, iceboats are like sailboats, but fitted with skis or runners to allow them to skate over frozen lakes. Iceboating clubs can be found throughout America, from **Maine**'s Chickawaukie Ice Boat Club to the Four Lakes Ice Yacht Club in Madison, **Wisconsin.**

islands, or cruise through the Cabrera natural marine reserve.

The Whitsunday Islands are a group of 74 mostly uninhabited islands lying approximately halfway between Brisbane and Cairns on the Great Barrier Reef in tropical North Queensland, **Australia.** Part of the Great Barrier Reef Marine Park, these islands are a nature lover's paradise. You can even see the abundant corals and thousands of fish from the boat. Start your trip from Hamilton Island, and the rest of the Whitsundays are within easy cruising distance. One of the most beautiful but little-known among Americans is Whitehaven Beach. Nara Inlet is another great one, and within easy hiking distance from the anchorage are aboriginal cave paintings. You're best off going in Australia's winter (May to September), when the weather is not oppressively hot and the deadly box jellyfish are gone.

The Sea of Cortéz is one of the richest ecosystems on the planet. Not only do dolphins and whales pass by, but you can also dive, fish, and swim with sea lions, rays, and other sea creatures. Big-game fishing is a huge draw as well, which is why most people prefer motor yachts—to get out into the deep-sea fishing grounds quickly. One really cool feature is the shore-side mangrove forests, where you'll encounter exotic birds, and you'll find plenty of open, unspoiled beaches at which to anchor. The desert brims with life, including small antelope herds, and the ancient forest of Cardon has cacti that stand more than 70 feet tall. Leave from La Paz, **Mexico,** and stop

Rent a Houseboat

Renting a houseboat with friends or family can be cheaper—and a lot more fun—than booking hotel rooms. Houseboat prices can range from $1,000 to $13,000 a week. You don't need to have a background in sailing. Most of these boats are easy to navigate, and there are experts at the marina who can help you out. Web sites such as Houseboating.org and Houseboatingworld.com allow you to browse vessels and destinations to fit your budget. Remember, one drawback to houseboat rentals is the price of gas. These boats burn through 8 to 18 gallons of gas an hour while moving at the slow pace of 5 to 10 miles per hour. To save money, anchor the boat as much as possible.

off at any number of seaside villages. Go between November and May, when the weather is mild and it's outside of hurricane season.

A little closer to home, take a motorboat to the San Juan and Gulf Islands, off the coast of **Washington** just south of the US-Canada border. This large sheltered body of water has short port-to-port passages, protected yet interesting waterways, and a great variety of onshore entertainment, which makes it a great cruising ground for bareboats in general and powerboats in particular. For more of an adventure, head north to Desolation Sound in Canadian waters, a pristine, remote location for those who want peace, dramatic scenery, and an abundance of wildlife.

SAILBOATS

Most people think of the Greek islands when they consider a Mediterranean yacht cruise, but the Dalmatian coast of **Croatia,** with its 1,000 offshore islands, offers an equally—if not better—sailing experience. The Dalmatian coast cruising grounds extend from Dubrovnik northwest to Zadar. An abundance of anchorages makes it easy to explore the rocky islets, ancient villages, unique flora and fauna, and translucent waters of the islands. Unlike other parts of the Mediterranean, this area still contains lots of fish and other sea life. Hotspots include Mljet, Korcula, and Lastovo, plus the harbors and coves along the rugged Peljesac Peninsula and the nearby Elafiti Islands. Though there are plenty of remote, bare-bones places to anchor and have a secluded getaway amongst the 500 or so anchorages, the Dalmatian coast also boasts at least 50 fully serviced marinas in which you'll find restaurants, hot showers, mini-marts, and weather charts. This makes things easy for first-timers without much boating experience. The best time to go? Anytime from April through the end of October.

For a variety of compelling reasons, not the least of which is cost, **Turkey** is another great alternative to Greece and has two seas you can sail: the Aegean and the Mediterranean. In addition to untouched bays and crystal clear waters, there are hundreds of off-shore islands. The scenery is replete with ancient ruins and archaeological sites such as sunken Roman harbors and crumbling crusader castles. You'll find the most amenities in Gocek, Bodrum, and Marmaris, all of which have modern, well-equipped marinas. But don't miss out on the chance to charter a *gulet*, a traditional two-masted Turkish sailing vessel. These schooners can be chartered with a full crew including captain, cook, and deckhands. Turkey is also host to several international sailing tournaments such as the Extreme Sailing Series, the Farr 40 European Tour and Championship, and the ISAF Youth World Championship.

Tahiti, comprised of 118 islands, offers a unique combination of lush tropical atolls, volcanic peaks, blue lagoons, and immense coral reefs. All of this and the good, steady trade winds make it an ideal place to cruise under wind power. There are literally thousands of anchorages from which to explore both the underwater and land-based wonders. You can go ashore on the main islands of Raiatea, Tahaa, Bora Bora, and Huahine, or immerse yourself in the numerous fringing reefs and lagoons. You'll see some of the greatest creatures of the ocean here,

Jet Boating

Jet boating is a favorite activity of adrenaline junkies. It involves whipping around a river in a small, powerful jet engine–propelled boat at speeds up to 50 mph. G-forces pull your body to and fro as you feel the wind in your hair and the mist on your face. Shotover Jet (www.shotoverjet.com) in Queenstown, **New Zealand,** was one of the first places in the world to offer commercial jet boating, and it continues to be a breathtaking ride of a lifetime. In **Montreal,** you can zip up the St. Lawrence River with Saute-Moutons (www.jetboatingmontreal.com) in a crazy, wet and wild ride. Take a spin with Whirlpool Jet Boat Tours (www.whirlpooljet.com) in the Niagara Gorge in **Niagara Falls.** In Portland, **Oregon,** you can go for a thrill ride up the Willamette River in the spring and summer with Willamette Jetboat Excursions (www.willamettejet.com).

including giant manta rays and sharks. Or go farther afield and explore the more remote island groups: the Tuamotu atolls; the unspoiled and mysterious Marquesas; the Austral Islands; or even the Gambier Islands, which are way off the beaten track. This region is so vast and varied that it would take weeks to cover it all, but the good news is you can sail year-round. The best time of all is when the trade winds are blowing between April and October.

Just like the Greece-Turkey comparison, look to **Fiji** for more affordable boat charters. Boating in Fiji has to be experienced to be believed. With 330 volcanic islands in a balmy, tropical climate, Fiji has some of the best water-based activities in the world, so it's no surprise that boating is also a must. This is a complex, often treacherous, reef system with unpredictable weather, so unless you're an experienced boater, charter a crewed vessel. Launch points are located on Taveuni and Savusavu, among others, where you can set out and either island hop throughout the archipelago or spend a day diving or snorkeling among the reefs.

The **Chesapeake Bay** is a 200-mile-long estuary that has cruising grounds all the way from Chesapeake City, Maryland, in the north to Norfolk, Virginia, in the south. There are hundreds of fishing villages, islands, marshes, coves, and tributaries to explore, plus many quiet anchorages to spend the night. You can go ashore and eat blue crabs and oysters, or stay on board for fishing and spotting seabirds (there are several bird sanctuaries in the bay). Since the bay is protected by land on both sides, the current and wind are not too strong, making it ideal for less-experienced bareboaters (some even use it as a training ground for the Caribbean). The climate is much milder than the eastern shore, and the season runs roughly from May 1 to November 15—but sometimes you can sail as early as April, depending on the weather. Tip: In the height of summer when the winds are less strong, you may want to consider chartering a motor yacht instead of a sailing yacht. However, during the edges of the season, when winds are more reliable, a sailing yacht is a good bet.

The **Great Lakes** are often overlooked, but those familiar with the area know that they offer a unique, grassroots, family-oriented sailing experience in the heartland of America. Despite the cold, the protected waters mean it's friendly even for amateur boaters. With five different lakes to choose from and more coastline than the East and West Coasts combined, there are plenty of options. For example, Bayfield, Wisconsin, is a popular launch spot on windy Lake Superior, whose north shore features lots of small islands that can be slowly explored. The Apostle Islands, Isle Royal National Park, and the Crown Land on the shores of Ontario, Canada, are other favorite spots. On Lake Erie, you can launch from western points such as Put-In Bay and explore the nearby small islands. (And even though Erie is the busiest lake of the five, there are still far fewer boaters here than in warm-water sailing destinations like Florida or the Bahamas.) Lake Ontario offers more than 1,000 islands to explore plus access to the St. Lawrence River, which is the gateway to the Atlantic (if you're really ambitious). Throughout the region, the season runs from mid-May through mid-October, but it can start a little earlier for the lower lakes.

TALL SHIPS

Tall ships are traditional old-fashioned sailing vessels with tall masts and full sails. Typical rig varieties include schooners, brigantines, brigs, and barks. The navies of many countries and merchant marine organizations use them to train sailors. There are many ways for travelers to experience the majesty and grace of tall ships.

Almost every major American port city has at least one resident tall ship that is open to tour, such as the *Pride of Baltimore* in Baltimore, the USS *Constitution* in Boston, or the *Californian* in San Diego. Sometimes they are taken out for short jaunts around the harbor. Check with your local harbor or maritime museum for details on this. Tip: The new Boston Tea Party Ship and Museum in Boston Harbor feature two full-scale replica tall ships built to historical specifications.

Every year, somewhere in the world there is at least one tall ship race or challenge. In 2012, which is the 200th anniversary of the War of 1812, Tall Ships America is organizing a commemorative Atlantic coast Tall Ships Challenge in May and July between Nova Scotia; Newport, Rhode Island; Charleston, South Carolina; and Savannah, Georgia. In 2013 there is a similar challenge on the Great Lakes between mid-June and late September. www.sailtraining.org/tallships/index.php

You can even learn to sail like our forefathers did by taking tall ship sail training courses. You learn not only navigation, rigging, and ship maintenance, but also bigger lessons about teamwork, self-reliance, and discipline. These courses are especially popular for teaching independence and leadership skills to older kids and teenagers. The American Sail Training Association has a searchable database of hundreds

Boat Races

The Rolex Sydney Hobart Yacht Race, held every December, is one of the iconic boat races in the world. It runs from Sydney, **Australia,** across the Tasman Sea to Hobart, the capital of the island of Tasmania. The best place to watch the New Year's Eve finish is at Lyne Park or Neilsen Park in Hobart. Pack a picnic and a bottle of wine, and enjoy the summer weather while you watch the yachts cruise in. http://rolexsydneyhobart.com/default.asp

At the Hong Kong Dragon Boat Festival every June, hundreds of these long, brightly colored paddle-powered boats race each other on the Shing Mun River in **Hong Kong** to commemorate an ancient Chinese hero. You can feel the excitement in the air as drums beat on the shore and crowds roar in support of their "team." The fireworks at the end of the three-day festival are spectacular. www.hkdba.com.hk/eng/index.asp

The International Festival of the Sea (Les Tonnerres de Brest) in Brest, **France,** is a unique event that happens only once every four years. More than 2,000 traditional watercraft from 25 countries converge on the waters around the tip of Brittany, including fishing vessels from Africa, towering windjammers, and tall ships from Russia. Festivities include the parade of classic yachts, the onshore Viking and Russian villages, plus lots of food and craft displays. www.lestonnerresdebrest2012.fr

of ships. www.sailtraining.org/membervessels/database.php

Last, but certainly not least, more than 100 commercially operated tall ships around the world are available to take you on a weeklong (or longer) vacation to various destinations around the world. These are a fun alternative to taking a traditional cruise ship because they are more intimate, less formal, and offer you a chance to see the day-to-day workings of the ship. Not to mention you can visit smaller, more interesting ports of call, which larger cruise lines cannot access. Sailing Ship Adventures (www.sailingshipadventures.com) is a niche agency that connects travelers with tall ships everywhere from the Mediterranean to the Caribbean to Scandinavia to Thailand. What's great about this agency is that they can match you up with exactly the kind of experience and ship you want, because not all are created

---

Luxury Yachts

For those who can afford it, or have about 25 friends who want to chip in, how about renting one of these mega-yachts? The *Delphine* is a 78-meter classic motor yacht that plies the waters of the **Mediterranean.** For a mere $74,000 per day, you (and up to 25 other guests) get to relax in the onboard Turkish bath and steam room (with mosaic dressing rooms), beautify in the onboard hair and beauty salon, work out in the fully decked out gym (with massage table and minibar), and watch the flat-screen televisions, which are normally hidden behind mahogany wood panels and original works of art.

Or how about the elegant sailing yacht *Southern Cloud*? This **Australia**-based boat that sails between the Great Barrier Reef and Sydney may be "only" 40 meters, but it packs a lot into the space. The teak decks, huge amount of water-sports equipment, and suspended poop deck make it seem like a bargain at only $10,000 per day. (Both of these yachts are available through CharterWorld.com.)

In the **Caribbean,** you and 11 of your closest friends can charter the 205-foot *Baton Rouge* from BurgessYachts.com. It's a steep $630,000 per week, but look at what you get: six—yes *six*—decks, a crew of 16, a pool with jet stream, a sundeck that converts to a party deck (complete with disco), and a sea-level beach club lounge with an impressive inventory of water toys and tenders.

equal. Some of the ships have been retrofitted with luxury fixtures, and you'll travel in top-notch comfort. Others are intentionally kept spartan, the way they were in the 18th century, for those who want a more "authentic" experience. Some of the ships encourage participation in helping to sail the ship (particularly on transatlantic voyages), while others (i.e., Caribbean) just expect you to sit back, relax, and enjoy the weather. Sailing Ship Adventures also offers voyages specifically for sail training, including for active disabled people who find other ships inaccessible.

LEARN TO SAIL CLOSE TO HOME

Annapolis Sailing School in Annapolis, **Maryland,** has a range of classes and prices for all levels, from a beginner's one-day Basic Seamanship course to an advanced Preparation for Bareboat Chartering course. The KidShip Program is aimed at kids learning to sail. They learn basic skills and water safety on small, responsive boats in 2- and 5-day programs. www.annapolissailing.com

With the **Florida** based Offshore Sailing School, you can learn to sail, cruise, or race in waters around the world, including New York,

Ecoboating

One of the most environmentally sensitive ways to see the world is by boat—but not just any boat. Here's where you can jump on for a green travel experience. Taking a gondola ride in **Venice** is a classic travel experience that won't spoil the environment. But there are also some options you may not have heard about, where you can be ecofriendly and enjoy the ride. In **London** a solar-powered shuttle sails back and forth on the Serpentine, a lake in Hyde Park. In **Australia** you can sail through a tropical rain forest on the remote Daintree River on the *Solar Whisper* and see crocodiles in action. On the Krabi River near Phuket, **Thailand,** bamboo rafts are available for floats down the river—the ultimate carbon footprint–free form of water transportation.

New Jersey, Maryland, Tortola (British Virgin Islands), and parts of Florida. If you're a beginner, try the 3- or 5-day Learn to Sail course. Or try the weeklong Fast Track to Catamaran Cruising course in Tortola. For those who feel the need for speed, there is an annual high-speed Performance Racing program in Captiva Island, Florida. www.offshoresailing.com

At Pacific Yachting and Sailing, you can learn to sail on the beautiful Monterey Bay in **California.** They offer a full array of group courses and certifications from beginner to advanced, plus women-only courses, private instruction, and multiday lessons where you get to live aboard the boat you're learning to sail. www.pacificsail.com

Boston Sailing Center is one of the best places to learn to sail in New England. Housed in a Louisiana riverboat just steps from Faneuil Hall marketplace. From May to September, a complete roster of beginner through advanced courses combines classroom learning with on-the-water experience. Specialty courses include Coastal Passage Making and Night Sailing. In winter you can take navigation courses and attend sailing seminars. www.bostonsailingcenter.com

Broker a Deal

Charter yacht brokers (and agents) take the hassle out of finding a boat. Contact one in advance of your trip to be the liaison between local yacht owners-managers and yourself. Brokers can find you a boat to rent that meets your specifications as far as location, size, type (crewed, power), and price, and you won't pay a cent for the service. CharterWorld.com is an independent broker-agent that specializes in luxury crewed yacht charters and sails on every continent except Antarctica. It can connect you with thousands of charter boats and even offers around-the-world charters. Moorings.com offers both crewed and bareboat charters worldwide and sunsail.com has yachts in 30 different locations.

CANAL BARGING

Speed has its limitations, and this is almost always true about travel. Getting there can still be half, if not most of the fun, especially if you pick the right mode of transport. And that's where barges come in. That's right—barges.

With nearly 5,000 miles of navigable waters, **France** has the largest and most intricate inland waterway system of any country, which is why it should come as no surprise that it is home to some of the best scenic canal barging.

Canal de Bourgogne in Burgundy is what many people envision when they think about cruising through French wine country. Served by barges like the 20-passenger *Litote* and the six-passenger *Fandango*, the canal twists through the Ouche River valley. It passes vineyards, Gothic churches, Renaissance châteaux, and picturesque villages such as Dijon and Beaune. The towpaths have been paved for easy cycling or walking when the barge docks for the day. Don't miss a side visit to Clos de Vougeot, a vineyard bound by stone walls where monks planted the first vine in the 12th century, as well as to the medieval Château de Châteauneuf and the hilltop basilica of St. Mary Magdalene in Vézelay. Best of all, this route will take you to Les Halles, the enormous covered market in Dijon. You'll find the lowest rates in the shoulder season, usually early March through late April and mid-October to early November.

INSIDER'S TIP

Europe is also a great place to get hands-on barging experience. Although driving a barge isn't difficult, the intimidating part is navigating the canal locks and lift bridges. If you're a first-timer, your best bet is the Canal du Rhone à Sète in the Camargue region of southern France. It has only three locks total, and it's a more off-the-beaten path option with old fishing villages and Mediterranean beaches. Le Boat (www.leboat.com) is the major provider of self-drive barges in Europe, and will set you up with instructions on how to operate the barge and provide emergency support along the way.

Food lovers can splurge on a Michelin cruise on the Burgundy Canal du Nivernais and Yonne River on board the *Randle*. You can charter the entire boat, which fits only four guests, and comes with a Cordon Bleu chef who prepares your breakfast and lunch. With brokers like Edge Charter (www.edgecharter.com), you create your own itinerary: Dine at four Michelin-starred restaurants in a week, including the two-star le Grand Hôtel de l'Espérance in the village of Saint-Père and the renowned three-star La Côte Saint-Jacques in Joigny. And to avoid the tourist wine trail, you can arrange visits with small, artisan winemakers in villages like Tennay and Irancy.

To explore a lesser known region, skip the well-trod Burgundy and Bordeaux regions in favor of the 300-year-old Canal du Midi in Languedoc-Roussillon. This is a considerably more laid-back region for wine lovers, and yet it's an unusual gem because of how difficult it is to grow wine grapes on the foothills of the Pyrenees Canal du Midi is a designated UNESCO World Heritage site, and its network of waterways stretches nearly 225 miles from the Atlantic to the Mediterranean. It's considered an engineering marvel, with hundreds of aqueducts, bridges, and locks connecting the waters, but to barge here feels like you've traveled back a few centuries. While sailing on a barge like the four-passenger *Alouette*, you'll travel between Béziers on the Mediterranean and the medieval walled fortress town of Carcassonne, passing by vineyards, Roman ruins, and medieval villages along the way. Languedoc-Roussillon has a typically Mediterranean climate, with hot summers and mild winters, so you can go any time of year, but wine lovers should go in October—this is harvest season when the region is alive with festivals and events.

Savvy travelers like the **Alsace-Lorraine** region because it's a little off the beaten path. The area borders France and Germany and features distinct architecture, the capital of Strasbourg, the town of Colmar with its "Little Venice" district, and the famous Saint-Louis-Arzviller inclined plane. This is a hill that the barge ascends via a specialized boat lift, which is considered an engineering marvel. It enables the barge to cross a stretch of the Vosges mountains without making a long detour.

Want a gourmet experience outside of France? The 10-passenger *Shannon Princess II* follows the lower River Shannon in **Ireland,** between Athlone and Killaloe. Chef Olivia Power, trained at Ballymaloe Cookery School (which is at the forefront of modern Irish cuisine), uses locally sourced ingredients from artisan cheese makers and bakers. She'll even take you on foraging excursions and bring you back to the barge for a seasonal cooking lesson. As you sail the river, you'll visit the ancient Clonmacnoise ruins, medieval castles, kitchen gardens, traditional craftsmen, and rural old villages along the way. www.shannonprincess.com

Llangollen Canal is a stunning 41-mile, 3-day journey through **England** and **Wales.** The canal starts near the town of Nantwich in Cheshire and ends near the Welsh village of Llangollen. Along the way, you'll span the border of both countries as you pass by sheep pastures, peat bogs, tree-lined lakes, the ruins of Castell Dinas Bran, and the foothills of Snowdonia. The canal also traverses the Pontcysyllte Aqueduct, a feat of masonry engineering, which carries

---

INSIDER'S TIP

Did you know that on many barge cruises, you can jump on and off the boat throughout the day? When the barge is in a lock, you can jump out and bike, walk, or jog along the towpath that parallels the canal. If you're near a village, you can even take a detour through town to see the sights. Since barges only go 3 to 4 miles per hour, there's little chance the barge will outpace you. When you're tired of exploring, simply hop back on. Many people fear that barges will be too claustrophobic, considering their small size, so knowing that they can hop off at regular intervals is reassuring.

---

the canal 120 feet over the River Dee. Another less-spectacular aqueduct carries the canal over the River Ceiriog and passes through several tunnels. Nature enthusiasts love the fact that the canal runs right through the Fenn's, Whixall, and Bettisfield Mosses National Nature Reserve on the border of Wales and England.

It's no surprise that you can barge through **Holland**'s ample waterways and even less of a surprise that the best time to do it is in spring tulip season. For a more unexpected itinerary, the *Marjorie II* is a 12-passenger luxury barge that sails from Haarlem down into Bruges. That means you cover many of the same sights as a traditional central Holland cruise—like the Keukenhof Gardens and Aalsmeer flower auction—but also stop in Antwerp, Ghent, and Bruges. Beer and chocolate, anyone? www.marjorie2.com

Want to stick closer to home? The Erie, Oswego, and Cayuga-Seneca Canals in central and western **New York** are popular with the slow-travel brigade—and families with children—who want to soak in the delightful scenery and see peaceful historic villages that have changed very little this century. You can have a perfectly Norman Rockwell experience over 10 days or so on the water. Swimming, fishing, and biking are plentiful along the route, while dozens of small towns, vineyards, museums, churches, and waterfalls beg to be explored during off-barge excursions. These canals are navigable via self-drive barges that can be rented from a variety of vendors along the route. Mid-Lakes Navigation (www.midlakesnav.com) operates daily cruises and 2- and 3-day journeys along the Erie Canal. And if you want to try your own hand, you can self-skipper a charter boat and get a full orientation on how to operate the boat and maneuver through a lock.

DUDE RANCHES

Whether you're a city slicker or a die-hard outdoor enthusiast, there's a dude ranch out there for you. The trick is figuring out what kind of experience you're looking for. Do you want hands-on experience on a working cattle ranch? Multigenerational activities for the entire family? Horseback riding followed by a gourmet meal?

HANDS-ON

Lozier's Box "R" Ranch is a true western working ranch 60 miles south of Jackson Hole, **Wyoming,** and Grand Teton National Park. It's so hands-on that you're assigned your own horse and tack to help drive 175 to 250 head of cattle over 26,000 acres of land. You can help with roundups, brandings, and breaking in new horses, as well as patching fences and other ranch chores. Activities depend on the season. There are "cowboy camps" several times a year, cattle drives in spring, summer horseback riding vacations, and fall roundups. As for the food, expect cowboy-size, meat-heavy meals. www.boxr.com

What better way to learn the fundamentals of running a ranch than to work alongside the owners? Burnt Well Guest Ranch is a family-run, 15,000-acre cattle and sheep ranch in Roswell, **New Mexico.** Guests are invited to help out in every aspect of ranch life, whether it's herding, shearing sheep, bottle-feeding lambs, repairing fences, or landscaping. For the full experience, go for the multiday cattle ride, complete with overnight camping and campfire cookouts. www.burntwellguestranch.com

Clayoquot Wilderness Resort on Vancouver Island, **British Columbia,** is located on the Clayoquot Sound Biosphere Reserve Area, a well-preserved temperate rain forest. Practically everything in this lodge combines comfort with a nature-based twist, whether it's grilling lessons in a 3,000-square-foot cookhouse or sleeping in a tent that's equipped with heated floors and antique furniture. You won't be roping cattle here, but there are plenty of outdoor traditions like wildlife spotting, horseback riding, and kayaking. www.wildretreat.com

For a working estancia experience without having to rough it, El Charabon, in the hills of Rocha, **Uruguay,** is a cattle and sheep ranch near the spectacular Atlantic coast. About 140 miles from Montevideo, this is an especially scenic ranch where you can be as involved as you'd like—from working alongside gauchos to having a laid-back day horseback riding on the sand dunes. www.elcharabon.com

FAMILY FRIENDLY

Latigo Ranch, located about 130 miles west of Denver, **Colorado,** is surrounded by 75 miles of mountains and valleys in the Rockies. While in winter it operates more like a ski lodge, come summertime the family-owned-and-operated ranch becomes a camp for families. Its summer programming is exceptionally kid friendly, with dozens of supervised activities such as nature walks, fishing, hayrides, arts and crafts, and pony rides. For both adults and kids, there's everything from rifle shooting to roping, archery, whitewater rafting, and hiking. But unlike traditional summer camp, the food is nothing to complain about: Communal dining and cookouts include plenty of kid-approved meals and gourmet options for parents. www.latigotrails.com

Although the Wild Horse Sanctuary in Northern **California** isn't technically a dude ranch (the sanctuary rescues mustangs), it's one of the best places to see real wild horses running free and to get involved in trail rides and cattle drives. They offer multiday rides between May and October on horses suitable for all levels of experience, but the ride itself can be challenging depending on the weather conditions. To get a real education, try a "work ride," which also includes trail and range maintenance. The sanctuary itself is rich in Indian and pioneer history, with remnants of homesteads, Indian camps, and petroglyphs. www.wildhorsesanctuary.org

Argentina has a long tradition of cattle ranching, and many of the historic estates have now been turned into estancias for those who want to immerse themselves in gaucho culture. Los Potreros in Cordoba hits all the marks for a great experience: family friendly, spectacular scenery, home-cooked organic food, and off-the-beaten path riding. Horse enthusiasts especially appreciate the fact that the 6,500-acre farm in the Sierras Chicas mountains breeds both Aberdeen Angus cattle and Paso Peruano horses. There are short rides and daylong tours, or you can go on overnight treks in which you stay in tents or village houses. www.estancialospotreros.com

FOODIE FOCUSED

Triple Creek Ranch in Darby, **Montana,** is an upscale resort ranch best known for its food and wine. Executive Chef Jacob Leatherman serves upscale western-style dishes, and the wine cellar boasts a whopping 3,000 bottles. If you want to venture out into nature, there are not only the typical outdoor experiences like horseback riding, hiking, and fly-fishing, but also more specialized activities such as photo safaris, moonlit horse rides, and winemaking lessons. www.triplecreekranch.com

How about a dude ranch in the middle of **California** wine country? Alisal Guest Ranch and Resort in the Santa Ynez Valley, in Santa Barbara County's wine region, is more of an all-around resort with horseback riding, golf, and fishing. But head there in fall for harvest season, and you can also get a real foodie experience—everything from casual barbecues to a winemaker's dinner, barrel tasting, and winery tours. Alisal offers a few different programs designed for couples and women, but my favorite has to be BBQ Bootcamp. This 4-day program teaches you all about Santa Maria–style barbecue, from grilling techniques to a spice-blending seminar where you'll blend your own seasoning. www.alisal.com

LUXURY

Of course, there are plenty of dude ranches in **Colorado,** but only one is a member of the upscale Relais & Châteaux. The Home Ranch in Steamboat Springs has all the amenities of a five-star property, but you still have the chance to disconnect and really get immersed in the great outdoors within the scenic Elk River Valley. There are no TVs or phones in the cabins (but there is wi-fi for those of us who like to have the option of staying connected). Since it's a year-round destination, you can go for activities like horseback riding, fly-fishing, and cross-country skiing, but the real attraction here is the gourmet, seasonal cuisine that's included in the rate. My advice? One of the best times to visit Colorado is in the shoulder season, after the summer rush and before winter, so head there in mid- to late September, when the aspen trees turn gold and the crowds have dissipated. www.homeranch.com

Located on 540 acres near the Routt National Forest in Colorado, Vista Verde is a small (only 10 guests at a time), upscale ranch where the highlight is horseback riding and skiing, but it also caters to those who want more than outdoor activities. We're talking wine tasting, hands-on cooking classes, nature hikes, and photography tours, not to mention three-course, wine-paired dinners by candlelight. www.vistaverde.com

The folks at Paws Up in Greenough, **Montana,** pretty much coined the term *glamping*, which combines the fun of camping and ranch life with the more luxurious comforts of home. This isn't a working

INSIDER'S TIP

The Dude Ranchers' Association is a great resource for insights and recommendations on dude ranching (www.duderanch.org). Though it does not include all the dude ranches in the United States, it allows you to search more than 100 member ranches by amenity or state, and gives advice on what to expect from your dude ranch. Or check out Top50Ranches.com to find ranch vacations worldwide—from rustic, hands-on experiences to luxury resorts.

ranch, but it has some of the best horseback riding through the Montana wilderness. And if you want the real cowboy experience, the resort's Saddle Club offers activities like wrangling and cattle roping. www.pawsup.com

About 27 miles from Buenos Aires is one of the largest estancias in all of **Argentina** and one of the most visually arresting. La Concepcion is actually a French-style mansion sitting on 200 acres of beautifully landscaped grounds (it even has a neo-Gothic chapel on site), but it's also a working dairy and cattle farm. Along with more highbrow activities like polo and carriage rides, you can participate in agro-tours and horseback riding along the Salt River. www.fitozuberbuhler.com

FALL FOLIAGE

Traditionalists always head to New England to watch the leaves change color, and there's certainly nothing wrong with that. There are a number of stunning destinations that almost consistently put on a dazzling fall foliage show, and some, like Oklahoma and Arizona, may not be on your list.

BY LAND

You'll step into a canopy of blazing colors as you drive through White Mountain National Forest in **New Hampshire.** Here, it's all about the brilliant red maple leaves and bright yellow birch trees, with deep evergreens dotting the landscape. Depending on when the nighttime cold snaps begin, foliage tends to peak in the northern part of the mountains the week before Columbus Day; in the central and southern parts of the forest, Columbus Day weekend is a truly amazing time to see the leaves. The Kancamagus Highway is an official Scenic Byway and travels through the heart of the forest. It showcases New England's foliage at its very best between mid-September and mid-October. You can drive the entire length of the 34-mile highway in about an hour. As you cut through the national forest, you'll get magical views of the fiery mountains and the Sabbaday, Lower, and Rocky Gorge waterfalls.

The White Mountain drive can get crowded during peak foliage season, so your best bet is to camp or stay at a B&B in the towns of North Conway or Sugar Hill, just outside of the park. That way, you can get up and out early in the morning. Loon Mountain is one of the best places to get a sweeping view of the region—just take the gondola up to the 3,050-foot summit and climb up to the observation tower. Loon Mountain also has a free shuttle to take you and your bike to Franconia Notch State Park, where you can hike or bike to the Flume, an 800-foot gorge at the bottom of Mount Liberty. The trail is manageable but a bit steep, so wear sturdy shoes and watch out for sprays from the cascading water. Keep going, and you'll be rewarded with close views of waterfalls, old-fashioned covered bridges, and, of course, the New Hampshire fall foliage.

You can't talk about fall foliage and overlook **Vermont.** Here the bountiful red and yellow maple leaves mix with oaks, evergreens, and other colorful deciduous trees, with hundreds of miles of trails, driving routes, and mountain overlooks to capture all the colors. If you're willing to hike, then head to the northern half of the famous Green Mountains into Camel's Hump State Park, named for its distinctive peak. This is truly undeveloped territory—no resorts, no concessions, no camps. Because the summit itself is free of foliage, you can get a clear, unobstructed view of the highest peaks in three states: Mount Washington in New Hampshire, Mount Marcy in New York, and Mount Mansfield in Vermont. Standing just over 4,000 feet, there is more than one way to go up, including Burrows Trail from the town of Huntington and the Monroe Trail from Duxbury. Although primitive camping is allowed on the mountain, my advice is to take advantage of the shelters and lodges supervised by the Green Mountain Club that are open between May and October.

Then there are the foliage hikes for those of us who don't want to do a lot of heavy lifting—or at least aren't comfortable hitting the trails without an experienced guide. Appalachian Trail Adventures has packages in Vermont that include guided day hikes based on your level of fitness, plus they throw in meals and spa treatments. Setting out from Killington, you'll explore the Appalachian Trail

INSIDER'S TIP

Accessible hiking to see the foliage is possible in Vermont's Green Mountains. Camel's Hump View Trail is a wide, easy path of just under a mile, with several viewing points to see the summit and surrounding foliage.

and the Long Trail within the Green Mountain National Forest. www.appalachiantrailadventures.com

The beauty of biking through foliage country is that you get to wind your way through places that aren't accessible by car, and you can cover a lot more ground than on foot. To make it even easier on yourself, book a biking trip with a company like Great Freedom Adventures, where they'll handle the logistics such as lodging, sightseeing, and schlepping your luggage from point to point. You'll set out from the quintessentially quaint town of Woodstock, Vermont, during peak foliage week, usually late September/early October, and embark on 6 days of biking anywhere from 20 to 50 miles a day. Don't worry, these aren't races and you can go at your own pace. The terrain varies from flat, paved roads to the occasional dirt roads and hills. As you look out into the dense foliage of bright maples and deep evergreens, you'll also make pit stops at working farms, do a tasting at the Plymouth Cheese Factory, and pick up baked goods at the King Arthur Flour headquarters. www.greatfreedomadventures.com

Practically the entire state of **Connecticut** is awash in colors come October, but if you have to choose, the best place to start is the Litchfield Hills. This northwestern region is a collection of small towns in the foothills of the Berkshire mountains, and a driving tour of Route 7 shows off the most classic of New England scenery. Drive north, along pastoral hills and valley, to pass through towns like Gaylordsville and Kent. Then it's south on Route 45 toward the shores of Lake Waramaug. The loop continues onto Route 47 and Route 67 back toward New Milford, past the Housatonic River and the historic covered Bull's Bridge where you can get out for a spectacular autumn photo op.

Oklahoma has a beautiful fall foliage season that peaks around late October. It happens in the southeastern part of the state, particularly in Kaimichi County. The Talimena Scenic Drive in Ouachita National Forest is the state's only Scenic Byway, which runs 54 miles along the Winding Stair Mountain Range, overlooking mountain scenery and changing leaves. It has several easy, self-guided hikes, as well as a 3.5-mile hike down the Billy Creek Trail (it's a steep climb back up), a longer 11-mile loop called Horse Thief Spring Trail, and the more rugged 23-mile Broadstand Trail. Real adventurers can try the full 223-mile Ouachita Recreation Trail.

And then there are the places that you wouldn't expect to see changing fall colors . . . like **Arizona.** Most people don't realize that the desert has a diversity of foliage. Even the cacti change to a beautiful red or purple when the temperature drops. Although you can't count on it as on the East Coast, there are desert drives, like the Apache Trail or along Highway 88 going to Canyon Lake. South Mountain Park is about a 10- to 15-minute drive from downtown Phoenix and is packed with hiking, mountain biking, and horseback riding trails. For prime viewing, take the Bajada Trail and the National Trail. Meanwhile, the Estrella Mountains offer almost 20,000 acres of desert and mountain scenery; start with the short, flat 2.4-mile Baseline Trail.

Great Smoky Mountains National Park, which straddles the border between **Tennessee** and **North Carolina,** is awash in autumn colors, with more than 100 species of native trees changing color. At

Bog Touring

Here's a crazy idea: touring a bog in fall. On the East Coast, there is an abundance of kettle hole bogs, which were formed thousands of years ago by peat moss creeping into depressions caused by melted glaciers. Because the land here is acidic and nutrient poor, the foliage tends to be different than nearby forests. In **New Hampshire,** both Ponema and Philbrick-Cricenti bogs actually have boardwalks so you can wander through about a mile of swampy land to see the changing colors, like blueberry shrubs that turn flaming red and conifers turning golden before losing their needles. In **Maine,** the Great Saco Heath bog is part of the Nature Conservancy, covering more than 1,000 acres with a nature trail and floating boardwalk. Here you can catch sight of rich colors from red maple and black gum trees (which also turn a brilliant red), along with white pines and white cedars. In Lubec, Maine, Quoddy Head State Park has a 1.5-mile bog trail that takes you along a raised boardwalk to see sheep laurel, cotton grass, and black gum trees.

the highest elevations, between 4,500 and 6,000 feet, leaves begin to change in mid-September with the yellow birch, American beech, and mountain maple. The colors peak in late October, when the sugar maple, scarlet oak, sweet gum, and dogwood turn to gold, orange, and deep red.

To avoid some of the crowds, try a drive on the eastern side of the park into the Cataloochee Valley. The 35-mile route there from Cosby, Tennessee, is one of the more scenic drives—just take Route 32, and about 20 miles into it you'll reach the border of North Carolina. Keep in mind, the road becomes mostly unpaved and gravely, and it winds uphill for a while. Once you reach the end, you'll be in one of the prettiest sections of the Great Smoky Mountains, where you can embark on a long and quiet hike.

In the **Napa Valley,** harvest season is when the grapes are plucked and the grapevine leaves explode into vivid reds and yellows. Napa's Mediterranean-like climate makes the fall season one of the nicer times of year to visit, with October temperatures ranging from the low 70s in the day and dropping down to the low 50s in the evening. The Napa Valley Wine Train travels an old rail line between Napa and St. Helena past miles of vineyards, where the plucked vines change into bright autumn colors.

Despite their northern positions, **Nova Scotia, Prince Edward Island,** and **Cape Breton Island** turn in late October due to the fact that the Atlantic Ocean keeps the weather more temperate. Sugar maple trees are a big deal here (just look at the Canadian flag), as are yellow birch and deep green firs, while bright red mountain ash berries speckle the countryside. Driving the 185-mile-long Cabot Trail is a great way to see the leaves, as the trail loops around the northern tip of the island, with craggy cliffs that drop sharply into the Atlantic. A portion of the trail is located in the protected Cape Breton Highlands National Park, which is renowned for its hardwood and softwood forests.

In **North Carolina**'s Black Mountains, Mount Mitchell is the highest peak east of the Mississippi, standing 6,684 feet. In Mount Mitchell State Park, the primary colors come from American chestnut and hickory trees, punctuated by green firs and spruce trees. With nearly 2,000 acres of wilderness, the trails are innumerable, but if you want an easy view, just drive along the scenic Blue Ridge Parkway from Asheville, and then hop on NC 128 to the summit. From the lot, there's a wheelchair-accessible walking path to the summit and an observation deck where you can look out over the majestic mountains awash in colors. www.ncparks.gov/Visit/parks/momi/main.php

You can't forget about **Colorado**'s aspen and cottonwood trees that turn a brilliant gold in the fall. Your best bet is to go between the third week in September and the first week of October; time your outing to late morning for the best light. For the best scenic view, take Kebler Pass, which sits at just over 10,000 feet between Crested Butte and Highway 133. From the town of Gunnison, take Highway 135 to Crested Butte and turn left on Whiterock Avenue, which turns into Kebler Pass Road. Kebler Pass is part gravel, part rough pavement, and winds through the aspen forest.

Unlike North America, red is not the dominant color of the Swiss autumn. Hues of yellow and gold are most prominent, with just a hint of red. This is because most alpine trees are coniferous and stay green all year, with the exception of the larch, whose needles turn golden before falling off. The dash of red comes from the blueberry bushes. The best time to see fall colors in **Switzerland** is late September through early to mid-October. The Nendaz Historic Water Trail actually takes you through one of the largest raspberry- and apricot-producing regions in Switzerland, with an ancient network of irrigation channels and 60 miles of walking trails. The Aletsch Panoramaweg hike sits in the middle of the Jungfrau-Aletsch-Bietschhorn UNESCO World Heritage area, which has more than 30 peaks that are more than 4,000 feet high, the breathtaking Aletsch glacier, cottony grass, and sparkling lakes. Getting there is half the fun: To get to the starting point of the hike to Bettmerhorn peak, you have to take a train, an aerial cableway, and a gondola lift.

Kyoto is a must-see destination to view fall foliage (*koyo*) in **Japan,** and Arashiyama is the spot in the city to see it. The vivid reds, golds, and yellows of the forested hills are almost too intense to be real and are best viewed in early October through mid-November. The location is rendered even more picturesque by the nearby antique wooden Togetsu-kyo Bridge, the Sagano bamboo grove, and the handful of small temples that sit at the base of the hills. One of the best ways to see the foliage is by bicycle, which you can rent at any train station in the district. Arguably the second most popular spot to see *koyo* is around Oirase Stream and Lake Towada, in the Aomori Prefecture. Best viewed from middle to late October and early November, the fall foliage in the 9-mile river valley is viewable by bus. But in my opinion, you're much better off strolling by the river. The trail is about 5 miles long and takes about 2 hours to walk one way. (You can return by bus.) As a bonus, more than a dozen waterfalls feed into the river from the walls of the surrounding gorge.

BY WATER

There's my favorite way to travel: by water. Most of the major cruise lines, like MSC and Holland America, sail along the coast of New England and Canada. But my advice is to find smaller ship experiences. American Cruise Lines has cruises along the **Hudson River valley** onboard the *American Star*, which fits 100 passengers, and the *American Glory*, which accommodates only 49. You'll set out from New York City and make your way into the picturesque Hudson Valley, stopping in maritime villages with the Catskill Mountains to your west and the Taconic and Berkshire Hills to your east. www.americancruiselines.com

Add a dash of culture to the trip with Smithsonian Journeys, which also charters the *American Glory* to sail along the Hudson River on an art-and-architecture-themed cruise. The trip is led by a museum curator, who will take you on private tours of artists' studios, Hudson Valley mansions, and even the cadet chapel at West

Point. And, of course, you'll sail past spectacular foliage views. www.smithsonianjourneys.org

Even the plains of the Midwest have an array of deciduous trees that burst into fall colors. Take advantage of this autumn beauty before **Illinois**'s frigid winter sets in. Head to the Chain O Lakes State Park in Spring Grove (north of Chicago) which—like its name suggests—is a chain of 15 lakes connected by the Fox River, canals, and channels. Through mid-October, you can paddle a kayak along the Fox River or rent a motorboat to take out into the lakes, affording ideal views of the 6,000-acre park's array of oak, hickory, cherry, elm, and spruce trees. dnr.state.il.us/lands/landmgt/parks/r2/chaino.htm

Combine foliage viewing with an intense adrenaline rush. Every weekend in October, waters are released into Russell Forks in Breaks Interstate Park on the **Virginia-Kentucky** border, creating some of the most challenging whitewater rafting in the country. Known as the Grand Canyon of the South, "the Breaks" spans 4,600 acres with a plunging 5-mile gorge that drops as deep as 1,650 feet. The trees are in full color in October, with dazzling oaks and beech. The whitewater here is among the most challenging in the country, so don't even attempt it unless you're experienced with Class IV rapids. For a more laid-back adventure, there's plenty of kayaking and canoeing. www.breakspark.com

BY SKY

They don't call it **Aspen** for nothing. Located high in the Rocky Mountains, Aspen, Colorado, is awash in golden yellow in the month of September. The area is known for its quaking, white-barked aspen trees mixed with rich evergreen trees. My advice: Take the Burlingame Lift in Snowmass Village or the Silver Queen Gondola up 3,000 vertical feet to the summit of Aspen Mountain, and hike or bike down to enjoy the scenery. Because of the altitude, the foliage comes in early—good thing, since the lifts usually close for the season by the second week of September.

Wine Country has beautiful foliage courtesy of the grapevines. Hop into a hot air balloon basket with **Napa Valley** Balloons, and soar high above the wineries, where you can see grapevines change from green to bronze in late September and early October.

For really incredible aerial views, how about hang gliding? If you're a first-timer, you'll likely start by practicing with a Scooter Tow, where you'll actually be towed along by a motor scooter. But then, when you're comfortable, you'll get to fly from a mountain launch point like Lookout Mountain in **Georgia,** near Chattanooga, Tennessee. You'll launch from the flight park and soar over the colorful scenery.

Timing Your Trip

If you're traveling east of the Mississippi in search of colors, how can you be sure that you'll get a show when you arrive? Unfortunately, there's no foolproof way to predict when the leaves will turn. Deciduous trees need a cold snap to change the leaves into bright fall colors, so we're at the mercy of Mother Nature. But a good rule of thumb is that foliage starts changing first in higher elevations in the Northeast and works its way down and west. So **Maine, New Hampshire,** and **Vermont** generally get colorful from the last week of September through early October. In **Massachusetts, Connecticut,** and **New York,** colors usually peak around Columbus Day weekend. If you travel farther east, **Nova Scotia** and **Prince Edward Island** actually have a later fall season because the ocean keeps the weather more temperate. So the leaves there change well into late October. Another late starter is the Arkansas River valley in **Arkansas,** which peaks as late as November. And in November, you can also find great foliage down south, in areas like the Cherokee Foothills Scenic Highway in **South Carolina,** and Lookout Mountain in **Alabama** and **Tennessee.** Fall foliage isn't just a one-shot deal. Travel like a contrarian and you can catch great color all around the United States.

FISHING

Ask anglers where the best fishing is, and they'll insist that they—and only they—know the best spot. But what you soon discover is that the location may have less to do with the kind of fish you're looking for (or the number of fish available) than with the total fishing experience. After all, in my experience, a day of fishing, even without catching a single fish, always trumps a day at the office. I often do my best work, and especially my best thinking, while holding a rod and reel.

Having said that, ask most anglers where the best salmon fishing is, and they'll likely point you to the Kenai River in **Alaska.** If you're vying for the bragging rights of a lifetime, this is the place to be between May and July, when there are two runs of wild king salmon. (The Kenai is where the current world-record salmon was caught in May 1985, weighing an incredible 97 pounds and 4 ounces.) Late summer into early fall is when silver salmon are at their peak.

But Alaska isn't your only choice. The waters around Vancouver Island, **British Columbia** (less than a day's drive from Seattle), also have some great salmon fishing. In the little village of Ucluelet, fishing is a year-round sport. Between March and May, king and silver salmon swim from Alaskan waters into the coastal streams and rivers on the west coast of Vancouver Island; between May and September, it's all about halibut; colder months are a great time to catch winter king salmon, crab, and oysters. If you go with Salmon Eye Charters (www.salmoneye.net), you'll be guaranteed at least 50 pounds of fish per day (on trips of 3 or more days). It has various

INSIDER'S TIP

If you go on a fishing excursion in Alaska and want to bring your catch home with you, don't try to transport it in your luggage! Companies like Alaska Sausage and Seafood will clean, vacuum-seal, and flash-freeze your fish, then ship it to your home so you can cook it there. Or for an extra fee, they can even process it into kippered salmon, smoked salmon strips, or lox before shipping. www.alaskasausage. com/Custom-Fish-Processing.aspx

fishing packages that include all gear, fish cleaning and packing, a cook-your-catch dinner, and accommodations.

Between spring and fall, **Lake Michigan** is well stocked with salmon and trout, and those numbers are boosted by natural reproduction in the streams and rivers that feed into the lake. There are plenty of launch points in Michigan, Wisconsin, and Illinois that yield great catches. Waukegan, Illinois, on the west side of the lake, is only about 40 minutes from Chicago, making it an easy excursion for first-timers. Head out between April and June for silver salmon and brown trout, or later in the summer to encounter the mighty king salmon.

Although you might associate Southern **California** with deep-sea fishing, believe it or not it also has a sizable lake fishing scene. Just north of Los Angeles is Castaic Lake, a prime spot for bass fishing, including a good amount of double-digit fish (more than 10 pounds), and even a handful of 20-plus pounders. Depending on what's been stocked, you might also come across trout and catfish, but it's the largemouth bass that most anglers are looking for. Between October and March, the lake is stocked with rainbow trout, which tends to send the bass on a feeding frenzy—and imitation rainbow trout (a.k.a. swimbait) is generally the best lure for the prized fish. Bass tend to hide around docks, submerged foliage, and rock piles. They also prefer mild temperatures, so in summer and winter, head toward deeper waters; in spring and fall, look for them in shallower coves.

The other option in Southern California is Lake Casitas in the Ojai Valley. It, too, is renowned for its bass population, and the waters warm up quickly in spring. In early spring, live swimbait or crawdads are usually the best lures; but April is shad spawning season, which then becomes prime bait for the bass. While morning is usually the best time to fish, you can often have a very productive afternoon in spring because of those shad. Need a tutorial? Marc Mitrany, a.k.a. the "Ojai Angler" (www.ojaiangler.com), has claimed record-size catches and can take you out on a guided trip to Castaic in the fall and Lake Casitas year-round. You'll learn the basics of bass fishing and practice catch-and-release techniques on largemouth bass. But if you catch a trout, catfish, or sunfish and really want to bring it home to show off, just ask.

Thailand's lakes and rivers are excellent places for freshwater fishermen looking for bragging rights. If it's your first time in Thailand, the easiest place to start is Bungsamran Lake in Bangkok. The site of several fishing world records, this lake is a draw for enthusiasts in search of monster-size Mekong catfish and Siamese giant carp. Once you've gotten your fill, your next challenge is to go about an hour outside of Bangkok to the rural Boon Mar Ponds, where prized barramundi lurk. Anglers from all over the world come here for lure or fly-fishing to bring in these difficult-to-catch fish, which range anywhere from 10 to 30 pounds.

You've heard of wild game safaris, but how about a fishing safari? **Africa**'s rivers and floodplains are a fisherman's paradise, and the mighty tiger fish is perhaps the most prized catch of all. These guys are real fighters, with razor-sharp teeth and bony jaws, which is why a catch is so coveted. These fierce creatures tend to peak in August on the upper Zambezi and in September on the lower Zambezi. Just head to Livingstone, Zambia, where any number of angling lodges and operators can set up charters or fly-fishing outings.

FLY-FISHING

Western **Montana** is about as good as it gets for fly-fishing, particularly from Bozeman to Missoula. Wild rainbow, brown, and cutthroat trout are what you'll find here, in numerous rivers such as the Flathead, the Blackfoot, and the Yellowstone. Trout are the main catch in these rivers. There are mountain lakes, too, which offer a different experience from the streams and rivers, but both give you some of the best trout fishing in the world. The scenery is astonishing no matter where you go, but the Blackfoot—surrounded by towering cliffs and ponderosa pine forests—offers that Zen-like atmosphere that makes fly-fishing such a magical experience. If it's your first time, try wade fishing at Rock Creek, which is located about 20 miles east of Missoula. It's easy to find, has plenty of access, and offers blue-ribbon fly-fishing for brown, rainbow, and cutthroat trout.

Western **North Carolina** has a great fly-fishing trail (www.flyfishingtrail.com) that encompasses 11 creeks and four rivers, and is the only trail of its kind in the country. Located in the Great Smoky Mountains, the trail takes you to Scott Creek, Panthertown Creek, the Whitewater River, and the Tuckasegee River (among others), which are prime grounds for brook, brown, and rainbow trout. You can self-navigate the trail, or if you're not an experienced angler, consider a guided tour along any number of waterways along the trail. For example, Endless River Adventures (www.endlessriveradventures.com) offers guided drift boat, guided oar-rig, stream side, and wet-wading excursions along the Upper Nantahala and Tuckasegee Rivers. Best of all, you can fly-fish in the unlikely month of November, when the weather is mild and waters are well stocked with trout.

Fishing season isn't over when winter arrives. All you have to do is go south. **Patagonia**'s rivers and lakes abound with freshwater fish, and high season runs between November and April. The fish are abundant in the Caleufu River, but challenging rapids and private land make it difficult to access on your own. Your better bet is to book a trip through one of the properties, like Estancia Alicura (www.estanciaalicura.net), where there's actually a director of fly-fishing on staff to take you to the best spots, depending on the day and climate. And within the Nahuel Huapi National Park (about an hour outside of Bariloche, **Argentina**) is Lake Hess, where you can fly-fish for brown, brook, and rainbow trout against the backdrop of the majestic Mount Tronador.

The Southland region of **New Zealand**'s South Island holds a special spot in the heart of fly-fishing enthusiasts. The dramatic and isolated backcountry terrain, the clarity of the water, and the size of the fish all explain why. It's no wonder this region has the highest rate of angling per capita of any part of New Zealand. Remote rivers such as the upper Mataura and Aparima teem with brown trout most of the year. Though you can get by with a fishing map from Fish and Game New Zealand (www.fishandgame.org.nz/Site/Regions/Southland/fishingAccess.aspx), the best way to navigate these rivers is with a guide, who can show you the hidden, unmapped spots, depending on the conditions and climate. Best of all, at the height of summer, the days are extremely long, with the sun rising around 5 a.m. and not setting until 10 p.m. Fly Fish Mataura (www.flyfishmataura.co.nz) has teamed up with Wentworth Heights Bed and Breakfast (www.wentworthheights.co.nz) to offer fishing packages.

SALTWATER FISHING (DEEP-SEA AND INSHORE)

The eastern Long Island community of **Montauk** offers classic Northeast fishing, with waters teeming with blackfish, sea bass, fluke, stripers, cod, bluefish, and tuna. The season begins the last weekend in June and runs through Labor Day weekend, but some charters will take you out in the off-season. A local favorite is Captain Jamie Quaresimo, who can take you aboard the 80-foot *Miss Montauk* (www.missmontauk.com) for fishing. Bait, tackle, and fishing poles are included. But if you're a landlubber, it's also possible to fish from Hither Hills State Park and Montauk Point State Park, among others.

Every year, between mid-March and mid-April, thousands of fishermen flock to **Panama City Beach** to catch the annual cobia run. Cobia, also known as lemon fish or ling, swim up from the Keys and range from 20 to 80 pounds. It's so coveted that the Florida Fish and Wildlife Conservation Commission actually has limits of one cobia per person, and six per day, per vessel, over 33 inches. Hook up with an experienced captain like James Pic of JP2 Fish (www.jp2fish.com), who'll help you catch not only cobia, but also pompano, jacks, sharks, king mackerel, and other migrating fish in these waters.

Farther south, the **Florida Keys** are known as a year-round destination for sportfishing enthusiasts. Nearly every species of saltwater game fish can be found in the surrounding waters, including sailfish, marlin, tuna, wahoo, and king mackerel. Tip: The Keys are also one of the world's best destinations for bonefishing, which is done in the flat, shallow waters of the backcountry. The season runs from March through October, but the biggest bonefish are found in September and October. Make sure you use a guide who is a specialist in bonefishing because it requires special boats and casting techniques.

The waters off the posh resort town of Los Suenos on Herradura Bay in **Costa Rica** offer excellent year-round deep-sea and inshore fishing. If you're in search of big game fish, you'll be impressed by the sailfish, mahimahi, tuna, dorado, and wahoo, and especially blue, black, and striped marlin. Those sticking closer to shore will

Ice Fishing

Crazy about fishing (or just plain crazy)? Why not go ice fishing? This growing sport isn't just about the challenge. Any enthusiast will tell you that dropping a line and sitting out on a frozen lake is an incredibly peaceful experience. There are obvious safety precautions involved (an important motto is "There is no such thing as 100 percent safe ice"), so if you're not familiar with the process, go with an expert guide. In **New York State,** there are dozens of lakes and ponds, including the very scenic Finger Lakes region where you can find trout, landlocked salmon, walleye, and northern pike. **Minnesota** has ample opportunities for ice fishing all over the state. North of Minneapolis, the area around Mille Lacs Lake has plenty of operators that can take you out for the day or rent you an ice-fishing house complete with heat, lights, and bathrooms. Ice fishing abounds in **Canada,** particularly in Ontario's larger lakes like Lake Simco and Lake Nipissing, where there are winter lodges and cottages open for the season.

Fishing Resources

As many anglers know, it's always the locals who know the best spots. But here's how you can find them, too. There are Web sites that offer hints on where to find the best fishing spots, based on everything from water temperature to water composition to time of year. Fishing.com tells you exactly what bait you need for each type of fish. LandBigFish.com lists well over 2,900 fishing spots in the United States and Canada. Plus, you can search for guides, schools, lodges, and marinas. GlobalAnglers.com gives independent, unbiased advice on 120 fishing destinations and charter companies in the United States, Central America, the Caribbean, and Australia.

find roosterfish, Spanish mackerel, and grouper. Fishing is available year-round, with fall being the best time for marlin and snapper, and December through March for sailfish. A good bet as far as charter companies is Captain Tom Carton (www.captaintoms.com), who was the first to offer a fishing charter service in the area. He holds several world records (including largest sailfish) and numerous tournament wins.

There are two reasons the waters around the **US and British Virgin Islands** have some of the best game fishing in the world: the North Drop and the South Drop. The North Drop is a 28,000-foot-deep underwater trench about 20 miles north of the islands that is reputed to produce more blue marlin bites per boat than any other place in the world. During peak fishing months from May to October (considered the off-season for tourism), you'll likely get between five and 10 strikes in a day. You can also catch white marlin, sailfish, and yellowfin tuna there. The South Drop, which is located 8 miles south of St. Thomas, is as deep as 12,000 feet in places and is where you'll catch similar fish, plus lots of mahimahi, kingfish, and wahoo. Charters from any of the US or British Virgin Islands can take you to either zone (although because St. Croix is so far south, those charters tend to hit the South Drop). Double Header Sportfishing (www.doubleheadersportfishing.net) in St. Thomas has been in the business for more than 25 years, and its guides have a solid knowledge of the waters.

There are numerous places to go fly-fishing or deep-sea fishing in Europe, but did you know that you can catch gigantic catfish in the Ebro River in **Spain**? One of Spain's largest rivers, it runs through a large swath of Catalonia on its way to the Mediterranean. In 1974 catfish were introduced, and ever since then, fishermen from around the world have been flocking to catch specimens that can reach up to 300 pounds. Though fish this size are not common, most anglers net at least one fish over 100 pounds on any given day. The best season for catching catfish is from mid-March through mid-November. Carp and zander can also be found in large quantities in the Ebro, and winter is actually the best carp season. Dozens of mostly United Kingdom–based companies offer guided expeditions with English-speaking guides, such as CatMaster Tours (www.catmastertours.com), with accommodations in picturesque Catalan towns such as Zaragoza and Mequinenza.

If you ever want to set out for some serious relaxation with your fishing, **Vanuatu** is the place to be. This volcanic archipelago in the South Pacific has long relied on fishing as an industry, but if you're just looking for a place of ultimate relaxation out in the deep blue sea, this is it. Fishing is a year-round business here. Blue marlin season is year-round, while black and striped marlin appear in the winter, between May and October. Mahimahi, wahoo, and oversize yellowfin tuna are also commonly found in these waters. To get out there, just go to the Waterfront Bar and Grill in Port Vila, where companies like Crusoe Fishing (www.crusoefishing.com.vu) are ready to take you out.

EXPERT FISHING

Seafood lovers may as well learn how to catch it, cook it, and eat it straight from the local experts.

Kapiti Island is a renowned nature and marine reserve off the west coast of **New Zealand**'s North Island. On a seafood-gathering excursion with Kapiti Island Nature Tours, you can join an island family to gather *paua* (abalone). Paua are considered a delicacy in Maori cuisine and are gathered from rocky shores, clinging to rocks underwater. After you learn to identify and collect the paua, you'll get a lesson in how to prepare it for cooking and eating. www.kapitiislandnaturetours.co.nz

There's always the option of chartering a boat to get that hands-on experience. Bohicket Marina on Kiawah Island in **South Carolina** offers guides, charters, and custom excursions for fishing, crabbing, or just observing the pros at work. For serious redfish and trout fishing, consider hiring an inshore fishing guide. For an afternoon that's more about fun and sun, catch a ride with Captain Harry, a colorful local character. He'll take you cruising or crabbing, and regale you with history and stories of life at sea. http://bohicket.com

Thousands of people head to St. Joe's Bay, **Florida,** between July and September for the recreational scallop diving season. This is a fun activity for the whole family. It's very easy to do: You can either wade right out into the bay with a snorkel, flag, and bucket and pick them off the seafloor, or you can rent a small boat or kayak to get a bit farther out. If you prefer to have an expert show you the ropes, there are numerous kayak and boat charter companies that can take you out, show you the best spots, and teach you the basics. Don't forget to get a saltwater fishing license before you go scalloping, and limit yourself to 2 gallons of whole bay scallops in the shell, or 1 pint of bay scallop meat, per day. http://myfwc.com/fishing/saltwater/regulations/bay-scallops

In **California** counties like Mendocino, Sonoma, and Monterey, you can go abalone diving from April through November (excluding July). Mendocino is California's most popular diving area, and sites like Westport, MacKerricher State Park, Glass Beach, Noyo Bay, Caspar Bay, Mendocino Bay, and Albion can get crowded on weekends. You can either go it alone, or find a guide who can direct you to the best spots (often in a kayak) and help you harvest, clean, and prepare the abalone for eating. Sub-Surface Progression is a good dive shop from which to rent gear like a wet suit and snorkel, and they'll recommend independent guides as well. www.subsurfaceprogression.com

In the **Florida Keys,** practically every oceanside restaurant and resort has a BYOF (bring your own fish) option. If you book a guided fishing tour with Robbie's Marina (www.robbies.com) in Islamorada, they'll clean and fillet the fish for free. Then you can take it to the marina's Hungry Tarpon (www.hungrytarpon.com) restaurant, where the chef will cook it up any way you like and serve it with vegetables, rice, and plantains. In Sarasota, the fourth-generation family-run Walt's Fish Market Restaurant (www.waltsfishmarketrestaurant.com) will clean, fillet, and cook (or smoke) your day's catch.

Epic Adventures (www.epicadventures.co.nz) and Cathedral Cove Macadamias (www.cathedralcovemacadamias.co.nz) in the

The Deadliest Catch-Your-Own

If you're impressed by the guys on *Deadliest Catch*, why not try out their job for a day? The Bering Sea Crab Fishermen's Tour in Ketchikan, **Alaska,** follows in their footsteps aboard the very crab boat that was used in the popular series. During the $3^{1}/_{2}$-hour tour on the *Aleutian Ballad*, you'll watch the crew at work catching and releasing crab, prawns, octopus, and possibly even shark. Some of the less dangerous creatures they catch are placed into a live observation tank where guests can touch and photograph them. The boat is located on the same dock where cruise ships berth, so it's a popular half-day excursion for cruisers. http://56degreesnorth.com

Coromandel Peninsula of **New Zealand** have teamed up to offer a unique fishing/cooking package. Spend a day fishing with Epic, a top-notch game-fishing outfitter, and try your hand at catching everything from crayfish to kingfish to scallops. Then go ashore to nearby Cathedral Cove, a macadamia orchard and merchant. Join the crew there in cooking up a seafood feast using macadamia-based ingredients and other fresh local produce. Macadamias are a great complement to seafood: Imagine snapper breaded with lemon macadamia crumbs, or fishcakes made with macadamia seasoning.

Deep in the **Nova Scotia** wilderness is the upscale Trout Point Lodge (www.troutpoint.com), which has a cooking program that focuses almost entirely on Canadian coastal seafood. You'll learn the basics of sourcing salmon, lobster, mussels, and oysters, along with preparation techniques from Mediterranean to Cajun.

Virginia Beach's seafood bounty is the stuff of culinary legend, so it's no surprise that plenty of local restaurants will prepare your catch for you. Just head out on a charter boat, and you can bring back your cleaned catch to places like Waterman's Surfside Grille (www.watermans.com) or Rudee's on the Inlet (www.rudees.com), where the chefs will cook it to order.

GOLF

Golf is one of the most frustrating and challenging sports. While I smartly don't play the game—I do, however, drive a mean golf cart—I love watching it. But for those of you brave enough (and patient enough) to pursue golf, I've got a few suggestions that, while they may not actually improve your game, will work wonders in improving your overall experience.

UNITED STATES

Shadow Creek in **Las Vegas** isn't just desert golfing at its best, it may well be one of the best golf courses you'll ever play. Surrounded by barren desert land, it's almost impossible that this Steve Wynn creation could exist where it does. The 350-acre site has the lushest landscaping imaginable, with rolling green hills, lakes, creeks and waterfalls, and thousands upon thousands of trees of at least 200 different varieties. Now here's a strange thing: No pictures are allowed once you get inside the gates, where you're whisked over to the links by chauffeur. Although back in the day, only guests of Wynn's could play, today it's owned by MGM Resorts International, so you just have to be a guest at an MGM resort to play. www.shadowcreek.com

The links at Bandon Dunes Golf Resort in **Oregon** is golf for purists. The four courses—Pacific Dunes, Bandon Dunes, Old Macdonald, and Bandon Trails—are carved into massive windswept sand dunes on the Pacific Coast. Though it's a public course, Bandon Dunes is not necessarily cheap, and it's not adjacent to a major metropolitan area. But golf fanatics will go to any length to get there. www.bandondunesgolf.com

The sheer beauty of Torrey Pines is just one of the reasons golfers love to come here. It's hard to beat the scenery. The municipal course in La Jolla, **California,** sits on a cliff overlooking the Pacific Ocean, and you could spend hours in the ocean breeze just absorbing the sweeping views. But the course here is so good that Torrey Pines hosts the annual PGA Tour's Farmers Insurance Open, bringing A-list players to the first city-run golf course to host a US Open. www.torreypinesgolfcourse.com

Life on a ranch doesn't usually involve golfing, but at Rancho de los Caballeros, it's the main attraction. This luxury resort in Wickenburg, **Arizona,** has one of the top courses in the golf-obsessed state. It's located about 55 miles northwest of Phoenix at the foot of the Bradshaw Mountains in the Sonoran Desert. The course itself is semiprivate, meaning it's open to the public as well as members. The par 72 course itself is a challenge with a slope rating of 135, but what's really special about the ranch is that it truly is family friendly, so no one will be stuck on the course who doesn't want to be. www.ranchodeloscaballeros.com

Kiawah Island Golf Resort, located on a barrier island a few miles from Charleston, **South Carolina,** has five pristine championship courses, each one seemingly better than the next—until you get to play the best of them all: the Ocean Course. This public course lives up to its name, with 10 holes alongside the Atlantic Ocean. The greens are so renowned that the Ocean Course has hosted the Ryder Cup, the Senior PGA, and the 2012 PGA Championships. www. kiawahresort.com

Amelia Island Plantation is home to three top courses in **Florida,** including the Tom Fazio–designed Long Point Club. Quiet, off the beaten path, and luxurious all around, this par 72 course covers different types of island terrain, from salt marshes to sandy dunes to dense foliage. www.aipfl.com

INTERNATIONAL

There's nothing more quintessentially Scottish than golf (except, perhaps whisky, but that's another chapter). St. Andrews aside, there are plenty of equally renowned courses to choose from throughout **Scotland.** One of the best, the historic Muirfield in East Lothian, is a private club, but they'll open their doors to you if you pay a steep greens fee on Tuesday or Thursday. www.muirfield.org.uk

Your other option in Scotland is a resort club, where you can get access as a paying guest. The upscale Gleneagles Hotel and Resort has three renowned courses on site: the King's Course, the Queen's Course, and the PGA Centenary Course, which will host the Ryder Cup in 2014. If your skills aren't, well, up to par, Gleneagles is also home to the PGA National Golf Academy, where you can get one-on-one instruction at every level. http://glenmor.gleneagles.com

New in 2012, Castle Stuart Golf Links in the town of Inverness is poised to be the next big thing in golfing, with a championship course overlooking Moray Firth and Chanonry Lighthouse. www.castlestuartgolf.com

When it comes to classic Irish golfing, the seaside town of Ballybunion is it. Located on **Ireland**'s southwest coast in County Kerry, the golf club has two courses: the Old Course and the Cashen Course. The Cashen is top notch, but the Old Course is the one you'll remember. With daunting holes that nudge up against the sea and incredible cliffside views, it's been said that this is as close to heaven as you'll get. www.ballybuniongolfclub.ie

Doonbeg Golf Club in County Clare, Ireland, is a relatively new

Unusual Golfing

And then there are those experiences you do just to say you did it. Like ice golfing. Uummannaq, **Greenland,** is home to the World Tce Golf Championship and has unbeatable views of icebergs and formations while you play. Then again, there's also the potential for frostbite if you're not careful. A round of ice golf is a lot like normal golf, except the greens are called whites and the golf balls are red.

The Coeur d'Alene Resort Golf Course in **Idaho** is certainly one of the prettiest courses out there, with the Rocky Mountains in the distance and the glistening Lake Coeur d'Alene. But that's not all there is to talk about: It's also home to the only floating green in the world. That's right, the 14th hole is on a floating island that is only accessible by boat.

The golf course at Furnace Creek Resort in Death Valley, **California,** is the lowest in the world, sitting 218 feet below sea level in one of the hottest, driest places on earth. So why would you want to spend hours standing out under the blazing sun? To say you did. In summer, temperatures average 109 degrees and have been known to top out at 130 degrees. And that's when the brave (or the foolhardy) like to play. The course has even hosted an event called the Heatstroke Open. The key: Stay hydrated, stay in the shade, and don't waste energy with practice strokes. www.furnacecreekresort.com

course that quickly became a favorite among golfers. Designed by Greg Norman, the old-fashioned course is naturally integrated into its environment. It is downright stunning, with grassy dunes and ocean waves crashing into a 1½-mile stretch of beach, and gusty winds making each tee its own challenge. www.doonbeglodge.com

It's not easy to get to Kauri Cliffs in **New Zealand**'s Northland region, on the Bay of Islands. But enthusiasts will make the 4-hour trek (or take a helicopter) from Auckland just to step foot on the greens. Why? Because the immaculate par 72 golf course affords panoramic views of the Pacific Ocean from its perch high on a cliff. Fifteen holes offer ocean views, and six of those take place next to the cliffs so you can look down and see the rocky walls plunging into the ocean. www.kauricliffs.com

Dubai is quickly making its name as a world-class golfing destination. What's cool, even for bystanders, is that the golf balls here are orange, to make them stand out in the desert! The Desert Classic Tournament is a premier event held at the venerated Emirates Golf Club (www.emiratesgolf.com), which is open to the public. There are two courses here: the challenging Majlis course and the Faldo course, where you can actually play night golf. At the Intercontinental, the Al Badia Golf Club (www.albadiagolfclub.ae) is known for its lush layout with water features, plus high-tech motion-capture clinics where you can perfect your stroke.

AFFORDABLE ALTERNATIVES

When someone says golf in **Scotland,** you probably think of St. Andrews. The famous Old Course usually means steep prices and long wait times. But just 10 miles away is the Crail Golfing Society. Here, you can tee off for about half the price and still be challenged by the par 69 course. About 25 miles north is Carnoustie, which has hosted several British Opens.

One of the top courses in the United States happens to be in southern New Jersey. Pine Valley Golf Club consistently tops nearly every best-of list out there, but it's a private membership, men-only club. Instead, drive north to Bethpage State Park on Long Island, **New York,** where the Black Course is one of the best municipal courses in the country. Its popularity means it's not easy to get a tee time, but at least it doesn't require a special invitation!

You've probably heard of the Master's Tournament at Augusta National Golf Club in Augusta, **Georgia,** where it costs several hundred dollars just to watch the tournament for a half day. But less than 18 miles away is the Bartram Trail in Grovetown, where tee time costs $35 on weekends. And Jones Creek Golf Club (www.jonescreekgolfclub.com) has exceptional, similar terrain.

While there are unbeatable views at **California**'s Pebble Beach (www.pebblebeach.com), the price tag can certainly be beat at the Bayonet and Black Horse golf club (www.bayonetblackhorse.com). It's only about 20 minutes away and also comes with beautiful views of Monterey Bay. On the other side of the peninsula is Pacific Grove Municipal Golf Links, known as the "poor man's Pebble Beach," that offers amazing value and scenery.

Finding Golf Deals

During off-peak times, many courses will drop their prices, specifically midmorning or late afternoon. In Scottsdale, **Arizona,** for example, Grayhawk Golf Club offers reduced "twilight" rates about 4 hours prior to sunset. Of course, you may not have time to finish all 18 rounds. Savvy travelers will also tee off in the low season to save. In destinations like **Arizona, Nevada,** and **California,** the high season is in the winter, while places like Hilton Head, **South Carolina,** peak in late spring and summer. So if you can stand the desert heat midsummer or brave the cold in winter, you can save up to 50 percent. Or try the shoulder season, which is that sweet spot in fall and spring when prices are lower and crowds have dissipated. Look for online promotions and sign up for e-mail newsletters that offer last-minute discounts to loyal followers. Check out online resources such as GolfVacationInsider.com and statewide associations for targeted deals and reviews of specific courses.

HIKING

There's no shortage of spectacular hiking trails around the world that cater to every level, from casual strollers to backcountry enthusiasts to thrill seekers. Are you looking for a challenging climb? A scenic payoff? Lots of natural wildlife along the journey? Bottom line is, there's a lot out there to choose from, but some of the best hikes in the world have a little something extra that really makes them stand out from the crowd. It's not just the terrain or the challenge of the hike—it's where the hike takes you.

UNITED STATES

Most people associate Las Vegas with outdoor adventures, but within a few miles are a variety of kid-friendly hikes. In Red Rocks Canyon, **Nevada,** the Children's Discovery Loop trail is level and well marked, making it a great desert option for beginner and young hikers. Follow the signs as they lead you from the Lost Creek parking lot to the petroglyphs, the waterfall, and a grotto area, and then loop you back to the parking area. After a good rain, you'll find the waterfall flowing strong. For some really unexpected scenery, head just 35 miles north of the Strip to Mount Charleston. The cool, evergreen-covered mountainside known for its waterfalls and wild-flowers is a welcome respite from the dry desert scenery. The Fletcher Canyon trail is an easy option for any age, stretching nearly 2 miles one way at a gentle elevation.

Shenandoah National Park in **Virginia** is an exceptionally family-friendly destination, with junior ranger programs, nature work-shops, and live music events. The park has more than 500 miles of trails catering to all levels of hikers, but the family-oriented trails are worth visiting: Little Stony Man Cliffs is an easy walk that mostly follows the Appalachian Trail, with rewarding views of Sky-line Drive; Blackrock Summit is an even easier option of about a half mile on level ground and affords one of the best views of the Shenandoah Valley. www.nps.gov/shen

It's not a family trip to Yellowstone National Park without seeing Old Faithful, but once you've checked that off your list, there are ample hikes in the area that are ideal if you have younger kids. In the nearby city of Cody, **Wyoming,** Cody Pathways is a system of trails in the Shoshone National Forest (which happens to be the first national forest in the country). For families, the Paul Stock Nature Trail is a manageable 1.3 miles along the Shoshone River. And just east of there is the Shoshone Riverway, which extends another 1.3 miles and offers plenty of wildlife viewing. fs.usda.gov/shoshone

Inside Rocky Mountain National Park in **Colorado,** one of the most family-friendly treks also happens to be a spectacularly beautiful one. Starting from the Bear Lake parking lot, you wander over to Nymph Lake and then set out on a more moderate climb to Dream Lake, until you reach Emerald Lake. The entire hike is only about 1.8 miles with an easy elevation gain of 600 or so feet. The only real challenge for young ones is climbing over some large boulder steps, but the payoff is more than worth it, with sweeping views of the alpine lakes surrounded by the snowy mountains. www.nps.gov/romo

For a more advanced hike with incredible views, head to Havasu Canyon (www.nps.gov/grca), a side canyon of the Grand Canyon in **Arizona.** The hot, arid climate and rugged switchbacks make this a moderately challenging climb, but the reward is a lush landscape at the bottom where waterfalls cascade over the red-orange sandstone cliffs. The 20-mile (round-trip) trail can be hiked in 2 or 3 days on foot. You can even chopper in or have your gear transported by mule. In fact, you're likely to pass by those pack mules during your hike— they're not just transporting gear, but also carrying US mail to the

INSIDER'S TIP

Truly family-friendly accommodations can have a lot more than just a roof and a bed and still be affordable. The YMCA of the Rockies' Estes Park Center is a 70-acre resort-style property surrounded on three sides by Rocky Mountain National Park. This is a value-packed stay that includes meals and seasonal activities like guided nature hikes and stargazing, and the national park is just steps away.

Havasupai tribe that resides in the canyon! If you're not comfortable hiking the entire way on your own, you can go with Austin-Lehman Adventures (www.austinlehman.com), which has an established camp (with someone else doing the cooking) so you can set out on day hikes without having to lug your gear.

Of the dozens of trails snaking around **Vermont**'s Green Mountain National Forest, intermediate hikers shouldn't miss the Skylight Pond Trail, which runs just over 5 miles round-trip. It start off climbing up an easy road. Once it enters the Breadloaf Wilderness, you'll ascend steeper switchbacks until you reach Skylight Pond and the rustic Skylight Lodge. On the south half of the forest, the Lake Trail is a long, meandering switchback to the Big Branch Wilderness until it connects to the quiet, scenic Griffith Lake area, running about 3.3 miles each way. www.fs.usda.gov/greenmountain

Hiking season in **Montana**'s Glacier National Park is relatively

Accessible Hiking

When seeking out wheelchair-accessible trails, the most obvious thing to look for is level, hard-packed, or paved ground. But also ask questions such as, how wide is the trail? Are there any potential roadblocks like sets of stairs, steep terrain, or fallen logs? Are the public facilities accessible? In **Colorado**'s Rocky Mountain National Park, Sprague Lake nature trail is a short path (about half a mile) of solid dirt that's lined with logs and observation decks overlooking the lake. The Green Mountain National Forest has a 900-foot boardwalk at Thundering Falls—which was the first fully accessible portion of the Appalachian Trail in **Vermont**—with a viewing platform that gets you an unobstructed view of the falls and the Ottauquechee Valley. In **British Columbia,** not only is the 8-mile Inland Lake loop trail at Inland Lake Provincial Park entirely wheelchair accessible, but it also has wheelchair-accessible cabin bathrooms spaced around the trail. Last, but certainly not least, there's the high-tech TrailRider, a lightweight, nonmotorized, one-wheeled riding device that can navigate even rugged and rough terrain. To use one requires the help of two able-bodied people, one to push, one to pull, but it's been instrumental in opening up trails to people with several mobility restrictions.

short, but with more than 730 miles of trails to choose from, the options are practically endless. You have to be in good condition to tackle the Highline Trail to the Grinnell Glacier Overlook, but it's a beauty: It's about 15 miles round-trip from the Logan Pass visitors center, with never-ending views of the towering mountains. After the first 8 miles, you'll hit the Grinnell Glacier Overlook Trail, which becomes quite steep and challenging, but the sweeping vista as you look down to Upper Grinnell Lake and the glacier are downright breathtaking. www.nps.gov/glac

Although most people flock to Yosemite National Park's valley floor, nearby Tuolumne Meadows in **California**'s High Sierra is where serious hikers go to avoid the heat and crowds. The Yosemite High Sierra Camp Loop features rustic lodgings where family-style breakfast and dinner are available. Spaced out every 6 to 10 miles, these camps allow you to tackle difficult hikes in the high wilderness without having to lug tents or cooking gear. The 35-mile Yosemite to Vogelsang Peak Loop, part of the iconic John Muir Trail, is a tough hike with a 3,000-foot elevation gain, but it offers some of the best scenery in the Sierra Nevada. We're talking crystal-clear alpine lakes and the Tuolumne River, unbeatable mountain views from Lyell Canyon, and miles of wildflowers. www.yosemitepark.com

The Precipice Trail is perhaps the most challenging trail in **Maine**'s Acadia National Park, on the eastern face of Champlain Mountain. The 1,000-foot climb is practically vertical, so it's crucial that you're in good condition before taking it on. This climb is best known for its view of the rare peregrine falcons from the cliffs—if the trail is closed during nesting season, ask the park ranger if there are spotting telescopes available. www.nps.gov/acad

Stretched along the Continental Divide, Bob Marshall Wilderness (a.k.a. "the Bob") in western **Montana** is part of the largest contiguous wilderness in the lower 48 states (over 1.5 million acres). Part of the Flathead National Forest, this area is one of the most completely preserved mountain ecosystems in the world. For wildlife enthusiasts, the grizzly bear population here is among the densest in the country, and you'll also see endangered wolves, moose, elk, bighorn sheep, wolverines, mountain lions, bald eagles, and ospreys. Don't miss the multiday hike to the Chinese Wall, an 18-mile-long, 1,000-foot-high chunk of limestone resembling the Great Wall of China, that juts into the Montana sky. www.fs.usda.gov/flathead

INTERNATIONAL

The Cotswolds hills, located about 100 miles from London, are ideal for country rambles. Designated an Area of Outstanding Natural Beauty, 3,000 miles of footpaths connect **England**'s rural villages and towns, primarily in the county of Gloucestershire, but also parts of Worcestershire, Oxfordshire, Warwickshire, Wiltshire, and Somerset. If you don't have a lot of hiking experience, opt for the Cotswold Way National Trail, which is the best-marked path and stretches about 100 miles from Chipping Campden to Bath, ascending a maximum of about 1,000 feet. Or lighten your load, as a handful of tour companies will arrange for self-guided walks in which they transport your luggage from one stop to the next.

France's first national park, Parc national de la Vanoise in the

Vanoise mountain range of the French Alps, is wild and remote yet accessible, making it an ideal escape. Enter from the mountain resort town of Pralognan-la-Vanoise and take a cable car up Mont Bochor. From there, follow the trail on a 4-hour (or so) hike to Vanoise Pass to catch sight of the Vanoise Peak and the Grande Casse, the highest point in the range that looms more than 12,000 feet.

Zermatt, **Switzerland,** located at the northern base of the Matterhorn, has nearly 250 miles of walking and hiking trails that wind around the mountainside—the largest collection of navigable trails in all of the Swiss Alps. One of the most amazing, midalpine hikes is the 3-hour trek up to Höhbalmen, starting from a 5,300-foot elevation. Once you catch your breath from this moderately steep, craggy climb that reaches an elevation of almost 9,000 feet at its highest point, you'll be rewarded with a panoramic view of the Matterhorn's north face looming over frozen glaciers and snow-covered peaks.

As one of the Seven Summits—the highest in **Africa**—Kilimanjaro

Hut-to-Hut Hiking

Many multiday hiking trails have huts at regular intervals with running water, electricity, cooking facilities, and beds so you don't have to sleep on the ground or eat freeze-dried food out of a bag during your trek. You generally need to book well in advance and abide by the rules of the hut, which means if they say lights out at 9:30, it means lights out. There are more than 250 shelters roughly a day's hike apart along the length of the **Appalachian Trail,** which stretches from Georgia to Maine. That's a shelter about every 8 miles, on average. They're located near freshwater sources so you don't have to lug your own. The 10th Mountain Division Hut Association operates 31 huts in Colorado's **Rocky Mountains** that connect 350 miles of trails. They have dorm-style rooms, electricity, and wood-burning stoves. The Alpine Club of Canada operates 28 huts in popular hiking spots like **Banff, Jasper,** and **Lake Louise.** Several of the famed walking tracks in New Zealand's **Fiordland National Park** on the South Island are also known for their hut lodging, including the Dusky Track, Milford Track, and Routeburn Track. You have to get a ticket in advance to stay in them, as the number of trekkers is limited by the park service and the huts fill up fast in high season.

Heli-Hiking

Sure, hiking is a common pastime. But have you ever heard of heli-hiking? The mountain ranges of eastern **British Columbia** are prime territory for multiday hikes, but some of the best spots are hard to get to. This is why companies such as CMH, one of the largest and most sophisticated heli-hiking operations in the world, can drop you in by helicopter and pick you up a few days later, after you complete your trek through the stunning backcountry. Since there are no trails, this is a truly wilderness experience, in which hikers are aided by experienced guides who can help navigate the difficult terrain.

is often considered the most attainable. The real trick with Kilimanjaro is the unpredictability, in terms of both weather and your own physical response to the trip. While the climb isn't considered technically difficult (most tour guides will tell you crampons are optional and poles are helpful but not necessary), there is no way to predict how your body will respond to the altitude. One of the best ways to assimilate to altitude is to give yourself time by choosing a longer, slower route. Skip the short, heavily touristed Marangu route (a.k.a. the "Coca Cola route") and opt for the longer, slower Machame route.

Located in the Southern Alps of **New Zealand**'s South Island, the Routeburn Track traverses a pristine rain forest landscape. Roughly a 3-day trek (or 4, if you take a more leisurely pace), it covers two national parks: Fiordland, with its glacial valleys, and Mount Aspiring, with its snowy peaks and mountain passes. Unlike other popular trails, this one features lodging along the way at simple but comfortable huts (which have gas stoves for cooking), so you won't need to carry tents and other equipment. Routeburn does not really lend itself to day hikes since it's not easy to get to and does not loop, but for the moderately to extremely fit, it is rightly considered one of the greatest hikes in the world.

HORSEBACK RIDING

I've been on horseback in Mexico, Bahrain, Peru, Utah, Texas, Arizona, Jordan, and Louisville. Am I an experienced horseman? Hardly. In most cases, I've been given a horse named Champ who takes one look at me and, 8 minutes into the ride, turns around at full gallop and races back to the barn, with me barely holding on! Having said that, the best places for horseback riding are divided by difficulty of terrain, location, and your own level of experience.

BEGINNER

Although you may associate the Big Island of **Hawaii** with ocean views and tropical forests, it's also home to a long cowboy culture with working ranches. At Dahana Ranch in Waimea, you'll be guided by third-generation Hawaiian horsemen (*paniolos*) through miles of sheep-dotted ranch lands with backdrops of the Waipi'o Valley and Mauna Kea. Best of all, no previous riding experience is necessary on these treks. If you're looking for a really immersive experience, go for the long-term horsemanship camp, which can run anywhere from 40 to 90 days (hey, I said it was immersive!). This includes basic training of ranch horses and working cow horses, as well as more specialized activities such as rodeo training, competitions, and ranch work. http://dahanaranch.com/horse_camp.htm

There are many farms and ranches that will allow anyone to walk slowly around a corral, but for beginners looking for a taste of trail riding, you want an area with easy, well-marked terrain with gentle horses and expert guides to lead the way. Griffith Park in **Los Angeles** has all of this, plus the benefit of being in the middle of the city. First-time riders are welcome at Griffith Park Horse Rentals, where you'll set out from the stables on an easy trail ride through the expansive park. www.griffithparkhorserental.com

It may seem counterintuitive for beginners to ride in the cold, but Icelandic horses (actually ponies) are tough, hardy, and tame, and you don't have to be an expert rider to ride one. This small breed has a gentle temperament and remarkable stamina. They are famous for their unique gait called the *tölt*, a kind of smooth running trot where one foot is always touching the ground. Most operators will supply you with head-to-toe insulated jackets and sturdy boots that can hold up even to frigid temperatures. As for the best places in **Iceland** to ride? There are a number, including Hornstrandir Nature Reserve in the west; Húnaflói, Skagafjörður, Dalvík, and Mývatn in the north; Landmannalaugar, Hella, Hvolsvöllur, and the Markarfljót valley in the south; and Breiðdalsvík and Borgarfjörður Eystri in the east.

Can't travel to Iceland to ride? Equitours actually supplies these gentle breeds on a novice ride through **Vermont**'s Green Mountains. Because of the stunning location, you're best off opting for the fall foliage ride, where you'll literally be surrounded by brilliant color. The best part about this trip is that rides start from the Vermont Icelandic Horse Farm, so you can spend as much or as little time as you want riding through nearby forests and farms, and you're within easy distance from the town of Stowe. www.ridingtours.com

MODERATE

I t's probably no surprise that Texans love their horseback riding. Big Bend Ranch, just northeast of Presidio, is the largest state park in **Texas**, where the Wild West meets the Chihuahuan desert. There are more than 200 miles of horseback trails plus acres of backcountry areas to choose from. The easiest option is to head to Sauceda Ranger Station, which offers guided horseback rides every hour. If you want a more rugged experience, take part in an actual longhorn cattle drive in which you set out on horseback on a 3-day adventure to drive longhorns to the ranch, alongside working wranglers. www.tpwd.state.tx.us

With more than 3,740 square miles of terrain, **Yellowstone National Park** has over 40 licensed outfitters that can take you on rides ranging from 2 hours to several days. The horse trails of Lamar Valley are especially worthwhile for more experienced riders, with multiday pack trips along the Lamar River. Pack mules carry all your gear, leaving you free to ride your horse through miles and miles of unsullied wilderness away from the crowds. Along the way, take a break from riding to go hiking or fly-fishing. The best time for riding tends to be in June and early July, before it's too hot and when the wildlife is at its most active—particularly bison and bears. Although the spring shoulder season will be less crowded, be aware that the altitude can mean very cold weather, especially on over-nights. www.nps.gov/yell/planyourvisit/stockbusn.htm

On **New Zealand**'s South Island, wild and often roadless land-scapes are some of the most scenic in the world, making it a favorite for horseback riding. The best part about riding in the South Island? The population is so small that you won't encounter any crowds. Dart Stables, about 45 minutes from Queenstown, has exclusive horse-riding access to Paradise Station near Mount Aspiring National Park. Here, moderately experienced riders can travel up to 6 hours for 2 days through streams and fields against the backdrop of the rugged mountains. www.dartstables.com

Headed to the North Island instead? Try riding along Pakiri Beach, about 2 hours north of Auckland. This unspoiled expanse of smooth, white sand is ideal terrain for beginners and families, with everything from hourlong to full-day rides along the coast.

EXPERT

I f you've ever wondered about the Great American Cattle Drive adventure, this one's for you. Twice a year, in June and October, cattle herds are moved back and forth between summer pastures near Bryce Canyon in **Utah** and winter ranges on the north rim of the Grand Canyon in **Arizona.** Operated by the original clan that has run cattle in the western United States since the Wild West days of Buffalo Bill, the Long Valley Cattle Drive is an 11-day saga of ranching, riding, cutting, and cantering. Guests assist real cow-boys in cutting particular cows and calves from the herd of 800, and then feast on meals cooked fireside. This ride is for intermediate to advanced riders—beginners will find it a bit too intense.

The Darhat Valley in **Mongolia**'s Khovsgol is wild, wide, and remote, with vast grasslands dotted with wildflowers that spread up to the snow-topped mountain peaks. Horse-riding enthusiasts can ride between Darhat Valley and the pristine Lake Khovsgol National

Park, where you may meet up with members of the nomadic Tsaatan tribe along the way. On a guided tour, you're likely to spend several hours a day on horseback and sleep in rustic cabins or tents, so previous experience and an adventurous attitude is a must. Look for a tour that takes place during the summertime Naadam festivities, a centuries-old tradition with horse racing and other sporting events.

One of the top outfitters for horseback riding is Equitrekking, which tends to focus on ecofriendly, culturally rich horseback tours. Advanced riders will want to opt for the **Jordan** Bedouin Trek. Led by a champion endurance rider, this is a 10-day journey on Arabian horses that starts from the world wonder of Petra and treks through the Wadi Rum desert, through massive canyons and caves, passing nomadic Bedouin communities. According to many, this is the only way to experience Jordan at its most natural. www.equitrekking.com

The owner of Equitours, which began operating on a ranch more than 40 years ago, was raised in East Africa and continues to take advanced riders to the Masai Mara in **Kenya.** Gallop alongside zebras and wildebeest, and yes, there is a chance you may have to sprint from lions while on horseback! www.ridingtours.com

LUXURY

Part country chic, part rugged outdoors, the Stonepine Estate in **California**'s Carmel Valley is a private family estate that calls for total equestrian immersion. My favorite part of this resort? You can actually get hands-on experience working with ex-racehorses, to train them for their new roles on the resort property. At one point, Stonepine was the largest thoroughbred breeding facility west of the Mississippi. There are about a dozen trail rides in and around the property, with guides at your disposal. www.stonepineestate.com

Ireland's Castle Leslie Estate in County Monaghan is a prime destination for every level of horse enthusiast. Ride along the Irish countryside, learn the fundamentals of dressage, learn to hunt on

A Horse of a Different Color

Instead of horse trekking, how about cow trekking or camel trekking? At Bolderhof, an organic farm in Hemishofen, **Switzerland,** you can ride one of Heinz and Doris Morgenegg's cows while exploring the banks of the Rhine river and the beautiful Swiss countryside—very slowly. www.bolderhof.ch

If camel trekking is more your speed, Nomadic Expeditions will take you on a multiday trek through the Gobi desert in **Mongolia** on the back of a Bactrian camel. In **Yellowstone National Park,** Llama Treks will set up a multiday pack trip with these gentle creatures. For a moderate, but totally accessible ride, head to the Black Canyon of the Yellowstone, a 3-day trip that runs along the Yellowstone River, with a side hike to Knowles Falls and plenty of trout fishing in the river.

horseback, or even take a horse veterinarian course. This particular castle is also unique in that it's one of the few remaining castles that's still in the hands of its founding family, Clan Leslie. www.castleleslie.com

Riding by horseback doesn't necessarily mean roughing it. With the Riding Company, a 7-day, 6-night ride to Machu Picchu in **Peru** includes stops in luxury lodges along the way. You'll ride Uruguayan quarter and Arabian horses from the Sacred Valley over the Salkantay Pass, past lakes and valleys, and end with a private tour of the world wonder of Machu Picchu. Just keep in mind, there is a good deal of walking involved as well, as the terrain can be steep and challenging. If you can, go during winter solstice over the week of June 21, when locals have massive celebrations in and around Cusco. www.theridingcompany.com

RIDE IN A HOT AIR BALLOON

My very first balloon ride, in Albuquerque back in 1973, was a terrifying experience. As a control freak (yes, I admit to this), I soon discovered I had no control. We were at the mercy of the wind. Then, about 5 minutes into our ascension, I realized that not being in control is the essence and the beauty of ballooning. It's not just the staggering views. It's the silence as I drifted over the desert and the cactus. One of the big—and refreshing—surprises about ballooning is the lack of wind, which means a lack of noise. Simple explanation: We are moving at the speed of the wind. The other great thing about ballooning is the other unknown: You obviously know your departure point, but you have no idea where you are landing. That's part of the excitement.

A few years later, over the Loire Valley in France, I benefited from that "unknown" firsthand, with legendary balloon pilot Buddy Bombard. Early each morning, before the wind picked up, or sometimes in the late afternoon—when the winds died down—we'd go up in his balloon. And every day, we'd end up landing in the backyard of a beautiful private estate and château. Despite our surprise arrival, the owners would invariably come out into their fields with an impromptu buffet of fabulous wine and cheese to welcome us!

UNITED STATES

There seems to be a natural connection between **California**'s Napa and Sonoma wine country and ballooning, and with good reason. Wine Country Balloons offers sky-high tours starting at the crack of dawn from Santa Rosa. Where you go depends on the weather conditions, but typical bird's-eye views include the Pacific coast, the rolling vineyards of the Russian River and Sonoma valleys, and the redwood forests. What's cool about this company is that you can also participate in the process of inflating and deflating the balloon by learning about it while still on the ground. www.balloontours.com

Talk about a year-round destination. Aspen and Snowmass, **Colorado,** are blanketed in snow in the winter, wildflowers in spring and summer, and foliage in the fall. So what better way to view it all than from above? Above It All Balloon Company takes off at sunrise and, depending on the conditions, can cross over some lower mountains toward the west (most other balloon companies stay in one main valley). Best time to go? September, when Snowmass holds both a balloon festival and a wine festival, and the mountains are blanketed with the golden glow of changing aspen trees. www.aboveitallballoon.com

Fall is undoubtedly the best time to take a balloon ride over New England, when the changing foliage creates a wild palette of colors. But the region also contains unique topography that makes the view from above particularly distinct. Balloons Over New England operates from Quechee, **Vermont,** home of the 165-foot Quechee Gorge, the deepest gorge in the state formed more than 13,000 years ago by glacial activity and the still-flowing Ottauquechee River. www.balloonsovernewengland.com

Albuquerque, **New Mexico,** is known as the Balloon Capital of the World for good reason. Its cool morning temperatures and predictable wind patterns make for excellent flying conditions, not to mention the unbeatable views of the Rio Grande Valley and the Sandia Mountains. Experts come here because of something called the "Albuquerque box," or a set of wind patterns that make it easier to navigate the balloons. Most enthusiasts will head to Albuquerque for the famous balloon festival, but those interested in the process behind the product shouldn't miss the Albuquerque Balloon Museum. The $12 million, 59,000-square-foot museum covers everything about ballooning history, navigation, and science with interactive exhibits and historic memorabilia. What's really wild is that the building even looks like a balloon inside!

Albuquerque is host to the International Balloon Fiesta every October, the largest balloon rally in the world, with 10 days of launches, fireworks, and festivities. What started off as a promotional stunt in

INSIDER'S TIP

Balloon festivals are a photographer's dream and a family-friendly event. It can be quite an emotional experience to see these colorful giants launch into the air all at once. To find a balloon festival anywhere in the world, check out www.hotairballoon.com.

1972 with 13 balloons has grown to more than 700 hot air and gas balloons with hundreds of pilots from 19 countries. The 10,000-foot Sandias form the backdrop, and the October wind patterns gently increase altitude of the balloons. In fact, on some mornings during the festival, you can see as many as 400 balloons floating in all different directions. My favorite time at this festival? At 5:45 a.m., when lighted balloons participating in the Dawn Patrol take off while it's still dark. Almost every evening around 5:45 p.m. is the Balloon Glow, where you can walk among the balloons as they are grounded, burners fired and lit up from within. www.balloonfiesta.com

How about a great balloon race that just keeps going and going? The Great Forest Park Balloon Race, a free event in St. Louis, **Missouri,** in September, stands out because the balloons actually launch from a park in the middle of the city. Crowds of around 130,000 gather to watch as 70 "hound" balloons chase the Energizer Bunny "Hot Hare Balloon." The balloon dropping a baggie of bird-seed closest to the Energizer Bunny balloon is declared the winner. www.greatforestparkballoonrace.com

INTERNATIONAL

I t's one thing to experience the dramatic vistas of the ancient city of Teotihuacan in **Mexico.** But to see it from above is an entirely different experience altogether. Located about 30 miles northeast of Mexico City, this archaeological site contains some of the largest pyramids built in the pre-Columbian Americas. (The name Teotihuacan loosely translates into "the place where the gods were created.") The multilevel compounds, temples, plazas, and caves are dominated by the 200-foot-tall Pyramid of the Sun, one of the largest pyramids in the world. On the northern end of the main boulevard sits the Pyramid of the Moon, and within the sprawling Ciudadela square is the Temple of Quetzalcoatl. When you think of the history of these holy sites, seeing them from above is a truly special experience.

France is the birthplace of hot air ballooning, so it's fitting that there is a full-service ballooning resort there. At Buddy Bombard's Europe, you can spend anywhere from 5 to 8 days drifting over medieval castles and vineyards, while spending your nights at an 18th-century château. One-third of each day is devoted to ballooning, which is done at such a low level you practically graze the treetops. In fact, you're so low you can even speak to people on the ground! The remainder of each day is spent land-based, sightseeing with private guides and exploring the restaurants of Europe. www.buddybombard.com

The closest thing to flying over the moon is taking a hot air balloon ride over Cappadocia, **Turkey.** The landscape is covered in tall rock spires known as hoodoos, or fairy chimneys, and a view from above is inspiring. Kapadokya Balloons sets off every day at sunrise, though the location varies based on the wind conditions of the day. Once you complete your journey in the sky, you head underground! Cappadocia is known for its underground cities and cave hotels that are actually carved into the unique rock formations. www.kapadokyaballoons.com

Sure, you might expect to see African game from the perspective of a 4x4, but how about from the sky? Since hot air balloons are nearly silent, you can creep up on wildlife without disturbing them. One of the best areas to view from above is the Masai Mara National Reserve in **Kenya,** simply for the diversity of wildlife packed in a relatively small area. Your best bet is to travel there in fall when game spotting is at its peak; a number of balloon companies take off at dawn for the best views and end with a champagne breakfast in the reserve.

In **South Africa,** a safari in Kruger National Park is a must. But make the experience even more memorable and personal by adding a dawn hot air balloon flight just outside of the park, overlooking the rolling Mpumalanga and the Sabi River valley. Beauty spills as far as the eye can see, with dense foliage, small hills, and views of the mountains off in the distance.

Not many Americans are familiar with the scenic beauty of Western **Australia,** which is exactly why you should go. Departing just outside of Perth, Windward Balloon Adventures will take you high over the bucolic Avon Valley, where you'll look over rolling farms and the wandering Avon River. Because of the hot, windy conditions in summer, these flights are only available between April and November. www.ballooning.net.au

Urban landscape or sprawling vineyards? In Australia, you can choose to fly over Melbourne—one of the only major cities in the world that offers hot air balloon rides over the city center—or over the famed Yarra Valley wine country. With Global Ballooning, the Melbourne flight gives an overview of the entire city at sunrise and then drifts into green outskirts. The wine country ride starts at Rochford Wines and soars over the Yarra Valley.

KAYAKING, CANOEING, AND PADDLEBOARDING

All three activities are thrill-seeking—yet accessible—water sports. They're some of my most favorite things to do in just about any kind of weather, short of a Category 5 hurricane. Perhaps the best part of kayaking, canoeing, and stand-up paddleboarding is that, with exceedingly few exceptions, just about anyone can do it, master it, and enjoy the experience.

RIVER

Just 2 hours south of the gridlock and noise of Washington, DC, **Virginia**'s Northern Neck boasts 1,397 miles of paddle-ready shoreline that covers a four-county area. Part of the Chesapeake Bay watershed, the Rappahannock is an exceptionally scenic river, flowing through pastoral farm country and Civil War battle sites. The waters and weather are at their best between April and November. The launch site from Mount Landing Creek is ideal for beginners, as is the easy, calm water at Kelly's Ford access point, where rapids max out at Class I. More advanced paddlers can also set off from Kelly's Ford and tackle the 2-day journey to Mott's Run, which courses through some Class II whitewater rapids on the 25-mile route.

Some of the best quiet-water paddling in the country can be found in **New Jersey**'s Pine Barrens coastal plains. For a really peaceful experience, head to the 55-mile Mullica River, where you can paddle all day and probably not see a single house or person. It's a real wilderness no-man's-land as it goes through the Wharton State Forest and groves of cedars, oaks, and pine trees. Those looking for beautiful scenery and a decent workout will appreciate the Upper Mullica bookended by Goshen Pond and Atsion Lake, a narrow stretch that's teeming with wildlife and is especially pretty during fall foliage season.

The Weeki Wachee is a spring-fed river that lets out into **Florida**'s central Gulf Coast. With waters that remain a constant 75 degrees year-round, this is a welcoming area for beginners, particularly between Weeki Wachee Springs State Park and Rogers Park. (Local outfitter Paddling Adventures, www.paddlingadventures.com, can transport you back to your vehicle at the end of the journey.) What really stands out along this peaceful, 7.5-mile stretch of river is the diversity of wildlife—otters, turtles, alligators, and, best of all, wild manatee. Bonus: In the town of Weeki Wachee Springs, you can watch the famous (but campy) mermaid show where costumed ladies perform song-and-dance numbers underwater.

Michigan is filled with rivers and lakes that are suitable for paddling, but locals know to go to the Au Sable River from Grayling to Oscoda. In fact, this 120-mile stretch of river is home to a popular nonstop canoe marathon that takes anywhere from 14 to 19 hours to complete, and spectators will literally stay up all night to cheer on the racers. Recreational canoers and kayakers can head out from a number of launch points, but a great low-key trip runs from Stephan Bridge to McMaster's Bridge, where the clear waters flow at a leisurely pace.

At 740 miles, the Northern Forest Canoe Trail is the longest inland recreational water trail in the country. This network of rivers, streams, lakes, and ponds starts off in **New York State** and flows northeast through **Vermont** and **New Hampshire,** and then meanders into the wilderness of northern **Maine.** In fact, the trail crosses the Canadian border twice. And yes, they will ask for your passport. There is an infinite amount of choice here, and so far, only about 50 people have completed the entire route in one go. Much of the water here is actually challenging whitewater, but for a more leisurely route, try a one-day trip from its starting point at Old Forge to Inlet, which is entirely on the flat waters of Fulton Chain of Lakes. Visit www.northernforestcanoetrail.org for an interactive map of the entire route, including inns and B&Bs, camping, and dining options along the way.

Not many people associate kayaking with a trip to **France,** but paddling along the Vézère River is a great way to get a historical perspective of the Dordogne region. You can float along shallow, quiet waters past medieval villages and ruins, castles, cliff dwellings, and the famous prehistoric caves filled with Stone Age paintings. Paddlers usually set out between April and September, but the best time to go is in early summer when the water levels are at their highest after the spring rains. Best of all, there are plenty of canoe and kayak companies that will drive you back to your starting point—Canoës Vallée Vézère (www.canoesvalleevezere.com) even allows you to choose your own beginning and end points. My advice: The famous Lascaux caves are located in Montignac, which is an excellent place to begin or end your trip.

LAKES AND PONDS

It's safe to say that most paddlers can find a great experience in the Adirondacks in **New York,** with thousands of lakes, ponds, and rivers that have several launch points, sand beaches, and kayak camping spots. The best part about this area is that the waters are safe and quiet, which means that most paddlers of all ages can tackle these waters (although the Hudson River has some challenging whitewater sections). Within this whole region, you probably want to head to the Saint Regis Wilderness Canoe Area, a 19,000-acre area of Adirondack Park that has the distinction of being the largest wilderness canoe area in the Northeast, including 58 ponds plus the headwaters of the Saint Regis and Saranac Rivers. There are several navigable loops here, like Rollins Pond Loop, which also connects to the Floodwood Pond loop for a manageable 8-mile journey. (Note: You will have to carry your canoe for short stretches.) Find an interactive map with dozens of suggested routes at www.adirondacklakes.com.

Along the **Arizona-Utah** border is the 150-mile Lake Powell. What makes this body of water really stand out are its still waters, multiple coves, and narrow slot canyons. These slot canyons are completely remote and are often inaccessible by motorized vessel. Kayaking or canoeing through Cathedral Canyon is an unbeatable experience, with towering red sandstone walls, yet it's entirely navigable for all levels of expertise. Another great ride is through Cascade Canyon, which is a much more adventurous option that requires backpaddling to get back out.

THE SEA

Avid kayakers love the low country around **Georgia**'s Sea Islands, which includes Tybee Island, Little Tybee, St. Simons, and

Cumberland. This area is a magnet for paddlers, who can explore the open water, tidal creeks and marshes, and sandbars. If paddling with kids or beginners, try an easy half-day excursion to Little Tybee Island, which is only accessible by boat. Go for a guided tour with an outfitter like Sea Kayak Georgia and you'll get an educational experience en route to this uninhabited barrier island, where you can spot dolphins, otter, osprey, and various birds, and explore its complex ecosystem. www.seakayakgeorgia.com

Where else can you paddle and be eye to eye with exotic wildlife and marine life and explore hidden coves and untouched mangroves? The **Galapagos,** of course. The Galapagos Marine Reserve is a prime spot for kayaking and canoeing. A great option is to go on an organized trip with a company that combines kayaking with hiking, snorkeling, and other natural adventures to get the best out of this region. OARS (www.oars.com) offers an 11-day tour in which you'll stay on a catamaran and set out on kayaks to access hard-to-reach coves and inlets, getting up close and personal with the richly biodiverse marine life and flightless birds.

Off the coast of **Mexico,** the Sea of Cortéz is famous for its warm, calm waters and rugged islands that are prime for exploring. Best of all, you can get close to diverse marine life wherever you go. Loreto National Marine Park is home to porpoises, sea lions, blue whales, and manta rays, while Magdalena Bay is where massive gray whales return every winter.

Glacier Bay, **Alaska,** is home to an array of astonishing scenery, from towering icebergs to tidewater glaciers. With Mountain Travel Sobek (www.mtsobek.com), a summer sea kayaking expedition starts with a charter boat to carry you across the strait, and then you'll paddle your way along 50 miles of shoreline. You'll catch sight of humpback whale feeding sites and other diverse wildlife such as sea otters and sea lions, as well as black and brown bears within the dense forests. Best of all, the tour operator has rare permits to camp inside Glacier Bay National Park.

One of the best sea kayaking destinations in **Canada** is Lake Superior, a freshwater inland sea. Naturally Superior Adventures (www.

naturallysuperior.com) will set you up on a base at Rock Island Lodge, near Wawa, Ontario, and set out on guided trips from there. Take the chance to explore some of the more remote parts of the lake on a multiday trip to Denison Falls. You don't need any kayaking experience (but keep in mind there is camping involved). You'll get to explore 35 miles of the northern coastline heading west and spend a day hiking to the impressive 100-foot waterfall on the Dog River. For the mildest paddling conditions, try to go between mid-July and mid-August.

STAND-UP PADDLEBOARDING

S tand-up paddleboarding is among the world's fastest-growing water sports. Why? It's accessible for all fitness levels and is a great alternative to kayaking. Since you're standing, not sitting, you get better views both into the water and out to the horizon. All you need is flat water, which can be on the open ocean (especially in calm tropical areas with reefs or small islands), in rivers, lakes, lagoons, or reservoirs.

Hawaii is known as the birthplace of stand-up paddleboarding, and the opportunities are practically limitless. Many hotels around Honolulu offer basic lessons and rentals for those who just want to tool around in the shadow of Diamond Head, but if you want to see more of what Hawaii has to offer, try Hanalei River in Kauai. You can either stick to the calm river itself—and catch sight of the historic Hanalei Bridge in the upper reaches—or try your luck in the sometimes choppy Hanalei Bay. The family-run Hawaiian Surfing Adventures is a favorite of Laird Hamilton, one of the most famous surfers in the world, who is credited with popularizing stand-up paddleboarding in the United States (www.hawaiiansurfingadventures.com).

On Oahu's north side, the Anahulu River lazily winds its way through the historic town of Haleiwa. On the Big Island, both Kamakahonu Bay and Kealakekua Bay are known for calm waters that are ideal for stand-up paddleboarding.

Paddleboarding in Newport Beach, **California,** can be an all-day experience. In the morning you can enjoy a paddle in the Upper Newport Bay, home to the Upper Newport Bay Nature Preserve and Ecological Reserve, to enjoy the scenic wetlands and wildflowers. At lunch you can paddle around the harbor to be side by side with sailboats. And here's an unusual idea: stand-up paddleboard surfing. All you have to do is head toward rolling waves—just by Blackie's by the Sea, where all the locals hang out—and get started. You'll likely spot seals, dolphins, and whales, depending on the time of year. Go early in the morning because both the wind and the crowds pick up by afternoon. Want an even harder workout? SUPcore Academy pretty much invented the concept of "gym on the water" by combining fitness and yoga programs atop a paddleboard (www.supcoreacademy.com). If you prefer to be a spectator, go to nearby Dana Point in September for the Battle of the Paddle, the world's largest stand-up paddleboard race.

The **Maldives,** a chain of 1,000 islands in the middle of the Indian Ocean, is a paddler's dream destination. You'll glide over brilliant coral reefs that sit just below sea level and paddle past atolls that jut above the surface of the absurdly clear water. If you've ever wanted to paddle at sunset, this is where to go.

The Bay of Islands, at the very top of **New Zealand**'s North Island, offers a huge variety of paddling experiences. The water is warm year-round, and even on windy days you can find a sheltered bay somewhere to get your paddling fix. With 2,000 miles of coastline, two marine reserves, and 17 harbors, you could literally spend years exploring the mangroves, bays, islands, rivers, and beaches. But my advice is to head to Kerikeri inlet, which has exceptionally calm waters and accessible launch spots like Skudders Beach and Opito Bay. It's also a beautiful area, surrounded by volcanic rock and a high population of dolphins that you can spot while in the water. Never attempted this sport before? Northland Paddleboarding (www.northlandpaddleboarding.co.nz) is one of the very few outfitters that offers stand-up paddleboarding instruction in this region. These guys are so confident in their training that they offer a "stay dry" guarantee with their lessons. They also offer inflatable paddleboards, which have better shock absorption in the event you hit a rock—and you don't have to worry about scratching or breaking them.

The tiny, off-the-beaten-path island of Koh Lipe in southern **Thailand** is an excellent spot because of its dense population of marine life. What you want to do here is combine stand-up paddleboarding with snorkeling: Simply paddle to one of the two smaller islands just offshore (Koh Kra or Koh Usen), then stop to swim with reef sharks in the balmy water. Visit between November and March for the best weather (the island is pretty much closed for business from May through October because of monsoon season). Koh Lipe can be reached by boat from Koh Phi Phi, Koh Lanta, and several other islands in the Andaman Sea.

Of course, advanced surfers know **Tahiti** for its legendary surf break, Teahupoo, which some brave adventurers have also attempted on stand-up paddleboard—but this is for the very experienced only. Otherwise, you're better off sticking to calmer lagoons, like the ones at Four Seasons Bora Bora or Le Meridien Tahiti. If romance is on the agenda, few places are better than this for an early morning sunrise paddle or a night paddle under the full moon. The months between May and October are usually the best because of cooler temperatures.

The Apostle Islands in **Wisconsin** are a series of scattered jewels along the southern shore of Lake Superior. Most people are surprised to learn that there are 21 islands and 12 miles of mainland to

Better Than the Gym

Paddling is not the only thing you can do on a paddleboard. Yoga, Pilates, core strengthening, and even jousting are just some of the many ways to utilize a paddleboard. The paddleboard is an ideal complement to core training and yoga because the extra effort required to balance on the board makes your abs and back muscles (not to mention your calves, shoulders, and feet) work even harder than usual. And it's a lot more fun than being a gym rat!

explore in this region, with rocky shorelines, sea caves, and sandy beaches in protected bays. Spend the day exploring the sea caves along the coast, and maybe spot a lighthouse or two, then paddle up to a cove for lunch, and explore the islands while paddling back.

The **Virgin Islands** are an attractive spot for all sorts of water sports, but for stand-up paddleboarding, you want to go to the broad, gorgeous Cinnamon Bay on St. John. This bay boasts tons of tropical fish, sea turtles, and brilliant blue waters. Since it's part of the Virgin Islands National Park, there's no development nearby, just densely forested hills and fine white sand. At the Baths at Virgin Gorda, you'll paddle around the massive granite boulders, and you can make frequent stops to inspect the tidal pools, rock tunnels and arches, and hidden grottoes.

Just off the coast of **Sweden,** running both north and south of Stockholm, is one of the world's largest archipelagoes, consisting of more than 24,000 islands and islets spread over 70 miles of ocean. It is divided into subsections, almost all of which can be paddled (just avoid the shipping lanes!). A favorite area is the Roslagen's archipelago in the northern end, which contains 13,000 islands. Each island has a different character—some are rocky and barren, while others are green and flower filled. There's even a national park on one (Ängsö). Bird-watching paddlers love the huge variety of seabirds that can be spotted.

The high-altitude Bow Lake in **Banff National Park** in the Canadian Rockies offers everything you'd expect from a mountain lake: unparalleled scenery, wildlife, and glacier-fed waters. Geese, fox, and moose can be seen on the shore, and you can get up close and personal (as you dare) with Crowfoot Glacier. Go in the morning, before the chilly wind picks up in the afternoon. And you'll need to wear more than a swimsuit for this one.

If you've never heard of Apulia, **Italy,** you're missing out. This area in the "heel" of Italy boasts more than 20 miles of coast from Vieste to Mattinata, and over 30 limestone caves that can be explored on a paddleboard. The sea caves are the result of thousands of years of wind and water battering the cliffs, and they often have bizarre and unusual shapes. In fact, stand-up paddleboarding is preferable to the more common motorboat tours, because paddleboards are less damaging to the fragile limestone.

Off the central coast of **Portugal,** within an hour's drive of Lisbon, there are all kinds of opportunities for paddleboarding. The calm waters of the Obidos Lagoon (Lagoa de Óbidos) are great for beginners and intermediates, while those who want to tackle waves can head to the surf beaches of Supertubos, Lagide, and Belgas. The middle and lower reaches of the Rio Tejo are wide and smooth, and as a bonus you'll paddle past beautiful gorges and a medieval castle. Lastly, the Luiz Saldanha Marine Park near Arrabida is a perfect place to spot bottlenose dolphins as you glide beneath soaring limestone cliffs.

Urban Kayaking

Where else but Austin, **Texas,** can you combine kayaking with spotting urban bats? That's right, a company called Live, Love, Paddle will take you at night by kayak up Lady Bird Lake to see the colony of 1.5 million bats as they make their nightly departure from Congress Bridge (www.livelovepaddle.com). New Yorkers can kayak along the Hudson free of charge! Downtown Boathouse is a nonprofit venture that provides kayaks in three spots around **New York City:** Pier 40 at Houston Street, Pier 96 at 56th Street, and at 72nd Street in Riverside Park (www.downtownboathouse.org). In Milwaukee, **Wisconsin,** there are 25 miles of reclaimed shoreline you can paddle on the Milwaukee, Menomonee, and Kinnickinnic Rivers. The Milwaukee Urban Water Trail map is available at http://mkeriverkeeper.org. In Vancouver, **British Columbia,** intrepid types can dip their boats in the Capilano River between North and West Vancouver. On days that the dam is releasing water, there are rapids up to Class IV. And believe it or not, you can even kayak in Venice, **Italy.** Bring your own inflatable kayak and take a self-guided tour of the city's mazelike canals, or go on a guided tour with a company such as Venice Kayak (www.venicekayak.com).

Best Places to Find

MARINE LIFE

My first encounter with marine life was at an aquarium in Palos Verdes, California, when I was 6 years old. It was called Marineland. You could look—from a distance—but you could not touch. As fascinating as the concept was of seeing these incredible creatures of the deep, my attention span was limited by my lack of access. My parents told me I got bored and wanted to leave after 5 minutes.

Thankfully, times have changed, and the definition of "spectator" when it comes to marine encounters has been amended.

AQUARIUMS AND MARINE PARKS

If you think aquariums and marine parks are overrated tourist attractions, think again. When looking for hands-on or family-oriented activities, there are specialized programs that can really make the experience memorable—much more than just eyeing these creatures from a distance or watching a rehearsed performance.

Underwater World is an oceanarium off the coast of **Singapore** where you can safely swim with sharks and stingrays, even if you're not scuba certified, or with pink dolphins if you prefer friendlier swimming companions. But here's what's really special about this place: Ask about the fish reflexology option. Dip your feet into water where two types of doctor fish will nibble off your dead skin, followed by a foot massage by (human) reflexologists. www.underwaterworld.com.sg

More experienced divers will want to head to the Blue Planet Aquarium just south of Liverpool, **England.** Here there are dives with dozens of sand tiger sharks, nurse sharks, zebra sharks, and lemon sharks in a 3.8 million-liter Caribbean reef tank. But what I like about this place is its family-friendly programming—even kids can swim with the sharks! Children between 8 and 15 years old will get expert instruction before a supervised dive experience in a tank, where they're guaranteed to get a close encounter with sharks, sting-rays, and an array of tropical fish. www.blueplanetaquarium.com

Dolphin Cove, **Jamaica,** is one of the top animal-encounter marine parks in all of the Caribbean, both in Ocho Rios and Negril. The best thing about this park is that the dolphins are in a natural ocean enclosure, not an artificial setting. My advice: Go for the "Sea Keeper for a Day" program, where you get to do more than just swim with marine life; you can feed, hold, and play with dolphins, Carib-bean sharks, and stingrays. www.dolphincovejamaica.com

Want to take a trip around the world? Istanbul Aquarium, the largest in **Turkey,** is home to 15,000 land and sea creatures. Each room is designed to reflect different parts of the world, from the Black Sea to the Pacific Ocean, to showcase the indigenous area of each creature. www.istanbulakvaryum.com/en-US/home

WILD ENCOUNTERS

BEGINNER/INTERMEDIATE

The waters around Kaikoura, **New Zealand,** are ideal for those looking for wild encounters. This is the area to see the dusky dolphin, which can only be found in the Southern Hemisphere. In fact, pods of more than 1,000 of these acrobatic dolphins can be spotted in the waters, often doing leaps and somersaults in the air. An operator like Dolphin Encounter can take you out on an open-water excursion to see these lively creatures from a boat or swim alongside them. www.dolphinencounter.co.nz

There's a good reason why you want to travel all the way to the Red Sea to see marine life: Dolphin Reef in Eilat, **Israel,** has eight bottlenose dolphins that live in ocean enclosures, not artificial pools, and the experience is as natural as possible. It's entirely up to the dolphins if they want to interact with snorkelers and divers, with no touching, chasing, or feeding to entice them. www.Dolphinreef.co.il

Just off the coast of Gansbaai in **South Africa** (near Hermanus, the world-famous whale-watching region and about 2 hours from Cape Town) is an area called Shark Alley, best known for great whites. Some of the best operators in the country will take you here. Marine Dynamics (www.sharkwatchsa.com), a Fair Trade–accredited operation, is owned by the founder of a shark conservation program, so you'll get to experience cage diving in the sharks' natural habitat and get an education in shark conservation from marine biologists on board. Meanwhile, certified divers will want to check out Shark Diving Unlimited (www.sharkdivingunlimited.com), which is run by a shark behavior expert. The best visibility is between May and October, but if you want to avoid the crowds, there is still high shark activity in the slower months between January and March.

Along the southern tip of South **Australia**'s Eyre Peninsula are the lagoons surrounding Port Lincoln. Baird Bay, in particular, is one of the few places in the world where you can swim face-to-face with Australian sea lions. Because this is a natural habitat, it's up to these friendly creatures how much interaction you'll actually have with them. If you really want to push the envelope, look for companies like Adventure Bay Charters (www.adventurebaycharters.com.au), which can travel farther out to sea, near the Neptune Islands, for cage diving with sharks. These guys actually have an interesting methodology. Instead of using chum or bait to attract sharks, they use . . . heavy metal music. (Apparently the great whites in these waters are big fans of AC/DC.) Meanwhile, the company Calypso Star Charters (www.sharkcagediving.com.au) has a following because of its ability to attract an 18-foot behemoth named Big Mamma while cage diving with the great whites.

There are now dozens of highly promoted dolphin "encounter" experiences around the world. But the key is to make your dolphin encounter a meaningful one. The 10,000 Islands Dolphin Project is a conservation project to protect coastal bottlenose dolphins in southwestern **Florida.** It's the only continuous study of wild dolphins in this area and the only educational program that actually encourages public participation. Twice daily, you can set out from Marco Island with a survey team, where you'll observe and record the activities of these playful creatures. www.dolphin-study.com

Just 27 miles off the shore of San Francisco are the **Farallon Islands,** a collection of rock islands and a marine sanctuary. There is a vast array of marine life swimming here, including great white sharks that feed on the elephant seals that live in the area. For a more hands-off approach, you can travel with the Oceanic Society (www.oceanicsociety.org) to spot blue and humpback whales, dolphins, seabirds, and more. And, yes, they also offer a shark-diving excursion—no scuba certification required.

Traveling solo or prefer to leave the planning to someone else? Hook up with an organized tour that offers packaged shark-diving trips around the world. Shark Diver (www.sharkdiver.com) is one of the leading shark dive expedition companies. In **Mexico** the Isla Guadalupe White Shark Cage Diving package transports you from San Diego, California, to Isla Guadalupe for a 5-day cage-diving excursion with the great white sharks. You don't even need to be certified to cage dive here. The 8-day **Bahamas** expedition goes to Tiger Beach and other sites to dive cageless with great whites, tiger sharks, lemon sharks, and bull sharks. In the Cayman Trench near **Honduras,** you can ride in a specially designed submarine to depths of up to 2,000 feet and see prehistoric six-gill sharks.

Thrill-seeking marine encounters aren't all about sharks. **Florida**'s Citrus County, comprised of communities like Crystal River and Homosassa, is the only place in the United States where you can snorkel with the West Indian manatees in their natural environment. Companies like Captain Mike's Sunshine River Tours (www.sunshinerivertours.com) and Bird's Underwater Dive Center (www.birdsunderwater.com) will take visitors on manatee tours, where guests are fully briefed on how to behave around the manatees. These creatures are so curious and friendly, it can be tempting to pet or hold them, but there are certain protocols in place. Also notable is the Homosassa Springs Wildlife State Park (www. homosassasprings.org), a rehabilitation center for more than 200 injured and orphaned marine and land animals.

Hawaii's massive manta rays can't be missed, whether you want to get up close and personal or view them from afar. One of the top places to interact with these graceful creatures is on the Kona coast of the Big Island, and the best time to dive or snorkel is at night— that's when the rays do their "ballet" as they feed on plankton. If you prefer to stay out of the water, the Sheraton Keauhou Bay Resort and Spa (www.sheratonkeauhou.com) has a local expert consultant, James Wing, who implemented special lights to attract plankton, establishing this area as a prime viewing site for the manta rays. On most nights, they can be seen from the shoreline (bring binoculars), or you can see them by boat on an excursion with Wing himself.

The Caribbean island of **Dominica** is a nature lover's paradise, and the whales seem to like it, too. Sperm whales live off the island's coast all year long, drawn to the warm, sheltered waters for mating and calving. Males migrate from the icy waters up north, but the females and young ones remain. The odds are excellent for sighting these toothed giants, along with other marine creatures like the pygmy sperm whale, spinner dolphins, and bottlenose dolphins.

Marine Festivals

Every July, the three-day Whale Shark Festival (www.whalesharkfest.com) in Isla Mujeres, **Mexico,** celebrates the 40-foot creatures that congregate off the coast. Of course, you can go underwater and see the sharks, either on your own or with a guided group tour with an operator such as Ceviche Tours (www.cevichetours.com), but there is plenty to do on land such as environmental education and local cultural programming. In the whale-watching capital of Hermanus, **South Africa,** the annual Two Oceans Whale Festival (www.whalefestival.co.za) takes place in late September, when southern right whales are easily spotted in Walker Bay. On the island of **Tobago,** the Underwater Carnival happens every July. For a week, there are daily dives off both northern and southern reefs, photography seminars, gear demonstrations, street parties, and more.

How about a wedding surrounded by more than 8 million gallons of water at the **Georgia** Aquarium (www.georgiaaquarium.org), touted as the world's largest aquarium? The crown jewel of the **Las Vegas** resort Mandalay Bay is the massive Shark Reef Aquarium (www.sharkreef.com), a 1.6 million-gallon exhibit with more than 2,000 predatory and exotic creatures. Sure, anyone can drop in and visit the aquarium, but why not take it a step further? Savvy couples can skip the drive-through chapels and arrange a Shark Reef ceremony, saying "I do" while surrounded by hundreds of bright tropical fish, 15 species of sharks, giant rays, and even an unusual golden crocodile. Prefer not to celebrate the big day in Vegas? Celebrate your nuptials underwater with a shark dive wedding at the Long Island Aquarium (http://longislandaquarium.com) in **New York.** That's right, in the midst of a 120,000-gallon shark exhibit, you and your beloved will be dropped into a shark-diving cage to say your vows surrounded by hungry predators. Last, but certainly not least, the renowned Dolphin Encounters (www.dolphinencounters.com) in the **Bahamas** will arrange a surprise marriage proposal among the dolphins for free, and it hosts in-water weddings with dolphin ring bearers and flower girls!

ADVANCED

Okay, don't say I didn't warn you. Ready to swim with the sharks cage free? The northern shores of **Tobago** are prime for scuba diving among nurse sharks, black tips, and hammerheads. You can look, but definitely don't touch. One of the best spots is the Sister site, which is for advanced divers only, where hammerheads congregate especially between December and March. Or head to London Bridge, an underwater rock arch where sharks are often sighted alongside less ominous creatures like turtles and octopus. Nurse sharks are abundant around Kelleston Drain and can usually be found under what is believed to be the world's largest brain coral. www.tobagoscubadiving.com

Real shark fanatics and experienced divers will travel far to catch a glimpse of sharks in their natural habitat. The uninhabited Cocos Island, a World Heritage site about 350 miles off the coast of **Costa Rica,** is home to enormous schools of hammerheads, tiger sharks, whale sharks, and Galapagos sharks. The catch? We're talking a 36-hour boat ride, which is offered by several local companies. Undersea Hunter (www.underseahunter.com) and Aggressor Fleet (www.aggressor.com) are both known for multiday diving trips to Cocos Island. But the biggest attraction here is diving at night at Manuelita Island, a submerged mountain just north of Cocos Island, to see whitetip reef sharks pack-hunting for their prey.

Richelieu Rock, **Thailand,** is a prime whale-shark dive site located in the Andaman Sea between the Similan and Surin Islands. Shark sightings aren't guaranteed, but chances are higher if you go between February and April. Regardless, divers can also look for colorful schools of fish, barracuda, and even manta rays in this diverse spot.

MOUNTAIN BIKING

For years, I equated mountain biking with the road to orthopedic surgery. But, thankfully, my approach to this outdoor experience has changed. Improvements in equipment and protective gear now make mountain biking accessible—and eminently survivable—for just about everyone. The real challenge is choosing which amazing scenery you want to look at as you ride.

MOAB, UTAH

This area of red-rock canyons is my mountain biking mecca. I actually discovered it by accident when I was a television executive at Paramount and we were producing the first episode of *Mac-Gyver* there. The large canyons, arches, and rock formations make for incredible views. Moab's trails consist of enormous slabs of visually striking red slickrock made of sandstone, which provide enough traction to climb and descend very steep grades.

Located to the right of US 191, 7.5 miles north of Moab, the Moab Brand Trails is a network of riding trails that accommodates novice to advanced bikers. Starting the course is the smooth, 8-mile dirt trail of Bar M, a perfect, family-friendly warmup, especially for those new to Moab.

Although the next track, Circle-O Loop, is only 3 miles long, it's for more advanced riders—the slickrock means you need to exercise caution while speeding through sharp dips and curves. For the next 1.5 miles, it gets even more advanced as you enter Rockin' A, a trail of short drops and curvy climbs, right into the last leg of your journey, Bar B. This final 2.5-mile stretch proves just as difficult as the rest, requiring you to dismount in a few sections. All the while, you're surrounded by spectacular views of the La Sal Mountains.

Advanced riders can attempt the challenging Slickrock Bike Trail in the Sands Flat Recreation Area, which twists for 12 miles through sandstone cliffs and affords beautiful views of the Colorado River. The alluring sandstone trail pulls more than 100,000 bikers each year to test their mettle. The unusual terrain will give you that adrenaline-pumping thrill needed to handle the twists and drops along the way.

Feeling up for a big challenge? Porcupine Rim is one of those must-do trails for serious bikers. At just about 14 miles (or you can make it a loop from and to Moab if you're suicidal), it's got difficult rocky climbs and seriously technical downhills with rocky cliffs and ledges. And don't worry, even the world's most experienced mountain bikers aren't shy about walking the more difficult sections.

CRESTED BUTTE, COLORADO

Crested Butte is home to some legendary trails, particularly the singletrack Trail 401, which takes you deep into the high country with spectacular mountain vistas and meadows of wildflowers. In fact, as you speed downhill on the singletrack, the vegetation is so thick that it's what keeps you centered and balanced. The entire route there and back is about 24 miles, climbing 2,800 feet in elevation. At one point, you can spot the famous Maroon Bells peaks, which is known as the most photographed spot in Colorado. If you're not up for the full 401 experience, a more intermediate ride is a pared-down version called Lower 401, which is about 7 miles round-trip through moderate elevation.

For beginners, there are several trails within easy reach from downtown. Head to the Lower Loop Trail from Butte Avenue, and you'll likely see plenty of locals on a leisurely hike or bike ride. Stretching It runs into the Slate River valley and connects to the

Bike to Brew

Oregon has a dual reputation as both a great mountain biking destination and a mecca for beer enthusiasts. If you want to combine both, try some of the following rides: 1) Post Canyon—Cycle the Post Canyon Trail or the Klickitat Rail Trail, and end the day at the nearby Double Mountain Brewery and Taproom in Hood River where you'll be treated to a variety of creative micro-brews; 2) Willamette Valley—Cycle the Alpine Trail, the Middle Fork Willamette River Trail, or the Salmon Creek Trail, and quench your thirst at the Brewers Union Local 180; or 3) Bend—Hit the Golden Triangle network of trails spread out southwest of the town, then cruise up to 10 Barrel for a brew. The roll-up garage doors and open-air fire pit are very welcoming to cyclists.

Oh-Be-Joyful wilderness area. You'll ride through alpine meadows blanketed in wildflowers, pass an abandoned mine, and view the mountain peaks off in the distance.

While you're there, be sure to visit the Mountain Bike Hall of Fame and Museum, which chronicles the sport's history through vintage bikes, classic photographs, and press clippings. Try to meet the facility's co-director, Don Cook, who helped build more than 100 of the nearly 400 miles of biking trails in Crested Butte.

WHISTLER MOUNTAIN BIKE PARK, BRITISH COLUMBIA

Seventy-five miles north of Vancouver, Whistler is not only a great ski spot (it was the official alpine skiing venue for the 2010 Olympics), it also has incredible mountain biking during its warm season, May through October. With riding and an active nightlife scene in its pedestrian-friendly village, Whistler is a place where all sorts of outdoor enthusiasts can feel at home.

Whistler Mountain Bike Park has 124 miles of lift-serviced trails, as well as beginner trails, all-day cross-country rides, and short but technically challenging trails for experts. If you're a beginner, stick to the lower mountain where there are wide, flat trails like Upper Easy Does It and After Atlantis. Intermediate riders have nearly two dozen options on this part of the mountain, including Upper B Line and Blue Velvet, which have some mild jumps and banked turns. See videos of every trail at Whistler Bike Park with the Camp of Champions iPhone app.

Feel like a challenge? Take the Garbanzo chair to higher elevation and advanced tracks like No Joke and Original Sin. And if you're an avid cross-country or all-mountain rider, there are some seriously expert tracks as well, including the double black diamond Captain Safety. www.whistlerbike.com

Watch the experts at the annual Crankworx festival, which takes place in late July or early August. There are races of every discipline throughout the week. The main event is the Joyride, where you can watch top athletes perform tricks over large jumps and obstacles near the base of the mountain. www.crankworx.com

ST. LUCIA

On the 600-acre grounds of Anse Chastanet Resort, you can combine a Caribbean getaway with the unusual experience of "jungle biking" down Bike St. Lucia's private trails. www.bikestlucia.com

Twelve miles of trails take you through a tropical forest filled with organic fruit trees, birds, and wild orchids, as well as the ruins of Anse Mamin, a colonial sugar plantation from the 18th century. Staff patrol the trail, and there's a 4,000-square-foot covered bike facility and retail center on site. If you're a beginner, you can take skill-training lessons before venturing out; if you're a more experienced rider, zip through singletrack loops to test your skills.

Tinker's Trail, created by world champion Tinker Juarez, offers skilled riders adrenaline-pumping steep uphills and tight switchbacks. Once you climb the challenging 1,000-foot-high peak, you can celebrate the victory by ringing Tinker's Bell at the top of the trail and taking in a sprawling 270-degree view of the Caribbean.

CORTINA D'AMPEZZO, ITALY

In Italy's northeast corner, Cortina d'Ampezzo sits in the heart of the steep and striking limestone Dolomite mountain range. The alpine village of about 7,000 permanent residents attracts serious skiers in the winter; in the summer, mountain bikers come for spectacular climbs and descents. In fact, many travel down rubble roads that the Italian, German, and Austro-Hungarian armies roughed in during World War I between May 1915 and October 1917.

Try the Cortina to Calalzo di Cadore route, a 23-mile journey along an old railway line that affords clear views of the Marmarole range and quiet mountain villages along the way. If you really want a challenge, you can take on all six passes around Cortina, riding a different route every day for more than 400 miles. A bike pass gets you access to all the mountain lifts.

Perched on the peaks are "bike hotels" that cater specifically to cyclists by offering services like washing your dirty bike clothes, while mountain refuges—or *rifugios*, literally "mountain huts"— provide meals and simple lodging to adventurers.

Companies such as Dolomite Mountains offer custom-guided excursions based on your skill levels, interest, and budget. For more independent types, the company can design an experience that takes care of all the essentials—including your itinerary, accommodations, and meals—but leaves out the guide. www.dolomitemountains.com

QUEENSTOWN, NEW ZEALAND

On New Zealand's South Island, Queenstown makes a great off-season destination, as their summer is our winter. The Skyline is a bike-carrying gondola—the only one of its kind in the Southern Hemisphere—providing access to an amazing network of downhill mountain bike trails in the Queenstown Bike Park (www.queenstownbikepark.co.nz). The park's nearly 20 miles of trails range from well-groomed to goat tracks, rocky gardens, and natural singletrack. There are beginner, intermediate, and advanced options. In fact, the trails here are so varied that many World Cup racers use them for training.

Hammy's Track is the trail for beginners. You can ride the gondola up and bike down about 4 miles of easy, gentle slopes. If you're feeling adventurous, the track also has some jumps and "log rides," where you're literally riding the bike along a horizontal log. Vertigo is the best option for intermediate riders, with some steep, challenging slopes. And if you're an expert, there are multiple options, including Rock Garden, which is accessible via Vertigo and features some steep drops before opening out onto an actual rock garden. Feeling suicidal? Try Grundy's Track, an extreme, technically difficult downhill ride.

If you're saddle sore from climbing hills in Queenstown, consider driving about an hour southeast to Clyde, where you can hop onto the flat Otago Central Rail Trail for a ride. It's about 90 miles long, but you don't have to ride that far to find local food and color at one of the many small towns along the scenic route. www.otagocentralrailtrail.co.nz

SCUBA DIVING

I remember my first diving experience. After being pool certified, I went down in shallow water in the Cayman Islands. But the most exceptional—and unforgettable— dive came a few months later in Micronesia, in the northern Caroline Islands, when I went deep off the island of Palau. Sunk beneath me seemed to be half the Japanese fleet from World War II—with still-live depth charges in their canisters, a car still strapped to the top deck of a destroyer, and more fish than I could have ever imagined.

For my Star Trek friends, I beg to differ: Underwater is the last great frontier, and no matter what your physical ability or challenges, it awaits you.

REEF DIVING

Known as the rain forests of the ocean, coral reefs are homes to incredibly rich biodiversity and marine life.

The Great Barrier Reef is more than 1,400 miles long and consists of 900 islands and coral cays, making it the most extensive reef system in the world. If you're a beginner, it's best to start at Agincourt Reef, which is located about 40 miles from Port Douglas, **Australia,** on the Great Barrier Reef. There, dive operators like Quicksilver (www.quicksilver-cruises.com) have fixed pontoons that make it easy for those with less experience to dive into shallower waters. The area itself, which is on the outer edges of the Great Bar-

---

INSIDER'S TIP

Every November, the conditions on the Great Barrier Reef are just right for a phenomenon called coral spawning. After a full moon, coral simultaneously releases its eggs into the waters, which makes for a dazzling nighttime display. The timing isn't entirely dependable, but certified divers can see this event on a night dive from the *Silverswift* catamaran, which departs from Cairns. www.quicksilvergroup.com.au

---

rier Reef, is made up of a series of smaller reefs and swim-through caves, with water depths up to 78 feet and visibility averaging around 65 feet.

The Ribbon Reefs are part of a 400-mile stretch of coral that includes some of the best dive spots in the Great Barrier Reef. Intermediate divers should head to Cod Hole on the northern end, which plunges about 98 feet and is home to a huge variety of exotic marine life. We're talking about the massive (and friendly) potato cod, emperor cod, Maori wrasse, and even whitetip reef sharks and giant clams. Definitely bring along an underwater camera!

If you're more advanced, then tackle Osprey Reef, which is located in the Coral Sea off Cairns. Sharks convene at wall drop-offs for feeding, so if you're lucky, you can see everything from whitetips to gray whalers to hammerheads. Manta rays, bottlenose dolphins, and even whales are also commonly sighted around this area. Be sure to see the North Horn feeding site, a sea mountain that looms more than 3,000 feet above the ocean floor. Depths around Osprey Reef range anywhere from 15 to 3,300 feet, and visibility extends from 32 to about 160 feet.

Want a "stay and play" type of experience? The Great Barrier Reef has a series of islands where you can practically swim off the beach and into the reef. The coral cay of Heron Island has more than 20 dive sites within just a few minutes from the beach, while Lizard Island is a granite piece of land that offers easy access to Cod Hole. Lady Elliot Island, a coral cay on the very southern end of the reef, is best known for the 40 or so manta rays that live in the waters. The water close to shore is shallow with nearby reefs, allowing you to swim off the shores and into the protected waters.

About 35 miles off of **Honduras,** the island of Roatan offers exceptional diving conditions because it's actually on top of an underwater mountain range known as the Bonacca Ridge, which also comprises Utila and Guanaja Islands. Roatan itself is surrounded by living coral reef. In fact, the Mesoamerican Barrier Reef System is the world's second-longest coral reef system and is home to a huge array of marine mammals, fish, and reptile. Anthony's Key Resort is a dedicated dive resort in the center of more than two dozen dive sites. Most dive sites are a short boat ride away, but for even easier access, try a shore dive to Front Porch Reef. www.anthonyskey.com

The nearby island of Utila is home to the Whale Shark and Oceanic Research Center, where you can arrange diving trips to see the native whale shark population. Even cooler? The research center offers underwater digital photography courses, which include two dives. www.wsorc.org

Lembeh Strait, off the northern tip of the island of Sulawesi in **Indonesia,** is one of the ocean's epicenters of marine biodiversity. You'll find a higher concentration of marine life here than anywhere else on the planet, including some of the most wondrous, otherworldly "critters," as the locals call them. These weird and wonderful creatures include the hairy frogfish, Pegasus sea moths, and flamboyant cuttlefish. Some of these animals are found nowhere else in the world and are so unusual looking that the area is a mecca for underwater photographers. The terrain consists of small coral reefs and "featureless" black sand, which is why the diving here is sometimes known as "mucking."

The island of Bonaire, off the coast of **Venezuela,** offers such pristine diving because much of the offshore environment has been protected marine parkland for some 30 years. With visibility up to 150 feet, many of the 86 underwater dive sites are accessible from shore, making it popular with beginning divers and weekend warriors. The water is so calm and the weather so mild that it is possible to dive 24 hours a day, 7 days a week. Self-guided diving is easy here, too, as there are yellow marker stones located all over the island that point to easily accessible offshore fringe reefs: The Alice In Wonderland dive site is best known for its double reef complex; Angel City features the wreck of the *Hilma Hooker;* and the Thousand Steps is popular among snorkelers for its calm, clear waters (just be aware that you have to navigate 67 or so steps onto the beach while carrying all your gear).

Off the coast of **Mozambique** in the Quirimbas Archipelago, Vamizi Island is home to one of the healthiest coral reefs in the world. It's teeming with life. Beginning and intermediate divers have plenty of shallower options like Skunk Alley, Fraggle Rock, and Cave Wall. But if you've got some experience under your wet suit and can manage strong currents, don't miss one of the best dive sites in the world: Neptune's Arm. The walls drop more than 2,500 feet and are teeming with exotic creatures like the giant potato cod, huge grouper, gray reef sharks, and barracuda.

More than 65,000 divers visit Monterey Bay, **California,** each year to explore its mysterious kelp forests, underwater canyons, and scenic coves. Though the waters can be chilly, the good visibility (10 to 30 feet) and safe conditions make this one of the top Pacific coast dive spots. The waters of the Monterey Bay National Marine Sanctuary are nutrient rich, which ensures that there is a lot of marine life to see. Beginning and intermediate divers like Whalers Coves, Lovers Point, Monterey State Beach, San Carlos Beach, and McAbee Beach. Advanced-level divers head to places like Bluefish Cove, Monastery Beach, and Carmel River State Beach.

WALL DIVING

Wall diving usually involves diving along the face of a vertical reef. These reefs can drop suddenly into the depths, without any seabed under your feet, making this a better option for more experienced divers.

Few places can top the **Cayman Islands** in terms of accessibility, diversity, visibility, and marine life—not to mention the balmy Caribbean waters. The islands comprise more than 150 dive sites, most of which offer a combination of precipitous walls, towering canyons, and reefs peppered with swim-through tunnels.

On Grand Cayman Island, wall diving is possible for beginners, particularly along the west wall, which is easily accessible from Seven Mile Beach and known for its calm waters and great visibility. More experienced divers will go north, to the spectacular coral walls of Eagle Ray Pass, Chinese Wall, and Ghost Wall. Potentially rough

Unusual Dives

Although the Kona coast of the Big Island of **Hawaii** has dozens of dive spots, don't miss a midnight dive among the giant manta rays. Your dive master will set up lights on the ocean floor to illuminate the plankton, which attracts the rays. As they feed, the rays bend, glide, and somersault around in an elaborate, mesmerizing dance, sometimes getting within inches of the divers. (Don't worry, they're harmless.) Prefer to observe from afar? Many of the beachside hotels turn on bright lights in the evening to attract the mantas to shore.

Silver Bank in **Dominican Republic** is one of only a handful of places on the planet where you can swim with humpback whales. Each year between early February and mid-April, up to 5,000 of the creatures migrate to Silver Bank, a 300-square-mile portion of the 1,000-square-mile Marine Mammal Sanctuary in the Dominican Republic. If you're fortunate, you'll see mother whales tending to their calves, and you'll actually feel the sound of whale song echoing through the water.

conditions and distance make the east wall better for advanced divers who want to get away from the tour boats and get to spots like Three Sisters, Snapper Hole, and Babylon.

Palau, my personal favorite, is a collection of 350 Micronesian islands situated at the intersection of the Pacific Ocean and Philippine Sea, 500 miles from Indonesia. Its rich biodiversity explains its appeal to divers: Its waters boast more than 1,300 species of fish and more than 800 species of coral and sponges scattered around the wildly varied underwater topography. The Ngemelis Wall starts extremely shallow and drops to nearly 1,000 feet, marked by soft corals, bright yellow pyramid butterfly fish, orange clown fish, and many more. In fact, this is such a great experience that even Jacques Cousteau gave it his stamp of approval as one of the best wall dives in the world.

FRESHWATER DIVES

Though freshwater dives aren't typically as rich and colorful as sea diving, it's an easily accessible option for those who don't want to stray too far from home—whether you're exploring lakes, rivers, or underwater caves.

Central and northern **Florida** are home to more than 600 freshwater springs, which explorer Ponce de Leon once dubbed the "fountain of youth." Whether or not you believe that claim, the waters from Ginnie Springs to Blue Grotto are the world's best collection of springs for snorkeling and diving. The 70-degree water is crystal clear, the bottom is sand and limestone, and the extensive cave system is intriguing to explore. No crazy tropical fish here, but unusual geological formations abound.

In **Missouri**'s Ozarks, the Bonne Terre mine is the largest year-round freshwater dive spot in the world. The abandoned mine is filled with more than a billion gallons of water. You won't see any exotic sea life here. But you will get a close-up view of cavern walls made out of calcium and even remnants of original mining equipment.

Or you can go diving in the desert in Santa Rosa, **New Mexico.** A natural phenomenon called Blue Hole is an 80-foot-deep pool, where the water is 64 degrees but is so crystal clear you can see up to 80 feet.

The cenotes of **Mexico**'s Yucatan Peninsula are something most divers want to experience at least once. These freshwater sinkholes allow divers to access the network of underground rivers that percolate through the peninsula. The clarity of the water is striking, the result of rainwater being filtered through limestone, so you can swim among rock structures and ancient fossils with practically unlimited visibility. Dos Ojos (Two Eyes) is located north of Tulum, and the original exploration of the entire cave system began through this particular cenote. Still, it takes some gumption and a lot of experience to tackle these waters. Dos Ojos also contains the deepest known cave passage in Quintana Roo, a 400-foot-deep area known as the Pit. The intricate labyrinth can be disorienting, so it's easy to get lost without the help of an expert guide. www.hiddenworlds.com

WRECK DIVING

Wreck diving refers to artificial reefs, historically made of sunken ships but also decommissioned ships, planes, and even subway cars that have been purposely sunk to create exceptional dive sites. Many training courses offer special wreck-diver

---

Diving App

If you're not familiar with dive sites in your destination, the Professional Association of Diving Instructors (PADI) has a mobile app that can direct you to the nearest certified dive center. www.padi.com/scuba/padi-mobile

programs to prepare you for the potential hazards of deteriorating or fragile structures.

Ever heard of scuba diving in a missile silo? That's right, just outside of Abilene, **Texas,** there's an Atlas intercontinental ballistic missile silo that has filled up with groundwater over the years. A company called Family Scuba Center can arrange dives of the silo, which is about 130 feet deep and 60 feet wide.

The coast off of **North Carolina** is known as the "graveyard of the Atlantic." Dozens of World War II wrecks, including American blockade runners and German U-boats, lie here.

Off the coast of Pensacola, **Florida,** you can explore the wreck of the USS *Oriskany,* a former US Navy aircraft carrier. It was sunk in 2004 to create one of the largest artificial reefs in the world.

Off the island of Oahu in **Hawaii,** intrepid divers can head down to a Corsair plane wreck. If you're lucky, you might even meet the moray eel that lives in the cockpit.

Off of Long Island, **New York,** and **New Jersey** are a number of unusual artificial reefs such as old subway cars, old army tanks, and donated Coast Guard vessels.

The **Grand Cayman**'s USS *Kittiwake* is one of the world's newest purpose-sunk wrecks. Within weeks of its sinking off the shores of Seven Mile Island, divers began spotting a 100-pound grouper and a huge barracuda, among other marine life. Because it's only 10 feet from the surface, it's both an easy dive and an accessible snorkel site.

Around the island of **Palau,** there are dozens of World War II wrecks, accessible either by shore excursion or via live-aboard boat.

Accessible Diving for Anyone

Even if you have a physical disability, traditional scuba diving is still easily accessible. When looking for an organized dive operator or tour, ask if they have instructors who have been certified by the Handicapped Scuba Association, which helped develop the current standards to accommodate divers with disabilities.

One of the best places in the world for accessible diving is Divi Flamingo Beach Resort and Casino in **Bonaire.** The resort has several handicap-accessible rooms and a customized accessible dive boat, along with specially trained instructors.

The Jean-Michel Cousteau **Fiji Islands** Resort has several dive masters who are certified in handicapped diving instruction. All but one of the resort's *bures* (thatched-roof bungalows) are handicapped accessible, and the piers leading out to dive boats are wheelchair accessible.

In **Maui,** Lahaina Divers (www.lahainadivers.com) has a fully handicapped accessible dive boat, which includes an accessible bathroom, and an HSA-certified dive crew.

You can find HSA members at www.hsascuba.com.

Note that there are three levels of HSA certification.

Level A divers are certified to dive with one person in the traditional "buddy system." This level can be achieved by divers with all types of disabilities, including amputees and paraplegics.

Level B divers require two people accompanying them. If a diver can't physically operate the mechanisms to control buoyancy, he or she will require a buddy who has been specially trained to operate someone else's equipment.

Level C divers must be accompanied by two buddies, including a rescue diver—i.e., if a blind diver is unable to participate in the buddy system, the third person is on hand to perform those duties.

HSA and Eels on Wheels (www.eels.org) regularly take groups on accessible dive excursions. Want to learn how to dive? The Diveheart Foundation (www.diveheart.org) teaches "dive therapy" to kids, adults, and veterans with all types of disabilities.

SKIING

The key to finding the best skiing is to first be honest with yourself. The real quality of skiing is, after all, directly related to how you match your ability to the terrain, how much or how little you challenge yourself once there, and not what the experience cost, but how much you valued it.

BEGINNER

With an entire mountain practically dedicated to beginner slopes, Sun Valley resort in **Idaho** is the place to get your "ski legs." The slopes on Dollar Mountain are gentle, well groomed, and treeless. Because more advanced skiers tend to go on Bald Mountain, there's no intimidation or competing for space—meaning even adult novices can feel comfortable starting out here. Fun fact: The world's first chairlifts were installed on Proctor Mountain and Dollar Mountain in 1936. www.sunvalley.com

Utah's powdery snow is the stuff of legends, and with more than 2,000 acres of skiable terrain, Deer Valley is no exception. Five of the six mountains have a green run from the top, but the real novice's haven is Wide West, a beginners-only area on Bald Eagle Mountain (not to be confused with the advanced Bald Mountain). It's accessible by three conveyer lifts that make the progression uphill smooth and easy for new skiers. Once you've gotten comfortable with going uphill, you're ready for the Snowflake and Burns chairlifts to access smooth, wide trails where you don't have to contend with more advanced skiers zipping by. Once you feel more confident, you can access midmountain beginner trails on the Silver Lake Express chairlift—and even better, it's a "downloading" lift, which means you can ride it down the hill as well! www.deervalley.com

The green trails at **Colorado**'s Breckenridge Ski Resort are long and relatively flat, so beginners have plenty of time to get used to

Lift Your Spirits

Canada's Peak 2 Peak gondola runs for 2.7 miles between Whistler and Blackcomb. The longest continuous lift system in the world, soaring more than 1,400 feet in the air, this is a true engineering feat.

the experience. Fourteen percent of the trails are for beginners—the really easy stuff is accessible on the Magic Carpet lift toward the bottom of Peak 9, but for longer routes, just go up Quicksilver Super 6 chairlift. www.breckenridge.com

Most people don't think of **Canada**'s premier mountains, Whistler and Blackcomb, as beginner territory. With their reliable snowpack and sheer volume, they are a favorite place for advanced and expert skiers. But what's really cool here is that beginners have access to the whole mountain at all altitudes—not just the bottom of the hill. On a high-altitude beginner trail like Burnt Stew Trail on Whistler, you get a gentle ski experience with phenomenal 360-degree views of the mountains. From midhill, you can take Upper Olympic and connect to Lower Olympic all the way into Whistler Village. Even better, there's more than 8,000 acres of skiable terrain spread over two mountains—200 marked runs and ample backcountry terrain—so the slopes rarely get crowded despite their popularity. www.whistlerblackcomb.com

Alpe d'Huez in **France** has everything a beginning skier would want: lots of sunshine (locals say it's sunny 300 days of the year), astonishingly beautiful scenery in the central French Alps, and . . . free skiing? That's right, this resort has four "drag lifts" that are free: Téléski Grenouille, Petit Rif-Nel, Petite Ecole, and Petit Poussin. This is ideal for first-timers and very young kids who really need to start on the bunny slopes to get comfortable. www. alpedhueznet.com

INTERMEDIATE

It doesn't get better than the powdery, fluffy snow in Eden, **Utah.** Known locally as "Pow Mow," Powder Mountain is still something of a local secret even though it is actually the biggest ski resort in the United States by size (more than 7,000 acres). It doesn't have the typical ski village that you associate with a resort, and its infrastructure is limited, with only four chairlifts and three tow lines. The locals prefer it that way! This is the place for powder purists who just want the sheer experience of skiing on clean, dry powder without having to contend with out-of-towners. As a bonus, it's one of the great value mountains—a full-day pass costs just $60. http://powdermountain.com

The bulk of Park City's slopes are geared to intermediate skiers. There are 11 blue trails clustered on the King Consolidated (a.k.a. "King Con") mountain zone, which is accessible from the Eagle, Silver Star, and King Con lifts. And if you want a long, almost leisurely run, just take the King Con Ridge run to the Temptation trail. www.parkcitymountain.com

Aspen's ski scene in **Colorado** seamlessly blends well-heeled elite with dedicated ski bums. Although this is not a spot for true beginners (nearby Buttermilk and Snowmass are better options), those with some experience under their belt have plenty of options. At Aspen Mountain, your best bet is to go up the Ajax Express lift to the intermediate slopes. But an even better option is Snowmass mountain, which has a ton of intermediate terrain. From Snowmass Village, just hop on the Elk Camp Gondola and you'll reach the mid-mountain Elk Camp area. www.aspensnowmass.com

Want to know the really cool thing about Zermatt, **Switzerland**? Its altitude means you can ski 365 days a year. This picturesque town, dominated by the mighty Matterhorn, has three ski areas that tower more than 10,000 feet. Its winter ski season usually runs from late November to early May and, in fact, you're better off going in spring when the north-facing mountains warm up and the snow is still in fine form. A huge glacial area translates into great summer skiing. There is a vast amount of terrain here with long runs. You can ascend the summit of the incredibly scenic Rothorn sector—which has the best and most symmetrical view of the Matterhorn—on a funicular railway, gondola, or cable car, and ski your way back down. Tip: You can even ski in two countries in one day. Cross over from the Swiss side to Italy on the Cervinia cable car.

Italy's Dolomite mountains are a ski wonderland, with 12 ski zones totaling more than 750 miles of terrain, with 450 lifts in all. If you're in it for the long haul, the Dolomiti Superski pass gets you access to each and every one of them, meaning you have breakfast in Alta Badia, lunch in Val Gardena, and dinner and an overnight stay at Rifugio Lavarella in Val de Fanes. For intermediate skiers, it's a must to tackle the Sella Ronda, a complete circuit around the Sella massif. It should take about 6 hours to complete (including about 2 hours of lift time), but you can brag about it afterward. And there's much more than great ski conditions and incredible alpine scenery. The Sella Ronda takes you to the heart of Alta Badia, which has a collection of Michelin-starred restaurants in its luxury mountain hotels, including Restaurant St. Hubertus, La Siriola, and Stüa de Michil.

EXPERT/SUICIDAL

Hard-core skiers know La Grave in **France,** and you should, too—if only to fantasize about a heart-stopping ride down one of the most dangerous ski slopes in the world. There's only one piste, or marked trail, on this entire mountain. The rest? It's up to you to figure out. Even if you think you know what you're doing, a guide is a good idea. That's because the terrain is filled with hidden drops, crevasses, couloirs, slippery snowpack . . . oh, and the occasional avalanche that might trip you up. And the scenery? It's simply amazing, dominated by the towering peaks of La Meije. www.la-grave.com

The sheer volume of terrain at Vail in **Colorado** means that every level of skier has plenty of options. Experts tend to stick with the vast Back Bowl where black diamonds abound. But on the front face, there's Prima Cornice for those with a death wish. Accessible by Chair 11-Northwoods, this slope is a short ride, but it's so steep you'll feel like you're lying on the ground.

At Jackson Hole Mountain Resort in **Wyoming,** Corbet's Couloir is the stuff that expert skiers talk about for years to come. It's been branded "America's scariest ski slope" and starts off with a massive drop in a cornice, essentially free-falling through the air before landing on a powdery run.

The light, powdery snow in **Canada**'s Banff National Park makes the resorts of Ski Banff, Lake Louise, and Sunshine a huge draw for skiers. But if you've got suicidal tendencies, there are a couple of runs to check off your list. Goat's Eye Mountain is expert territory, where Hell's Kitchen is a steep, narrow, death-defying run; and Lookout Mountain is known for an extreme run called Delirium Dive, where you'll face a 40-degree pitch with death-defying chutes and couloirs. Bring a shovel and an avalanche receiver.

One of the legendary mountains of the world is at Ski Portillo in **Chile,** about 2 hours from Santiago. What's cool about this place is that its ski season takes place in our summer, so this is where all

What If You Don't Ski?

Mountain resorts have a lot more to offer than simple downhill skiing, and that doesn't mean being stuck inside the lodge drinking hot toddies (you can save that for later!).

Ever heard of snowbiking? It's not as scary as it sounds, and it's becoming a trend in resorts all around North America, including Sunshine Village in **Banff** and in Vail, Keystone, and Telluride resorts in **Colorado.**

It doesn't get much more adventurous than heli-skiing. Some mountain routes aren't accessible by chairlift or gondola, so you have to be choppered in! This extreme sport is happening in places like the Western Chugach mountains in **Alaska, Washington**'s North Cascade mountains, the Columbia Mountains in **Canada,** and the Tomamu Alpha Resort on **Japan**'s Hokkaido island.

Then there's always the great workout of snowshoeing across the terrain. Lone Mountain Ranch in Big Sky, **Montana,** has 12 miles of trails and gets as much as 400 inches of snow a year. Northstar-at Tahoe has moonlight and stargazing snowshoe tours. And for a more aerobic workout, Queenstown, **New Zealand,** has miles of trails on the Remarkables range.

If you're like me, it's all about the scenery—which is where a simple gondola ride comes in. At Heavenly ski resort, the gondola takes you up 2.4 miles for the best panoramic view of **Lake Tahoe.** And in Aspen, the Silver Queen Gondola takes you from the center of Aspen to the 11,212-foot mountain summit.

the pros and athletes go to train in their "off" season. Not only that, but there is no village around the mountain and only one main hotel, the bright yellow Hotel Portillo, where almost everyone stays, so you can get that community feel while drinking *pisco* sours among locals and pros. Portillo has slopes for all levels, but experts—and some suicidal skiers—love it here for the variety of challenging chutes and wide-open bowls, namely the Garganta run. www.skiportillo.cl

You have to be a seasoned skier to take on the near-perfect powder slopes of Asahidake in **Japan.** The mountains on the northern island of central Hokkaido get abundant amounts of fine, powdery snow each year, making it one of the best-kept secrets among enthusiasts. Of all the resorts in the area, Asahidake is the highest peak on the island with some of the best snow. It's actually a national park, not a traditional ski resort, so the accommodations are spartan and the skiing is essentially all off-piste, backcountry terrain.

CROSS-COUNTRY SKIING

An entirely different animal than downhill skiing, cross-country skiing is a great full-body workout. The trails are long and meandering, and there's nothing easy about them. Here are my top picks:

In **Colorado,** the Aspen Snowmass Nordic Trail system is 56 miles of trails connecting Aspen, Snowmass, and Basalt, and it's free. Craftsbury Outdoor Center in **Vermont** has 53 miles of trails that meander through meadows and forests in rural New England.

Mont-Saint-Anne, **Quebec,** has 130 miles of trails in the Laurentian Forest and alongside the Jean Larosse River near Quebec City. If you get tired and need a rest, you'll find five heated shelters along the trail (two of which can accommodate overnight visitors) and a bed-and-breakfast.

Geilo, **Norway,** 155 miles northwest of Oslo, is home to more than 135 miles of marked, well-maintained trails taking you past unbelievable scenery with snowcapped mountains, along the banks of the

Ustedalen fjord, and through the wooded Hardangervidda plateau.
www.geilo.no

St. Moritz, **Switzerland,** has 117 miles of trails through the Engadine Valley and the shores of St. Moritz Lake.

ADAPTIVE SKIING

Disabled Sports Eastern Sierra runs a ski and snowboarding program from Mammoth Mountain Ski Area in **California.** The instructors create a customized program depending on your needs. www.disabledsportseasternsierra.org

In Denver, **Colorado,** the National Sports Center for the Disabled has therapeutic, recreational, and competitive programs. Participants can try a range of accessible activities from alpine skiing and snowbiking to snowshoeing and ski racing. With group or individual tour options, trips go from Denver to ski resorts in Winter Park. www.nscd.org

Lodge-to-Lodge Skiing

The idea is that you can set out from one lodge, and cross-country ski your way to your next one. Usually there's a network of nearby trails so you can take day trips from a home base. In **Maine,** the Appalachian Mountain Club has more than 66,000 acres of protected land, with four lodges where staff members cook meals and provide information on trail conditions. If you're not comfortable on your own, AMC also has 2- to 4-night guided packages. It's less than $200 a day and includes meals and guided group skiing, and they'll even shuttle your gear for you. In **Minnesota,** they've got "yurt skiing." You can ski along the Banadad Ski Trail and stay in fully equipped yurts along the way. Last, but not least, **Colorado**'s 10th Mountain Hut Association is a network of 29 huts connected by 350 miles of routes and trails. Just keep in mind that this is real backcountry skiing. If you're not confident, consider snowshoeing. Or wait until summer comes back around and make it a hiking trip.

Colorado's Challenge Aspen has a series of programs throughout the winter, including visually impaired skiing, mono-ski camp, and sit-down skiing lessons. The organization can also arrange for a ski buddy for the day if needed. www.challengeaspen.org

Also in Colorado, you can work with the Adaptive Sports Center of Crested Butte to arrange private and semiprivate lessons for all types of winter sports. www.adaptivesports.org

The nonprofit organization Northeast Passage hosts the Adaptive Sports and Recreation program, which offers a range of sports and challenges throughout all six states in **New England.** Yes, they have skiing programs, but if you want to try something different, check out the winter sled hockey games. http://nepassage.org

Vermont Adaptive Ski and Sports is now the largest adaptive program in the state, servicing Pico Mountain, Sugarbush Resort, and Bolton Valley. Their programs aren't just limited to skiing and snowboarding: We're also talking rock climbing, snowshoeing, and even dogsledding. www.vermontadaptive.org

STARGAZING

Look up at the night sky, and you get to see quite a show. Look up at the night sky from special locations, and you see the best star performances. It's not about the quantity of the stars up there. It's about the quality of the gazing.

UNITED STATES

Start by learning about the stars from the experts, the National Optical Astronomy Observatory at Kitt Peak, **Arizona.** It's surrounded by the Sonoran Desert, and the night skies here are some of the finest in the world. The observatory's 27 telescopes are entirely accessible to the public, so you can get hands-on experience using high-tech equipment, interact with astronomers, observe the research process, and explore the equipment there. The advanced observation program (no experience required) even includes an overnight stay with access to telescopes, Web cams, and cameras to observe and record the night skies. The best time to go is between April and June, when nights are clearest. Avoid stargazing trips from mid-July through September, which is monsoon season in this part of Arizona (and the program is closed).

Thanks to tough lighting ordinances in Flagstaff, the clear, dark skies make this mountain town another must for astronomy lovers, particularly at the Lowell Observatory (www.lowell.edu). You can see the telescope where astronomers discovered Pluto, and in the evening, powerful dome telescopes allow you to see everything from Jupiter to star clusters to supernovas. But that's not the only place to gaze at stars in Flagstaff. The Coconino Astronomical Society (www.coconinoastro.org) often provides telescopes for free public viewings in Heritage Square. Flagstaff is typically driest and clearest in June but you can also get some great night viewing in September and October.

The dark skies are also well protected in West **Texas,** home to McDonald Observatory, which is part of the University of Texas at Austin. Located 6,500 feet up on Mount Locke and Mount Fowlkes in the Davis Mountains of West Texas, this area has some of the darkest skies in the continental United States. See sunspots and solar flares during the solar viewing program and get an up-close look at massive research telescopes. But what you don't want to miss are the outdoor Star Parties that take place on Tuesday, Saturday, and Sunday nights, where you can view the skies through powerful telescopes. www.mcdonaldobservatory.org

You can also throw your own stargazing party. The New Mexico Skies stargazing "resort" near Alamogordo, **New Mexico,** features six observation domes containing state-of-the-art equipment and separate living units. Couple that with low light pollution and high elevation overlooking the Sacramento Mountains and the Lincoln National Forest, and it's an ideal spot for amateur astronomers to gaze, stay, and relax. If you're a real beginner, instruction and stargazing assistance is available for a fee. During the day, the grounds provide ample opportunity for nature walks and wildlife viewing. www.nmskies.com

In Santa Fe, Astronomy Adventures offers guided night sky tours led by an astrophotographer and park ranger. Although locations can vary based on the conditions, the primary stargazing site is along the Turquoise Trail, one of New Mexico's most scenic byways. www.astronomyadventures.com

The Coca-Cola Space Science Center in Columbus, **Georgia,** has nothing to do with the soft drink. Instead, you can participate in free Astronomy Nights at the center and in local parks. They provide

Guided Astronomy Tours

Whether you want an expert leading the way, or you're chasing a timely event like a solar eclipse, a guided astronomy tour is often the way to go. Smithsonian Journeys (www.smithsonianjourneys.org) offers specialty tours like a behind-the-scenes look at several **Arizona** observatories led by a member of the Harvard-Smithsonian Center for Astrophysics. MWT Associates (www.melitatrips.com) has a series of stargazing tours worldwide, whether it's viewing the northern lights in **Iceland** or following in the footsteps of **German** astronomers with the editor of *Astronomy* magazine as your guide. Or travel with QuasarChile (www.quasarchile.cl) to examine the stunningly clear skies of the Atacama Desert and to get a close look at **Chile**'s renowned observatories.

Hotel Stargazing

The Loews Ventana Canyon resort not only has guided nighttime hikes into the desert around Tucson, **Arizona,** but stargazers can get help from the Celestial Concierge who sets up a high-powered telescope and helps novices spot major constellations and planets. www.loewshotels.com/en/Ventana-Canyon-Resort

In Sedona, join astronomer Dennis Young twice weekly at L'Auberge de Sedona as he leads you on a tour of the night skies. Attendance is limited to L'Auberge guests and offered free of charge. It takes place on Tuesdays and Fridays, but times may vary (check with concierge) and sessions are subject to weather conditions. www.lauberge.com

The Post Ranch Inn in Big Sur, **California,** offers stargazing talks on the patio of its restaurant four nights a week between 8 and 9 p.m. View the stars through the 12-inch reflective lens telescope and learn from an amateur astronomer, who describes the constellations and planets while you eat. www.postranchinn.com

The Hapuna Beach Prince Hotel in Kohala, **Hawaii,** offers stargazing on Sunday and Wednesday evenings where a professional astronomer will guide you through the night sky. www.princeresortshawaii.com/hapuna-beach-prince-hotel.php

In **New Hampshire**'s Waterville Valley, join educators from the Christa McAuliffe Planetarium for a North Country Skywatch each month. Start with an indoor presentation of the night sky at the Margret and H.A. Rey Center, followed by an outdoor stargazing session. http://thereycenter.org

the sky maps and telescopes, and the head of the observatory introduces you to the wonders of the world overhead. www.ccssc.org

The summit of Mauna Kea volcano on the Big Island is not only the highest point in **Hawaii,** it's also home of some of the world's largest telescopes within a collection of 13 independent observatories. You can only see the telescopes by day, but by night, you don't need any special equipment to see the stars. The high elevation, thin dry air, and lack of light pollution make this peak one of the best places in the world to see the universe. Getting here is a challenge on its own, as it's only accessible by four-wheel-drive vehicle. Go slow so you can acclimatize to the 14,000-foot climb, or stop off at the information station, which sits at only 9,300 feet, where you can join in a nightly stargazing session that's free to the public. www.ifa.hawaii.edu

INTERNATIONAL

For a really educational experience in stargazing, you want to head south—to the Southern Hemisphere, that is. The constellations and stars in the skies viewed from south of the equator are entirely different than those in the United States. **Tahiti**, with its low levels of light pollution, is a prime spot for viewing, and La Société d'Astronomie de Tahiti invites the public to peer through its equipment including the largest telescope in Polynesia. There are planned sessions for one weekend every month, but private sessions can also be scheduled. www.astrosurf.com/sat

If you really want to escape the bright lights of the city, travel to Ayers Rock in **Australia**'s Outback. The ultra-remote location and lack of light pollution make it one of the best locations on earth from which to see the Southern Hemisphere skies. Ayers Rock Resort offers guests a 4-hour Sounds of Silence excursion, in which a resident astronomer explains the visible constellations and planets, and shares ancient Aboriginal stories of mythology and creation as they relate to the cosmos. www.ayersrockresort.com.au

A stargazing safari? **South Africa**'s Kruger National Park (www.krugerpark.co.za) has no light pollution and is probably one of the best places for do-it-yourself observations—all you need is a pair of binoculars and a hammock. Or if you prefer a more hands-on approach, head to the South African Large Telescope (SALT) in the town of Sutherland (about 4 hours from Cape Town). As part of the South African Astronomical Observatory, this is the largest optical telescope in the Southern Hemisphere. You can see the research equipment by day, but nighttime stargazing tours actually involve other telescopes where you can view the constellations. www.saao.ac.za

SURFING

In the interest of full disclosure, my uncle, David Rochlen, was a legendary surfer, and he rode with the best in Southern California and Hawaii. (He was later inducted into the Surfing Walk of Fame.) Thanks to him, I first learned how to surf on Sandy Beach in Oahu. That Hawaiian experience led me to mistakenly think I was good enough to try my luck on the treacherous North Shore. And *that* experience ultimately led me to realize my true limitations! Instead, I'm now a practicing stand-up paddleboarder on the East Coast, on the Great South Bay on Fire Island in New York. But every once in a while, in a fit of stupid nostalgia, I'll return to Hawaii and try my luck again.

ALL-AMERICAN SURFING

When you think of surfing in the United States, what comes to mind first? Most likely **Hawaii.** Home to some of the most legendary big waves in the world, Hawaii is practically the birthplace of modern surfing. The good news is, you don't have to be a local pro to get started. First-timers and novices can learn to surf right on Waikiki Beach, where the gentle Canoes surf break is located right in front of the Royal Hawaiian Hotel. Just rent a board and hire an instructor at the beach shack—you'll know you're in the right place if you can see the statue of Hawaiian surfing legend Duke Kahanamoku. Definitely get there early and on a weekday if you want to avoid the crowds.

On the island of Maui, you want to head to the beautiful Launiupoko State Wayside Park for a beginner lesson. The waves are broken up by coral reefs, making them gentle and smooth enough for newbies to handle. (And with a children's wading pool, snorkeling, and picnic tables, this is also a great spot for a family day out.) On Kauai, Hanalei Bay on the northern shore has a 2.5-mile-long, white-sand beach where the waters tend to remain calm and easy to manage in the summer, making it perfect for learning.

Prefer to watch, not surf? Go to the North Shore of Oahu, where the locals go. The waves are at their highest in the winter months. Although there's no guarantee of where and when the big waves will hit, you can usually get a great view of the surfers on massive waves at Waimea Beach Park. If you want to bring your board, remember, winter waves on these beaches are for the experts only, so be prepared. (However, the waters calm down tremendously in summer.) The famous Banzai Pipeline reef break, considered one of the most challenging waves in the world, is located at Ehukai Beach Park on the North Shore.

North Carolina's Outer Banks, a string of barrier islands more than 175 miles long, is a surfer's paradise, with big swells on the ocean side of the peninsula. On the northern end of the Outer Banks, Corolla is ideal for beginners. What happens here is that waves break when they encounter water that is shallower than they are tall (so, for example, a 3-foot wave will not break in 4 feet of water). The barrier sandbar makes the waves break at manageable heights, and surfers can walk out to the breaks rather than exert energy by paddling. On the northern end, you don't have to worry about rocks, the water is shallower, and the beach is much flatter. Summer is a great time to go—there are fewer crowds, shallower waves, and warm water. Those looking for more of a challenge just need to head south of Corolla at the peak of hurricane season between August and November. And last, but certainly not least, experienced surfers should try Cape Hatteras, which holds the biggest, most consistent waves along the islands. Your best bet for lessons is Corolla Surf Shop (www.corollasurfshop.com), whether you're a first-timer or looking for a refresher course.

On the West Coast, one of the great surf spots for beginners isn't in Southern **California,** it's in the Central Coast town of Santa Cruz. Cowell's Beach, just north of the main beach, receives long, easy waves, while Capitola Beach is an even less crowded alternative for beginners. Both Cowell's Beach Surf Shop (www.cowellssurfshop.com) and Santa Cruz Surf School (www.santacruzsurfschool.com) can show you the ropes. If you're a skilled surfer, there's a place for

INSIDER'S TIP

Every November, the Triple Crown of Surfing is held on Oahu's North Shore in three breaks: Haleiwa Ali'i Beach Park, Sunset Beach, and Banzai Pipeline. www.triplecrownofsurfing.com

you as well: Steamer Lane is a longtime favorite among big-wave surfers and downright dangerous if you're not very experienced. Keep in mind, the waves in Santa Cruz tend to be largest and most consistent between September and March.

Believe it or not, one of the easiest places to pick up a board for the first time is in my favorite place in the world: Fire Island, **New York.** Robert Moses State Park has an easy break near the Field 5 lot, and it's a lot less crowded than the more well-known Long Beach and Jones Beach.

MEXICO

In **Oaxaca,** Mexico, Puerto Escondido, a.k.a. the Mexican Pipeline, is one of the top surfing spots in the world. Although there are places for less experienced surfers, the big draw here is the annual Quiksilver Pro surf competition in August. But you have to be flexible. The waves here are so powerful that officials will frequently postpone the event until they reach safe levels. Between April and November, surfers hang ten at Playa Zicatela, where the breaks and riptides are among the most powerful in the world. This spot is no joke, so unless you're extremely comfortable out on the waves, you're best off watching from the shore.

If you're in the mood for an adventure, head to the more remote, laid-back Oaxacan spots. San Agustinillo, about 40 miles south of Puerto Escondido, sits on a small bay where it meets the Pacific Ocean. The area has two surfable beaches: Playa San Agustinillo on the west end, and the eastern Playa Rinconcito, which has calmer, more sheltered waters.

Bahias de Huatulco is a well-kept secret among surfers. It's barely on the tourist radar and an especially beautiful spot where the Sierra Madre del Sur meet the Pacific Ocean. Several protected bays, including La Bocana, have some powerful surfing breaks.

Troncones, in the Mexican state of **Guerrero,** isn't a major tourist destination—which is exactly why you should go. The point that juts out into Manzanillo Bay is suitable for many levels and the surf is good year-round, but newer surfers should stick to November through April, when the waves are smaller (watch out for the rough, rocky bottom). Summer brings a larger but more consistent swell. Many hotels in the area offer surfing lessons for beginners, including the Inn at Manzanillo Bay (www.manzanillobay.com), which has a beginner package that includes rentals and lessons, as well as non-surfing activities like snorkeling and horseback riding. If you're a longboarder, La Saladita, which is not far from Troncones, is an ideal spot.

Most people are familiar with the resort town of Puerto Vallarta. But the **Riviera Nayarit** runs for about 200 miles, including some excellent surf spots. That includes the popular surf town of Sayulita, where waves range from ultra-beginner to intermediate. Or head to Punta Mita, once a poor fishing village that has become a major destination (the Four Seasons and St. Regis have both taken up residence here), where there are four breaks to choose from: Beginners will appreciate the long, slow waves at La Lancha, while experts can take on the faster, rougher sea currents at the Cove. The other two breaks, Anclote and El Faro, are beautiful and remote. As with other parts of Mexico, the peak season is in winter, between November and April, when the waves are stronger and more consistent. Summer here means fewer crowds but the potential for hurricane swells.

EUROPE

France's Basque Coast, which stretches from Bordeaux to the Spanish border, is practically the surf capital of Europe. The chic resort town of Biarritz is at the center of the action, known for its consistent conditions and ritzy social scene. In town, La Côte des Basques has gentle, long waves that are great for beginners, while La Grande Plage tends to be a little more challenging for more advanced surfers. Biarritz beaches get crowded in summer, so pick the slower shoulder seasons or head out of town for a more local experience.

If you're an intermediate surfer, you want to go to spots like Miramar, Port Vieux, Aquitaine, Hossegor, and Seignosse. Expert surfers should go up north to the town of Anglet, where the Chambre d'Amour is pretty much credited as the birthplace of surfing in this region, or head south to Guethary for powerful swells.

AUSTRALIA

Most out-of-towners will head to Australia's famous Sydney beaches, Manly and Bondi, to test the waters. But don't over look Maroubra Beach, a.k.a. the "Bra," a national surfing reserve just outside of **Sydney.** This small beach is more of a local hangout than a tourist attraction, but it's a favorite spot for its consistent surf and long waves. Just watch out: This is the beach that spawned the notorious Bra Boys gang, so while the surfing itself is great, be careful to respect the locals and general surfing etiquette. If you're not an experienced surfer, opt for a lesson with an outfitter like Sydney Safe Surf Schools (www.safesurfschools.com.au), with locals as your guide.

Pro Surfing Competitions

Most of the major surf brands have competitions on the coast throughout the year, so if you prefer to watch the experts at work, this is the place to do it. Probably the biggest and the best is O'Neill Surf de Nuit (night surf) contest, which takes place in mid-August on Anglet's Sables d'Or beach in **France.**

Bells Beach, also known as the gateway to **Victoria**'s Surf Coast on the Great Ocean Road, is host to the world-famous Rip Curl Pro competition, the longest-running event in professional surfing.

The famous Gold Coast in **Queensland** is considered to have the best surfing conditions in all of Australia—so much so that there's actually a beach called Surfers Paradise that's a main hub for tourists and locals alike. But for beginners, locals will take you a little farther north to an area called the Spit, where a break wall makes the waves much easier to handle than the more exposed beaches. You can take surf lessons from a local company like Surf in Paradise (www.surfinparadise.com.au), where instructors are intimately familiar with the swells in this area.

Intermediate surfers will want to head to nearby beaches like Narrowneck, an exposed beach break where an artificial reef was built to protect the coast from erosion and to improve surfing conditions. Or head to Kurrawa Beach, in the heart of Broadbeach, where the Australian Surf Life Saving Championships are held each year. Or, to go a little off the beaten Gold Coast path to Mermaid Beach, which is known for its strong breaks but is much quieter and more family oriented than the more mainstream beaches.

If you're an expert, some of the world's longest waves can be found in Queensland at Snapper Rocks, on the northern side of Point Danger. This point break marks the beginning of the man-made sandbar surf break known locally as Superbank. The surf here has become something of a rite of passage—meaning it can get crowded with advanced surfers taking on the challenge.

Surf and Yoga

The Sol Sessions (www.solsessions.com) camps in La Saladita, **Mexico,** and Block Island, **Rhode Island,** offer twice-a-year surfing and yoga retreats to work out both your mind and body. Pura Vida Adventures (www.puravidaadventures.com) offers a similar type of experience in **Costa Rica** several times a year, so you can combine the art of wave riding with yoga within a beautiful natural setting. Former pro surfer Richard Schmidt (www.richardschmidt.com) runs weeklong surf clinics in Nosara, Costa Rica, every year, which include classroom and water-based instruction plus daily yoga sessions.

In the state of **Victoria,** a handful of coastal stretches feature long, mellow waves that are ideal for beginners. Near Torquay is Jan Juc and farther up the coast is Point Impossible, both of which have reliable conditions.

In Western **Australia,** monster waves and swells can be found on the beaches south of Perth in the Margaret River region. Experienced surfers will want to tackle the waves at North Point, a right-hand reef break, or at Three Bears, which is comprised of three major swells—Papa, Mama, and Baby. Or head out to Rottnest Island, where Strickland Bay, aka Strickos, has some of the top coral reef waves in the world.

TAHITI

What's great about Tahiti is the islands get swells from all directions. The main surf season runs from April to September, when trade winds push Antarctic swells onto the south shores. More advanced surfers can also tackle the waves between October and March, when the waves swell from tropical storms.

On the island of Tahiti itself, beginners can learn to surf on the long, black beach of Papenoo. The beach is so narrow that it's not a great place for sunbathing, since it can be swallowed up at high tide, but the exposed waters and consistent break make it ideal for beginners. On the south side of the island, Papara Beach has fewer crowds and is also accessible for beginning and intermediate surfers.

But even with its plethora of manageable swells, Tahiti is most famous for its world-class, extremely dangerous break known as Teahupoo. On the southwest corner of the island, Teahupoo has challenged even the world's most experienced surfers. The shallow coral reef below creates an unusual, hollow-breaking wave that can reach a whopping 10 feet, but that's also what makes it so deadly. Don't even bother attempting this wave, but you can witness the pros at work at the annual Billabong Pro Tahiti surf competition.

SOUTH AMERICA

Believe it or not, **Chile** offers a landscape not unlike central California. It's got a slightly cool climate and even cooler waters, dark sand, and craggy coastlines (rather than the balmy weather and white sand usually associated with surf spots). The resort town of Pichilemu in central Chile, about a 3- to 4-hour drive from Santiago, has two main beaches: Punta de Lobos and Puertecillo Beach, which offer a great variety of point breaks—everything from huge waves that the pros like to tackle, to "shadowed" swells that are good for beginners. This is the Southern Hemisphere, so the waves are at their best in April and May.

For spectators, there are some major surfing competitions at Punta de Lobos, namely the Quiksilver Ceremonial Big Wave Invitational. www.quiksilver-ceremonial.cl

Cold-Water Surfing

This is for the adventurous surfer. The town of Tofino on **Vancouver Island** is known as the surfing capital of Canada. The floor is flat and sandy, which means it's appealing for all levels, and the waves range from beginner to expert, depending on how exposed the surf is and the time of year. (Winter brings the biggest swells, while summer is much more manageable for beginners.) Long Beach is your best bet, but advanced surfers should tackle the hardier swells at Cox Bay. It's definitely cold, but that's what the wet suit is for—and the views of the rugged landscape are incredible.

Surf America's "third coast" by heading to **Lake Michigan,** which is actually a pretty hot—er, cold—surfing spot for a dedicated few. The wind is best in November, even though the water and air temperatures are chilly. But if you grab a thick wet suit, it's an experience you won't forget. The trick is to find a jetty or pier, because a swell will actually form around it, or you may be dealing with a relatively flat surface.

Windsurfing

First-time windsurfers can have a great experience on South Padre Island in **Texas,** where the waters of the 120-mile-long Laguna Madre are warm and shallow, and the wind is steady and not too strong.

In the Outer Banks of **North Carolina,** Hatteras Island acts as a sandbar, creating calm, shallow conditions in Pamlico Bay, which are perfect for those just learning.

In Naxos, **Greece,** July and August bring the famous Aegean wind, also known as the Meltemi. The swells can be challenging in some spots, but look for sheltered inlets like Mikri Vigla and Agios Georgios that are protected from the winds.

The inner part of Lac Bay on the island of **Bonaire** is well protected, so it's a great beginner spot. As you get toward the mouth of the bay, the winds become stronger and create conditions for more skilled windsurfers.

Want a serious challenge? Lake Arenal in **Costa Rica** sits between two mountain ranges, so it acts like a wind tunnel, creating waves up to 5 feet high. Not only that, but it has an incredible view of the active volcano from below.

Visitors to **San Francisco** are sometimes surprised at the sight of wind-surfers streaking under the Golden Gate Bridge and zigzagging around the waters of Alcatraz. But believe it or not, San Francisco Bay offers some of the best urban windsurfing in the country. The strong summer wind creates great conditions for more seasoned athletes, but there are also wind-sheltered areas like Alameda, Foster City, and the Sacramento River delta.

Exotic Kite Boarding

Cabarete, a beach town on the north coast of the **Dominican Republic,** is a huge kite boarding destination. The calm water and trade winds make it an ideal spot for beginners or experts. Don't miss the annual Cabarete World Cup in mid-June. Or how about kite boarding in . . . **Vietnam**? That's right, the small fishing village of Mui Ne (about 5 hours north of Saigon) has enormous sand dunes and constant winds, attracting kite boarders from around the world. And in Namibia, **Africa,** the shallow lagoon at Luderitz gets a strong wind every March and August to create perfect conditions. It's home to the well-regarded Luderitz Speed Challenge.

URBAN BIKING

There have always been a number of great cities overseas best explored by bicycle. But the good news is that a growing number of US cities are also best seen on two wheels. And even better news: Bicycles are becoming more readily available and affordable for out-of-towners.

BIKE-SHARING PROGRAMS

With 850 miles of off-street paved bike trails and a well-developed bike-sharing program, biking **Denver** is a no brainer. B-Cycle, the bike-sharing program, offers 500 bikes in 50 stations around the city that can be rented for a membership fee plus a nominal fee after each 30 minutes. Stations are located at well-known attractions such as the convention center, the Denver Art Museum, and the botanic gardens. More ambitious cyclists can venture beyond the downtown area because the city bike trails connect with a network of long-distance trails that go all the way to places such as Red Rocks amphitheater in the foothills and on into the Rocky Mountains. Bike culture in Denver extends to happy hour, and you're always welcome to join locals on the Wednesday cruiser bar crawl.

E-Biking

You've heard of electric cars, but electric bikes? That's right, this eco-friendly trend is growing rapidly in cities around the world. E-bikes involve battery-powered vehicles, so you have the option to pedal the old-fashioned way or with a great boost from electric power. One of the best places in the world to try it out is the **Swiss Alps,** where you can use the extra boost to ascend steep hills and passes. I've done this, and it makes a huge difference in what you're able to see and experience, and at what pace. And you don't have to worry about running out of juice because there are at least 600 spots throughout the country where you can swap batteries for free. You can arrange an e-bike journey through an organized tour company, or download a map of bike routes and swap points at www.Veloland.ch. The Alps are not the only place where e-bikes are becoming a trend. Hertz rents out electric bikes in **Spain** and the **United Kingdom,** while the Electric Bicycle Network (www.electricbikenetwork.org) is a great resource for e-bike rentals and routes throughout England. In the United States, electric bikes are growing especially popular in major urban zones like **San Francisco** and **New York.**

Even more bike friendly is the city of **Boulder,** which is now home to Valmont Bike Park, the largest free urban bike park in America. It's a 40-acre (think 30 football fields) off-road bike park with competition-grade racing rails, jumps, and trails. But this isn't just an expert destination. It caters to families with a tricycle track and an easy loop for new riders. www.valmontbikepark.org

Perhaps the best-known self-service bike rental program is Vélib' in **Paris,** France. There are at least 20,000 bikes available at more than 1,400 stations throughout the city. Users sign up for a subscription that allows unlimited rentals within a specific time period. Swipe the card, choose the bike from an on-screen menu, and you're off. If you keep a bike for longer than 30 minutes, the card is charged incrementally at a nominal fee. It's one of the coolest ways to get around town, like a local. http://en.velib.paris.fr/How-it-works

Taiwan's second-largest city of Kaohsiung has a public bike program known as C-Bike that is definitely worth a mention. The city-run bike-rental program has at least 70 kiosks open almost 24/7 (they shut down for 30 minutes to reset the system), and the city's flat terrain makes it ideal for exploring on two wheels. Best of all, kiosks have English translations, so even if you're at an unstaffed location, it's easy to figure out the rental process. www.c-bike.com.tw/eng/knowing.html

BIKE RENTALS

It's not just the number of bike rental shops in **Minneapolis** that makes it the best place for renting. It's also the ease of finding available bikes and using them throughout the city. For short-term rentals, Nice Ride Minnesota, the bike-sharing program, is available 24/7 April through November. Full-day rentals require a $50 deposit but cost just $5, with access to 95 locations. Niceridemn.org is an excellent resource for bike rental shops, as the site keeps an updated list with Web site links, contact information, and phone numbers. Freewheel Bike has been around since 1974 and helped launch the NiceRideMN public bike-sharing system. Its permanent locations are the West Bank Store, Midtown Bike Center, and Eden Prairie, and there is the Freewheel Mobile, a van that travels around all of Minnesota offering repairs and other services. After you've biked along some of the 43 miles of bicycle lanes and 80 miles of off-street bike paths, try to stop at the Angry Catfish Bicycles + Coffee in Minneapolis. Customers are served more than espresso. The shop has fittings, tune-ups, and a wide selection of cycling gear. My favorite thing about the Angry Catfish? Its baked goods come from the bakery next door, which is run by a former pastry chef from the Plaza Hotel in New York City.

Considering that **Amsterdam**'s narrow, winding, medieval streets aren't really well suited to travel by car, biking is a great way to explore and get to know the city and blend in with the locals (almost every one of its 750,000 residents owns a bike). Bike rentals are widely available and tend to be found near main hubs such as Centraal Station, Leidseplein, and Dam Square. Short-term rentals (3 hours minimum) average 8 euros for a full day, depending on the kind of bike; mountain bikes, tandem bikes, children's bikes, and kick-scooters along with standard city bikes are available at many shops. Rental shops also offer instruction on how to read the signs, where the bike paths are, and what the rules of the road are. For example, bicycles are allowed on the subway but not the tram; and streets may be marked one-way, but that only applies to cars and trucks, not bikes. The city has 400 kilometers of bicycle paths leading just about everywhere a visitor could want to go.

With narrow roads set up in a grid pattern, the Japanese city of **Kyoto** lends itself to being bike friendly. (Just be aware that the roads heading north into the city tend to slope uphill.) Kyoto Cycling Tour Project has four bike-rental terminals across the city: Kyoto Station, Golden Temple, Nishiki Ichiba, and Fushimi. Usually you have the option of choosing from city, mountain, and kid-size bikes.

The Kyoto bike-rental program works with several hotels, including the Hyatt Regency Kyoto and the Holiday Inn Kyoto, to coordinate tours with English-speaking guides. www.kctp.net/en

BIKING EVENTS

Portlanders commute by bike more than residents in any other city in the United States, and motorists are respectful of bikes here. With a 320-mile network of trails, lanes, corridors, and bikeways; a well-developed biking culture; and "rain or shine" dedication, **Portland,** Oregon, is considered one of the bike-friendliest cities in the nation. Come summertime, it's bike central, with summer bike-oriented festivities and events such as Pedalpalooza, the Cirque de Cycling family ride and parade, the World Naked Bike Ride, bike-in movies, mobile dance parties, and unicycle jousting. Near the festivals, local favorite spots to explore are Forest Park, the Vera Katz Eastbank Esplanade, and the Springwater Corridor.

The **Montreal** Bike Fest started in October 1985 with 3,500 cyclists, and today it attracts more than 30,000 cyclists a year. There is no limit to the number of cyclists who can participate, and participation is as simple as registering. The event lasts for 1 week and

Portland's Pedicabs

If you want to enjoy the scenery from the back of a bike but don't want to do any actual pedaling, hitch a ride in Portland with PDX Pedicab, a company that offers pedicab tours of the downtown area. Its knowledgeable guides stop at breweries and distilleries and give an overview of Portland's history. PDX's pedicabs even offer enclosed compartments and warm blankets for days when the weather is cold or wet.

has a range of experiences to accommodate different levels of riders—from the Tour de l'Île (tour of the island of Montreal) to programs like the Night Tour for less experienced bikers.

GUIDED TOURS

Boston has a reputation for being unfriendly to bikers, but Urban Adventours in the North End offers a few guided tours that might change that. The City View Bicycle Tour heads out from the North End, taking you past the USS *Constitution* down by the Charles River on the esplanade, Boston University, Fenway Park, Back Bay, Copley Square, and Boston Common. But a really special experience is the bike tour of the Emerald Necklace, a 1,100-acre chain of parks in Boston and Brookline. Each bike group has a tour guide at the front, middle, and back, and they use bike paths when they can. All the tours supply you with a hybrid city bike, water bottle, and helmet. www.urbanadventours.com

Barcelona prides itself on being one of the most bike-friendly cities in Spain. Dozens of bike tour companies such as Bike Spain, Barcelona CicloTours, Fat Tire Bike Tours, and Barcelona By Bike

Biking Apps

Avoid fees for late returns—they add up fast, to the point where you might have been better off buying a new bike. Spotcycle is a free mobile app available on iPhone, BlackBerry, and Android with bike-sharing program and bike path support information. Bike-sharing information is now available for Capital Bikeshare in Washington, DC/Arlington, Virginia; BIXI Toronto; Capital BIXI in Ottawa-Gatineau, Canada; BIXI in Montreal; Nice Ride Minnesota; Melbourne Bike Share; and Barclays Cycle Hire in London, England. The app shows and locates the status of bike stations around you.

can all take you on guided tours in English (or self-guided tours with a map). We're talking classic city tours, tapas tours, architecture tours, gay-friendly tours, and nighttime tours. With 90 miles of designated cycle paths—and even cycle traffic lights as of 2011—plus a mild and sunny climate, biking is possible year-round. And with a few exceptions (i.e., the hilltop Olympic Village), the city has flat terrain, which means you won't have to exert yourself too much. It takes hours to get around Barcelona by public transit, but on a bike you can zip from Ciutadella Park to the Sagrada Família to Las Ramblas without traffic or hassle.

WHALE WATCHING

Until you've seen a whale up close and in person, your appreciation for nature hasn't been fully charged. It is, to say the least, an electrifying moment to see these behemoths, and it's one of those bucket list items you won't check just once and move on. You will want to return, if you can, as often as you can to watch these giants who are, by the way, watching you.

The finback, which is the second largest of the whale species in the world, is seen on a regular basis in the waters around **Cape Cod.** The best time to go whale watching in this region is between the months of June and September when, after nursing their young in the tropics, whales return to Cape Cod to feed. Although there are plenty of charter services that will take you out into the water from Provincetown, check out Race Point and Herring Cove beaches, which are a short bike ride from Provincetown.

Olympic National Park in **Washington** is a prime spot to see gray whales heading north in spring, and they can easily be spotted from shore. For the best views, just head to Kalaloch Lodge, which sits high on a bluff within the Olympic Coast National Marine Sanctuary, which shares 65 miles of coast with the park. In summer, the national park service itself holds interpretive beach and tide-pool walks led by park rangers. www.nps.gov/olym

One of the most anticipated events in Maui, **Hawaii,** in December is the arrival of the humpback whale. As many as 3,000 whales come to mate and give birth in the warm and protected waters that flow between Maui, Molokai, and Lanai. However, the best place to view this phenomenon on Maui is at Papawai Point, near the 8-mile marker on the Honoapiilani Highway. What's really unique about the whale-watching experience here is that it's one of the best spots to eavesdrop on whales' mating calls, and boat captains will drop an underwater microphone so you can hear them.

Whales will travel thousands of miles to feed in the waters of **Alaska,** and you've got a good chance of spotting humpback and orca whales in summer. Beyond that, species such as beluga, bowhead, gray, minke, and northern right whales also inhabit Alaskan waters so it's a no-brainer that you'll see something. For the best chance of spotting these marine creatures, take an excursion in the Glacier Bay and Kenai Fjords National Parks. Glacier Bay Lodge operates the only day tour in Glacier Bay, an 8-hour experience that runs from late May through early September. You'll likely spot a humpback whale here, as a pod of about 15 to 20 lives here during the season. If you prefer to skip the tour, you can still spot the whales from the lodge itself. www.visitglacierbay.com

All up and down the coast of **Vancouver Island** is prime viewing for orcas, gray whales, and humpback whales. More than 85 orcas (a.k.a. killer whales) reside off the coast of southern Vancouver Island, comprised of three pods. You can spot them easily from Amphitrite Lighthouse on the coast of Ucluelet, along the 6-mile Wild Pacific Trail. Or go during the gray whale migration between February and May, when the majestic creatures travel the thousands of miles from Baja California to their feeding grounds in the Bering Strait. If you really want to get the full experience, the Pacific Rim Whale Festival takes place every March and includes various whale-watching excursions, interpretive lectures, and other events.

Between the Baja California peninsula and the mainland of **Mexico**, the Sea of Cortés is a favorite spot for migrating whales between December and April. Why? It's a combination of balmy waters, high salt content for buoyancy, and protected lagoons that keep the whales safe from predators. In fact, this migration route is thought to be the longest of any animal on earth, as the whales voyage some 12,000 miles from their Arctic feeding grounds to the Sea of Cortéz. For an eye-to-eye view, many experienced whale watchers will rent kayaks to get a close and personal view of the whales. Near Los Cabos, Mexico, whales tend to stick to the shallow lagoons around San Ignacio, Magdalena Bay, and Ojo de Liebre and often get close enough to shore to be visible from land.

The seaside town of Kaikoura on **New Zealand**'s South Island is one of the best places on earth to see the mighty sperm whale—in fact, what makes this such a prime destination is that these mighty giants can be spotted year-round. You're also likely to see orcas between December and March and humpbacks in June and July. There's no shortage of whale-watching tour companies here, but for a really unusual perspective, hop on a low-flying 30-minute flight for an airborne view.

The little town of Hermanus, located about 70 miles southeast of Cape Town, is the center of **South Africa**'s aptly named Whale Coast.

Between July and November, southern right whales migrate from Antarctica to Walker Bay, usually peaking in October; humpbacks are also known to frequent the area starting in May. What's exceptional about this place is that you don't even need to go out on a boat: The whales are easily spotted right from the shore. A stretch of cliff paths feature telescopes and benches where you can sit back and enjoy the show. And here's something you didn't know: Hermanus actually has its own official "whale crier," who patrols the town and blows his kelp horn to signal sightings.

Whale Watching for Free

There are plenty of places where you can catch a glimpse of whales for free.

In the Julia Pfeiffer Burns State Park in Big Sur, **California,** the end of the overlook trail is a great spot to watch whales migrate. San Simeon State Park in San Luis Obispo County has plenty of whale-watching spots along the boardwalk that runs parallel to Moonstone Beach.

The Point Vicente Interpretive Center in Palos Verdes, near Los Angeles, is one of the best places in California to see the gray whale migration, with docents helping visitors spot the whales offshore.

In **Oregon,** good viewing points include Cape Lookout State Park and Boiler Bay State Park. In fact, volunteers from the Oregon parks and recreation department are stationed at 28 different locations along the coast to help visitors see the great whales.

In the state of **Washington,** whales pass right by the town of Westport, on the Olympic peninsula, about $2\frac{1}{2}$ hours from Seattle. In summer, orcas migrate past Washington State.

And on the west side of San Juan Island, a state park nicknamed Whale Watch Park (officially called Lime Kiln Point State Park) is considered one of the best spots to view the whales, which come right up to the shoreline.

Here's a tip: If whale watching is high on your priority list, come prepared with portable chair, a cooler, and a pair of binoculars to enjoy the show.

THRILL-SEEKING ADVENTURES

BUNGEE JUMPING

I've been lucky enough to have had some great thrill-seeking experiences over the years. I've flown back or right seat in F-15s and F-16s, F-4s and F-5s. I've been on a classified mission on an attack nuclear submarine. But I admit—I have never bungee jumped. And although I hesitate to use the "n" word, in this case I'll make an exception: I *never* will. But that's not to mean you shouldn't or can't bungee. Though its popularity peaked in the mid-1990s, bungee (or bungy) jumping is still a favorite activity for thrill-seeking adventurers and an exhilarating way to experience some of the world's great cities, attractions, and natural beauty from a completely different and somewhat adrenaline-fueled perspective.

NORTH AMERICA

Combine hiking and bungee jumping in the mountains above **Los Angeles** for a full-day outdoor adventure. Bungee America operates a jump from the so-called Bridge to Nowhere, 5 miles into the Angeles National Forest. The bridge is accessible only via the popular Sheep Mountain Wilderness Trail, a hike that takes 2½ hours each way. The 100-foot jump is not the most scary or difficult, but it's good for newbies or amateurs—or just folks who don't have the time or money to go to some of the more far-flung bungee sites around the world. www.bungeeamerica.com

The Navajo Bridge in **Arizona** does not have an official jump operator on-site, but it is popular with seasoned bungee jumpers. The trick is you have to either come with your own equipment or with an out-of-town operator such as Bungee Expeditions. At 470 feet high, with a 725-foot span, the bridge arcs over the Colorado River in the northern reaches of the Grand Canyon, with an unbeatable view of cliffs and raging rapids below. www.bungee-expeditions.com

INTERNATIONAL

One of the highest bungee jumps in all of the Americas straddles the Colorado River 1 hour west of the **Costa Rican** capital of San José. What makes the Colorado River Bridge special is its height—265 feet—and extreme beauty: You'll drop into a raging river gorge amid green forest canopy. Thousands have jumped from this disused bridge since 1991, courtesy of Tropical Bungee. For an additional rush, try the combo "adrenaline tours," which combine bungee jumping, rock climbing, and paragliding in a 1-day excursion. www.bungee.co.cr

The jump off the top of **Macau** Tower claims to be the world's

Did you know that France offers more bungee jumping than any country in the world? Dozens of small licensed sites dot the countryside, making it easy to jump if you happen to get the urge while you're there. You can jump off old bridges, over cave entrances, from cranes, near dams, and more.

highest, boasting a 764-foot drop. However, bungee purists claim it's not a "true" jump, as the rebound is not uncontrolled but rather guided by a cable system (which, incidentally, prevents you from actually hitting the tower). Nonetheless it's still a thrill ride: The initial 5-second free fall is the longest in the bungee world, and you reach speeds of nearly 150 mph. Not to mention you come within about 100 feet of the ground before rebounding back up and then slowly being lowered to the ground. http://macau.ajhackett.com

If you can put aside the butterflies for a minute, enjoy the view from 364 feet in the air at the Victoria Falls Bridge in **Zimbabwe/ Zambia.** Then go for the adrenaline rush as you hurtle headfirst toward the mighty Zambezi River with Victoria Falls in the background. The Victoria Falls bungee jump drops through the mist between tree-lined cliffs from the bridge, which divides the nations of Zambia and Zimbabwe. www.victoriafalls.net/bunjee_jumping.htm

For real thrill seekers, Face Adrenaline runs jumps off the Bloukrans Bridge in **South Africa.** It is recognized by the Guinness World Records as the highest bungee jump from a bridge in the world, with the top of the arch at a little over 708 feet tall. It's located in the Tsitsikamma area of the Garden Route, where jumpers are secured in a full-body harness. If you aren't up for doing the jump, there are walking tours along the catwalk. As the highest and largest bridge in Africa and third-highest bridge in the world, this bridge walk is nothing to laugh at either. www.faceadrenalin.com

Feeling suicidal? Try bungeeing into a volcano. That's right, in Villarrica, **Chile,** a helicopter will fly you up over a volcanic crater and let you dive from 10,000 feet in the air. A $10,000 package from Bungee.com includes the jump, whitewater rafting, accommodations, and transportation from Pucón. Yes, it's possible you could perish . . . but the company will require you to sign a waiver.

Most people head straight to the Kawarau Bridge in Queenstown, **New Zealand.** But more extreme thrill-seekers know to go to the Nevis Bungy highwire: It's higher, wider, and more dramatic than its sister site. It's the third-highest jump in the world, towering 439 feet above the Nevis River in a dramatic red-rock gorge about 10 miles from Queenstown. Even getting to the platform is dramatic: You take a cable car shuttle across a wire from the edge of the cliff to the center of the gorge. The process is a little unique as the bungee cord has a ripcord that lets you unhook your legs when you're done, so you can sit upright and enjoy the incredible view while they pull you back up to the top. www.bungy.co.nz

INSIDER'S TIP

Bungee jumping not your style? AJ Hackett's original bungee jumping operation in Queenstown has a viewing platform designed for spectators. You can spend hours watching jumpers dive off the old wooden bridge—and count how many try to chicken out before being encouraged with a 10-second countdown.

Cliff Diving

When it comes to thrill seeking, just surviving the fall would earn a "best" in the cliff diving category. So the use of that word is relative. Cliff diving is usually an activity "best" left to experts or those with a death wish or both, because of the obvious inherent dangers. But there are a few places around the world where novices have been known to successfully give it a try—often on small cliffs near larger ones used by pros.

While I can't condone or condemn, I *can* say that if you decide to try it, follow some basic rules:

1. Don't dive in a spot that's above your ability (novices should stick with heights of 20 feet or less).

2. Dive with a companion who knows the area.

3. Test the water and weather conditions first.

4. Always dive FEET FIRST and enter the water completely vertical.

5. When in doubt, always observe rather than participate.

The South Point cliffs on Hawaii's **Big Island** tower at heights of 30 to 50 feet, but this is expert territory only. As an alternative, in Keahou Bay just south of **Kailua-Kona,** you can kayak out to the easy/intermediate-level cliffs and jump off. At 15 feet, Black Rock on Kaanapali Beach in **Maui** is also a pretty tame jump. If you prefer to just watch, every night the Sheraton Maui puts on a scheduled show where a hotel employee lights tiki torches and then plunges into the water below.

The limestone cliffs adjacent to Rick's Cafe in Negril, **Jamaica,** are a popular spot for cliff diving. In fact, the waitstaff might even encourage you to take the plunge. However, it is only recommended for experienced divers since the height is around 35 feet and there have been plenty of injuries, which seems to correlate with the amount of drinks consumed beforehand!

As opposed to most other dive spots worldwide that are found in coastal areas, the Kimberley region of Western **Australia** is known for inland diving. The lakes and rivers that crisscross this rugged landscape cut through spectacular gorges and are framed by waterfalls and mountain peaks. The Ord River has multiple cliffs of various heights, but don't attempt the highest one (80 feet) unless you're a pro—seek out smaller ones nearby.

You may have never heard of **Bluff Island** in the Adirondacks, but its cliffs were allegedly featured in a silent movie. In 1914's *The Perils of Pauline*, the heroine leaps off the cliff, on horseback no less. In modern times, you have to kayak out there from the Second Pond launch, and if you're a novice, don't jump off the top (it's 70 foot). Try the 15 foot jump-off point to the right-hand side.

What about the famous Quebrada Cliffs near Acapulco, **Mexico**? Don't even *think* about it unless you're a professional. These cliffs are not only a whopping 100 feet high, but the seafloor below is only 13 feet deep. A good time to watch is during mid-December's Festival of the Virgin of Guadalupe. On the evening before the festival, hundreds of divers make a procession to the cliffs and pray to their patron saint. Then they start diving in quick succession, often five at a time.

DOGSLEDDING

Although dogsledding may sound like an extreme sport, the reality is that it's just a different sport. And the good news is that you don't need any prior experience (unless you want to actually drive the sled yourself). Even better news: When looking for the best places to go dogsledding, there are options for all levels of expertise, not to mention best ways to dogsled when there's no snow on the ground!

BEGINNER

Song in the Woods offers rides in rural **Maine** tailored for beginners. Stephen Madera and his crew take guests through the icy winter wonderland around Gulf Hagas and the Roach Ponds area, just east of Moosehead Lake (about 75 miles north of Bangor). You'll cross frozen lakes while hearing nothing but the quiet of the woods and the sound of dogs' paws on the snow. Set out midmorning or, even better, head out at dusk to mush under a moonlit sky. www.songinthewoods.com

Dog Sled Rides of Winter Park is a full-service kennel and sledding operation within easy driving distance of Denver, **Colorado,** making it popular with day-trippers. Jeff Martin and his 80 dogs offer 45-minute, 5-mile guided winter and summer trips that pass by 13,000-foot peaks and the Continental Divide. In winter, you get to ride in a traditional dogsled. But if riding in the cold isn't for you, summer rides involve dog-pulled scooters or golf carts. There are educational kennel tours where you get to learn how a kennel is run and what goes into the care and training of a sled dog. Best of all, if you fall in love (which you will), you can even join a volunteer program to spend time grooming and exercising the dogs. www.dogsledrides.com/winterpark

---

Learn from the Pros

Husky Homestead in Denali National Park, **Alaska,** is home of four-time Iditarod champion Jeff King and his 75 award-winning huskies. No sledding excursions here, but the kennel offers an excellent tour to help visitors understand the art of racing and raising sled dogs. Guides describe the special relationship between musher and dog; show off their arctic survival gear, sleds, and racing equipment; and teach visitors how the state-of-the-art dog-powered training carousels work. If you cruise to Alaska on Princess Cruises, this is one of the featured shore excursions.

FAMILY FRIENDLY

Mitch Seavey's Ididaride in Seward, **Alaska,** is run by an Iditarod champion whose family has been racing dogs for three generations. In summer, you can hop on an easy 2-mile trek over dirt and gravel through the Alaskan wilderness to the base of Resurrection Mountain and along Box Canyon Creek. This option is especially family friendly since the weather is mild and, after the sledding experience, you'll tour the kennel and hang out with husky puppies. If that seems too tame, the winter ride emulates a more authentic Iditarod experience and includes a tour of a glacier that's only accessible by dogsled. You can actually learn to drive a dog team and then mush one down Resurrection Valley to Exit Glacier. www.ididaride.com

Head to Lake Elmore, **Vermont** (just outside of Stowe), for a unique dogsledding experience with Peacepups Dog Sledding. A team of Siberian huskies will race through the Vermont wilderness. These are serious racing dogs that have been trained to work with beginners. The trails are well maintained to avoid a bumpy ride, and the pace averages an easy 8 to 10 miles per hour. But here's something really cutting edge for those with moderate cross-country ski experience: skijoring. Basically, you get on the skis, and the dogs pull you along the backcountry trails. www.peacepupsdogsledding.com

Jamaican Dogsledding?

That's right, at Chukka Caribbean Adventures, you can participate in the experience with a real musher named Newton Marshall. He is the first person from the Caribbean ever to compete in the Iditarod. There are 15 dogs on the sled—all of them SPCA rescue animals. There is, of course, no snow, so the dogs pull you through the mud on warm weather–adapted sleds! Trust me, this is a really wild experience that you can't do anywhere else in the Caribbean. www.chukkacaribbean.com/dogsled.php

ADVANCED

Talk about remote: The **Yukon Territory** in Canada is about as unspoiled as it gets. Hans Gatt, the current record holder in the Yukon Quest, a 1,000-mile Alaskan dogsled race, has partnered with Sky High Wilderness Ranch to host a Chance of a Lifetime ride. You'll learn all the basics of training, riding, and dog care, and set out on an 8-day loop from the ranch. Each day will get progressively more difficult, averaging about 20 miles a day, compounded by the challenges of winter camping. www.skyhighwilderness.com

Wintergreen Dogsled Lodge near Ely, **Minnesota,** focuses almost entirely on the hands-on experience. Not only can you learn how to drive your own team of dogs, but you can harness, feed, and care for them, too. Tip: Ask about adding on an extra day for a special photography workshop run by a pro outdoor photographer. Ely and the surrounding area offer some of the most pristine conditions for winter photography, not to mention the dogs themselves make great subjects! For more extreme types, Wintergreen also hosts trips to the Russian Arctic, Greenland, and the Scandinavian Arctic. www.dogsledding.com

EXTREME

Although the Svalbard archipelago of **Norway** may be better known for its polar bear population, the frozen fjords make solid grounds for dogsledding. Activities Abroad takes extreme adventurers to Spitsbergen, one of the islands in the Arctic Ocean. Not only do you get to ride your own team of dogs, but the trip includes a 1-night stay on a ship frozen in the ice. When I say there's wildlife here, I'm not kidding—we're talking Svalbard reindeer, Arctic fox, and polar bears—and that's why your guides travel with rifles. www.activitiesabroad.com

Aurora Borealis Adventures in Lapland, in northern **Sweden,** has both winter and summer dogsledding through the Nordic forest teeming with reindeer, moose, eagles, and other wildlife. But for an extreme adventure, the most over-the-top of all is a 450-mile, 12-day mushing trip along the Vindel River that takes you through the winter wilderness and into some of Europe's most pristine, untouched nature reserves. At night, you'll get the added bonus of seeing the northern lights, which are a regular occurrence at this latitude. www.auroraborealis.nu

How extreme can you go? How about Lake Baikal in **Siberia**? Considered the world's oldest and deepest freshwater lake, this is where approximately 20 percent of the world's unfrozen freshwater exists, along with thousands of species of animals, fish, insects, and plant life. Here, instructors from Baikal Dog Sledding, which is owned by world-renowned champion musher Oleg Tyuryumin, will introduce you to the huskies, teach you the basics of hitching and driving, and take you along the ice trails. Rides can last anywhere from 3 miles to multiday dogsledding and winter camping excursions, based on just how adventurous you feel. www.baikalsled.ru

Best Places to Go

OFF-ROADING

In my experience, sometimes the best way to travel off the beaten path is to drive off of it—literally. Off-roading can be done in a 4WD car like a Jeep or Land Rover or in an ATV or dune buggy. But there are some cautions. Just because you're driving a 4WD vehicle doesn't mean it's legal to go off-roading, or even safe. And if you're not familiar with the car you're driving, it's frighteningly easy to roll it. So with those advance warnings, here are the best places for off-roading.

The Oceano Dunes State Vehicular Recreation Area is among the last remaining coastal dunes in **California** still open to off-roaders. Dune buggy enthusiasts know this area as an iconic site since the 1940s. Because of its proximity to Pismo Beach, it tends to be a lot cooler than the more inland off-road desert parks, and it's got truly spectacular ocean views. As for the dune buggying experience, it's one of the best. We're talking about 1,500 acres of land dedicated to off-highway vehicle use, with 200,000-year-old sand dunes that span all sizes, from small "rollers" to massive bowls. Beginners prefer the gentle slopes on the windward side, while more advanced drivers can tackle the crests on the leeward side. Want to make it a family trip? There are also 6.5 miles of beach here, so you can drive your 4WD vehicle along the shore and stop for fishing, kite boarding, and swimming. www.ohv.parks.ca.gov

When talking about **Utah**'s parkland, most people think of its great national parks. But off-road enthusiasts have a well-kept secret: Coral Pink Sand Dunes State Park. Of the more than 3,700 acres of open dunes, a whopping 90 percent is open to riding. And best of all, it's rarely crowded. Think of ATVing here as a free-form roller coaster ride on extra-fine sand. (Tip: Don't bring your SUV here as it will likely get stuck.) But what really draws the locals here is not the size of the dunes, but rather the scenic beauty in this aptly named park: soft, coral-colored dunes; looming, red sandstone cliffs; and ponderosa pine forests. Unfortunately for out-of-towners, the closest vehicle rental spot is about 60 miles away, so it's best for one-tank trippers who can tow their own ATV. www.stateparks.utah.gov/parks/coral-pink

Vast desert dunes meet giant desert cactus forests meet ocean views in Baja California, **Mexico,** a mecca for off-road racing. This region is something akin to the American West of days gone by, with wide-open spaces and low population, making it a great choice for off-roaders. And here's something really special: Occasionally it snows in higher elevations, which means you can drive your vehicle from sand to snow. If you're a first-timer or want to travel with other enthusiasts, Wide Open Excursions offers everything from half-day to 7-day loop trips around both Cabo San Lucas and Ensenada, with former pro off-road racers as your guides, using $100,000 open-wheel touring cars. If you really want to get the full experience, these guides can also help you compete in the renowned Baja 500 and Baja 1000 races. www.wideopenbaja.com

Polihale State Park in Kauai, **Hawaii,** isn't your typical off-road site, but it's a very remote beach park on the western side of Kauai, where simply getting there is an experience in itself. From the main road on Highway 550 (between mile markers 12 and 13), drive for 5 miles on Polihale Ridge Road, which is a bumpy, sandy, winding adventure. The terrain means you're best off in a 4WD vehicle (smaller cars can get stuck in the sand, and it costs a pretty penny to hire a tow truck). But the payoff is worth the effort: At the end of the road is 5 miles of Na Pali Coast with sand dunes looming 50 to 100 feet high in the distance. Even cooler, this is the westernmost point in the United States that's publicly accessible. You can swim in Queen's Pond, but anywhere else, the sea is too rough to enter. www.hawaiistateparks.org/parks/kauai/polihale.cfm

Off the coast of southern Queensland in **Australia,** Fraser Island is the largest sand island in the world, and it's strictly 4WD territory. Also a World Heritage site, the island is known for its long, uninterrupted white sand beaches, towering sand cliffs, and more than 100 freshwater lakes. But what really makes this place stand out is that there are rain forests growing alongside sand dunes, with tracks connecting scenic areas. My advice? Go straight to Seventy-Five Mile Beach, which is an actual sand highway that runs up the surf side of the island. You take a guided off-road tour through the island resorts like Kingfisher Bay Resort (www.kingfisherbay.com) or from a mainland resort on the Fraser Coast like Hervey Bay Resort (http://herveybayresort.com.au).

Or you can opt for a self-guided tour, which requires you to rent a vehicle on the island from a company like Aussie Trax 4X4 Rentals (www.fraserisland4wd.com.au), or rent on the mainland and transport the vehicle on a vehicle barge (www.visitfrasercoast.com/destinations/fraser-island). The best time to go is between October and March, not just because of the warm weather, but for the spectacular wildflower display. This is an exceptionally remote park, so be sure you've got a full tank of gas plus food and drinks.

Where else can you find an exceptional desert ride than in the **United Arab Emirates**? This region is known for the craggy Hajar Mountains, riverbeds (known as wadis), and miles and miles of sand dunes. This challenging region is best navigated on a guided desert safari through a company such as Arabian Adventures, which will also incorporate cultural experiences with your ride. Within the mountains, the Umm Al Quwain desert is the place to tackle the rolling dunes. Throughout the day, you'll remain on rough terrain while visiting a camel farm and driving through small villages and communities. www.arabian-adventures.com

And in **Dubai,** hop onto a Toyota Land Cruiser for their version of dune bashing. Any hotel can set this up for you. But my advice: Don't drive. Let your driver handle the wheel. Whether you're driving or not, you'll need to plan some extra time when you return to your hotel to attempt to remove sand from orifices in your body you didn't even knew existed!

INSIDER'S TIP

Find parks and trails and meet up with other enthusiasts at www.offroadnorthamerica.com, and check out ATV adventures throughout the United States at www.atvpathfinder.com. You can find racing events and vehicle reviews at www.off-roadweb.com.

On the northern tip of **Chile** is the Tarapacá Region, best known as the crossroads of the Pan American Highway, the Atacama Desert, the Pampa del Tamarugal, and the Altiplanico. With so much to see both on and off the road, this is a huge destination for adventurous drivers. Natural and man-made sites include the renowned petroglyphs in the Atacama Desert and the prehistoric geoglyphs carved into the landscape in Unita, as well as the impressive Isluga Volcano National Park and the ruins of an Indian fortress at Putre. A guided expedition will help you cover a lot of ground—for example, Extremo Norte has a 4-day overland trip through the Altiplanico (high plains), which includes a trip to a Biosphere Reserve, the Surire salt flat, and natural hot springs through mountainous terrain surrounded by cliffs and rock formations. If you go on a self-guided trip, you can rent a 4WD vehicle in Iquique from a company such as Lys Car Rental (www.lys.cl). Note this region is hospitable most of the year except for December through March, when heavy rains can flood the roads to dangerous levels. And remember to stock up on supplies because gas stations are few and far between.

HANG GLIDING/ PARAGLIDING

First, let's get down to a definition of terms: Hang gliding and paragliding are collectively known as free flight. Hang gliding uses a kitelike contraption with a rigid frame that a rider is strapped into, while paragliding requires a modified parachute. Paragliding involves flying in engineless aircraft, using air current to stay aloft. These two activities give you the closest feeling to flying like a bird.

BEGINNER

Beginners will want to fly—actually, they'll *need* to fly—tandem with an expert, so head to the historic Torrey Pines Gliderport in La Jolla, **California,** which has been host to soaring pilots for more than 80 years. Smooth onshore breezes create consistent lifting air, enabling Torrey Pines to offer one of the most reliable sites for hang gliding and paragliding tandem flights in the world. A paragliding school operates from the site overlooking the Pacific Ocean. www.flytorrey.com

Also in Southern California is the beginner-friendly Dockweiler State Beach, where locals have been hang gliding for decades. This is a safe environment, with west-facing dunes, consistent shore breezes, and as many as 300 flyable days. You can simply stand on the 3 miles of shore and watch the hang gliders soaring above, or take a lesson with Windsports, which has the only flight training facility in the area. www.windsports.com

If soaring over snowcapped mountains is more your style, beginners can take tandem rides at Jackson Hole Mountain Resort in **Wyoming.** Because it's easily accessible by the resort's aerial tram, this is one of the best spots in the Rockies for beginners to get an instructional tandem flight. www.jhparagliding.com

The Wright Brothers first soared at the dunes near Kitty Hawk, **North Carolina,** more than 100 years ago, and Kitty Hawk Kites continues the tradition of soaring there today. The forgiving sand dunes make this an easy option, with short flights of 30 to 100 or so yards up to 15 feet in the air. If you're ready to advance to a more extreme option, go for the high-altitude tandem flights that can take you 2,000 feet in the air or higher. www.kittyhawk.com

Valle de Bravo is a small colonial town located about 2 hours from **Mexico City.** It is surrounded by mountains and situated in the middle of a big forest next to Lake Avándaro. The views over the area are stunning, as are the air currents, which is why it draws thousands every year from all over North America who fly the skies. The opera-tor Fly Mexico offers 7-day package tours with lodging, transfers, and gliding equipment. www.flymexico.com

MODERATE

Santa Barbara, **California,** has near perfect conditions for glid-ing, as ocean breezes collide with sheer cliffs to create the cur-rents and lift required for the sport. The consistently nice weather means you can do it year-round. And what better view than the beautiful Pacific Ocean and the colonial town of Santa Barbara, sur-rounded by beaches, forests, and rolling coastal mountain ranges? In addition, the area has one of the finest training hills in the country to learn to paraglide and hang glide. Top-notch schools include Eagle Paragliding (www.eagleparagliding.com) and Fly Away Hang Glid-ing (www.flyawayhanggliding.com), which makes Santa Barbara a great place to spend a week or two to learn to fly.

Wallaby Ranch in Orlando, **Florida,** features the first full-time Aerotow Hang Gliding Flight Park in the world (this means a small ultralight aircraft pulls the tandem hang glider into the air, so no running is necessary). The 100-acre takeoff and landing field is ded-icated to gliding only, so you don't have to share space with airplanes or other craft while you're learning to fly. All beginner instruction is done tandem, with the instructor guiding your every move. If you're traveling with kids, the ranch offers more amenities than most hang gliding parks, including tent and RV camping facilities, swimming, a climbing wall, and ample mountain bike and hiking trails through the woods. www.wallaby.com.

For those with some experience who want to learn more, head to the Ellenville, **New York,** flight park, located 60 miles north of New York City. A nationally famous site since 1973, it has two major teaching facilities that offer full instruction and tandem instruc-tional flights. Flying in Ellenville in the fall when the leaves are full of color is an incredible experience and worth the trip. www.flyhighhg.com and www.mtnwings.com

EXPERT

In Chattanooga, **Tennessee,** Henson's Gap is one of the most revered places among hang gliders. Located high above Chattanooga, the site features the "radial ramp"—a downward-curving wooden launch plank custom-made for gliders. Once you've taken off, the gentle thermals of the Sequatchie Valley below facilitate long, sustained flights over cornfields and forests. But be aware that this site is for experts only, and you must be a member of the US Hang Gliding and Paragliding Association and the local gliding club, the Tennessee Tree Toppers, to launch from here.

The vertical cliffs of Makapuu on the island of **Oahu** are expert territory only. Located on the eastern end of the island, the 2,000-mile ridge has strong trade winds, and on a good day, you can spot gliders launching from several spots among the cliffs. To get a sense of just how heart-stopping this jump is, you can hike along Makapuu Hang Glider Trail with its sweeping coastal views.

Mieussy, 30 miles west of the ski resort town of Chamonix, **France,** claims to be the birthplace of paragliding, in 1974. Here, cool nights and hot days create temperature gradients that create powerful thermals and strong valley winds. The views of the Chamonix Valley, the mountains, the glaciers, and the lakes are second to none. Many flock to Mont Blanc, the massive peak nearby that dominates the skyline, to try their luck off its slopes, but it's best reserved for experts. Good flying starts in March, and the season ends in October. You can also learn "speed riding" here—a blend of paragliding and skiing that lets you fly down the slopes at incredible speeds.

SKYDIVING/ PARACHUTING

I've had the opportunity to fly right seat or back seat in an F-4 phantom, an F-5, an A-10, and an F-15. In order to be approved to fly, I had to go through ejection training with the Air Force. That just confirmed something I already knew about myself: The only time I'd ever willingly jump out of a plane is if the plane was about to disintegrate or we were about to hit a mountain. For those of you who actually *enjoy* jumping out of planes, I've compiled some of the best areas of sky for flying through the air.

What makes certain places appealing to skydivers? From the flight up to the jump down, the only thing that tempers the adrenaline is the beautiful scenery along the way. Jump sites near coastal or mountainous areas are usually the most attractive, since you get a bird's-eye view for miles in every direction.

It's hard to go wrong in **New Zealand,** where you can get an astonishing view from pretty much every angle, including from above. Most people associate Queenstown with adventure activities, and there are definitely beautiful views here, including the Remarkables mountain range and Lake Wakatipu. But I say if you're going to go for it, opt for a glacier dive in the Southern Alps. You'll get unobstructed views of the pristine Fox Glacier and its smaller counterpart, the Franz Josef Glacier; the looming peaks of Aoraki/ Mount Cook; crystal-clear mountain lakes; and the Tasman Sea. www.skydivingnz.co.nz

Or how about a beach landing? On the far north coast of the North Island, a company called Ballistic Blondes lets you choose between landing on the white sands of Ocean Beach in Whangarei or along Paihia Beach in the Bay of Islands. www.skydiveballisticblondes. co.nz

You can skydive all around **Switzerland,** but perhaps the most visually stunning spot is in Interlaken. You'll hurtle to the earth at 120 miles per hour over the achingly beautiful Swiss Alps, with the trio of mighty snowcapped peaks—Eiger, Mönch, and Jungfrau—in the distance. Directly below you are the emerald-green foothills and the two gorgeous lakes that give Interlaken its name, Thun and Brienz. My advice? Go for the more extreme experience: With Skydive Switzerland, you can actually jump out of a helicopter! It's the best way to combine a memorable scenic flight with a nail-biting adrenaline rush. Advanced skydivers can even request to land on the Petersgrat glacier during winter jumps. www.skydiveswitzerland.com

Skydivers love the **Emirates** because of its unusual desert vistas: sand, sea, sky . . . . and skyscrapers as far as the eye can see. On a really clear day, you can see all the way to Saudi Arabia or across the Strait of Hormuz to Iran. Not to mention the air at 10,000 feet is a lot cooler than on the ground, which can top 110 degrees in summer. Skydive Dubai (www.skydivedubai.ae) is one of the best operators in the UAE, with two jump zones; one is easily accessible in the urban Dubai Marina area, right beside the Palm Jumeirah. Not quite ready to jump out of a plane? Skydive Dubai is cohost of the annual Dubai International Parachuting Championship and Gulf Cup, where you can be an extreme sport spectator.

The great thing about skydiving in **Hawaii**? From 14,000 feet up, you can see almost the entire island of Oahu: the North Shore, Kaena Point, Pearl Harbor, and Diamond Head. The clear blue sky, 360-degree ocean view, green landscapes, and bird's-eye view of the island's famous beaches can't be beat either. Two well-established companies are Pacific Skydiving Center (www.pacificskydivinghawaii.com) in Wailua and Skydive Hawaii (www.skydivehawaii.com), which cater to both novice and experienced parachutists.

There's nothing like seeing a rugged mountain range from above, and in Portland, **Oregon,** you can tower over the Cascade Mountains for unbeatable views of Mount Hood, Mount St. Helens, Mount Rainier, the Three Sisters, and sometimes even Mount Shasta in the distance. Meanwhile, the nearby nonmountain terrain is a vibrant

Flying Festivals

The Coupe Icare in Saint-Hilaire-du-Touvet, **France,** is the largest free flight festival in the world. Every September, pilots from all over the world congregate to celebrate flying. More than 60,000 people attend this event to cheer throngs of pilots flying with ornate costumes draped around their wings. Telluride, **Colorado,** hosts the largest free flight festival in the United States. During the second week of June, top hang gliders from around the world come here to soar and spin above Town Park. The last day of the weeklong event is the competition for the World Acrobatic Championship, in which fliers skid, loop, somersault, and pirouette from the heights of the ski mountain, trailing colored smoke from their wingtips. And in **Canada,** the Atlantic Festival of Paragliding and Air Sports is an annual May event held in Parrsboro, Nova Scotia.

emerald green. In fact, this jump zone is so attractive that several world-record-holding skydivers choose to make this area their home. A favorite outfitter is Skydive Oregon, which is located just 20 minutes north of Portland and has an airport in Molalla that's only for skydiving flights. Even better, this facility is great for nonjumping family and friends, with a dedicated picnic and spectator viewing area perfectly located for watching jumpers dive and land their parachutes. www.skydiveoregon.com

With dozens of stunning locations and a favorable exchange rate, **South Africa** is a great and relatively inexpensive place to skydive. While skydiving is normally not a cheap activity anywhere (dives can cost from $250 to $550), in South Africa you can do it for as little

INSIDER'S TIP

Did you know that the first parachute jumps in Hawaii took place before airplanes even existed? On November 18, 1889, Joseph Van Tassell launched a hot air balloon off the slopes of Punchbowl, a mountain overlooking Honolulu. When the trade winds blew his balloon out to sea, Van Tassell parachuted down into Keehi Lagoon, thus becoming the first man to skydive in Hawaii! Unfortunately he was never found, so this was something of an unsuccessful attempt. He was followed eight years later by James Price, who in February 1897 flew a hot air balloon 3,000 feet above Remond Grove on Oahu, then parachuted back to earth—safely.

Rock Climbing

Think you have what it takes to be a rock climber? Places that are great for learning the ropes are not necessarily the iconic spots but are rather easy-to-access local crags or lesser-known parks.

In **North Carolina,** the Appalachian Mountain Institute (www.appalachianmountaininstitute.com) can set up first-timers to try rope climbing, which means a rope is firmly anchored above you. Good starting points include Looking Glass Rock in Pisgah National Forest, about 40 miles south of Asheville, and Crowders Mountain (www.ncparks.gov/Visit/parks/crmo/main.php) in Gastonia.

Other beginner options include Devil's Lake State Park in **Wisconsin,** Joshua Tree National Park in **California,** Smith Rock State Park in **Oregon,** the Red River Gorge in eastern **Kentucky,** City of Rocks National Reserve in **Idaho,** or Queen Creek Canyon in **Arizona.** These areas may not be as inspiring in height or stature, but they're much better schoolrooms due to the lower levels of commitment and the greater concentration of moderate routes.

More advanced climbers have endless options in **North Carolina**'s Linville Gorge such as Table Rock Mountain and the Ampitheater's three major climbs: the Mummy, the Daddy, and the Prow. www.linvillegorge.net

Situated in the northern side of Yosemite National Park in **California,** El Capitan is a challenging climb even for experts. Why? Because the granite cliffs have almost no joints. The crowning achievement for most climbers is the Nose at El Capitan, but for another option within Yosemite, try the equally challenging and classic Salathé Wall. www.nps.gov/yose/index.htm

More off the beaten path in Yosemite's high country is Tuolumne Meadows, where the higher elevation makes it a great option in hot, summer months to cool off.

Also known as "the Gunks," the Shawangunk Mountains, about 90 miles north of **New York** City, is one of the East Coast's greatest climbing areas. At 12 miles long and 300 feet high, this escarpment towers over the farmland of the Hudson River valley. With 1,200 or so routes, there are cliffs for all experience levels. Most of the famous crags are found in the Mohonk Preserve, such as the Trapps, Near Trapps, and Millbrook. www.gunkguide.com

West Virginia's New River Gorge region is among the most popular rock climbing and rappelling destinations in the eastern United States. Choose from thousands of climbs along the rim of the New River Gorge, and rock climbing guides can be secured almost any time of year. www.nps.gov/neri/index.htm

as $170. The area around Cape Town offers some of the most stunning vistas imaginable. On the way up, you have a fantastic view along the west coast, and you can see the Lagoon of Langebaan to the north and Robben Island out to the west. Once you're at maximum altitude, you'll see the famous Table Mountain, as well as the whole Cape Peninsula over to Cape Point. African Skies offers not only one-time tandem dives for novices, but also weeklong certification courses with accommodations. And, since you're in South Africa, there are plenty of ways to combine skydiving with other activities, like jump-and-drive tour packages where you can add in safaris, wine tasting, and hiking. www.african-skies.de

There are few places more visually exciting than the striking terrain of **Rio de Janeiro.** Most never get a chance to see what Copacabana Beach, Sugarloaf Mountain, or the Christ the Redeemer statue look like from 13,000 feet up. Not to mention the Tijuca National Park, the favelas, the coastal islands . . . and everything else that makes Rio one of the most dynamic cities in the world. Rio Turismo Radical can take you on a tandem jump during your visit to Rio and has bilingual guides. www.rioturismoradical.com.br/skydiving.htm

STORM CHASING

In the annals of thrill-seeking behavior (hint: there are no real annals . . . yet), storm chasing barely registers. But it should. It's one thing to accidentally observe wild weather, but it's another to intentionally seek it out. Watching a tornado or hurricane will almost certainly reward you with a spectacle like no other. It's awe-inspiring to see a powerful twister spiraling across the plains while massive lightning bolts shoot down from dark, heavy clouds.

Many storm chasing enthusiasts will justify their decision to get up close and personal with tornadoes as merely academic: They're just following the storm and capturing the spectacle on film. Of course, sane people know better!

But if you want to tempt fate, then you need to know the best times to go.

Of course, the best time of year to go storm chasing varies by region. In late April and May, storms take place in the southern plains of Kansas, Oklahoma, and Texas; in June and July, the storms are in the northern plains of North Dakota, South Dakota, Nebraska, and Iowa. Between July and September, southern Arizona is a great place to see spectacular monsoon rains and lightning.

Many storm chasing operations kick off from a base in Dallas, Texas; Oklahoma City, Oklahoma; Omaha, Nebraska; or Denver, Colorado. Small groups usually travel by van, along with all the storm-tracking equipment. Tour leaders track the weather and figure out the night before (or morning of) where you're going to travel. You can drive anywhere between 100 and 600 miles a day to catch multiple storms. Although there's never a guarantee that you'll

Storm-Watching Hotels

Watch storms from the safety and comfort of a hotel. The best place to experience winter storm watching is the Pacific Northwest, which gets huge gale-force winds and heavy rains, but not a lot of snow. On Vancouver Island, **British Columbia,** the Wickaninnish Inn is known for its storm-watching packages, where guests get prime ocean views from every room and public space. Even the spa and restaurant offer close-up views of 20-foot-high waves. On Cannon Beach in **Oregon,** the Stephanie Inn is another popular spot for storm watchers, where you can see the Pacific waves crashing over Haystack Rock from the comfort of your own room. And in northwestern **Washington,** Whidbey and Camano Islands are located in what's called a "rain shadow" between the Cascade and Olympic mountains, so you can view the effects of the Pacific storms without getting slammed by all the precipitation. On these islands, there are more than 130 lodges with water-facing windows to experience storm waves at their best.

catch a storm, there are occasions when you can see up to 10 tornadoes in one day and sometimes well into the night.

Major caveat: This is a potentially dangerous activity best pursued with the aid of trained professionals. (My interpretation of "trained professional" here: someone who is slightly more crazy than you are!)

Silver Lining Tours usually starts out from **Denver** and **Oklahoma City.** But for a more unusual option, try a tour of the **Canadian Prairies** from the foothills of the Canadian Rockies in western Alberta eastward across the lakes of Ontario. Supercell thunderstorms are common here and are some of the most dramatic tornadoes. You can also be a part of Silver Lining's "on-call" storm chasing—short-notice trips that operate in the earlier part of tornado season and invite you to drop everything to chase a storm. Are you a serious weather buff? Ask about the master class workshop, which teaches the fundamentals of forecasting, chasing strategies, and observation techniques. www.silverliningtours.com

Storm Chasing Adventure Tours holds its trips in May and June, starting from base camps in **Oklahoma City** and **Denver.** They use exceptionally high-tech equipment, including the Doppler on Wheels on select tours. If you aren't able to catch a storm, you may go sightseeing wherever you happen to be located that day and perhaps see the Severe Storms Laboratory in Oklahoma, local National Weather Service offices, or the Tornado Museum in Amarillo, Texas. www.stormchasing.com

INSIDER'S TIP

For up-to-date information on storm chasing, go to www.stormtrack.org, which provides details on recent storms, FAQs on storm chasing, and equipment information.

TRADD (Tornado Research and Defense Development) has 5-day storm chasing tours in May and June—but if you get hooked, you can extend for as many weeks as you want. TRADD also offers a guarantee: If you don't catch two storms in a weeklong trip, you get a discount off your next trip. www.traddtornadochasingtours.com

Cloud 9 Tours holds three trips per year, starting out in **Oklahoma City.** While meteorologist guides try to chase as many tornadoes as possible, you may also target severe storms, dust devils, hail, and sites that have been damaged by severe weather. www.cloud9tours.com

Tempest Tours is made up a team of veteran chasers and tornado scientists, and seven storm chasing tours are arranged in May and June in the Great Plains. Groups intercept the storms from a distance to view the event and take photographs, and may stay in place to catch nighttime lightning storms. www.tempesttours.com

Hurricane Museums

The **Nantucket** Shipwreck and Lifesaving Museum offers an exhibit that commemorates Hurricane Bob (made famous in the 1991 movie *The Perfect Storm*) and tells real stories about real people. The **Louisiana** State Museum in the French Quarter has a $7.5 million exhibit that tells personal stories of the 2005 hurricane, as well the science behind these natural weather phenomena. If it's the science that intrigues you, keep your eyes open for the Field Museum's traveling exhibit, *Inside Natural Disasters*. **Chicago**'s Museum of Science and Industry has a permanent exhibit called *Science Storms* that goes into the physics behind all the major types of natural disasters.

WHITEWATER RAFTING

Whether it's a mild immersion equivalent to the force and speed of a kiddie pool, or an experience that brings you as close to death as you'd ever want—or could ever imagine—whitewater rafting is an all-season sport accessible to everyone.

UNITED STATES

The Colorado River in **Arizona**'s Grand Canyon is 50 percent about rafting and 50 percent about the scenery, making it one of the best whitewater rafting experiences in the country. Since the water is controlled by a dam, the rafting season generally runs between April and October.

For beginners, the best bet is to pick a guide company like Colorado River Discovery, which operates one of the easiest smooth-water experiences between Glen Canyon Dam and Lees Ferry. This leisurely, 15-mile trip is a Class 1A (because it's so close to the dam, there are no rapids) that you'll navigate on a motorized pontoon raft. The canyon walls soar high above, and as you venture farther into the water, you'll start seeing ancient petroglyphs engraved on the rocks. www.raftthecanyon.com

For a beautiful—but not too bone-jarring—multiday trip, you can try a 6- to 8-day adventure from Lees Ferry to Phantom Ranch offered by OARS. Experts navigate the fast-moving water using oar-powered rafts. As the rapids gradually get larger, this helps less-experienced rafters acclimate to the movement, while soaking in the unbeatable views of the naturally vibrant colors and the grand scale of the canyon's many cliffs and rock layers. www.oars.com

Adrenaline junkies should go for a multisport option that combines whitewater rafting with other thrill-seeking adventures in the canyon. The Hualapai tribe's daylong trip takes on churning whitewater for first 12 miles, followed by fairly calm waters. Once you dry off, you'll take a hike up to Travertine Falls. You'll end the day with a helicopter ride up to the western side of the rim, where the Skywalk juts out into the expanse for one of the best—and most heart-stopping—views of the Grand Canyon. www.hualapaitourism.com

The Upper Canyon is especially known for its scenic beauty. Intermediate rafters can take on the 88-mile run from Lees Ferry to Phantom Ranch, passing by ancient rock formations, the natural springs at Vasey's Paradise, and the hugely expansive Redwall Cavern. Make sure you're in good condition for this one: The journey usually ends with a steep, 10-mile hike from Phantom Ranch to the South Rim Village.

The Lava Falls Rapid is widely considered the most challenging run in all of the Grand Canyon. This heart-pounding rapid tops out at a Class IV (or 8–10 on the "Grand Canyon Scale"), hurling even the most experienced rafters within the churning waters. If you're expert enough to navigate these fierce waters, go for it—it's an experience you won't soon forget.

Prefer to go at it alone? Professional River Outfitters has a "Painless Private" service that provides the boat, gear, food, and shuttle service to the handful of people who are awarded the few noncommercial river permits issued every year by Grand Canyon National Park. www.proriver.com

To find a guided whitewater rafting tour, visit the Grand Canyon River Outfitters Association's Web site, www.gcroa.org/Pages/outfitters2.htm.

Alpine beauty meets foaming whitewater rapids where the Salmon River has carved the deepest canyon in North America. Known as the River of No Return, the Salmon flows west through **Idaho** before emptying into the Snake River on the Oregon border and is one of the most iconic whitewater rafting spots in the country. Large, sandy beaches and natural hot springs make this more than just a rafting vacation. There are also ample hiking trails among the ponderosa pines, including a tough hike up to Rabbit Point.

Beginners and families with younger kids will want to stick to the Main Salmon, a Wild and Scenic National River. The rapids tend to be manageable Class II and III, like Gunbarrel Rapid and Kilum Rapid. Come June, you'll face high waters and the occasional Class IV, while August tends to bring choppier waters. Trails follow the river until Black Canyon, so you can easily get out and start hiking.

To make it a real adventure, go for a guided multiday rafting trip. River Time has a 5-day whitewater rafting and camping trip from Salmon, Idaho, to McCall, Idaho. You're out on the water by 9:30, sitting on the shores for lunch by 1:30, and setting up camp by late afternoon. www.mainsalmonrafting.com

Traveling solo? OARS has trips along the Main Salmon geared specifically to solo travelers, rather than families and couples. What's even cooler is that you get to use all different types of vessels, including an oar boat, a wooden dory, and the traditional paddle raft or inflatable kayak to tackle the whitewater. www.oars.com

Running for about 100 miles in central Idaho, the Middle Fork tends to be a tougher ride with mostly Class III and IV rapids along the way. Come spring, the rapids grow even higher and cooler—with the occasional Class V rearing up. Very experienced rafters will want to take on the Class V rapid known as Dagger Falls. The river flows through largely roadless wilderness areas. Along with the stunning mountain scenery, expect to see plenty of wildlife, and be sure to stop at a hot springs for some relaxation after a hard day of paddling.

Why not combine a culinary adventure with a rafting vacation? Canyons River Company, one of the largest outfitters that organize rafting trips on the Salmon River, has a "Wine and Whitewater" experience that combines 6 days of rafting with gourmet meals paired with wine. Ingredients are sourced from local farmers' markets and bakeries, and the beer and wine highlight the best of the Pacific Northwest. Dine outdoors at a table or—my preference—sit on the sand facing the rushing river. Believe me, nothing tastes as good as eating outdoors after a day of physical exertion, and the fact that the meal is high-end, seasonal, and local puts this experience over the top. www.canyonsinc.com

Seriously Expert Rafting

Not to be confused with its Idaho counterpart, the Salmon River Gorge in the Central **Oregon** Coast Range is known as the "Mount Everest of Oregon kayaking." This is real wilderness territory, plunging in a steep canyon rimmed by black cliffs, with six named waterfalls, including the aptly named Frustration Falls and Vanishing Falls. Believe me, this is expert territory only.

Beginner and intermediate rafters will want to raft the Nantahala River, aka "the Nanty," in western **North Carolina.** The majority of this 8-mile run is easy Class II rapids, where you can acclimate to the conditions and experience. But for a final adventurous kick, you'll enter the whitewater rapids of Patton's Run and the Upper Nantahala Falls, a Class III spot that can actually top out at Class IV depending on the water levels. Not only is the river and the surrounding Nantahala National Forest a destination in its own right, but you're also a stone's throw from the Great Smoky Mountains National Park.

For more of a challenge, head to the Ocoee River in eastern **Tennessee**'s Cherokee National Forest. Sound familiar? That's because the 4-acre Ocoee Whitewater Center hosted the whitewater course in the 1996 Summer Olympics in Atlanta. The Upper River is teeming with Class III and IV rapids, and best of all, you can raft like an Olympian. After tackling a few miles of fun rapids, you'll enter a short stretch with five sets of Class IV rapids. This is challenging stuff, with ledge drops and "hydraulics" (also known as a hole, when the river actually flows back on itself), broken up only by huge waves. The waters at the Ocoee Whitewater Center are carefully controlled, meaning you can only raft in summer Thursdays through Mondays. (The center also offers hiking, biking, and birding). Your best bet is to go on a guided excursion with a local outfitter like Nantahala Outdoor Center (www.noc.com). Ocoee Outdoors (www. ocoeeoutdoors.com) takes you on a neat experience where you can get out of the raft at Jump Point and bodysurf the waves.

Last, but certainly not least, there's some extreme whitewater rafting to be found in the southeastern United States. The Cheoah River in **North Carolina** is known for its Class IV+ rapids, a demanding 9-mile course that you should only attempt if you're an experienced rafter. This river has giant waves and drops as deep as 15 feet—some of the steepest commercially rafted waters around. This adventure has only been available for a few years, and release dates are limited, so make arrangements ahead of time. Looking to really push the limits? Guided tour operator Endless River Adventures (www.endlessriveradventures.com) has a doubleheader trip that

Whitewater Parks

Not all rafting has to be done on natural rivers. The US National Whitewater Center (www.usnwc.org), located just 10 minutes outside of downtown Charlotte, **North Carolina,** is a man-made course with rapids, 7-foot plunges, and 10,000-pound boulders, with options for all levels of expertise. In **Maryland,** Adventure Sports Center International (www.adventuresportscenter.com) features a 1,700-foot man-made course on a mountaintop. The course closely replicates the conditions of a natural river, where you can experience a 2-hour thrill ride with at least four descents. And in downtown Cañon City, **Colorado,** the Whitewater Kayak and Recreation Park funnels water from the nearby Arkansas River into a series of wild twists and turns. If you prefer to watch, you can see the action from sideline bleachers.

combines the Ocoee and Cheoah Rivers over the course of 2 days—a great option if you want to brush up on your skills before attempting the even more difficult Cheoah.

INTERNATIONAL

There's remote and then there's . . . **Siberia.** The Snezhnaya River offers heavy-duty expert rafting in the wilderness of Siberia. It's not your everyday whitewater rafting—this is "heli-rafting" territory, where you have to be choppered in via an MI-8 helicopter. This river has some seriously challenging Class VI rapids, including two of the toughest in the world, and astonishing scenery as you pass through remote and untouched landscape, with dense forests, shimmering glaciers and white-topped mountains. The river eventually empties out into the vast Lake Baikal, the oldest and deepest lake on the globe. Not sure how to go about whitewater rafting in Siberia? Wandrian Adventures (www.wandrianadventures.com) has an 8-day rafting tour that meets in Irkutsk. From there you get choppered to the put-in point at Zun Bairy, with nightly camping and access to some of the best, most remote fishing in the world.

If you thought Siberia was remote, try the Franklin River in southwestern **Tasmania.** Located at the edge of the Franklin-Gordon Wild Rivers National Park, this river passes through some of the most remote and rugged land in the world. A dedicated World Heritage site, this region is known for its dense temperate rain forest, deep gorges, and abundant wildlife that can only be found Down Under. Along the Upper and Lower Franklin, the majority of rapids are Class II and III, but the water levels here are unpredictable, so it's not for amateurs. Several multiday, guided trips are available from Hobart-based outfitters like Water by Nature (www.franklinrivertasmania. com) and Rafting Tasmania (www.raftingtasmania.com). If you're feeling extra fit, tack on an extra day or two to ascend the imposing—and strenuous—Frenchman's Cap mountain peak.

Inner Tubing

Tubing is a low-key alternative to rafting, and there are dozens of places to do it within a 1- or 2-hour drive from major urban areas. On the Delaware River, between **New Jersey** and **Pennsylvania,** you can tube along a 5-mile stretch close to the waters that George Washington famously crossed during the Revolutionary War. In **Texas,** you can explore Hill Country from the vantage point of the Guadalupe River. The 1-mile Horseshoe Loop is a nice, easy, scenic trip. One hour from Gainesville, **Florida,** is the Ichetucknee River, where you'll float alongside long-legged waterbirds in the natural spring water of the Ichetucknee Springs State Park.

Another version of this is called cave tubing, or blackwater rafting, which involves floating along underground rivers on huge inner tubes. Wearing a headlamp to illuminate the caves, you'll float over small waterfalls and down easy rapids. Most blackwater rafting is done in **New Zealand,** where the sport was more or less invented. Inside the Waitomo Caves, you can float in pitch black to see a magical sight: thousands of glowworms showing pinpricks of light on the cavern walls. In **Belize,** the Caves Branch River was once a sacred spot of the ancient Mayans, where you can see ceremonial sites and petroglyphs while rafting the caves.

Queenstown, **New Zealand,** is known as the Adventure Capital of the World for good reason. Part of the fun of the nearby Shotover River is getting there, as the precarious dirt road that leads to the launch point clings to the sides of the cliffs in Skippers Canyon. The waters are deceptively peaceful at first and then give way to fast-moving rapids. Ride the waves into the 560-foot-long Oxenbridge Tunnel before taking on the exhilarating Cascade Rapid. You can raft this river year-round, but in winter the put-in point is only accessible by helicopter—which is worth it for the scenic views alone. www.nz-rafting.co.nz

Costa Rica's Pacuare River runs through a protected zone in the Caribbean Basin, near the town of Turrialba. What's great about this warm-water river is that it ranges from Class II to IV rapids, meaning it's got some of the most scenic whitewater for amateurs and some of the most challenging for experts. This is one of the best ways to experience this region, surrounded by towering green walls, thick vegetation, tumbling waterfalls, and an incredible variety of rain forest wildlife. A ride along the Lower Pacuare starts with a few miles of easy, fun rapids and then becomes a wet and wild adventure in the Huacas River Gorge.

More advanced rafters can take on the Upper Pacuare, which contains Class IV and V rapids. You can run this river year-round, but Costa Rica's rainy season produces the best rapids, usually between May and November. Although there are a number of outfitters offering daylong or multiday trips, Rios Tropicales (www.riostropicales.com) includes overnight stays in its rain forest ecolodge. This outfitter has been at the forefront of efforts to oppose damming the river, and it works to protect and reforest the land and does educational outreach in conservation and sustainable resource management.

Africa's Zambezi River (aka Great River) has some of the most adventurous whitewater rafting in the world but also contains some fairly gentle sections. Along the Middle Zambezi, the Batoka Gorge has soaring black rock walls and features 23 rapids in 15 miles, with Victoria Falls providing the dramatic backdrop. For an easier ride, try the lower part of the river, where you can actually go on a canoeing safari in the Lower Zambezi National Park, spotting big game and spending the nights in bush camps on the banks.

How about whitewater rafting in **Ethiopia**? The Omo River is a wild ride through muddy rapids as you travel through a little piece of paradise. Gorge walls tower thousands of feet high, with waterfalls crashing down and thick brush lining the river, which empties into Lake Turkana. The river snakes all the way through Omo Valley, a UNESCO World Heritage site, where you'll encounter local tribes like the Karo and the Mursi. And yes, that might just be a hippo peeking its head out of the water. Don't get too close! Currently, the building of the Gibe III dam has raised concerns about the integrity of the river and its surrounding communities, but most outfitters are continuing to operate rafting tours.

ZIPLINES, ZORBS, AND ZEPPELINS

Attention, thrill seekers. If you want to push the envelope in a different way, I've found the best of the three *z*'s. Each has its own challenges and respective exhilaration levels—and the good news is that each can be done at your own pace (although I strongly suggest not eating a heavy meal before you go).

ZIPLINES

O nce an activity associated with rain forest canopies, ziplining has grown into a popular adventure sport worldwide, including some notable spots right here in the United States. Although it is considered an extreme adventure, it's not one that requires any previous experience. And, as most people will attest, it's not that intimidating once you step off the first platform. Unlike an extreme roller coaster or more intense sports like skydiving, there's no heart-in-your-throat sensation.

What you want to look for in a worthwhile zipline is one that combines the thrill of flying in the air with exceptional views. That's what makes ArborTrek Canopy Adventures in **Vermont**'s Smuggler's Notch such a great choice. It's a 4,500-foot-long course with eight treetop ziplines and—because it's open year-round—the view changes with the season. Fall is when you'll get the prettiest views of the Green Mountains' maple and birch trees, but don't overlook winter as a great time to zip through forests. The route is a little bit shorter in winter, but the views of snow-covered branches and white-capped mountains is truly special. www.arbortrek.com

Other East Coast standouts: Bretton Woods Canopy Tour in **New Hampshire**'s White Mountains, near the Omni Mount Washington Resort. Nine levels of ziplines are connected by bridges and trails, taking you over a ski slope and through the scenic mountain canopy.

INSIDER'S TIP

Ziplines are known as "foefie slides" in South Africa, "flying foxes" in Australia and New Zealand, and "zip slides" or "zip wires" in Europe.

And the really fun part? The last stretch is a dual zipline where you can race another rider.

In **New York,** Hunter Mountain's SkyRider is one of the best ways to see the foliage of the Catskill Mountains, especially when you consider that this is the longest (4 miles) and highest (600 feet) zipline course in North America.

On the West Coast, it's all about ziplining and wine. Okay, there's no wine actually included in Sonoma Canopy Tours in Occidental, **California,** but you easily find a tasting room after you finish the exhilarating ride. Standing 200 feet high, there are seven separate ziplines, including an 800-foot stretch that takes you into a forest of ancient redwoods—some of which are more than 700 years old. In fact, one of the ziplines is only reachable by climbing an impressive, 30-foot spiral staircase that's built around a redwood tree. www.sonomacanopytours.com

Believe it or not, the steepest zipline in the world is located in the United States. Just outside of Park City is the Xtreme Zipline in **Utah** Olympic Park, where a 1,500-foot-long zipline has a vertical drop of a whopping 500 feet, with an average grade of 34 percent. In fact, it runs parallel to the park's Nordic jump, so you might be able to watch competitive athletes in training as you zip down at speeds of up to 60 miles an hour. Prefer a less extreme ride? The ZipRider is a gentler ride and only 750 feet long. http://utaholympiclegacy.com

Ziplining is practically a rite of passage inside a rain forest, and Mystic Mountain in Ocho Rios, **Jamaica,** has an experience you don't want to miss. Inside a 100-acre park, you can zip from the top of the mountain over the rain forest canopy. But for a really memorable ride, ask about nighttime ziplining, when you'll use helmets with lights to slide to and from platforms ringed with lit torches. www.rainforestadventure.com

If an extreme adventure is what you're looking for, your best bet is to head south, to Sun City, **South Africa.** This ride is more than a mile long and reaches up to a whopping 100 miles an hour, with a vertical drop up to a massive 325 feet. Along with the speed and height, this ride also has the distinction of allowing riders to go in tandem while hanging horizontally, Superman-style. You'll fly down the course headfirst while taking in sweeping views of the South African plains. For an extra bit of fun, try the bombing run—where you try to drop a bomb and hit a target below while zipping down. www.zip2000.co.za

Talk about a crazy combination. In **Florida**'s Gatorland, the Gator Zipline is a nail-biting series of five ziplines. It's certainly not the longest or the fastest zip ride (up to 25 miles an hour), but what makes this one special is that you fly right over a collection of Cuban and Nile crocodiles and over the alligator breeding marsh, which holds 130 giant alligators. www.gatorland.com

Most ziplines include multiple lines and platforms, but for the best variety of experiences, head to Kipu Ranch in **Kauai** for the Zipline Trek Nui Loa. The whole circuit time is more than 5 hours, where ziplines include two tandem rides (one of which is 1,800 feet long); a "water zip," which ends by plunging into a swimming pool; and a "zippel," which combines ziplining and rappelling. The day also includes swimming and hiking, but the real highlight is the sheer thrill of zipping over Kauai's astonishingly beautiful rain forest, valleys, and waterfalls, with the Ha'upu mountains looming above. www.outfitterskauai.com

Chances are, when someone says "ziplining," you think of **Costa Rica.** After all, this is the country that practically invented the experience in the 1970s. So why not do it in the best spot of all? The Cloud Forest Reserve is unique because you can zip through the magical mist, along the tops of 200-foot trees, and see monkeys, toucans, sloths, and countless other creatures. Ask about a night tour,

Zipline at Sea

Did you know you can fly over seas on a zipline? Royal Caribbean's *Oasis of the Seas* and its sister ship, *Allure of the Seas,* have a zipline that hangs nine decks over an open-air boardwalk. So you can fly diagonally for 82 feet while other passengers watch from below. www.rccl.com

where you can see the forest's nocturnal animals. Even better, there are different ways to zip through the reserve. One tour operator, Selvatura, has ziplines built into the canopy, rather than above it, which is a more intense experience (you also have to brake yourself). If that's not enough thrill, the company has a Tarzan-style swing where you swing out over a giant canyon. Another outfitter, Sky-Trek, has a more leisurely zipline on traditional elevated platforms above the treelines. www.monteverdeinfo.com

Not all ziplines are in tropical places. In fact, perhaps the most scenic of all can be found in the Swiss Alps. Travelers come from all over the world to the village of Grindelwald, **Switzerland,** to hike, bike, or ride the train to experience the spectacular beauty of the snowcapped Alps. But why not make it an adventure by ziplining more than 2,500 feet, 165 feet above the ground, at a speedy 50 miles per hour?

ZORBING

Ever heard of Zorbing? It's a wild—and dizzying—experience where you roll down a hill inside a giant ball. The New Zealand company that originated it coined the term *Zorb,* but the more generic phrase for other operators around the world is "globe riding" or "hill rolling."

Zorb has two locations: Rotorua, **New Zealand,** and Pigeon Forge, **Tennessee.** The interior of the ball can be dry (Zorbit) or wet (Zydro), which makes for a slippier-slidier ride (not unlike being in a washing machine). You can also choose between a speedy zigzag track or a slower zipper track that has turns to stop you from picking up speed. www.zorb.com

Another globe-riding company called Sphere Mania has a few different options, including filling the ball with up to 50 liters of water or "eclipse sphering" in an opaque ball so the interior is entirely dark. But probably the craziest of all is in Milton Keynes, about 50 miles south of **London.** Known as "air-sphering," it's a combination of globe riding and indoor skydiving. The ball is actually placed inside a 160 mph wind tunnel, so you and a friend are flying in the air—no harnesses involved! www.air-sphere.com

ZEPPELINS

Though zeppelins were once a staple of the skies for both military and commercial uses, they went out of fashion during World War II for safety and economic reasons. However, they are starting to make a bit of a comeback with recreational fliers. I love them because they remind me of the glamorous golden age of travel, when people got dressed up, the service was impeccable, and it was more about the journey than the destination.

If you're plagued by visions of the Hindenburg, don't worry. Modern zeppelins are filled with nonflammable helium and have carried more than 80,000 passengers safely since they were reintroduced to the world a few years back. They also shouldn't be confused with ballpark blimps, which don't have rigid internal frames like zeppelins.

Airship Ventures, based near **San Francisco,** started flying people over various parts of the Bay Area in 2009 in its state-of-the-art Zeppelin NT aircraft called Eureka. It cruises at an altitude of 1,200 feet at 35 to 40 mph. Flights depart from either Moffet Field or Oakland, and float over either the city of San Francisco or Silicon Valley/South Bay. The San Francisco tour gets you a bird's-eye view of the Golden Gate Bridge, Coit Tower, Treasure Island, Sausalito, Alcatraz, and the Marin headlands. On flights that go to Silicon Valley, you'll see little hillside homes, vineyards, and mega-mansions, plus the headquarters of Google and Apple. The airship regularly heads down to Southern California and offers flights out of Los Angeles and San Diego, and occasionally goes on special journeys to other parts of the country. www.airshipventures.com

Zeppelin NT in Friedrichshafen, **Germany,** has been offering 30-, 45-, 60-, 90-, and 120-minute sightseeing flights since 2001. Tours head out on 12 different routes around the foothills of the Alps and over Lake Constance (Europe's third-largest freshwater lake), on the German-Austrian border. Occasionally it makes special trips to big cities like Munich. Prices range from 200 to 745 euros per flight, depending on the length. The parent company actually manufactures the aircraft that you fly in (and also the one used by Airship Ventures in San Francisco). The town of Friedrichshafen, which has been building airships since the 1920s, is also home to the Zeppelin Museum, where you can see a re-creation of the Hindenburg. www.zeppelinflug.de

GREAT FOODS AND DRINKS OF THE WORLD

BEER

There's hardly a country in the world that doesn't make beer, and between obsessive nationalism and outright pride, just about every country claims its beer is the best. For me, it's not just the beer, but the ambiance that surrounds the beer experience, the stories behind the brew, and the brewmasters. And, needless to say, some of my friends use the quest to find the best beer in the world as a transparent excuse to travel.

UNITED STATES

Northern California may have made its name in wine, but **Mendocino County** is a beer lover's paradise. These are truly local beers, and yet you're likely to see them appearing in bars and restaurants all around the country because they're just that good. North Coast Brewing Company was at the forefront of the microbrewery movement before it was a movement! It made a name for itself with intense beers like the Brother Thelonious Belgian Style Abbey Ale and the barrel-aged Old Rasputin Russian Imperial Stout. Stop by the brewpub and brewery in Fort Bragg for a sampler of beers with a platter of garlic fries. While you're on Route 128, stop in the Anderson Valley Brewing Company in rural Boonville (www.avbc.com) and see the old-school copper brew kettles that were imported from an old German brew house.

Where else but in **Sonoma County** does beer meet wine? Russian River Brewing Company in Santa Rosa ages its beers in used wine barrels that once stored Chardonnays and Pinot Noirs. They'll even go against tradition and blend beers, just as vintners do with wines, to create new flavor profiles. There are no tours available, but you can see the barrels in full view from the brewpub. www.russianriverbrewing.com

Milwaukee, once home to big names like Pabst, Schlitz, and Blatz—and still home to the MillerCoors factory—also has a booming craft beer industry, with standouts like Sprecher Brewing Company (www.sprecherbrewery.com) and Lakefront Brewery (www.lakefrontbrewery.com). Don't know where to start? Milwaukee Brewfest (www.milwaukeebrewfest.com) is an annual summer event that celebrates craft beers and microbrews from Wisconsin and around the world.

Ask any **Madison** locals where to get a great beer, and they'll point you to the Great Dane Pub and Brewing Company downtown. The atmosphere is casual and publike, but what you'll remember most is the variety of beers—cask ales, German pilsners, English porter styles, and the occasional oddball brew like the tri-pepper pilsner, made with habenero, poblano, and jalepeño. www.greatdanepub.com

Why is **Portland** so obsessed with beer? Some say it has to do with the Oregon rain. In a city that soggy, it's no wonder it's brimming with bars, coffee shops, and bookstores. Combine that with easy access to locally grown hops, and you've got the perfect conditions for brewing. There are dozens of breweries within the city limits, including the headquarters of the venerated McMenamins Pubs and Breweries (www.mcmenamins.com) and Cascade Brewing Barrel House (www.cascadebrewingbarrelhouse.com). Or, skip the traditional bar crawl and get your own designated driver. EcoTours of Oregon will take you to some of Portland's best brew houses while explaining the microbrew process as you sample the goods. www.ecotours-of-oregon.com/brew.htm

Bend, Oregon, is an outdoor playground, but it is rapidly becoming Oregon's next beer haven. With nine breweries in town, it's got the Bend Ale Trail that you can explore on foot. Bend is the home base of Pacific Northwest favorite Deschutes Brewery (www.deschutesbrewery.com), and the local McMenamin's pub is located inside a former Catholic schoolhouse!

San Diego's beer scene doesn't get the same love as the Pacific Northwest, but with more than 30 craft breweries in the county, it's on the verge. Its breweries, such as Ballast Point (www.ballastpoint.com) and AleSmith Brewing Company (www.alesmith.com), have been collecting one award after another. The beer culture here is growing so big that there's actually something called San Diego Beer Week, with beer dinners (and breakfasts), brewing workshops, and plenty of tastings.

Denver is a beer enthusiast's dream, with more than 70 craft breweries within a 90-mile radius—which is why they call it the Napa Valley of Beer. It's the home of not only iconic breweries like Coors and Anheuser-Busch, but also of notable local producers like New Belgium Brewing, the first wind-powered brewery in the country.

Move over, Oktoberfest. The Great American Beer Festival in Denver is *the* place to get to know America's beer scene. The September event is a 3-day beer extravaganza with a tasting pavilion, beer and food pairings, and a competition that's become an industry standard in the brewing world. www. greatamericanbeerfestival.com

St. Louis, Missouri, may be Budweiser country, but it's not all about the big brands. The local Schlafly Bottleworks and Tap Room (www.schlafly.com) has also claimed this turf. One of the newer contenders, Six Row Brewing Company (www.sixrowbrewco.com) has six beers on tap including the Honey Weizen, made with a generous portion of honey from Missouri Honey in Florissant, Missouri.

INTERNATIONAL

You can't talk about beer without mentioning **Munich.** Between pubs, brew halls, beer gardens, and Oktoberfest, so much happening in this city that it's hard not to find a place to drink. Bavaria's major breweries are known as the "Big Six"—Löwenbräu, Hofbräuhaus, Augustinerbräu, Paulaner, Hacker-Pschorr, and Spaten.

Hofbräuhaus has one of the oldest beer halls in Germany—it's right in the city center, but the venue remains a local favorite (translation: it's crowded) and is a lot of fun. To get off the beaten path and still have the loud, local experience, a good bet is Hirschgarten, an enormous beer garden that seats up to 8,000 people and is located about 20 minutes west of central Munich. Then there's the 111 Biere, or House of 111 Beers, located in northern Munich, which literally offers you 111 different types of beer.

Munich isn't your only bet for a great German beer experience. In **Berlin,** PraterGarten (www.pratergarten.de) is one of the oldest in the city—it was established in 1837, surviving World War II bombings and Soviet rule. Today, it's a hip enclave where locals pack the sprawling, tree-filled garden sipping on Prater pilsner and dark lager. And sitting on an urban beach on Museumsinsel (Museum Island), Strandbar Mitte is one of the prettier beach bars to have a beer, with the majestic Bodemuseum on the other side of the shore and boats sailing by.

Holland may be best known for Heinekin and Grolsch, but one very cool stop is the Koningshoeven Brewery, located in a monastery in Berkel-Enschot (about 90 minutes from Amsterdam). It's one of seven Trappist breweries and is open to the public. Learn the history of the Trappist monks who have been brewing beer for centuries (the idea was to fund the monastery's operations, not make any profit) and then taste the intense dubbel and tripel ales that make these guys a force to be reckoned with in the beer world. www.latrappe.nl

Beer and Bikes

How about beer combined with biking? Sounds dangerous, but if you drink in moderation, it's actually a lot of fun. In Milwaukee, **Wisconsin,** many of the smaller riverfront breweries and brewpubs are connected by a network of bike trails, lanes, and bridges, making it easy to hop from one to the next. Cog Wild (www.cogwild.com) offers the weekend Bike and Brew tour in Bend, **Oregon,** where you combine the best mountain biking trails with local brewery visits. **Colorado**'s New Belgium Brewing Company has taken its amber ale flagship beer, Fat Tire, and turned it into an annual beer and bike event. The Tour de Fat is a free bicycle festival across the country and features New Belgium beer (of course), circus-type acts, bicycle dance troupes, and a giant group parade around town. www.newbelgium.com

What better place to taste Guinness, Ireland's national drink, than at the source? First take a tour of the state-of-the-art St. James's Gate Brewery in **Dublin**, where Guinness has been made since 1759. The master brewer shows you how water, barley, hops, and yeast are combined to make the distinctive draught and stout. There are tastings all over the facility, but your best bet is the seventh-floor Gravity Bar, which offers a panoramic view of the city. www.guinness-storehouse.com

If you've done the Guinness thing, it's time to explore the dozens of other options in Ireland. Notable brands include Moylan's Dragoons, Murphy's Irish Stout, the Franciscan Well Brewery, and the Dungarvan Brewing Company, to name a few. Start your tasting tour at the Stags Heads (www.louisfitzgerald.com/stagshead) pub in Dublin, one of the most historic in the city and tucked in a narrow alley off Dame Street. Overwhelmed by the choices? The annual All-Ireland Craft Beerfest (www.irishcraftbeerfestival.com) showcases the country's "other" beers in one place.

INSIDER'S TIP

Like champagne or Roquefort cheese, some beers can only be brewed in a specific region to merit the name. A true lambic style can only come from a region of Belgium's Senne Valley, where wild fermentation means it's exposed to indigenous yeast and bacteria. Meanwhile, the original (and some say the only) pilsner, Pilsner Urquell, is a Czech beer brewed since the mid-19th century in the Bohemian city of Pilsen and made specifically with the local mineral waters.

It's not a trip to **England** without a pub crawl of sorts. So why not check out some of the quirkier pubs in the country? In St Albans, Hertfordshire, Ye Olde Fighting Cocks is supposedly the oldest pub in Britain, with reports dating back to 1129. It's even thought that monks were selling beer here as far back as the year 700. And in Bury St. Edmunds, Suffolk, there's the Nutshell (http://thenutshellpub.co.uk), the smallest pub in England, standing a mere 15 feet wide by 7 feet deep.

The Danish beer scene is booming, and the best way to experience it is at one of the best beer fests in the world. No, not Oktoberfest. It's the **Copenhagen** Beer Festival. The 3-day event is held every May and brings together hundreds of beer makers, including several dozen craft breweries. It's held on the grounds of the old Carlsberg Brewery, but the point is to showcase just how far the industry has grown beyond its most recognized brand. www.beerfestival.dk

Grab a brew at an outdoor cafe in **Brussels,** the city of beer and beer lovers. Fin de Siècle boasts an impressive list of Belgian beers, from Mort Subite ("sudden death" in French) to Duvel ("devil" in Flemish) to the sublime Leffe. Sip Hoegaarden outside during the summer and watch the sun pour through the art nouveau windows. Set on a busy intersection in the St. Gilles neighborhood, the artsy SiSiSi cafe is a great spot for sipping a Chimay and people-watching.

Explore ales, pilsners, lagers, and more at 35 microbreweries in the Australian state of **Victoria.** This region (of which Melbourne is the capital city) has a microbrewery scene that has been booming in the last 10 years. In the Yarra Valley, which is better known for its wine production, Coldstream Brewery (www.coldstreambrewery.com.au) has large windows where you can see the brewing process firsthand; the White Rabbit (www.whiterabbitbeer.com.au) boutique brewery in Healesville is one of the few to ferment its beer in open vats; the Otway Estate Winery and Brewery (www.otwayestate.com.au) in Barongarook brews 12 different preservative-free beers; and the iconic Holgate Brewhouse (www.holgatebrewhouse.com) in Woodend also has a restaurant and B&B on the premises.

Vietnam's tradition of making *bia* (beer) stretches back to the French colonial period in the 1890s. From *bia vang* (golden lager) to *bia den* (dark lager) to *bia hoi* (cheap, fresh, unpasteurized draft beer), the Vietnamese have an enduring beer culture. Hanoi beer gardens don't have names and are usually just known by their address or location. You drink while sitting in tiny plastic chairs, and the beer is super-cheap—we're talking 20 cents a glass. The intersection of Luong Ngoc Quyen and Ta Hiens Streets in the old quarter is known as "bia hoi corner" and has a number of good, cheap joints.

At the Kiuchi Brewery, an hour north of **Tokyo,** you can brew your own custom beer on the premises. First you consult with the brewer to decide what type of beer you want to make (ale, stout, or wheat) and what bitterness level and alcohol content you desire. Then they walk you through the steps of measuring the malts, milling, mashing, boiling, chilling, and bottling. You can even design your own label. The whole process takes 3 or 4 hours, but the beer is not ready for another 3 weeks or so. They deliver to your door (in Japan only) when it's done. www.kodawari.cc

Best Places to Taste and Make

CHEESE

I've actually been known to travel thousands of miles just for a particular kind of cheese. I've sampled amazing blue cheese in Tasmania and Comté in France. I went to school in Madison, Wisconsin, so it's not unusual for me to find any excuse to go back to America's Dairyland, or to towns like Monroe and New Glarus, or even to Babcock Hall on the Madison campus, where they still sell cheese from the Agriculture School. It's delicious!

The key to understanding cheese is to participate in the process. I've always felt that if you can understand the process, you will definitely value the product.

EXPERIENTIAL

The Ielpi Major family makes some of the best aged, raw milk sheep cheese in the country at the 250-acre Vermont Shepherd Farm in Westminster West, **Vermont.** At the farm store, you can purchase their award-winning cheeses from late August until the year's supply runs out in the spring. Several times a year, they do tastings and farm tours, during which time they open the vast underground cave where they age their cheeses. At any time of the year, you can see the sheep in the fields by walking along the rural valley trail, which weaves its way alongside the farm and into the town. www.vermontshepherd.com

Perhaps the most well-known producer in Vermont is Cabot Creamery Cooperative, which is actually run by 1,200 farmers throughout New England and upstate New York. Their Vermont Cheddars are renowned, and you can get an up-close view of the process in the flagship store. But if you really want to have a local experience, head to the Cabot Annex Store in the Waterbury area. Not only can you taste the cheese along with Vermont microbrews and wines, but you're just a few miles away from the Ben & Jerry's factory! www.cabotcheese.coop/index.php

Three Shepherds Farm (www.threeshepherdscheese.com) in Warren, Vermont, offers 3-day cheese-making courses designed for the average cheese lover, amateur cheese makers, and more advanced artisans. The courses, which offer a hands-on approach and individual instruction, stress the science behind cheese making, including how ingredients are combined, processed, and aged. Meanwhile, master cheese maker Peter Dixon (www.dairyfoodsconsulting.com) offers a series of 2- and 3-day workshops on making and aging cheese in Westminster, Vermont.

Shelburne Farms is another can't-miss stop, not just for its cheeses, but also for its educational programming and sustainable practices. You can actually stay overnight at this 1,200-acre farm, at the edge of Lake Champlain, and get a hands-on agritourism experience. We're talking working with the livestock, an on-site bakery that sources its ingredients locally, and, of course, learning about the artisan cheese-making process between May and October. www.shelburnefarms.org

Practically the entire state of **Wisconsin** has a love affair with the product. At least 60 local cheese makers produce more than 600 different types of cheese, many of whom can be visited on the Wisconsin cheese trail. There are also hundreds of stores, festivals, towns, and restaurants that all promote and celebrate the state's most famous export. While you're at the famous Dane County Farmers' Market in Madison, Wisconsin, don't overlook the booth of local cheese celebrities Tony and Julie Hook from Hook's Cheese Company. They offer samples of their renowned Cheddars, Colby, blue cheese, and more every Saturday from late April to early November. Or take a drive about 50 miles to their plant in Mineral Point to see how it's made. www.hookscheese.com

---

INSIDER'S TIP

The Vermont Cheese Trail consists of a whopping 42 artisan cheese makers throughout the state who produce more than 150 varieties. Farms range from small mom-and-pop operations to large commercial creameries. Visit www.vtcheese. com/cheesetrail.htm to print out a map and get started.

Just about 45 minutes north of Madison, in Sauk City, is Carr Valley Cheese, where "rock star" cheese maker Sid Cook produces top-of-the-line stuff. And what's great about this place is that you can join cooking classes that highlight both tasting and cooking with the local cheeses. www.carrvalleycheese.com

The town of New Glarus, Wisconsin, is another cheese destination. Home to one of the largest Swiss population outside of Switzerland, it features gems like the New Glarus Hotel Restaurant (www.newglarushotel.com), where Swiss-trained chefs can do fondue demonstrations at your table; and the Edelweiss Creamery (http://edelweisscreamery.com), which brought back the ancient art of producing giant wheels of Emmentaler cheese.

A couple of hours west of Madison is Hidden Springs Creamery in Westby, which actually makes unique sheep's milk cheeses by hand using sustainable and organic practices. Owners Dean and Brenda Jensen also run the farm as a bed-and-breakfast, so you can get a taste of life on the farm: Meet the 250 sheep, take part in the milking or spring lambing, and even learn to make cheese, depending on the season. www.hiddenspringscreamery.com

You'll be up to your elbows in curds and whey at the **Massachusetts** branch of the Northeast Organic Farming Association. They supply the milk; you bring home the cheese, which could include Parmesan, Swiss, Monterey Jack, ricotta, and goat cheese. www.nofamass.org/programs/extensionevents/cheesemaking.php

INTERNATIONAL

Just like real champagne can only be produced in **France**'s Champagne region, there's only one place in the world that can produce the famously pungent Roquefort cheese. The reason for that is the caves of Roquefort-sur-Soulzon, carved into Mont Combalou, where a certain mold contributes to the specific characteristics of flavor, odor, and texture. In fact, only a handful of producers actually make blue cheese, which is made from the milk of a very specific breed of sheep called Lacaune. That's why a visit to this region isn't just about tasting the product; you also want to go underground to the cellars to see the ripening process in action. Between January and June, check out the cellars to see cheeses ripening on the shelves. Société is the largest producer in Averyon, but don't miss a visit to the caves of Roquefort Papillon and Gabriel Coulet as well.

France's Franche-Comté region is famous for one exceptional product, with more than 3,000 dairy farms and aging cellars. The best way to experience this region is along the Routes du Comté. In the town of Poligny is the headquarters of the Comté Cheese Association (www.comte.com). But for a really authentic experience to see how this cheese is made in the traditional methods, go to Fort Saint-Antoine, near the town of Malbuisson. The cream of the crop, so to speak, comes from Marcel Petite, a family-run operation that ripens more than 100,000 wheels each year in an ancient stone fort.

Fans of Wallace and Gromit won't want to miss Wensleydale Creamery in the heart of the Yorkshire Dales National Park in **England.** Not only is it one of the few cheese makers that opens its

Cheese Events

C an't get enough cheese? The **Seattle** Cheese Festival is held every May at the famous Pike Place Market. There is a grilled cheese contest, to see who can create the most inventive sandwich, plus a self-guided cheese tour takes you to nearby Delaurenti, Beecher's, Paris Grocery, Pike Place Creamery, the Spanish Table, and Quality Cheese. www.seattlecheesefestival.com

California's Sonoma County is famous for its local goods, and cheese is no exception. Get a taste of everything this area has to offer at the Artisan Cheese Festival, held every March in Petaluma. Dozens of local producers come together to showcase their wares, along with winemakers and other artisan food makers. www.artisancheesefestival.com

Want to observe a really ancient cheese tradition? It doesn't get any wackier than the annual cheese-rolling festival at Coopers Hill in Gloucestershire, **England.** Yes, locals actually have a race rolling giant cheese wheels down the hill to see who comes in first.

doors to visitors for tastings and classes, but Wensleydale was put on the map when it became the favorite cheese of the famous Aardman Animation characters. And yes, you can pick up a special Wallace and Gromit cheese round while you're there. www.wensleydale.co.uk

If there's one place I always make sure to visit, it's **Tasmania**'s King Island Dairy (www.kidairy.com.au). If you love cheese, you will never leave this area. We're talking organic, grass-fed cows that produce an unbelievable blue cheese called the Roaring 40s and a Cheddar cheese that actually rivals most Wisconsin products. In Tasmania's northeastern region, you want to go to Pyengana Dairy, which makes a unique Cheddar using a very old-school "stirred curd" method.

CHEESE SHOPS

C'est Cheese is a small family-run cheese shop in Santa Barbara, **California,** that offers 120 different types of cheese, a small cafe, and tasting events during the third week of every month that explore cheeses from different parts of the world. They also stock cured salumi, pâté, charcuterie, wine, and tea that pair well with their cheeses, so just ask for help when picking out items to bring home. www.cestcheese.com

In Madison, **Wisconsin,** don't miss the cheese shop Fromagination in Capitol Square, which carries international, national, and local cheeses, including more than 60 artisan Wisconsin cheeses. Best of all, it's just across the street from the Dane County Farmers' Market. www.fromagination.com

The town of Monroe, Wisconsin, noted for its large Swiss community, is home to the state's oldest cheese store. Baumgartner's Cheese Store and Tavern has been in operation since 1931 and is a great place to stock up on Wisconsin cheeses to bring home—or eat right there and enjoy the tavern's huge selection of local beers. www.baumgartnercheese.com

The Artisanal Premium Cheese Center in **Manhattan** offers dozens of workshops that let you not only taste, but also learn how to pair cheese with different kinds of wine and beer. But the really fun class here is the Fromager's Favorites, which explains how a fromager assesses cheese from a professional standpoint. Ask about the five "caves" where they store and age each type of cheese in ideal conditions. www.artisanalcheese.com

Another cool New York experience takes place at Murray's Cheese, one of the oldest cheese shops in Manhattan. The one class you definitely want to take here is the Mystery of Caves, where you get to tour underground cellars to taste aged cheeses. www.murrayscheese.com

The town of Gouda, **Holland,** is known for its famous product. But if you stop in only one place, it should be Kaasland Singel, west of Centraal Station in Amsterdam. The creamy cheese comes in a dozen different flavors, including some really unique options like stinging nettle and coriander. www.kaasland.com

The Epicurean Connection in Sonoma, **California,** doesn't just sell an enormous variety of locally produced cheeses. You can also learn the stories behind these cheeses with owner Sheana Davis, a local fixture in the artisan food community. Cheese making, pairing, and serving tips are all available in her series of classes in the Sonoma Valley, the Bay Area, and beyond. www.theepicureanconnection.com

CHOCOLATE

This was a tough chapter to compile, simply because you have to look long and hard to find bad chocolate, and every connoisseur traveler is adamant about what he/she considers the best chocolate. In the end, it really comes down to the big three: Switzerland, France, and Belgium, with a few surprises (even one in Brooklyn!).

CHOCOLATE TOURS

Some culinary experts consider **Paris** the world capital of chocolate. Judging from the sheer number and variety of chocolate and pastry shops in the city—over 300, more than any city in the world—this may well be true. Everything from gourmet dark chocolate to pastries to ice cream to mouthwatering *chocolat chaud* (hot chocolate) can be found here. ChocoParis (www.chocoparis.com) offers a handy Paris chocolate shop map, which features pastry and chocolate stores by arrondissement, and offers three self-guided "chocolate walk" itineraries. Opt for the Right Bank walk and you'll come across the flagship store of Jean-Paul Hévin Chocolatier (www.jphevin.com) on rue Saint-Honoré—where not only can you get any number of ganaches, decadent gateau, or sinful mousse, but Hévin's famous chocolate stiletto shoes! You can also indulge at the upstairs cocoa bar with unbelievably rich hot chocolate.

Or go for the créme de la chocolate and join acclaimed Parisian food writer David Lebovitz on one of his high-end tours. A weeklong trip through Paris and Lausanne includes guided walking tours of chocolate shops, dinner at secret "underground" restaurants, and in-depth market tours. www.davidlebovitz.com

If you want someone else to do the driving while in **Belgium,** consider taking a comprehensive chocolate tour with InTrend International. Its 7-day escorted tours are a chocoholic's dream. You'll sample the sweets from some of the world's most famous chocolate makers in Brussels, Bruges, and Antwerp; participate in chocolate-making demonstrations at chocolate factories; and have delicious chocolate desserts every night. www.intrend.com

All aboard the chocolate train! **Switzerland**'s Chocolate Train goes from Montreux to Gruyères on board a vintage Pullman. Since it's Gruyères, your first stop will be the famous cheese-making factory and Gruyères castle, followed by a visit to the Cailler-Nestlé chocolate factory in Broc. Second only to the chocolate tastings are the views from the train, including vineyards that surround Montreaux, Lake Gruyère, and, of course, the Alps. www.goldenpass.ch/goldenpass_chocolate_train

You'll find plenty of chocolate tours in the United States, but among the most comprehensive—tastings, walking, historic information—are those offered by **Chicago** Chocolate Tours. Guided walking tours take you to various neighborhoods to experience everything chocolate: candy, cupcakes, bread, steamed buns, ice cream, and even teas. The same company also operates the Philadelphia Chocolate Tours and Boston Chocolate Tours. www.chicagochocolatetours.com

Did you know that **Ecuador** has a cacao route? The tour company Equatortrekking offers an immersive experience that covers the full spectrum of the cocoa process, from farm to factory to table. You'll learn the distinction in flavors between small and large farm production, and taste the difference between chocolate made from varying levels of cacao. Visit the homes of local villagers and learn how the art of chocolate making has been passed down among generations. To round out the experience, you'll also participate in a cooking workshop that incorporates cacao and try out local restaurants that include the ingredient in their everyday dishes. www.equatortrekking.com

In Limon, **Costa Rica,** the company Cacao Trails has a chocolate tour inside a rain forest. Start at an authentic plantation to learn about traditional chocolate-making techniques, and then try your hand at the actual process. We're talking everything from harvesting to drying to roasting . . . and finally, tasting. www.cacaotrails.com

Chocolate has huge historical significance in Oaxaca, **Mexico.** Follow your nose to Calle Mina, where a handful of chocolate makers line the street, including the renowned Chocolate La Soledad. But for a really immersive experience, join up with Seasons of My Heart cooking school in Guelaguetza. Owner Susana Trilling has in-depth courses in Oaxacan chocolate, where you'll learn to incorporate it into both sweet and savory dishes: moles, tamales, drinks, desserts, and even salad dressing. www.seasonsofmyheart.com

If real chocolate education is your goal, talk to the guys at Sweet

Earth Chocolates. Based in San Luis Obispo, **California,** the shop focuses almost entirely on organic, fair-trade chocolate and will take interested chocolate lovers to Africa to learn about the process from the ground up. We're talking visits with local farmers in five Ghanaian villages, tours of cocoa-bean drying plants, seeing the product being shipped from the ports, and even meeting with locals at the Ghana Cocoa Board (Cocobod). In Cameroon, you'll travel throughout the southwestern region, visiting cocoa villages and meeting with locals to learn about how the industry affects the local economy and sustainability. This is no luxury trip, involving little to no running water and nights sleeping on floors and even church pews.

CHOCOLATE MUSEUMS AND FACTORIES

Belgians take their chocolate very seriously, to the point that in order to be called "chocolate," the confection has to contain at least 35 percent pure cocoa. Choco-Story is a chocolate museum in Bruges, **Belgium,** that explains the process of Belgian chocolate making from the ground up. The museum is housed in a former 16th-century wine tavern (later repurposed as a bakery and a furniture factory). What's unique about this place is that it's not a marketing gimmick to push one brand—it's really all about the chocolate. Don't miss the third floor, which is packed with materials extolling the virtues of chocolate, good information to keep in mind if you visit any of the 50-odd chocolate shops in town. www.choco-story.be

They don't call Villajoyosa, **Spain,** the "Chocolate City" for nothing. Its chocolate history began in the 18th century, when it began importing cocoa beans from Venezuela and Ecuador. Today chocolate production is still booming as the town is home to Spain's oldest gourmet chocolate producer, Valor, which was founded in 1881. Villajoyosa boasts an excellent chocolate museum that showcases not only the history of its chocolate production but also how local favorites are made. But here's the real reason you want to go: to sample the famous local specialty, chocolate with churros.

Though entirely on the beaten chocolate path, I'm mentioning Hershey's Chocolate World (in Hershey, **Pennsylvania**) because the company goes beyond the typical chocolate factory tour with its hands-on experiences. You can customize your own candy bar (pick from white, milk, or dark, and add in your own ingredients); create your own treat in the dessert creation studio; or even become a factory worker for the day where you package your own Hershey's Kisses. The Chocolate Lab is another worthwhile stop for participatory classes, where you can examine the cacao from pod to nib, mold edible art, or make your own bar. www.hersheyschocolateworld.com

Even chocolate making can have an artisan approach. Brooklyn, **New York**'s Mast Brothers focuses entirely on small-batch production of organically farmed cacao. You can see the whole bean-to-bar process and get a hands-on experience actually cracking the beans. You'll taste five different types of chocolate to get a better sense of how individual beans lend themselves to distinct flavors. www.mastbrotherschocolate.com

CHOCOLATE TASTING

It doesn't get more chocolatey than Un Dimanche à **Paris**. Founded by renowned chocolatier Pierre Cluizel, this "concept store" features three levels of all things chocolate. Don't overdo it on the truffles before you leave the shop, because the 2,400-square-foot complex also has a cocktail lounge and a restaurant where the hip staff can whip up creative treats, all of which feature cocoa in some way (think layers of white chocolate and Roquefort cheese drizzled with chocolate balsamic vinegar). If you're inspired by what you see, eat, and drink, there is also a modern teaching kitchen for chocolate and pastry workshops. www.un-dimanche-a-paris.com

Craving chocolate while shopping in **London**'s most famous department store? You're in luck. Harrod's Chocolate Bar features melting chocolate fountains and fondues, seven types of hot chocolate, chocolate smoothies, pastries, cocktails, ice cream, and more, alongside traditional nonchocolate appetizers and entrees. www.harrods.com/visiting/restaurants/chocolate-bar

The Chocolate Boutique on Parnell Road in Auckland, **New Zealand,** offers more than the standard sweet-shop fare. Don't miss the chance to sit for a while at the tiny but outstanding cafe, which has an extraordinary menu of drinks and treats—from the super-thick flavored hot chocolates that come in varieties such as Mexican spice and chili pepper, to the "submarinos," which are chocolate bars submerged in hot steamed milk. www.chocolateboutique.co.nz

MAKE YOUR OWN

My Chocolate is one of the first companies in the **United Kingdom** exclusively dedicated to chocolate-making workshops. Several are held inside stores in London, Manchester, or Brighton, but the one you want to opt for is the workshop with partner Green & Black's. This one traces the history of chocolate, beginning with the cacao bean, followed by a sample tasting of raw cocoa nibs and pure chocolate. It's got both demonstrative and hands-on components—everything from dark chocolate truffles to chocolate ganache and milk chocolate praline. Best of all, you get to take home a box of 15 to 20 handmade chocolates. www.mychocolate.co.uk

Who better to teach you about chocolate than the French? Le Notre–trained Guy LeBlanc, a maître-patissier, has 4-day workshops at the Cuisine et Tradition School of Provencale Cuisine in Arles, in the south of **France**. Already have some experience under your belt? Join the Intensive Professional Chocolate Class, which includes three professional workshops, market tours, a visit to a professional chef's supply store, wine and chocolate tastings, and lodging. www.cuisineprovencale.com

The new ChocoMuseo in Cusco, **Peru,** is an ode to the country's chocolate heritage. The museum delves into the history of the cacao bean, from ancient Mayan times to the present. There is an artisan chocolate factory right on the premises, and overnight stays/tours of an off-site cacao bean plantation are available as well. The 2-hour chocolate-making workshops walk you through the entire process of authentic Peruvian-style chocolate making. After a lesson in how cacao is grown and harvested, you'll get a chance to actually roast the beans, remove the husks, grind the nibs with Aztec or Inca tools, and refine the paste. Then you get to customize the chocolate with additional ingredients and pour the finished chocolates into the molds. After that's over, you'll have a chance to taste cacao tea and Peruvian hot chocolate while you wait for your bar to finish hardening. http://peru.chocomuseo.com

Chocolate Festivals

The first week of October, the medieval town center of Perugia, **Italy,** turns into a river of chocolate during the annual Eurochocolate festival. The Umbrian streets are packed with stalls selling anything and everything made of chocolate. There are also exhibitions, workshops, cooking classes, tastings, and other celebrations of the "brown gold." www.eurochocolate.com/it/home.html

Also in October, **Paris** is host to the original Salon du Chocolat, an annual 5-day chocolate festival that brings more than 400 chocolatiers from around the world for a taste of chocolate heaven. The show covers more than 150,000 square feet filled with stands where visitors can sample chocolate, watch chocolate demonstrations, enjoy music, and indulge in one of the world's favorite foods. Best of all, the event is famous for its chocolate fashion show, where models walk down the runway wearing—what else?—haute couture chocolate dresses. www.salonduchocolat.fr

ChocoTravels in Italy offers a 4-day trip in **Tuscany** in which you'll visit some of the best chocolatiers in Florence, Pisa, and several smaller towns in the area. Ask about extending the itinerary for 2 days in order to take part in a hands-on course at the workshop of master chocolate makers Cecilia and Paul De Bondt. Why? Because De Bondt Chocolate, just a few miles outside of Pisa, is one of the top chocolatiers in the world. Paul will teach you how to choose the raw materials for chocolate, how to temper and blend it, and how to make fillings and decorations. Cecilia will give you ideas for how to present your masterpieces and how to create gift boxes. www.chocotravels.com/viaggi.html

Schokolade Artisan Chocolates & Cafe is a small shop in downtown **Vancouver** that makes unique chocolates in small quantities using only fresh, organic ingredients. It's known for inventive flavor combinations like chocolate paired with passion fruit, mango, jalapeño, and ginger. The last Friday evening of every month (except August, December, and February), chocolatier Edward Suter teaches the basics of how cocoa is grown and processed, and how to select and store chocolate for home use. But more interesting are his lessons in how to mold three-dimensional shapes, how to decorate with contrasting chocolate colors, how to roll and dip truffles, how to dip fresh fruit, and even how to write with chocolate! Of course you get to bring home all your finished chocolate pieces. The class includes the chance to taste Schokolade's artisan candies and the signature Ancient Aztec Hot Chocolate. www.schokoladecafe.com

Best Places to Find

COFFEE

This isn't about just drinking good coffee. This is about drinking *great* coffee but finding it first at its source. And taking the time for a second cup—probably long enough to cut a deal to buy it and then bring it home. It's also about finding the best coffeehouses in some pretty incredible places.

COFFEE FARMS

Only one US state grows coffee: **Hawaii.** And it does a great job. The combination of sunshine, volcanic soil, and moderate altitude make it an exceptional place for growing and processing. Most of the coffee industry is centered around Kona, on the west side of the Big Island of Hawaii. You can get up close to the beans on a tour of the Kona Lea Plantation, a family-owned, organic estate with free tours of the plantation, on-site roasting facilities, and a tasting room. What you'll get out of the experience is more than just a basic understanding of the coffee-making process; it's also an education in sustainable farming practices. Kona Lea composts the organic matter from coffee-bean growing and uses only natural pest control practices—and, perhaps best of all, it relies on a flock of geese for mowing and fertilization! www.konalea.com

Although coffee plantation tours aren't traditionally a kid-oriented activity, the Kona Coffee Living History Farm does a great job making history—and coffee—a fun, educational experience. It tells the story of Hawaii's early coffee industry by depicting the daily lives of early Japanese immigrants from 1920 to 1945, with interpreters, artifacts, and historic landscaping. On top of that, the 5.5-acre spread features coffee orchards, a processing mill and drying platforms, and a Japanese bathhouse. www.konahistorical.org

Costa Rica is known for its rain forests and ecolodges, but did you know that coffee is its second-largest industry? Costa Rican coffee is known to have a medium body in both taste and acidity. In the village of Heredia, the Mercedes Norte neighborhood is home to the Britt coffee plantation. You can tour the working farm, which is also a roastery and a turn-of-the-century mill to observe every step in the milling process, from receiving to sun drying. But what's really special about this tour is not just that there's a tasting at the end—it actually teaches you how the pros taste brews, along with proper brewing techniques. www.cafebritt.com/coffeetour

In Costa Rica's Monteverde cloud forest, the Santa Elena Cooperative was among the first fair-trade coffee farms in Costa Rica. The fair-trade label ensures that the coffee is sold for a guaranteed fair price, enabling members of the 75 participating farms to sustain their land and families. The 3-hour tour begins with an introduction to the history of the unique and rugged coffee-producing region. You'll then visit a working farm and learn about the coffee-growing process, tour the mill, taste a cup, and watch coffee being roasted and packed. www.monteverde-coffee.com

Most coffee lovers know about the Blue Mountains of eastern **Jamaica.** The coffee's distinct, mild flavor comes from the area's mineral-rich soil. But instead of a traditional plantation tour, you're better off exploring the small farms and roadside stands by car or, even better, by bicycle. Blue Mountain Bicycle Tours, for example, starts outs by driving you to Hardwar Gap, the highest part accessible by vehicle, then letting you bike down through the jungle roads. You'll pass by coffee plantations, see how the beans are processed, and sample a cup during an outdoor brunch. As an added bonus, the daylong experience includes a swim at a hidden waterfall. www.bmtoursja.com

In **Australia,** head straight to the Cairns Highlands in North Queensland, the heart of the Aussie coffee industry. The Skybury Tropical Plantation is Australia's oldest coffee farm. Owner Ian MacLaughlin has been in the coffee industry for more than 20 years and is truly an expert on the tiny bean. An hourlong tour explores the plantation grounds, the dry processing plant, and the coffee lab

"Specialty" Coffee

In the center of the Indonesian island of Sumatra, there's a special type of coffee made from beans that were "previously digested" by a small Indonesian creature. Called *kopi luwak*, the coffee is made with droppings collected after the native raccoonlike animal has munched on the beans.

where guests can experience the art of grinding, roasting, and tasting—also known as "cupping." Finish up with a full cup at the Australian Coffee Centre, which sits on top of the Great Dividing Range, on the peak of the Eastern Highlands overlooking the plantation. www.skybury.com.au

Experience the really exotic with Indonesian coffee. The tiny island of **Java** is the homeland of coffee's best nickname. Early Dutch explorers brought arabica trees to Java, and the small economy soon became almost totally supported by the even smaller bean. MesaStila sits on 55 acres of vegetation in the highlands of Magelang and is surrounded by eight dormant volcanoes. This is both a working coffee plantation and an upscale resort and spa, with villas built to resemble the original Javanese coffee plantation houses. The plantation tour is about as authentic as it gets. You wander through terraced fields, see beans being roasted and ground using traditional Javanese processing techniques and equipment, and taste the brew in a wooden coffeehouse at the center of the plantation. www.losaricoffeeplantation.com

Meanwhile, the island of **Sumatra** is known for its varied roasts. Among the most popular is the darker arabica variety grown in northern Sumatra. The Taman Simalem Resort is located northwest of Lake Toba, right in the middle of Sumatra's coffee-growing region, and offers a luxury look at coffee. The beans are harvested right on the property, and tours are easily arranged through the property's concierge. www.tamansimalem.com

The boutique hotel Hacienda el Roble, located 1 hour from Bucaramanga, **Colombia,** is a colonial-style coffee hacienda situated amid a Smithsonian-certified coffee plantation. The plantation grows 60 varieties of coffee amid hundreds of acres of native forest. You don't have to be a guest to tour the organic herb nursery and the coffee garden, learn about the roasting and milling processes, and experience a professional coffee "cupping." You can also hike or horseback ride along forest trails, and see some of the 123 species of native and migratory birds. www.cafemesa.2wpymes.com/hotel

COFFEEHOUSES

In **Vietnam,** the love of coffee dates back to the days of French colonialism. There are thousands of coffeehouses around Hanoi, but a favorite is Hué Café in the Old Quarter. Run by the third generation of the same family, this tiny, friendly shop serves great Vietnamese drip coffee from hand-roasted premium coffee beans. Try the Dalat, a bean grown in the Central Highlands of Vietnam, served iced with condensed milk. Or if you're really brave, try the Golden Weasel variety, a bean which is, er, "excreted" from a weasel's rear end.

In **London,** Kaffeine is tucked into a nondescript side street just north of Oxford Street, but is worth seeking out. They take their coffee so seriously that the baristas are required to have at least three years' experience at an espresso machine. www.kaffeine.co.uk

Café Passmar is located in the heart of Lazaro Cardenas Market in **Mexico City.** Don't miss its house blend coffee, made entirely of beans from the Mexican states of Guerrero and Chiapas, which are roasted in the micro-roastery next door. www.cafepassmar.com

Café de las Infusiones in **Havana,** Cuba, was recently restored to its colonial glory. This is the place to try the famous Cuban coffee (strong, black, and sweet, in small espresso-size cups), along with alcohol-spiked coffee drinks. If you want a little privacy, try the hidden patio at the back, through the stone archway.

Folks in **Melbourne,** Australia, are fanatical about their coffee, and Pellegrini's Espresso Bar is one of the best. It hasn't changed much in the 40-plus years since it's been in business, and regulars like it that way. It is owned by an Italian family who serves the coffee Italian style: either seated at a stool or standing at the bar.

Sant'Eustachio Il Caffè, which dates from the 1930s, is perhaps **Rome**'s most celebrated coffee shop. It still has the original mosaic tiling and furniture, and a device from 1948 in which they wood-roast the coffee beans. Coffee junkies sip brew made from water that comes in via an aqueduct built in 19 BC. Be sure to try the gran caffè, which is made by whipping the first few espresso drops into a frothy paste with several teaspoons of sugar, then adding the remainder of the coffee to the cup. www.santeustachioilcaffe.it/en

Seattle is known for more than just Starbucks. Caffé Vita, with six locations around the city, has some of the most well-versed baristas on staff and innovative coffee blends. Try their Americano and you'll be a fan for life. www.caffevita.com

Caffè Florian in **Venice** dates all the way back to 1720 and is one of the oldest continuously operating cafes in the world. Nobility, writers, and artists have eaten and drunk here throughout the centuries. It's also a cultural hub for the city: The Venice Bienniale exhibition was planned here in the late 1800s, and in modern times it hosts contemporary art shows and live music. The decor is unbelievable: frescoes on the walls, gilded paneling, hand-painted mirrors, wood wainscoting, and Oriental motifs in some rooms. You can buy not only coffee, tea, chocolates, and cookies here, but also art glass, jewelry, and other objets d'art. www.caffeflorian.com

The Viennese have had coffeehouses almost as long as the Turks, who invented the concept. Demel **Vienna**, founded in 1786, is a multistory emporium with airy salons on the second and third floors where aristocracy as well as the bourgeoisie used to rub elbows. House specialties include the Brauner (espresso with cream), Anna Demel (house coffee with orange liqueur and whipped cream), and the Melange (small espresso with warm milk and foam). On the ground floor, there is a glass-walled bakery where you can watch pastry chefs at work. www.demel.at

The Turks pretty much invented the coffee shop about 1,000 years ago. They continue to worship kahveh, which they like strong, thick, black, and sometimes with a hookah. Ethem Tezçakar Kahveci, which is run by the fourth generation of the Tezçakar family in **Istanbul,** dates back to 1909. Located near "Rug Street" in the Grand Bazaar complex, it's small (fits only about four people at a time), noncommercial, and nondescript—except for the silver- and copper-plated dishware displayed on glass shelves. But it serves some of the most authentic Turkish coffee you'll find anywhere in the city, and the baklava is amazing, too.

LIQUOR, SPIRITS, AND COCKTAILS

Okay, you've been properly warned: Proceed with caution. Embrace the words *designated driver*. And then be prepared for a magical mystery tour of the best alcohol, spirits, and cocktails in the world.

UNITED STATES

Y ou can't explore **New Orleans** without trying at least one of its famous cocktails. I'm not talking about a to-go cup full of cheap bourbon in the French Quarter. Venture out to find the places that make the best. Start with a deceptively refreshing Ramos Gin Fizz at the revolving Carousel Bar at the Hotel Monteleone (www.hotelmonteleone.com), follow it up with a Pimm's Cup at the Napoleon House (www.napoleonhouse.com), and end your night at the Roosevelt hotel's Sazerac Bar (www.therooseveltneworleans.com) for its world-famous Sazerac (rye whisky and bitters). If you want some guidance, you can get a good overview of the city's classic spots with Gray Line's New Orleans' Original Cocktail Walking Tour (www.graylineneworleans.com), a 2½-hour tour of the French Quarter . . . with a twist.

The **Kentucky** Bourbon Trail (www.kybourbontrail.com) connects six bourbon distilleries in bluegrass country, roughly between Lexington and Elizabethtown: Jim Beam, Four Roses, Heaven Hill, Maker's Mark, Wild Turkey, and Woodford Reserve. If you have to pick one, locals will probably point you to Woodford Reserve in

---

INSIDER'S TIP

Each year, New Orleans hosts Tales of the Cocktails, where top mixologists come together to create both classic and creative drinks. Organized tastings, seminars, and competitions go hand in hand with late-night drinking sessions and hangover beignets at Cafe du Monde.

Lexington, the oldest distillery on the trail. Once you've learned the traditional process of bourbon making, stop at the Bluegrass Tavern where they serve 178 different kinds of Kentucky bourbon. Beyond the trail is Buffalo Trace Distillery (www.buffalotrace.com), in the town of Frankfort, where you can stop for a tour and tasting, and then head over to the nearby Serafini, which serves more than 90 bourbons. Then go next door to Capital Cellars Wine and Spirits Cafe, where you can pick up bottles of hard-to-find bourbon.

INTERNATIONAL

Most first-timers get stuck at the Scotch Whisky Experience (www.scotchwhiskyexperience.co.uk) in **Edinburgh.** It's only helpful in realizing how big the scotch business really is. The tour involves a barrel ride through a replica distillery, a lesson in how to detect different aromas, and a glimpse of the 3,500-bottle collection. Of course, the real learning comes with hands-on experiences, so opt for the daylong blending course, where you can learn about all nuances of Scotch whisky. There's no shortage of whisky bars in Scotland, but for a really traditional Edinburgh experience, look for the extensive single-malt lists at the Abbotsford (www.theabbotsford.com) and Leslies Bar (www.lesliesbar.com).

Now it's time to leave Edinburgh for a literal taste of reality and an authentic immersion into a genuine distillery experience. In the ancient town of Forres on **Scotland**'s Moray coast, Benromach Distillery is one of the smallest producers in Speyside. Not only can you tour the facilities, but you can also sit down with the manager to get a one-on-one tasting lesson and create your own bottle of whisky to bring home. www.benromach.com

For the classic Glenfiddich single-malt whisky, skip the typical distillery tour and ask to see the Solera vats (normally used for sherry and cognac). They'll take you into the warehouse to see how it's done and do a private tasting. And if buying a bottle off the shelf isn't enough, you can bottle your own scotch straight from the cask, followed by a master class in tasting aged whiskies (www.glenfiddich.com). Fly to Scotland's windswept island of Islay to visit the old distilleries such as Bowmore and Lagavullin. These single malts are truly the best, but the deep, smoky, peaty flavor is definitely an acquired taste for many folks. Sip slowly.

Then there's the real surprise: In St. Moritz, **Switzerland,** is the Hotel Waldhaus am See. It's a pleasant hotel with a decent, small restaurant. But walk into the bar, and your world changes. You've now entered the bar with the largest whisky collection in the world. In Switzerland. Who knew? There are more than 2,500 different bottles, brands, ages, and strengths. It's called, perhaps appropriately, the Devil's Place and is a mecca for single-malt aficionados from all over the world. Most, like me, stumbled upon the place and had no idea it existed. There are not just single malts, but also blended, Irish, and Japanese whiskies. Best of all, the bartenders are expert historians and storytellers, because every bottle has a story or a mythology. There are nearly 1,000 different bottles on sale, some going for as much as $600 apiece! www.waldhaus-am-see.ch

Jalisco, **Mexico,** is the state where the world's best tequila is made from the blue agave plant. The landscape consists of miles and miles of fields of agave, as far as the eye can see. Industry giants such as Jose Cuervo and Sauza have their factories here, as do smaller operations. At the Cuervo factory (known as Mundo Cuervo or Cuervo World), visitors can take a 45-minute tour of the modern-day facility that shows all stages of the process, from the cooking of the agave to the milling, fermentation, distillation, and aging. You'll also visit the historic factory—which features an underground stone oven, an animal-powered stone mill, and primitive copper stills—and see where the tequila is aged. Don't leave without buying a bottle of the special family reserve.

Although you naturally associate sake with **Japan,** if you have to pick one place to visit, it's the Nada district of Kobe where you'll find dozens of breweries. In particular, the Kobe Shu-shin-kan Brewery (www.enjoyfukuju.com) has been making sake in that city since the mid-18th century. It's also one of the few places that actually invites people into the brew house, where you'll see the entire process from rice washing to filtration. In Kyoto, the Gekkeikan Okura Sake Museum (www.gekkeikan.co.jp) is located in a disused 1909 factory building, which re-creates the atmosphere of an old-time sake brewery. The museum has a huge collection of artifacts and memorabilia from Kyoto's 350-year tradition of sake making. And, of course, there's the requisite tasting at the end.

For a really immersive experience, you can travel to Japan with the only non-Japanese authority on sake. You can visit either the prefecture of Akita or the traditional San-in coast, both off-the-beaten-path areas that are difficult to navigate without a local expert. You'll meet master brewers, visit with local merchants, and learn to pair sake with country-style cuisine. http://saketours.com

In **Amsterdam,** Wynand Fockink has been making distinctive hand-crafted liqueurs and *jenevers* (Dutch gin) since 1679. The tasting room has one of the largest selections in Amsterdam, including apricot, licorice, and coffee-flavored liqueurs, served 17th-century style: Don't touch the glass, and keep your hands at your sides. Every Saturday afternoon is an English-language distillery tour, with a tasting afterward. You'll smell the mash and see the antique collection of Delft jugs and liquor bottles. But to really understand the process, take a workshop where you'll learn how to distill, blend, and bottle using the 300-year-old equipment. www.wynand-fockink.nl

Though rum has been a staple product of many Caribbean islands since the days of pirates, only one has a distinct rum trail for visitors. The 12 distilleries on **Martinique**'s Rum Route (Route des Rhum) make 17 varieties of rum, and all are open for tours and free tastings. What makes Martinican rum unique is the method used to produce it, called *rhum agricole*. While other rums are made from molasses (a by-product of sugar production), Martinican rum uses fresh sugarcane juice taken directly from cane stalks. It's so high quality that some Martinique rums carry the prestigious French designation AOC (Appellation d'Origine Contrôlée). A good place to start is the Rum Museum, located at the Saint James Distillery on the east coast. Other highlights include the Saint-Etienne Distillery in Gros-Morne for its white rum, and Habitation Clément in François, which is part of an 18th-century estate with 1.5 million liters of rum aged in oak barrels. It also boasts a 17-acre botanical park with more than 300 tropical plants. Plan a visit to coincide with one of the twice-yearly rum festivals on the island: the Sugar Cane Harvest Festival in July, and the Sainte-Marie Rum Festival in December.

BEST HOTEL BARS

When life gives you lemons, is your first reaction to break out the tequila and salt? If so, head south to Scottsdale, **Arizona**'s Phoenician Hotel. The Relish Burger Bistro has a menu of more than 400 types of tequila sourced from the top producers in Jalisco, Mexico It is one of the largest collections in North America, including its own private tequila label that is aged over 8 years. Prices range anywhere from $6 to $500, so ask for some guidance before you buy. www.thephoenician.com/dining/relish-burger-bistro

Prefer vodka? Just head to Mandalay Bay in **Las Vegas,** where the Russian-themed Red Square bar has its own private vodka "vault" with more than 200 varieties of frozen vodkas, infusions, martinis, and Russian-inspired cocktails. The hotel supplies mink coats and hats for tasting in the freezing room. And your drink is sure to stay cold because the surface of the bar is made of ice. As a bonus: At "Cavi Hour" from 4 to 6 p.m. on weekends, you get a free ounce of caviar if you buy four standard premium cocktails. www.mandalaybay.com/dining/signature-restaurants/red-square.aspx

In the **Bahamas,** the Graycliff Hotel has a collection of 250,000 bottles of wine from more than 400 vintners in 15 countries. It has literally one of the largest wine collections in the world. You can sample some of the goods during the daily wine luncheons, in which the master sommelier takes you on a tasting and tour, followed by a four-course gourmet meal paired with the appropriate wines from the cellar. www.graycliff.com

With nearly 200 choices of champagne, patrons of **Chicago**'s Pops for Champagne bar and nightclub have enough reasons to say "cheers!" Sip enough of the bubbly in this jazz bar, and you may feel like you stepped back to 1920s Paris. The menu includes shareable champagne-complementary items like oysters and caviar, cheese and charcuterie, and various desserts. http://popsforchampagne.com

The Quaich Bar in the Craigellachie Hotel in Speyside, **Scotland,** is the holy grail of whisky, with nearly 700 types available. The small, cozy room's walls are literally covered with shelf after shelf of single-malt scotch. Be careful which one you pick, because a single bottle can cost as much as $350. www.oxfordhotelsandinns.com/ourhotels/craigellachie

If you're traveling with a group, head to the Hotel Monaco in **Seattle,** where bartenders at the Sazerac restaurant teach guests how to make five different martini cocktails. Two drinks and an hors d'oeuvre are included in the price, plus a custom recipe booklet and souvenir stainless-steel Sazerac cocktail shaker. www.sazeracrestaurant.com

The Bar at the Dorchester hotel in **London** offers private or group mixology lessons courtesy of Giuliano Morandin, who has managed the bar for nearly 30 years. During the 2-hour bespoke session, you'll learn whatever you like, whether it's how to make the perfect cocktail, mocktail, or martini of your choice, or ideas for hosting a cocktail party at home. As a bonus, the bar will give your creation a name and put it on the menu for the rest of the day. www.thedorchester.com/the-bar

INSIDER'S TIP

Not sure where to start? Just follow the Malt Whisky Trail, which connects 10 of Scotland's famous highlands whiskies in the Spey Valley. www.maltwhiskytrail.com

Best Places to Enjoy

TEA

You can tell a lot about a place by following what the locals drink and where they drink it. This is especially true of tea—and the entire tea culture. It's more complex than you might think, but the good news is that it is also more welcoming and interesting than you might imagine.

TEA TOURS

Darjeeling, **India,** is synonymous with tea, and Glenburn Tea Estate is run by the fourth generation of a local family (it was originally founded by a Scotsman). The estate sits against the imposing Kanchenjunga range of the Himalayas, with 1,000 acres of private forest. You can participate in a half- or full-day tour that explains the process firsthand, whether it's harvesting, pruning, or withering the tea leaves. At the end of the experience, you can join in a tea-tasting session to discern the subtle flavors. This tour is a definite draw for foodies, as the owners also grow their own produce, herbs, and spices; overnight rates include three meals a day. You can even opt for a cooking class upon request. www.glenburnteaestate.com

Goomtee Resort, in the village of Mahanad, India, is a tea plantation and colonial B&B where you visit a working factory to see how the tea is withered, rolled, dried, sorted, and packed. Don't miss the hands-on tasting session that teaches the intricate system of grading, valuation, and flush. Go between March and November when you can also watch workers harvesting tea leaves in the fields. www.goomteeresorts.com

Ceylon Tea Trails is a working tea estate in **Sri Lanka**'s lush Bogawantalawa Valley, a.k.a. the Golden Valley of Tea. The trail actually combines four tea planters' villas, where you can stay overnight and get access to the insider tea-making experience. A resident tea planter shows you the step-by-step production, from picking "two leaves and a bud" to seeing the factory where black tea is processed using traditional methods. This is upscale all the way, with overnight accommodations in a Relais & Châteaux villa, gourmet meals, and butler service . . . and, of course, all the tea you can drink. www.teatrails.com

The Bigelow Tea Company has the only tea plantation in America: the Charleston Tea Plantation on Wadmalaw Island in **South Carolina.** The plantation spans 127 acres, where you can take a trolley ride to see the more than 320 varieties of tea plants in their various stages of growth. On the factory tour, you'll learn firsthand about the process of turning freshly cut leaves into finished product, and learn about the difference in the production of green, black, and oolong teas. Don't miss the 125-foot-long gallery window, from which you can peer into the production area. www.charlestonteaplantation.com

You've heard of Celestial Seasonings, right? Well, this company is based in Boulder, **Colorado,** and offers free tours every day around its active tea production plant. You'll see how the teas are blended, packaged, and shipped; free samples are offered at the end, of course. You can also view the gallery of artwork that graces the company's famous tea boxes. www.celestialseasonings.com

TEA TASTING AND EDUCATION

What's a trip to **China** without buying some tea? The Fangcun Tea Market in Guangzhou isn't just any tea shop—it's thought to be the largest tea-vending complex in the world, packed with more than 1,000 vendors from all over China selling loose leaves, tea sets, and ceramics. Want a memorable dining experience? Start the day at Lai Heen Cantonese restaurant inside the Ritz-Carlton Guangzhou and order the dim sum, which is specially paired with teas selected by the in-house tea sommelier. www.ritzcarlton.com

Happo-en is a traditional Edo-era garden in **Tokyo**'s Shirokane-dai district. Within this urban oasis of cherry trees, streams, and azaleas is a traditional teahouse called Muan. There, you can witness a Japanese tea ceremony where green tea (matcha) is brewed using a centuries-old method. www.happo-en.com

Tondaya, a historic restored merchant's house in **Kyoto,** tends to be on the tourists' path, but it's an excellent place to experience several Japanese traditions in an authentic setting. A private tea ceremony takes you through each intricate step of the process of preparing three different teas. http://www.tondaya.co.jp/English/indexE.htm

Teatime in **Britain** is practically a rite of passage, and almost all of the upscale hotels—from the Ritz to Claridge's—offer a traditional afternoon high tea. The Ritz in London has perhaps the most visible (and expensive) high tea service. Even if you can afford it, here's a caution about the dress code: It's jackets and ties only—no jeans of any kind are accepted. If you're going to splurge, the trick is to find a tearoom with a unique feature, like the Berkeley Hotel in London's Knightsbridge, which has an afternoon Prêt-à-Portea. It's teatime with a fashionable twist. That means the cakes and pastries are actually hand-crafted in the form of high-fashion tiny handbags, shoes, and clothes to reflect the latest fashions. www.the-berkeley.co.uk

Outside of London, the Rocke Cottage Tea Rooms has all the elements of a classic English tea without breaking the bank. The country tearoom is inside a 17th-century building in Shropshire's Clun Valley, with vintage decor from the '20s and '30s to round out the experience and locally sourced produce, cheeses, and clotted cream. www.rockecottagetearoom.co.uk

Make it a real foodie day and drive 20 minutes to the Ludlow Food Centre (www.ludlowfoodcentre.co.uk) in the village of Bromfield. It's a full marketplace and kitchen where 80 percent of ingredients come from only four nearby counties.

The famous Harney & Sons tea company doesn't grow its own tea, but there are two tasting rooms in **New York** where you can learn from the experts while sampling goods from around the world. They have more than 250 varieties of tea, which are prepared by master brewers; the temperature of the water they use is exactly calibrated for each type of tea. One location is in New York's SoHo district, and the other is in Millerton, New York (near Poughkeepsie). Don't miss SoHo's special weekend tastings and brewing demonstrations. www.harney.com

Discover the complex world of tea . . . in **Paris**? That's right. Even though the French capital isn't known for its tea culture, the Mariage Frères tea museum is. The main museum follows the history of tea, from lacquered chests to sample cases used by traveling merchants, and has a huge collection of teapots made of everything from porcelain to terra-cotta to cast iron (there's even a British piston system that fills the cup without moving the teapot from the table). Don't miss the old-fashioned *tasse à moustache*—teacups with a ledge to protect gentlemen's mustaches from getting wet. Mariage Frères also has salons and emporiums around France, Germany, and Tokyo where you can try dishes infused with tea, with a sommelier to pair your meal with various types of tea. www.mariagefreres.com

Who hasn't heard of Twinings tea? The manufacturer has been located at 216 Strand in **London** since the early 18th century, but you may not know that tucked in the back of the shop is a small museum chronicling the history of the famous family. It's tiny, but it's packed with curiosities such as an old wooden tip box (it actually reads, "To Insure Promptness"), ornate teapots and caddies, and archival images of tea being shipped from India to Britain. The shop also has a tasting counter so you can sample the goods. http://shop.twinings.co.uk/shop/Strand

A little closer to home is the Ippodo Gallery in **New York City.** It's a Japanese contemporary arts and crafts gallery, but not only do they showcase tea utensils, they also have a tearoom where practitioners can hold ceremonies. You can observe a lesson for free or sign up to actually participate in the experience yourself. www.ippodogallery.com

Southern **California** tea lovers know about Chado Tea Room, which features hundreds of teas from around the world in both Beverly Hills and Pasadena. But to go beyond just tasting, head to its newest location at the Japanese American National Museum in downtown LA. The tearoom (grab a seat in the outdoor garden) has a huge selection of teas and a traditional afternoon service, but you can also take advantage of the museum's programming that includes topics like Japanese pastries, hands-on workshops, and author lectures. www.janm.org

WINE

In all of my travels, I've become a firm believer in participatory journeys—getting up close and personal wherever and whenever I can. When it comes to wine, tasting is surely important, but I also want to learn about the history and experience the winemaking process. There's a lot to learn about the wine industry, and you don't have to be an oenophile to appreciate all the information. But you might be surprised at how fascinating (and useful) it can be.

HANDS-ON EXPERIENCES

Learn how to make wine from master winemakers at the Sonoma County Grape Camp in **California.** During this intense 3-day, hands-on seminar in late September, renowned winemakers work side by side with guests and show them the art behind the science of winemaking. Spend your time picking grapes and blending wine on the banks of the Russian River in Healdsburg, and participate in food-pairing lessons, cheese-making demonstrations, and gourmet dinners. If you'd prefer the contrarian approach, go to Sonoma in spring during the off-season pruning festival—it's a much more local experience that gets you out into the vineyards. www.sonomagrapecamp.com

During the intense 2-day harvest boot camp at Hall Wines in Napa Valley, winemakers walk you through every step of the winemaking process. You get up at dawn to handpick and sort grapes and bring them to the tanks for fermentation, and participate in barrel tastings and blending workshops. www.hallwines.com

Check out the Harvest 101 seminar at McIntyre Vineyards in Monterey County. You can learn about the process of winemaking from ground to bottle from Steve McIntyre, the proprietor. You'll learn how to determine the proper time to harvest by tasting grapes, analyze acidity, and test pH levels. The whole thing takes about 3 hours and includes a lunch in the vineyard and tastings of several wines. www.mcintyrevineyards.com

On **Long Island,** the North Fork wine region hosts a winemaking camp in spring. This is a real boot camp for wine lovers, with two sessions spread over 4 days that include hands-on classes, wine tastings, farm-to-table dining, and your own case of wine to take home. www.winecamp.org

The Chêne Bleu Extreme Wine Experience is an intensive 5-day winemaking class for serious wine aficionados that takes place every June in **France**'s Vaucluse region of Provence. The course blends theoretical teaching with hands-on learning. You'll be taught in English by top European winemakers on all aspects of the craft, from planting the seed to bottling. Of course, you'll also be treated to multiple tastings of exceptional wines and take part in hands-on activities out in the vineyard. The course is based at the wine estate of La Verrière, where you'll stay in a restored medieval priory and eat meals prepared by a renowned Provençal chef. www.laverriere.com

Champagne Drappier is a small, family-run champagne house in Urville, without the bus tours and the crowds. During harvest season, you not only visit the winery, but you can also participate in the harvest. Start with a small *casse-croutû* (pickers' breakfast). Put on some knee pads, grab a basket and some special shears, and you're in for a great time. After about 2 hours in the field, you'll have a family-style lunch with the crew, followed by a tour of the cellars and a champagne tasting. End the day with your own bottle of Drappier to bring home. www.champagne-drappier.com

Foxeys Hangout is a winery on the Mornington Peninsula of **Australia** (an hour south of Melbourne) that produces sparkling and still wines. It also offers the unique opportunity to create and bottle a sparkling wine blend of your own. During the finishing stages of the complicated winemaking process, you'll first observe the disgorgement—when the bottle neck is frozen and opened, and the sediment that has formed in the neck is popped out as a chunk of ice. Then you'll select your own dosage, the mixture of wine and sugar syrup that is added before final corking and sealing of the bottle. You determine what blend you want by trying test samples, and you'll instruct the winemaker on how many grams of sugar should be added to your bottle and which base wines to use to finish the blend. Then bring it home and wait for it to finish aging before popping it open. www.foxeys-hangout.com.au

Club Tapiz is a guesthouse located on a 22-acre vineyard in the Mendoza Valley town of Maipu, which is the heart of **Argentina**'s wine country. In addition to using the hotel as a base for wine tours of the region, you can tour the in-house winery and help prune, plant, and harvest alongside the local workers during harvest time. Every evening there are free wine tastings, and staff give lectures on the winemaking process.

In Ontario, **Canada**'s Niagara-on-the-Lake, Peller Estates hosts the Intense Icewine Weekend, a 2-day January boot camp that lets you experience the sweet, intense wine (made from frozen grapes) in many ways. You'll brave subzero temperatures in the vineyards with winemaker Lawrence Buhler during a chilly grape-picking session, learn to press and taste grapes, get a lesson in ice wine food pairing, and participate in a blind tasting of six local ice wines. And don't forget the gourmet dinner and a visit to the Niagara Icewine Festival. Throughout the weekend, you'll taste more than 25 ice wines. www.peller.com

In **Washington**'s Yakima Valley is the October Winemaker for a Day seminar at Two Mountain Winery. During this very technical, hands-on vineyard session, you'll learn how to measure sugar levels, take temperature readings, and make sure the wine stays properly mixed, as well as learn about the fermentation process. Four times a year is the Vineyard Crew session, where you get down and dirty helping staff prune or harvest the vines (depending on what time of year it is). www.twomountainwinery.com

WINE TRAILS

If you really want to immerse yourself in a region, just follow the trail. The wine trail, that is.

Sonoma County, **California,** has 13 American Viticultural Areas and hundreds of wineries, so covering it all in one go is near impossible. But the best way to get a taste is to snag a Ticket to the Wine Road pass (www.wineroad.com), which gets you access to 50 wineries. Not only do you get free tastings, but you can also bypass the crowds with extra perks like barrel tastings and behind-the-scenes tours with the winemakers.

On the other side of the country, **New York**'s Finger Lakes region has gained a reputation for producing exceptional cool-climate wines like Pinot Noir, Riesling, and Gewürztraminer. There are multiple trails clustered around the Cayuga, Seneca, and Keuka Lakes. If you have to choose one, go for the Cayuga, the oldest of the bunch, with 15 wineries along the way. Stops include Sheldrake Point and the Cayuga Ridge Winery, which actually has a "vine-leasing" program where you can work with the experts to grow your own vine and, in the fall, harvest the grapes. The program also includes a blending workshop and barrel tastings, so you get the full winemaker experience over the seasons. www.cayugawinetrail.com

Missouri has a surprisingly huge wine scene, and it's got five wine trails to show for it. The industry's roots date back to the 1830s, when German immigrants began producing wine in the town of Hermann. Today, the Hermann wine trail has seven wineries in a 20-mile-long route along the Missouri River, including the venerable Adam Puchta Winery—thought to be the longest continuously owned and operated family winery in the United States. www.hermannwinetrail.com

Although the state of Victoria in **Australia** is best known for its Yarra Valley wines, there's a new trail in the region. The King Valley Prosecco Road connects six wineries—from Milawa to Cheshunt in northeastern Victoria—that produce the relatively new offering of sparkling white Prosecco. Each winery has its own experience, but be sure to participate in a master tasting class at Chrismont Prosecco, along with a tour of the vineyards with the winemaker.

The wine trail in the Mendoza province area of **Argentina** is actually accessible by bike. Just east of the city of Mendoza is Maipu, the heart of the winemaking region. From here, you can rent a bike from a handful of bike shops like Mr. Hugo. They'll give you a rough map of the trail, which runs about 7.5 miles, covering six wineries, the Maipu Wine Museum, and a chocolateria that also produces an assortment of liqueurs (be careful when mixing wine with absinthe!).

In South **Australia**'s Barossa Valley, forget about the tourist van. Travel in style in a rare 1962 Daimler with wine expert John Baldwin. You'll visit up to six wineries, sit down for tea at Maggie Beers Farm Shop, and if you want, stop at local cheese makers, olive oil producers, and craft brewers. www.barossadaimlertours.com.au

Known as the culinary capital of **South Africa**'s Western Cape, Franschhoek has more than 40 wineries within a relatively small region. To get around, you can drive, hike, or go on horseback! Paradise Stables has wine rides through the scenic valley, with the mountains as your backdrop, stopping at Rickety Bridge Winery and Mont Rochelle along the way. www.paradisestables.co.za

LESSER-KNOWN WINE REGIONS

With 220 wineries spread out over nine distinct regions, **Virginia** has a surprisingly robust wine culture. Its wine-producing regions vary in both climate and geography, from Loudun County just outside of Washington, DC, to the locavore's paradise of historic Hampton Roads and the rural Blue Ridge Mountains. You can tour most Virginia wine areas by car, but there is also another way: by sea. Southeast Expeditions (www.southeastexpeditions.net) has kayaking wine treks on Virginia's Eastern Shore, where you'll launch from Bayford and paddle for about 40 minutes before stopping at Chatham Vineyards in Machipongo, where the owner will give you a behind-the-scenes look at the winemaking operation.

Believe it or not, **Texas** has a long wine history dating back to the 17th century. The wineries here are so sprawled out that there are 11 different wine trails to choose from. The Hill Country Wine Trail highlights favorites like Becker Vineyards (www.beckervineyards.com), while the High Plains region near Lubbock features the highly regarded Llano Estacado, among others.

Washington State is actually the number-two wine-producing state in the country, after California. Its regions range from the revered Walla Walla Valley to laid-back Woodinville, just outside of Seattle, to the sunny Yakima Valley. And because Washingtonians tend to love the great outdoors, plenty of wineries have activities beyond just tasting. The prestigious Chateau Ste. Michelle winery holds a summer concert series on its front lawn, bringing A-list names to this small, agricultural town.

Portugal is renowned for its port wines that come out of the Douro River valley. But do you know about *vinho verde*? Produced in the Minho region in the northern part of the country, vinho verde literally means "green wine," referring to how young and light the wines are. Though the land is ancient, some wineries are adopting more modern philosophies—like Afros (www.afros-wine.com), which relies on biodynamic agriculture to make the soil healthy and fertile.

Unusual Wines

Sure, your options for wine are pretty much limited to red, white, or rose. But that doesn't mean it has to be made from grapes. At Bartlett Maine Estate Winery in Gouldsboro, **Maine,** red varietals are made from Maine blueberries and apples, while its whites are made from pears, apples, and honey. And we're not talking about sweet dessert wines—these are well-balanced, sophisticated blends that are meant to be served with savory dishes. www.bartlettwinery.com

And while South **Florida** is hardly known for its grape-friendly climate, it does produce a bounty of tropical fruits. So why not turn those into wine? Schnebly's Winery, which also happens to be the southernmost winery in the country, makes wine from produce like guava, coconut, star fruit, and even avocados. No, it's not the best wine you'll ever taste in your lifetime, but it's certainly one of the most unusual. www.schneblywinery.com

Though the fertile grounds of **South Africa**'s Cape Wineland region produces renowned wines, it's also got a more unusual offering: mead. Made from fermented honey and water, this traditional brew has been a staple among South Africa's native Khoisan people for thousands of years (they call it *iqhilika*). At the Makana Meadery outside of Grahamstown, there's a new twist on the ancient drink: The facility, located in a decommissioned power plant, uses only sustainable and indigenous ingredients, like honey from an on-site beehive. Honey Sun African Mead can be made both dry and sweet, and is flavored with some unusual ingredients like Cape fig. www.iqhilika.co.za

Usually when someone says "Spanish wine," you think of reds from La Rioja, sherry from Jerez, or cava from Catalonia. But there are two lesser-known regions in **Spain** that you need to know about, both in the north: Geteria and Galicia. Geteria, in Basque Country, has difficult growing conditions, so locals are very proud of their light, slightly sparkling *txakoli*. Head to any tapas bar and watch the bartenders pour the liquid from high up, to maximize the bubbles. In Galicia, the signature wine is a white Albariño. In the Ribeira Sacra region, you'll marvel at how the grapes grow on impossibly steep terraces that rise up from the river.

Move over, Bordeaux and Burgundy. Languedoc-Roussillon is rich and fertile wine country in the south of **France** on the Mediterranean coast. Once known for its anchovy industry, the region is now known for its herbacious reds. This region begs to be explored by barge, where you can wander through the small villages and along the towpaths as you meander along the Canal du Midi.

Wine and Art

We've all heard of wine and food pairings, but what about wine and art pairings? There are a number of wineries that also double as art galleries. For example, the tasting room at the award-winning McKeon-Phillips Winery and Art Gallery (www.mckeonphillipswinery.com) in Santa Barbara County has a 45-foot wall to display the works of founder Ardison Phillips, as well as rotating exhibits of local California artists. In Sausalito, **California,** Bacchus and Venus (www.bacchusandvenus.com) features a collection of wine country–inspired art that includes still lifes and scenes from the Napa Valley, California, and Italy. The owners of Hall wines (www.hallwines.com) in the Napa Valley are avid art collectors. You can see fine works regularly in its facility in Rutherford, as well as take a tour of the winemakers' home to see their own extensive collection, followed by lunch overlooking the valley. Silver Coast Winery (www.silvercoastwinery.com) in Ocean Isle Beach, **North Carolina,** displays a mix of paintings and sculptures by local artists that reflect the owner's eclectic tastes. And in Ripley, **New York,** the Sensory Winery and Art Gallery (www.lakeeriewinecountry.org) highlights paintings by dozens of celebrated artists from around Lake Erie wine country.

Urban Wine Tasting

You don't have travel to the countryside to try great wine. Urban wineries are becoming increasingly common in cities around the United States. Of course, the big drawback of urban wineries is that you miss out on the vineyard experience, but you can save that for another trip. Brooklyn Winery (www.bkwinery.com) in **New York** offers a lot more than just tastings. Located in a former nightclub, it allows visitors to get hands-on experience with the entire winemaking process. You can follow your wine from grape selection to de-stemming, crushing, and eventually bottling. While California is known for its wine production, most people are surprised to hear that there's a winery located in downtown **Los Angeles.** It's called San Antonio Winery (www.sanantoniowinery.com) and offers free tastings and tours. New Bedford, **Massachusetts,** is better known for whaling than winemaking, which makes Travessia Urban Winery (www.travessiawine.com) such an unexpected attraction. It uses only Massachusetts grapes, so you know you're getting a local experience. And in the little hamlet of Castemola, **Italy,** there's a little cafe called San Giorgio that has tastings of . . . almond wine!

Chile's wine industry has grown immensely over the years, and it's become easier than ever to navigate the Aconcagua and Colchagua regions with the growth of B&Bs and wine lodges. But what you may not know is that Chile is home to a very cool project that is bound to get attention in the coming years. Viña Vik is attempting to make Chile's first 100-point wine, using modern, scientific technology and ancient techniques . . . and lots and lots of money. Santiago Wines can take you on a tour of the 800 acres of vineyards to meet with the winemakers (who are very excited about this project!) and sample the first batches of wine straight from the barrel and even spend a night in a wooden cabin in advance of the full-service hotel that is being planned.

Israel is home to some very sophisticated viticulture, with five wine-growing regions and more than 300 wineries (many of which are kosher). You can tour individual wineries, of course, but another way to savor the grapes is at an urban wine bar, another concept that Israel excels at. A clutch of wine bars in Tel Aviv and Jerusalem serve vintages from Israel's boutique wine producers, such as the Golan Heights Winery, Domaine du Castel, and Carmel Winery. At the deluxe Mamilla Hotel (www.mamillahotel.com) in Jerusalem, the intimate wine bar stocks more than 300 bottles of Israeli wines, with many available by the glass.

New Zealand's wine industry is booming, and most people follow the classic wine trails: Hawke's Bay, Wairarapa, and Marlborough. But an even better option is off the beaten path to Waiheke Island, off the coast of Auckland. Only 36 square miles, the island has an eclectic mix of residents—winemakers, olive growers, and artists, among others. The summers are hot and dry, and the stony soil provides ideal grape-growing conditions for the excellent red wines produced there. Boutique wineries include Te Whau Vineyard (www.towhau.com), which is located on such a steep slope that its barrel cellar is dug into the side of the hill; and Mudbrick Vineyard (www.mudbrick.co.nz), which makes the Shepherds Point Label and has a restaurant made of mud-hewn brick with spectacular 360-degree views over the Hauraki Gulf toward Auckland.

FOOD MARKETS

Wherever I travel, I make it a point to seek out the best local food markets. Not only do I usually find fresh, healthy food, I also get to interact with the locals and learn the secrets that no guidebook could ever provide about that location. It's the best way to get insider info and a great meal at the same time.

UNITED STATES

Guess where my favorite farmers' market in the country is located. Napa Valley? New York City? Nope. It's in Madison, **Wisconsin.** The Dane County Farmers' Market On the Square is the largest producer-only farmers' market in the United States. The "no resale" rule means that the person behind the table is the same person who grew or made the product. It's also one of the few midwestern farmers' markets that remain open year-round. In summer, it takes place at the square by the Capitol every Wednesday and Saturday; in winter, it moves indoors and is just on Saturdays. Not only is this where you can buy produce grown from area farms, but it's the best place to sample Wisconsin's famous cheeses. Ever heard of cheese curds? It's a midwestern specialty made from solidified soured milk during the cheese-making process. They're usually served within hours of production, which you'll know if you hear that satisfying "squeak" between your teeth. Check out the free samples from Farmer John. And if you can't wait till you get home to eat your purchases, go for the Winter Market Breakfast, which is a full meal made entirely from farmers' market products. The menu changes every week, depending on the harvest. But get there early. There are only about 250 meals, and it's first come, first served. www.dcfm.org

On **Hawaii**'s Big Island, the tropical climate makes for fertile grounds, and the bustling Hilo Farmers Market has more than 200 vendors selling their products every Wednesday and Saturday year-round. There is also a pared-down version of the market open every other day of the week except Friday. In addition to predictable tropical fruits like coconuts and pineapples, you'll be able to find more exotic options like sugar apples, lychees, and Buddha's Hand—all of which look more like underwater creatures than edible fruit. But it's not just about the produce. You can graze your way through the market, tasting all of the local delicacies: fruity *haupia* (a coconut milk and gelatin dessert), coconut milk-flavored tea, and even vegan baked goods. Score one-of-a-kind souvenirs at Secondhand Sundays, which is essentially a highly organized community garage sale. Fun fact: Hilo was the first farmers' market in the country to accept electronic food stamp benefits, helping to put healthy local produce onto families' plates. www.hilofarmersmarket.com

The Capital City Farmers Market in Montpelier, **Vermont,** won't win any awards for size or volume, but it is a standout for the specialty and small farmers who supply it. There are only about 40 vendors any given week, but they provide an amazing array of products, including ripened berries, emu oil, kimchi, flavored honey, grass-fed beef, mead, artisan bread, and raw-milk goat cheese. There's always live music and special events such as ice-cream-making demos and lectures on various food topics. In summer, the event is held Saturdays on State Street downtown; in winter, it's indoors at the Vermont College of Fine Arts gym on the first and third Saturday of every month. www.montpelierfarmersmarket.com

Here's one you probably haven't heard of: Zern's Farmer's Market in Gilbertsville, **Pennsylvania,** about 40 miles west of Philadelphia. The name is a bit misleading, because Zern's is so much more than just a farmers' market—it's a glimpse into the long history of the Pennsylvania Dutch community. The 100 outdoor and 300 indoor stands offer authentic regional treats such as corn relish, shoofly pie, and chowchow relish, plus a huge array of fresh produce, baked goods, and proteins. Don't forget the funnel cakes and homemade ice cream. There's also a flea market that sells vintage clothing, antiques, and thousands of other items, not to mention on-site butchers, bakeries, and a spice shop. Be sure to stop by on a Friday or Saturday to see the live auctions in progress. www.zerns.com

Want to see celebrity chefs browsing for the freshest ingredients? **Los Angeles** has a number of farmers' markets throughout the city, but your best bet to see familiar faces from TV food shows is the Santa Monica Farmers Market on Wednesday mornings. This is a certified organic market where the produce comes straight from California farmers, and you're likely to see those ingredients appear on menus all around the city. www.smgov.net/portals/farmersmarket

INTERNATIONAL

The farmers' market in Marylebone, **London,** is not huge, but it is one of the city's loveliest. The 35-odd stalls cater not only to locals going about their weekly shopping, but also to foodies from all over the city looking for something delectable and unusual. We're talking homemade soups, seasonal pestos, and handmade sausages from nearby producers. Best of all, these items are truly local, sourced from no more than 100 miles away from the M25 (London's ring road). The market takes place every Sunday in the Cramer Street parking lot. www.lfm.org.uk/markets/marylebone

Markets are the heart and soul of **Mexico,** and they're among the best places to mingle with the locals and capture the flavors of the region. In Mexico City, Mercado San Juan is a gastronomic wonderland for foodies. It offers some of the freshest produce, herbs, and exotic meats (like ostrich and alligator), and also has a huge selection of artisan cheeses and meats. Check out the western side of the market where the *comedores* are a cluster of prepared food stands, serving everything from fresh quesadillas to hot pozoles (Mexican stew).

The Edinburgh Farmers' Market in **Scotland** definitely has the most dramatic location of any farmers' market: It's located on Castle Terrace, with the imposing Edinburgh Castle in the background. The market attracts close to 60 stallholders, the majority of whom grow the specialty items they sell—free-range eggs to organic meats. Meat vendors sell organic beef, chicken, lamb, and pork, as well as rarer finds like water buffalo and wild boar. Plenty of artisan producers sell cheeses, jams, and even organic beer. Cold-pressed grape seed oil, artisan pretzels, and handbags made of wild Scottish deerskin are all souvenir options. Market grub makes a good accompaniment for a day trip/picnic into the Scottish countryside. www.edinburghfarmersmarket.com

Although most people are familiar with the Central Market in Florence, there's another place where you can get the really rustic

Italian experience. The medieval hill town of Colle di Val d'Elsa, **Italy,** is an exceptionally charming Tuscan village, just north of Siena. On Friday mornings, the market at Piazza Arnolfo is filled with locals doing their weekly shopping—and it carries everything from local cheeses and cured meats to crafts and antiques.

Located between Jaffa and Agrippas Streets is the open-air Mahane Yehuda in **Jerusalem.** Most stalls sell fruits and vegetables, but there are also butchers, bakers, and Shabbat candlestick makers. This is a great place to mingle among the locals while snacking on falafel and shawarma, and picking up exotic spices to bring home.

Although it's heavily trafficked by tourists, La Boqueria in Barcelona, **Spain**'s La Rambla district is truly a must-see. Somewhere in between a farmers' market and a supermarket, the covered market hosts 300 vendors who sell a wide variety of fresh and dried produce, cured meats, cheeses, Spanish olives, and other specialty items. Vendors are often very specialized: One sells only different types of salt cod; another has 40 types of wild mushrooms. You can easily spend hours here marveling at the huge piles of brightly colored veggies, whole rabbits hanging from meat hooks, and even edible beetles. Around the edges are various excellent tapas bars, where you can grab a quick meal while you shop. You can even learn how to cook at the market's own cooking school. I also go there to eat—when I have time. And by that I mean, time to wait. Inside La Boqueria, you'll find a little place called Bar Central. It's just one counter and about eight bar stools. Opposite the counter is a stack of all kinds of freshly caught fish. When you arrive, the stools will likely all be occupied. Be patient. (You may have to wait for about 20 minutes, but it will be well worth it.) Once you sit down, you simply point to the fish you want, and they cook it right in front of you. A little olive oil, a little garlic, and . . . well, you get the picture. Delicious. www.boqueria.info

The Viktualienmarkt (victuals market) is a main attraction in central Munich, for good reason. Not only do you get access to local produce, but you can also track down traditional bratwurst and salamis, as well as find vendors selling spices, bread, and, of course, apple strudel. And, because it's **Germany,** there's a huge beer garden that opens at 9 a.m., where you're allowed to bring your own food. Stock up at the market, order a beer, and enjoy the people watching.

The exceptional Östermalms Saluhall in Stockholm, **Sweden,** dates back to the 1880s and offers a smorgasbord of gourmet Scandinavian foods and restaurants. Located in a covered red-brick building in the smart Östermalm district, the market is light on produce but heavy on quaint stalls that sell uncooked seafood, sausages, smoked fish, and prepared foods like pastries, pies, and chocolate. Of course, you'll find native fruits like lingonberries and cloudberries, and herring prepared a million different ways. In addition to food stalls, there are a number of restaurants within the market that offer delectable Swedish specialties like gravlax, open-faced sandwiches, and international fare such as sushi and kebabs. www.saluhallen.info

Queen Victoria Market is an enormous sprawling market in the heart of Melbourne, with a unique layout consisting of "precincts" devoted to meats, produce, organics, general merchandise, and more. At least 50 percent of the market offers fresh items, including exotic and international goods like Greek cheese, Italian sausage, and lychees. The rest is divided into sections for art, children's clothes, coffee and tea, jewelry, wine, and innumerable other items. There's a very cool weekend wine market, and you can see some of **Australia**'s top chefs demonstrating how to cook with all the local produce at the Electrolux Cooking School. www.qvm.com.au

MUSHROOMS AND TRUFFLES

It's one thing to shop for mushrooms or truffles at a farmers' market, or order them at an upscale restaurant, but quite another to make them part of your overall travel experience. In my opinion, it's those hands-on activities and educational components that make it a more rewarding experience.

MUSHROOMS

The largest concentration of mushrooms—edible and other-wise—can be found in the Pacific Northwest. The damp conditions are ideal for growing fungus throughout Washington, British Columbia, and even parts of Montana. But there are some lesser-known regions where this humble ingredient has been gaining notoriety, and some experiences you don't want to miss. (Just one tip: If you're not an experienced forager, always go with someone who is. Mushrooms can be dangerous business if you don't know what you're hunting for in the great outdoors.)

Late fall means mushroom madness in Mendocino County in Northern **California,** where there are more than 500 types of edible mushrooms and educational, hands-on experiences throughout November. Ricochet Ridge Ranch has guided horseback tours to lead guests on mushroom hunts, while the Botanical Gardens in Fort Bragg has weekly walks with a local expert (yes, there is such a thing as a mushroom expert). But the season's highlight is the 10-day Wine and Mushroom Festival. There are more than 100 events, everything from mushroom dinners and wine- and beer-pairing workshops to foraging walks, kayaking along the Noyo River to hunt for water-dwelling mushrooms, and learning to dye wool with mushroom pigments. Don't miss the daylong train ride from Fort Bragg into the heart of the redwoods for a mushroom cook-off and wine-tasting event. www.visitmendocino.com

Most people are surprised to learn that **Colorado** is home to up to 3,000 varieties of mushrooms (although only a fraction are edible), making it the country's second-largest concentration after the Pacific Northwest. The epicenter of Colorado's mushroom scene is the Telluride Mushroom Festival (www.shroomfest.com). This event calls out to foodies, counterculturalists, and nature geeks, with hunts for the coveted meaty King Boletus porcini, seminars on medicinal mushrooms, and a look at the chemistry and physiology of fungi.

There are also plenty of ongoing mushroom events during the May-through-October foraging season. The Colorado Mycological Society offers guided forays near Boulder and Denver, while Myco-tours (www.mycotours.com) provides private hunts in the Rocky Mountains. Even some of the top hotels, like the Little Nell (www.thelittlenell.com) in Aspen and the Four Seasons Resort Vail (www.fourseasons.com/vail) offer foraging experiences followed by gourmet meals and cooking lessons.

They don't call it the mushroom capital of the world for nothing. Although Kennett Square in **Pennsylvania**'s Chester County is clear across the country from the Pacific Northwest, it cultivates more than a million pounds of mushrooms a year, or about half of the nation's mushroom crops. Your first stop should be the Mushroom Cap (http://themushroomcap.com), which is the central spot for all your mushroom needs and educational programming. Phillips Mushrooms is the largest grower of specialty mushrooms, and right in Kennett Square is the Woodlands retail store, a historic venue that sells Phillips mushrooms, where you can learn to cook with locally grown fungi. But, like other major mushroom regions, it's the annual festival that really shines the spotlight on the famous product. The Kennett Square Mushroom Festival takes place every September, and includes farm tours and hundreds of food vendors who highlight the ingredient (mushroom ice cream, anyone?).

There are thousands of mushroom varieties growing in **Nova Scotia,** and there's no better place to experience this local specialty than the aptly named Chanterelle Country Inn and Cottages (www.chanterelleinn.com). The property sits on 150 acres in Cape Breton, where chef-owner Earlene Busch focuses on local and seasonal cuisine. In fact, it was the abundance of Nova Scotia chanterelles that convinced Busch to move there from Boulder. Every fall, she and mycologists from around the world take guests on a hunt for the wild mushrooms that dwell in Cape Breton's forests. Return to the inn to feast on the "catch" prepared in gourmet meals.

Believe it or not, one of the best places on earth for mushrooms is **China**! There are as many as 800 varieties of mushrooms growing in the Yunnan Province in southwestern China, including the elusive matsutake mushroom. Restaurants all over town serve dishes featuring an assortment of the prized fungi, including a street devoted to serving mushroom hot pot. You can see a huge selection at the wild mushroom wholesale market in the capital city of Kunming. Want to go foraging? You'll have to head to nearby areas like Qiexi Village where foragers gather each morning during the rainy season (usually July and August). But let me reiterate: A local guide is a must because of the high risk of toxicity if you ingest the wrong kind of mushroom.

TRUFFLES

Feel like elevating the fungal experience? Then concentrate on the coveted truffle. Both the black and white varieties are renowned in the culinary world as the "diamonds of the kitchen," served shaved, diced, or infused into sauces.

Italy is practically synonymous with the pungent, delicate, and expensive white truffle (*tartufo biaco*), which becomes a star attraction in the fall. White truffles can be found in a handful of regions, but come October and November, the place to be is the Langhe region of Piedmont, Italy. Set smack in the middle of wine and chocolate country, Piedmont is a foodie's dream come true. This is where the white truffle is most widely celebrated during the International White Truffle Fair in Alba. In nearby Roddi, you can participate in foraging expeditions, complete with truffle-hunting dogs. Or you can opt to stay an hour and a half away in Milan, where the Hotel Principe di Savoia (www.hotelprincipedisavoia.com) will arrange a chauffeur for your own truffle hunt and a tour of the truffle fair, among other truffle-y dining experiences.

But if you want a less touristy option, my advice is to head to other parts of Italy where the quality of truffles isn't as prized, but the experience is just as fun only without the crowds. In San

Giovanni d'Asso in Tuscany, a truffle fair takes place the second and third weeks of November. This is where you can really mingle with the locals while shopping at food stalls and participating in truffle dinners in local restaurants. To get a hands-on experience, Asso Tartufi (www.assotartufi.it) can arrange a morning truffle hunt and tasting with an expert.

If you've never heard of the Marche region in Italy, you're not alone. Located between the Apennine Mountains and the Adriatic Sea, this little-known gem is a great alternative to Tuscany, particularly for its culinary scene. The town of Aqualagna is prime truffle grounds. For a splurge, go to the Michelin-starred Symposium, an unassuming restaurant/inn that's tucked deep in the woods on a country road. An Aqualagna truffle dinner here is an experience you won't soon forget, especially because it's paired with gems from the three-room, 25,000-bottle wine cellar. www.symposium4stagioni.it

One of the youngest industries can be found right here in the United States, in **Oregon,** where the soil and climate are ideal for truffle growing. Oregon has only been in the business for a few years, but it's certainly made a name for itself. Truffle season is in January, and the Oregon Truffle Festival in Eugene is the place to experience these gourmet treats. This is a well-organized, 3-day event—the first of its kind in the English-speaking world—where you can get hands-on experience growing, cultivating, cooking, and eating truffles prepared by high-end chefs. The culinary apex is the Grand Truffle Dinner, which includes a five-course meal of native winter white and black truffles paired with Oregon wines. There's even a truffle dog training seminar, where 20 pups can learn how to recognize Périgord and Oregon truffles and get to try hunting them in the wild. Or just sit back and watch a truffle dog demonstration in action with trained canines. www.oregontrufflefestival.com

When the Italian and French varieties are out of season, chefs and connoisseurs turn to Western **Australia.** This part of the continent produces more black truffles than any other region in Oz and supplies top US chefs with black truffles in the summer months. The

Wine and Truffle Company is the largest producer of fresh truffles in the Southern Hemisphere and is the largest mainland truffle-growing company in Australia. Located 4½ hours south of Perth at Hazelhill Estate, an area where climatic and soil factors are similar to truffle-producing regions of France and Italy, the company produces about 5,500 pounds of truffles each year, which grow around the groves of hazel and oak trees. You can join a hunt with the estate's truffle-hunting dogs every weekend between June and August, and participate in truffle dinners featuring pairings with Australian wines. www.wineandtruffle.com.au

Just 45 minutes from Perth is Mundaring, home of the picturesque Sculpture Park and the Mundaring Truffle Festival. This event is considered *the* food festival on the Western Australian calendar. We're talking everything from "master" classes in the art of the truffle to high-end truffle dinners presented by leading Australian chefs, truffle dog demonstrations, an open-air market, and much more. www.mundaringtrufflefestival.com

Alternate Truffle Regions

The Périgord region in **France** is famous for its aromatic black truffles. The town of Lalbenque is home to the chaotic Marché aux Truffes, a weekly market that takes place for the few short weeks in midwinter when truffles are harvested. In the Istria region of **Croatia,** truffles are found that command just as high a price as those harvested in Italy and France. The tiny town of Livade hosts two truffle fairs each fall, Zigante Tartufi Days (www.sajamtartufa.com) and Tuberfest. They are both in October and showcase white truffles. They feature auctions, foraging demonstrations, and a contest for the biggest and most beautiful truffles.

Best Places to Find

SIGNATURE DISHES

I have a general rule about travel and restaurants: I don't have a favorite restaurant; I have favorite dishes at individual restaurants. There's no better way to get to know a destination than to fall in love with one signature dish everywhere you go. So I'm guilty as charged.

APPETIZERS

Bread is something that is usually overlooked by many restaurants, and by customers as well, but not by me. The bread served at A Figueira Rubaiyat in São Paulo, **Brazil,** is nothing short of extraordinary. The food at this restaurant is great, but the bread is the best. It's a chewy, rich interpretation of *pão de queijo*, Brazil's famous cheese bread. How many times have you been warned by your mother (or a close friend) not to "fill up" on bread and ruin your appetite? This Brazilian restaurant is the exception to that rule—ignore the admonition, and please fill up. www.rubaiyat.com.br

For me, Indian food is all about the naan and the appetizers. We're talking about something called *chaat*, or savory Indian street snacks. In Cape Town, **South Africa,** go to the Bombay Brasserie inside the Taj Hotel. Don't worry about the entrees. Ask for the *bhalla chaat*, which is made of soft lentil dumplings in yogurt with sweet mango relish. www.tajhotels.com

In **Washington, DC,** Rasika serves the best garlic naan with herbs, and its signature dish is *palak chaat*—crispy baby spinach, sweet yogurt, tamarind, and date chutney. And if you don't order seconds (my bet is that you will), then move on to a main dish of tandoori salmon, made with organic Scottish salmon, cinnamon, and black pepper. www.rasikarestaurant.com

The best tapas can be found in a place called El Carajo, located in a decidedly unsexy part of **Miami.** This place looks like 7-Eleven merged with a liquor store and a gas station. In fact, it *is* a wine store, and, yes, you can also buy motor oil and a spare battery. But you really go there for the tapas. Try the *coquetas de bacalao* (codfish croquettes) or the amazing *pulpo a la gallega* (octopus Galician style, from northwest Spain). www.elcarajointernationaltapasandwines.com

SEAFOOD

Never underestimate the quality and inventiveness of the menu at small American strip mall restaurants. In Juno Beach, **Florida,** I found one that serves the best tuna on the planet and in the most inventive way. The place is called Captain Charlie's Reef Grill, and it's located in a strip mall so tiny that it's easy to miss (drive on Highway 1 and look for an interior design store and a fire station). Folks (myself included) will drive more than an hour to get there, just to stand in line for 45 minutes waiting for a table. What's even more amazing is the menu—handwritten and photocopied each day on three legal-size pages. The entrée and appetizer creations number in the dozens, and how they manage this menu in such a small place is still baffling. But one thing on that menu stands out and is a local favorite: peppered tuna medallions with blueberry teriyaki sauce. Doesn't sound great, until you put it in your mouth and find yourself unabashedly ordering seconds.

How about the best grouper in the world? It's at Laurel's Restaurant and Bar in **St. Lucia.** Here, there are only about six tables and a small bar. Talk about the catch of the day: It's great *every* day. The shrimp and the chicken are also excellent, but when you order the grouper, they throw it in the pan and make culinary magic right in front of you, since the kitchen is about 5 feet away. The restaurant isn't easy to find in the Bois d'Orange section of Quarter of Gros-Islet—there are no street signs or lights. So get them on the phone and have them direct the cab driver.

My pick for the best sushi might surprise a lot of my sushi-snob friends. I'm not picking Nobu in New York (although their black cod is amazing). There are two great sushi experiences: The first are the sushi stalls right next to the Central Fish Market in **Tokyo.** Go to the fish auction there around 4:30 a.m. each day. The auction ends just before 6 a.m., and that's when you walk about a hundred feet to any one of a half dozen or so sushi stalls with the freshest fish ever. Strange as it may seem, nothing beats incredible eel rolls at 6:15 in the morning.

In the United States, the place to go for an almost religious sushi experience is in Honolulu, **Hawaii.** Sushi Sasabune is located on King Street, and it's almost easy to miss it. Once there, be prepared to wait for your table, but leave all your past sushi dining experiences at home. Why? Because the sushi masters (as well as the waiters there) all wear shirts that say "trust me." Translation: You don't order. They order for you. They present the sushi, and then they tell you how to eat it and what sauce to use (or avoid). In my experience, they've never been wrong. So I can't tell you to order the sesame calamari wrapped around blue crab. But I can tell you to beg the waiter to bring you another order. His answer (when I asked) was, "Wait . . . you will eat in order, and I will get you one later." If I could eat there every night, I would.

Tasmania and seafood go hand in hand, so it's no surprise that some of the best shrimp in the world comes out of here. Tasmania has very strict quarantine regulations, which keep its environment pristine and disease free. The seafood industry also practices sustainable techniques. Top-notch shrimp is available year-round. Along with shrimp, the area is known for its incredible oysters, wild abalone, and scallops. Waterfront seafood restaurants abound in Tasmania, including some local favorites like Blue Skies (www.blueskiesdining.com), located in a working port in Hobart and featuring an extensive wine list and a must-order tasting plate of hot and cold Tasmanian seafood. Or you can go even more casual at Fish Frenzy (www.fishfrenzy.com.au) in Hobart's Sullivan's Cove, which has some of the best fish-and-chips in Tasmania.

Some regions are known for a certain food for good reason. **Norway** produces what is known as fjord trout, a red, sea-farmed salmon with firm, tender flesh. It can be eaten raw, as well as smoked, salted, grilled, etc. You can go fishing for trout along the bridge to the island of Garten—an old fishing port that's considered one of the top fishing areas in Norway, located about 8 hours north of Oslo. A little more convenient to travelers, the Oslo fjord is also a good spot for fishing, and you can arrange guided fishing tours with companies like Oslo Fjord Boat Fishing (www.oslofjordboatfishing. com). Any foreigner can fish for free in saltwater, but fishing for sea trout from rivers and lakes does require a state fishing license, which can be bought at any local post office. Many lakes and rivers are privately owned, so a local fishing permit must also be acquired from landowners and is available at gas stations or at Inatur.no.

For the best mussels, head to Brasserie Beck in **Washington, DC** (www.beckdc.com). What makes these mussels so wonderful isn't just the creamy garlic sauce they're cooked in. It's also the incredible Belgian fries that come with them. Another option is Flex Mussels (www.flexmussels.com) in **New York,** which has two locations. The options on this extensive mussels menu are staggering. Why just order them the traditional way in white wine and garlic? Instead, order the Parmesan-crusted mussels. But be careful. The serving pan is almost molten hot when it gets to the table.

Last, but certainly not least, the Utah beach oysters are out of this world at L'Ecailler du Bistrot in the 11th arrondissement in **Paris.**

MAIN COURSES

Like a hearty breakfast with every single possible option? Then try Hash House a Go Go in **Las Vegas.** It's not on the Strip, and it will take you a little while by cab to get there. It's also not open 24 hours a day, which is a rarity in Sin City. Breakfast is served starting at 7:30 a.m. As its name implies, this place is hash and more hash, ranging from roasted chicken hash to corned beef hash to smoked salmon hash to japaleño hash. And don't forget its signature griddled meat loaf with smoked mozzarella. The portions, I should caution you, are huge. www.hashhouseagogo.com

The best steak tartare is in **Paris,** of course. And the best steak tartare in Paris can be found at a legendary place that hasn't changed in more than a hundred years: Brasserie Lipp, on boulevard Saint-Germain (walking distance to the Musée d'Orsay). This is the

classic preparation, made tableside in the most traditional manner
www.ila-chateau.com/lipp

When you think of pizza, about the very last place you'd imagine finding the best is in **Switzerland.** But that's where it is, in the Engadin region—more specifically, St. Moritz. What mountains! What lakes! What pizza! Head up the mountain (Corviglia) on the ski lift to the top. When you get to 8,000 feet, that's where you'll find Mathis Food Affairs. It looks like any other mountaintop ski restaurant, but owner Reto Mathis, who is a legend in the region, disabuses you of that notion the minute you sit down. It's okay to look at the menu, which boasts contemporary alpine cuisine, but only order the pizza. Important note: It's not called pizza; it's actually a *tarte flambée,* or a *flammkueche,* an old Alsatian specialty. It's made with an extremely thin and crispy dough, topped with *fromage blanc* (ricotta), and then layered with raw onion rings, bacon strips, Brie, and coarsely grated Fontina. It's baked very hot, at 300 degrees Celsius (!) for about 2 minutes. Then Reto adds shaved truffles and truffle oil. I always order two, and if a friend goes with me, I order three. I won't share! www.mathisfood.ch

When it comes to food and wine, stop. Do not pass Go. Head directly to an airport and fly to Cape Town, **South Africa,** and the tasting room at Le Quartier Français in Franschhoek. Owner Susan Huxter has a menu that you can only dream about (after you leave and, of course, before your return visit). The wine pairings are phenomenal, and there is no one best dish. Surrender your plans and have Susan order for you. www.lequartier.co.za

Argentina is a beef-oriented country. The dollar is still king there, which means you can dine like one and walk out of the restaurant with your wallet as full as your stomach. When dining in a Buenos Aires steakhouse, don't expect to get out before midnight—and only after dining on platter after platter of top-quality cuts of meat, to the point that you might wonder if you just ate a whole cow. Skirt steak, in particular, comes from the belly of the cow. It's an inexpensive cut, tougher than many other cuts, which makes it prime for marinating and braising. It may be called *churrasco,* but that usually refers to any thin, boneless slice of meat that's grilled or cooked in a hot pan. One of the top steakhouses in Buenos Aires is Cabaña Las Lilas, which raises its own cattle. Even before you dive into the meat selection, you'll gorge yourself on cheese, olives, tomatoes, anchovies, and garlic bread. www.laslilas.com/restaurant.php

The famous muffuletta from **New Orleans** is made of soft, round Sicilian bread loaded up with salami, ham, and provolone, and then topped with the all-important savory olive salad—made with a blend of olives, vegetables, garlic, seasonings, and olive oil and marinated for at least a day. (You can buy jars of this addictive topping as well.) The name *muffuletta* translates into "little muffin" and originally referred to just the bread. Although it is available all over New Orleans, the best place to get it is Central Grocery, the birthplace of the muffuletta. But arrive early, as the lines get long. One important caution: A number of my friends go there en route to the airport and order two to go, with many extra napkins. Why two? Once you open the sandwich on the airplane, your seatmates will want to sample it.

SIDES

Yes, there really is such a thing as the best coleslaw. And if you want some, you should go to the Cherry Creek Grill in **Denver.** Their coleslaw is nothing short of amazing. Served with a special peanut and soy sauce, it is so great that I actually fly to Denver at least once a year and make a coleslaw run and order it as an entree. It's so good I've even had friends go there and do coleslaw takeout! www.hillstone.com/#/restaurants/cherryCreekGrill/

A lot of places claim to have the best macaroni and cheese in the world. But the one place that does it exactly right is a restaurant called 1300 on Fillmore in **San Francisco.** Here, they serve soulful American cuisine, including a phenomenal macaroni and white Cheddar cheese. Ask them to add just a little extra cheese and burn it slightly on top. www.1300fillmore.com

FARM TO TABLE

Madison, **Wisconsin,** has the best farmers' market in America, and Harvest Restaurant, just 30 feet from the Dane County Farmers' Market, has the best evolving, seasonal, farm-to-table menu I've found. Try the heirloom tomato salad or the house-made tagliatelle served with pork sausage and arugula. www.harvest-restaurant.com

In Aurora, **New York,** on Route 90, the Pumpkin Hill Bistro is located inside a 19th-century farmhouse. The best dish of all? A signature smoked gouda and artichoke dip, which is a seductive blend of four cheeses, spinach, and roasted artichokes served bubbling hot with toasted wheat pita chips. www.pumpkinhillbistro.com

In Cape Town, **South Africa,** do lunch at the truly five-star, 24-room Steenberg Hotel. It's the oldest farm in the Constantia Valley; the land grant goes back to 1682. Order the cured Franshhoek salmon trout (with prawn and avocado). But leave the wine ordering to Gaby Gramm, the hotel's general manager. www.steenberghotel.com

DESSERTS

Firinda sutlac is a creamy rice dish from Istanbul that is vastly different (most say superior) from American rice pudding. It dates back to royal kitchens of the Ottoman Empire and can be found in pudding shops and restaurants all over Turkey. The best rice pudding in **Istanbul** is in a small restaurant called Tarihi Subasi Lokantas, near the famed covered bazaar. When you get to the covered bazaar main entrance, do *not* go inside; instead, turn right and walk to the end of the block. You'll find the restaurant on your right. The word *tarihi* means historic, and this rice pudding, which is torched on the top (much like the better crème brûlées) is epic. I don't go to Istanbul without stopping there. Twice.

For chocolate mousse, there is absolutely no comparison. I travel at least once a year for my chocolate mousse fix at a little restaurant in **Lisbon** called Papa Açorda, in the Alfama District. Make sure your hotel concierge gets you an exact address for the place and a map, because many cab drivers don't even know about it. And be prepared to eat a lot of chocolate mousse. At Papa Açorda, it's not just how good the mousse is, but how much there is. You won't be served in a small pudding dish or an even smaller champagne glass. At Papa Açorda, the server brings an empty dinner plate to your table. Soon after, a waiter appears behind you with a very large bowl and an oversize serving spoon, and simply holds the bowl while you dig deep and serve yourself as much as you want. Okay, you've been warned!

Lebanese *kanefi* is dessert is made of a layer of shredded dough and a layer of cheese stuffed inside a dough with sesame seeds. You can find it all over Lebanon. But a little closer to home, you can find an outstanding version of it at Tanoreen Restaurant in **Brooklyn**'s Bay Ridge neighborhood. *Knafeh*, as they spell it, is their signature dessert. The shredded dough is stuffed with two kinds of sweet cheese, topped with pistachios and homemade syrup flavored with orange and rose water. It takes 15 minutes to make, and it's served fresh and hot. (While you're there, be sure to try chef-owner Rawia Bishara's eggplant dishes for which she's renowned.) www.tanoreen.com

The best black-bottom pie comes from a little joint called Weidmann's Restaurant, thought to be **Mississippi**'s oldest restaurant (operated almost continuously since 1870). The Meridian Amtrak station is down the street from Weidmann's, and people have been known to come from Louisiana and Mississippi just for a taste of that pie. The Crescent line departs New Orleans at 7 a.m. and arrives in Meridian at 11:02 a.m., before departing again at 11:07 a.m. People literally run off the train, grab an entire pie, and run back on the train! Want to know the secret of Weidmann's famous recipe? The black-bottom pie crust is made from crushed gingersnaps and butter, and topped with a layer of chocolate and then a creamy bourbon-flavored filling.

Most Expensive Cuisine

FleurBurger 5000 is a $5,000 burger at Fleur by Hubert Keller restaurant at the Mandalay Bay Hotel and Casino in **Las Vegas.** The burger is made with Wagyu beef and topped with foie gras, truffle sauce, and shaved black truffles on a brioche. But that's not all: It's served with a 1995 Château Pétrus from Bordeaux in Italian stemware that will be shipped to your home.

Nino's Positano Pizza in **New York** can create a caviar pizza for $1,000 (that's $125 a slice, if you're counting). The crust is topped with crème fraiche, four different types of caviar, sliced lobster tail, and salmon roe, and drizzled with wasabi sauce. Not surprisingly, this pizza has to be ordered 24 hours in advance.

Norma's restaurant dares you to choose its Zillion Dollar Lobster Frittata inside Le Parker Meridien Hotel in New York. This supersize dish is made with six eggs, roasted Maine lobster tail, and 10 ounces of caviar, for a grand total of $1,000.

On the Upper East Side of New York, Serendipity 3's Frrrozen Haute Chocolate goes for a whopping $25,000. Made with 28 types of cocoa, including some of the most expensive types from South America and South Africa, the hot beverage is infused with 0.2 ounce of edible gold and topped with whipped cream, more edible gold, and shavings of the world's most expensive chocolate truffle from La Madeline au Truffe. Don't worry, you won't be left empty-handed once the drink is gone. You also get an 18-karat gold bracelet with diamonds and the diamond-encrusted gold goblet and spoon that it's served in.

The founder of Three Twins Ice Cream, Neal Gottlieb, is so invested in his certified organic ice cream that he'll personally deliver 100 pints to you (almost) anywhere in the United States for the cool price of $3,333.33. Visit the store at Oxbow Public Market in Napa, **California,** you've got even more options: The World's Most Expensive Ice Cream Sundae is $3,333.33—a banana split made with syrups from three rare dessert wines (a 1960s vintage port, a Château D'Yquem, and a German Trockenbeerenauslese), served with an ice-cream spoon from the 1850s. Order it a day ahead and it will come with a performance by a cellist. If you've got $60,000 to spend, go for the World's More Expensive Most Expensive Ice Cream Sundae: It comes with first-class airfare to Tanzania, where you'll climb Mount Kilimanjaro with Gottlieb and he'll hand-churn a batch of ice cream made with glacial ice from the summit. The price also includes five-star accommodations and, of course, all the ice cream you can eat. http://threetwinsicecream.com

STREET FOOD

PORTLAND

The Pacific Northwest is home to high-quality local ingredients, and Portland is a food-obsessed city. The result? A glut of specialty food carts selling everything from Cuban fare to crepes. What sets these vendors apart from other cities is that they tend to stay in one place in rented spaces, with more than two dozen lots scattered throughout the city. Just keep in mind that due to the weather, many carts close up for the winter. Your best bet is to check www.foodcartsportland.com for the latest news in food carts throughout Portland.

Join the late-night scene at Hawthorne and SE 12th, where Whiffies (www.whiffies.com) serves up fried pies, both savory and sweet, from barbecue beef brisket to a Mounds bar–inspired confection with coconut cream and chocolate chips.

The Mississippi Marketplace, at North Mississippi and Skidmore Street in North Portland, has 10,000 square feet of space loaded with carts, including the Big Egg, which focuses entirely on breakfast using cage-free, organic eggs.

On SE 43rd and Belmont, the Good Food Here hosts nearly 20 carts, including a local favorite, the Sugar Cube (www.thesugarcubepdx.com), where chef-owner Kir Jensen makes every gourmet cupcake, milkshake, and smoothie inside her 8- by 14-foot cart.

LOS ANGELES

Street food has long been a part of Los Angeles's food culture in the form of taco trucks. But the concept of gourmet trucks went mainstream in LA with the Kogi barbecue to-go (www.kogibbq.com) truck, which brought Korean-Mexican fusion to the streets. From there was an explosion of gourmet eats.

The Grilled Cheese Truck (www.thegrilledcheesetruck.com) has one of the best things you can get: the cheesy mac and rib sandwich. Even restaurants have gotten into the food truck game, like the

Border Grill (www.bordergrill.com), which serves modern, upscale Mexican food both from a truck and from brick-and-mortar restaurants. Meanwhile, other trucks have evolved into stand-alone restaurants, like the local favorite, Coolhaus (http://eatcoolhaus.com) gourmet ice-cream sandwiches.

In a city as spread out as LA, there is no one good place to catch these trucks. But a good bet is to head to the Miracle Mile on mid-Wilshire Boulevard during lunchtime; the lot of Figueroa Produce in the Highland Park neighborhood every Tuesday; Venice Beach on the first Friday of the month; and downtown's Art Walk on the second Thursday of the month.

AUSTIN

Austin's Sixth Street is buzzing with nightlife, making the surrounding streets a natural magnet for food carts serving late-night eats.

A local favorite is Lucky J's Chicken and Waffles, which has both a trailer on Sixth and Waller, and a brick-and-mortar restaurant on Burnet Road. It serves the classic fried chicken over waffles, and uses the humble waffle as a tacolike vehicle filled with savory (bacon, egg, potato, onions, and Cheddar) or sweet (bananas, peanut butter, Nutella, and honey). www.luckyjs.com

It's not easy for a barbecue joint to stand out in Texas, but Franklin Barbecue has done just that with its hand-cut, slow-smoked (up to 18 hours!) brisket, pork rib, and pulled rib. It started out as a food trailer, but has since expanded into a brick-and-mortar establishment that's always packed with hungry locals. www.franklinbarbecue.com

Everything is bigger in Texas—even its doughnuts. At Gourdough's, the tagline is "Big. Fat. Donuts." And they're not kidding: Ask for a knife and fork when you order. The big seller here is the Flying Pig, a doughnut topped with crispy bacon and maple syrup icing. And for a "lighter" touch, opt for the Son of a Peach, stuffed with peach filling and topped with cinnamon, sugar, and . . . cake mix. www.gourdoughs.com

PUERTO RICO

When someone says "foodie destination," Puerto Rico may not be the first place that comes to mind. But the culinary culture here is diverse and exciting, with Caribbean flavors known as *cocina criolla* that come from Spanish, Taino Indian, and African influences.

Old San Juan is packed with vans and stalls selling snack foods, and on a hot day, don't miss the local treat known as *piraguas*, fruit-flavored shaved ice. But the real treat is at the Tico Triplet truck at the corner of Calle Comercio an Calle de San Justo (near the pier), which serves up a meaty sandwich filled with thin slices of beef, pork, and chicken, smothered in ketchup, mustard, and mayonnaise.

The real foodie destination is just outside the town of Luquillo, where dozens of kiosks line the beach—each with its own menu and personality. Look for seafood kiosks to sample Puerto Rico's legendary conch. La Parilla is among the best for authentic *mofongo relleno*, made of mashed green plantains stuffed with vegetables, and is known for its fiery homemade hot sauce.

PARIS

Though not exactly a mecca for food trucks, Paris is known for its cafe culture, and that's just as satisfying when it comes to experiencing the local street food flavor.

The quintessential street foods of Paris? Crepes, of course. These thin crispy-soft pancakes can be sweet or savory, whether layered with Nutella and bananas or egg and cheese. Crepe stands in the farmers' markets generally make them with the freshest ingredients. Marché Richard Lenoir off rue Oberkampf is an outdoor market with outstanding crepes. In the evenings, crepe stands open up in and around Montparnasse and around any nightclub area.

Then there are those Parisian sandwiches. Some of the best combos are salami-olive-cheese, tuna-crudité-egg, or a simple ham and cheese, each served on a fresh-from-the-oven baguette. For a great selection of *boulangeries*, head to the Latin Quarter in the Left Bank near Saint-Michel. But if you want a sandwich made on one of the best baguettes in the city, you have to go to the flagship store of Philippe Gosselin on boulevard Saint-Germain. Light and crusty, these *baguette de tradition* are so coveted they've twice been awarded the honor of being served at the presidential Élysée Palace for a year. Most recently, baker Pascal Barillon was awarded that honor for the baguettes served at his Au Levain d'Antan on rue des Abbesses in the Montmartre district.

BANGKOK

Bangkok is the world capital of street food, and there are literally thousands of places to get it. In fact, the best food in Thailand is served by street vendors and cafes, so you can get an amazing culinary experience without ever stepping foot in a high-end restaurant. The food you'll find in Bangkok is not just Thai food: You can also find stalls serving Chinese, Indian, Malay, and more.

Yaowarat Road in Chinatown is one of best places in Bangkok for street food. You'll find dozens of stalls serving up Chinese and Thai dishes such as grilled duck, river prawns, sweet black sesame dumplings, *pad kii mao* (drunken noodles), and red pork rice. Stalls are open from evening till the wee hours of morning. Nearby Phahurat Street is a small Indian community with dozens of street food stalls.

Sukhumvit Soi 38, near the Thonglor skytrain station, is a small lane that comes alive at night with its huge variety of food stalls. Locals, expats, and visitors all flock here for late-night eats, everything from traditional pad thai to crab wontons to sweet mango sticky rice. Come morning, if you're still hungry, Sukhumvit Soi 55 has numerous stalls that offer Thai breakfast staples such as rice noodles in soup and *johk* (rice porridge).

You can't miss the giant red swing monument that marks Sao Ching-Cha. It's known as one of the most diverse areas for street food—particularly cheap noodle shops as well as local favorites like barbecued duck and *mee krob*.

JAMAICA

The West Indies have a long tradition of street food, which has African and sometimes Latin American influences. Some of the most authentic culinary experiences can be found by heading out to the roadside stands, beach shacks, and cafes alongside the country's roads and rivers. There's even something called a Jerk Trail, with 22 restaurants across the island serving Jamaican jerk.

The good news is, there's little possibility of getting sick because fruit is usually freshly picked and seafood is sourced from nearby. Other dishes are either jerked or slow-cooked for hours over a low flame. And the capsicum in jerk seasoning is one of nature's most potent and effective natural preservatives.

If there's one place I always make time to visit in Jamaica, it's Scotchie's. This is the place to get traditional Jamaican jerk. There's an outpost in Ocho Rios, but my advice is to go to the original stand in Montego Bay, just outside of Rose Hall. These guys cook over an open flame over traditional sweetwood—believe me, it gets hot back there. No need to dress up or spend a lot of money here. This is the real island experience. And speaking of hot, if you don't otherwise mention it, your food gets a liberal dose of hot sauce. Result: More than one Red Stripe beer will be needed!

Billy's Grassy Park in Middle Quarters, St. Elizabeth, in the southwestern corner of the island is one of the best, most out-of-the-way places. (There's no street address and no landmarks nearby, so just ask around and someone will point the way). It specializes in shrimp, including spicy pepper shrimp, crunchy french-fried shrimp, and shrimp soup with potato, plus Jamaican specialties like peanut porridge, and peas and rice.

Miss Wissy's (a.k.a. Belinda's Riverside Canteen) isn't technically a "roadside" stand, since it's only accessible by taking a rafting trip down the Rio Grande from Port Antonio. But it's worth the trip just to taste the exquisite local cuisine like curried goat, pepper pot soup, fried dumplings, and plantain tarts—which are all Miss Wissy's specialties.

EVERYTHING ELSE

Beyond being on a destination quest, the true global traveler is an experience junkie. And part of that experience addiction involves seeing the journey as one big meal, both literally and figuratively. Eating your way through a trip can reveal all sorts of new and interesting flavors—from olive oil to octopus to currywurst!

SPECIALTY SHOPS

Although most people think of salt as a basic seasoning in the form of iodized table salt, the varieties of finishing salts are truly staggering. To get a primer, just check in with "selmelier" Mark Bitterman at the Meadow in Portland, **Oregon,** a gourmet shop that specializes in artisan salt, both quarried and from the sea. He carries more than 100 different kinds of *fleur de sel*, flake salt, and *sel gris*; smoked salts; infused salts; and even blocks from Himalayan quarries that you can use as a plate. There's an outpost in New York, but the original location is really the one to see. www. atthemeadow.com

Ever heard of mahlab? Do you know the difference between Hungarian and Indian paprika? How about the price of saffron per gram? It's all there at the Spice Station in Santa Monica, **California.** Bins and jars of spices, herbs, salts, and chiles are on full display. Browse, ask questions, and then figure out the right seasoning for your next dish. http://spicestationsilverlake.com

The olive oil industry in the Napa Valley is relatively young, but the St. Helena Olive Oil Company has some of the best extra-virgin olive oils and wine vinegars in the state. You can shop in the St. Helena store (housed in a former nightclub), but a better choice is the more industrial production facility and shop in Rutherford, where you can ask for a private tasting. www.sholiveoil.com

You won't find more Italian specialties under one roof than in Eataly, in **Manhattan**'s Flatiron District. Based on a concept from Turin, Italy, this 5,000-square-foot culinary mecca is part-owned by beloved chefs Mario Batali and Lidia Bastianich. The selection is almost overwhelming, which is why locals are willing to brave the crowds (and the prices) to go again and again—whether browsing in the marketplace for fresh pastas, cured meats, olive oils, or produce from the "vegetable butcher," or sitting down for a complete meal. Finish it off with a drink on the rooftop bar, Birreria. http://eatalyny.com

There's no shortage of sandwich shops in the college town of Ann Arbor, **Michigan,** but Zingerman's Delicatessen is an experience unto itself. Along with mile-high sandwiches, this local institution sells a selection of cheeses, honey, jams, olive oils, teas, and pretty much any other gourmet specialty food you can think of. www.zingermansdeli.com

You may not think a grocery store could top a food list, but when you're talking about the flagship Whole Foods in Austin, **Texas,** it's worth the trip. Located on Sixth Street and Lamar, this enormous center has a mind-boggling array of organic produce, meats, international cheeses, and a huge array of packaged and prepared foods. There's also a culinary center for a hands-on experience or for watching chef demos. www.wholefoods.com

Consider Edible Canada as a one-stop shop for the best of Canada's culinary scene. Located inside **Vancouver**'s foodie haven, Granville Market, the retail shop features northern products like lobster oil made from Nova Scotia lobsters, jams and jellies from an organic farm in British Columbia, and hazelnuts from an organic orchard in the Fraser Valley. There's also an on-site bistro showcasing Canadian cuisine, regular market tours, chef dinners, and even a "kayak to your dinner" trip to the Gulf Islands. www.ediblecanada.com

Japan has dozens of offbeat and wonderful specialty food museums, "theme parks," and emporiums that allow you to taste a variety of versions of one dish or food in a single location. The Shinyokohama Ramen Museum in Yokohama is exactly what it sounds like: a museum dedicated to ramen. (Believe it or not, this Japanese staple actually came from China.) It became hugely popular in Japan in the 1950s, hence the midcentury theme of the two basement restaurant floors, which feature a replica of a Tokyo neighborhood. Here you can choose from nine different ramen restaurants, each of which offers noodles from a different region of Japan. www.raumen.co.jp/ramen

Or, simply do what I do. Before leaving home, buy a box (or two) of toothpicks. Then when landing in Tokyo, head to the Daimaru (www.daimaru.co.jp) or Mitsukoshi (www.mitsukoshi.co.jp) department stores. Look for the food halls, with the most amazing displays of fruits and vegetables and other delectables. (Want to see a $100 perfect melon? It's right there.) Here's how you play the sampling game. The stores routinely put out samples of their food on counters throughout the food halls. But you've come prepared—armed with an ample supply of toothpicks. Need I say more?

REGIONAL FOOD

The Germans know how to do sausage, and Zum Schiffchen (little boat) in the Old Town section of Düsseldorf, **Germany,** is a great, atmospheric place to get it. In addition to trying different types of sausage, you can also chow down on stews, sauerkraut, herring, and oxtail soup, and quaff cold German beers amid the high beams and crystal chandeliers of this 380-year-old brew haus (which Napoleon reputedly ate at). www.brauerei-zum-schiffchen.de

Ever heard of currywurst? It's basically a pork hot dog smothered in curry sauce and served with greasy fries. The best place to get it?

Best Butchers

The movement to embrace local and organic foods has even extended to butchers! Instead of buying prewrapped meat from your grocery store, you can actually talk to someone behind the counter of a neighborhood butcher shop who knows where the meat comes from and which cut is the best. In **Los Angeles,** Lindy & Grundy (www.lindyandgrundy.com) is owned and operated by two women who work with area ranchers to sell only pastured and organic meats. **Brooklyn**'s The Meat Hook (http://the-meathook.com) is a hipster haven with an old-school butcher shop that works closely with New York State farmers. (Ask about a butchering class, where you can break down an entire pig from nose to tail!) And in **Portland,** Oregon, Laurelhurst Market (www.laurelhurstmarket.com) is part organic butcher shop, part steakhouse, where practically everything is made in-house, from charcuterie to smoked sausages.

Curry 36 in the Kreuzberg neighborhood of Berlin. Don't expect any-thing fancy—this is basically a fast-food joint where you stand and eat curry meatballs, curry cutlets, and bratwurst. This is especially a hit for the late-night crowd looking to soak up the liquor, so it's usually open until 4 a.m. www.curry36.de

Sicily is where the cannoli was invented, so it makes sense that Palermo would have one of the best places in the world to buy them: Pasticceria Cappello. But that's not all it has. This half-century-old bakery makes pastries that are practically miniature works of art. The chocolate *torta Setteveli* is a seven-layer cake made from alter-nating layers of chocolate, hazelnut, and mousse. Or try the *cassat-ina*, a traditional Sicilian sponge cake filled with ricotta cheese and smothered with pistachio paste. www.pasticceriacappello.it

Hot dogs in **Iceland**? That's right, Bæjarins Beztu has been selling *pylsu* (basically lamb dogs), since 1937 at the Reykjavik harbor. As if there were any doubt that Bæjarins Beztu's are the best in town, the store's name actually translates to "the best in town." There's even a hot dog named after Bill Clinton, one of the many famous folks who've eaten here while on a visit to Iceland. http://bbp.is/en

Sure, you have to try Key lime pie when you're in **Florida,** and of course the best is in the Keys. Pepe's Cafe (www.pepescafe.net) in Key West has been around since 1909, and makes its tart pie with a graham cracker crust and serves it in a bowl, not a plate. While every guidebook mentions Joe's Stone Crab in Miami Beach (www.joesstonecrab.com), it's partly because the Key lime pies (and the stone crabs!) are that good.

Of course, the debate over who has the best lobster roll in **Maine** could go on forever. After all, its coastline stretches 3,500 miles, and there are countless unassuming ocean-side shacks serving buttery lobster chunks in soft hot dog buns. (There's also some debate over whether lobster salad, bound with mayonnaise, counts as tradi-tional.) My pick should come as no surprise among lobster roll aficio-nados: Red Eats, located in Wicassett, where mounds of tail and claw meat are served on a toasted buttered bun. Mayo is optional.

That said, there are plenty of places outside of Maine that can rival even the best. In Newport, **Rhode Island,** try Flo's Clam Shack (www.flosclamshack.net) across the street from First Beach. And in Clinton, **Connecticut,** Lobster Landing wins for its quarter-pound lobster rolls served along the Long Island Sound.

Ventura, **California,** is a quiet seaside town halfway between the better-known enclaves of Los Angeles and Santa Barbara. On San Buenaventura State Beach, you'll find the Jolly Oyster, a unique stand that offers sweet-tasting Kumamoto and Pacific oysters, grown by the owner at a farm in Baja California. You can eat them raw right there, or bring them home to shuck and prepare yourself. www.thejollyoyster.com

Mangonui is a quiet seaside town in Northland, **New Zealand.** It's a bit of a trek to get to Mangonui Fish Shop, but once you take your first bite of one of their offerings, you'll know what all the fuss is about. Everything is made from fish caught fresh that day, which consists of New Zealand species such as John Dory, hapuka, and blue nose. In addition to the classic Kiwi fish-and-chips, you can get crayfish and various types of smoked fish. Enjoy it while sitting on the deck (built on piles over the harbor) and admiring the stunning view of Doubtless Bay.

You might expect the best fish-and-chips to be in London, but in fact, you want to head toward the coast to get the really fresh stuff. Harbour Lights Traditional Fish and Chips in the seaside town of

Chef Demos

Not sure what to do with all that produce you picked up? Many farmers' markets will feature chefs demonstrating their skills, using items straight from the market. The famous Union Square Greenmarket in **New York City** has cooking demos every Monday, Wednesday, Friday, and Saturday mornings. The Ferry Plaza Farmers Market in **San Francisco** is another hot spot for local chefs—you'll see them shopping here. They also put on demonstrations every Saturday in a series hosted by the Center for Urban Education about Sustainable Agriculture. In **Dallas,** a Chef at the Market series takes place at the Dallas Farmers Market (www.dfmfriends.org) between late May and October.

Falmouth in Cornwall, **England,** is known for more than just its fried food. It was one of the first "chippies" to take a stance on sustainability by refusing to serve any endangered species (like cod roe and skate), so you know you're dining on fish that's fresh, local, and ecoconscious. www.harbourlights.co.uk

Naples, **Italy,** is the birthplace of traditional Italian pizza and has more than 12,000 pizzerias. But they're not all great . . . or even that good. Fortunately, Pizzeria da Michele makes what is possibly the perfect, simple margherita pizza: tomatoes, mozzarella, basil, and oil. There is only a handful of tables in the small shop, so the line can go out the door—but just wait it out because it's worth it.

If a trip to Napoli isn't on your agenda, how about New Haven? Pizza has been part of the fabric of this **Connecticut** city for decades, when Italian immigrants who perfected this hometown favorite opened up dozens of holes-in-the-wall around Wooster Square. Frank Pepe Pizzeria Napoletana continues its long tradition as the best, which is why you'll often see long lines. But don't balk—the legendary white clam pizza is well worth the wait. www.pepespizzeria.com

The debate over which region, state, or city makes the best barbecue could rage on for centuries. When it comes to the sweeter **Kansas City** style, Fiorella's Jack Stack Barbecue in the historic Freight

Market Tours

If you're overwhelmed by all the options, try a farmers' market tour, where a local can take you to the best stands, explain the history of the market, and score free samples along the way. Melting Pot Tours (www.meltingpottours.com) takes you through the Original Farmers Market in Los Angeles, where some stands have been in place for decades. In the Napa Valley, chef Julie Logue-Riordan (www.cookingwithjulie.com) will take you to the Napa Farmers Market on Tuesday or the St. Helena Farmer's Market on Fridays to meet the purveyors and sample everything from locally grown olives to a diverse array of cheeses. In Colle di Val d'Elsa in Italy, American expatriate Judy Witts Francini (www.divinacucina.com) leads Friday market tours followed by a cooking class using those ingredients.

House not only serves slow-smoked barbecued ribs, beef, and chicken, but also has a fantastic ambiance—25-foot ceilings girded with exposed wood beams, a see-through fireplace, giant windows, and outdoor dining overlooking Union Station and the city's rail yards. www.jackstackbbq.com

Without a doubt, the best Philly cheesesteaks are in . . . **Philadelphia,** of course. For old-school ultra-authentic cheesesteaks, head to Pat's King of Steaks (www.patskingofsteaks.com), the place where the steak sandwich was invented in 1930. It's still owned by the Olivieri family and still in the same location at the corner of Nineth and Passyunk after all these years. Order "one wiz wit" (a cheesesteak with Cheez Whiz and onions), and you'll understand why people come here at all hours to satisfy their cravings. However, there's some stiff competition to this classic from Cosmi's Deli (www.cosmideli.com). Order the Sam's, with cheese, mushrooms, peppers, and onion.

When it comes to Texas-style barbecue, preferred cooking styles vary based on whether you're in east, central, or west **Texas.** But if you're going to pick one place to go, it's Franklin Barbecue (www.franklinbarbecue.com) in Austin, which makes its incredible barbecue brisket over indirect heat over slabs of wood for a slow, 18-hour cook. Of course, in Texas Hill Country, you also can't miss the Salt Lick (www.saltlickbbq.com) in Driftwood, where meats are slow smoked over an open pit with the rolling hills as your backdrop.

EDUCATIONAL TRAVEL

Best Places for

MAKING AND FINDING (AND EATING) THE BEST FOODS

Part of being smart is admitting what you *don't* know. I'll admit: I'm just an okay cook. But I'm an extremely enthusiastic eater! I love to find great opportunities to both learn how to make new dishes and find the best places to sample new and exciting flavors. Even if I never become an expert in the kitchen, I've learned to become a pretty great taste tester. What better job is there?

HANDS-ON CLASSES

I f you've never heard of Walland, **Tennessee,** now is the time to get to know it. Here, tucked in the foothills of the Great Smoky Mountains, is a surprising food nirvana. Blackberry Farm is a luxury property located on 4,200 acres of land, where not only can you go horseback riding and fly-fishing, but you can roll up your sleeves and join in the work on the farm. Its Life on the Farm program gets you up close and personal with the farm's artisan producers: the butcher, the baker (there is no candlestick maker), a cheese maker, and a "jam lady." And you get to work alongside them to make preserves and cheese, help harvest the day's produce, or work with the chef to make the day's meals. www.blackberryfarm.com

For a really immersive experience, Artisans of Leisure will personalize your culinary vacation based entirely on your interests. It won't be cheap, but you will come away from it with a much deeper understanding of the culture through its food. You can travel through Bangkok and Chiang Mai, **Thailand,** taking cooking classes in every setting—from a private lesson inside a rural home, to local programs at the Blue Elephant Cooking School in Bangkok and the Chiang Mai Thai Cookery School, to the internationally known classes at the Four Seasons Resort Chiang Mai. Add on market and street food tours as well as an introduction to Thailand's extensive restaurants, and you've got an education worth traveling for. www.artisansofleisure.com

You don't have to be a die-hard food lover to know that traveling through **Italy** means eating, eating, and more eating. The question is, are you going to eat a plate of hastily cooked pasta in a tourist trap or delve into the local scene to find those special moments that make every calorie worthwhile? Delicious Italy focuses on those bragging-rights experiences, like learning to make cheese in the Abruzzo Mountains, picking olives and chestnuts in north Tuscany, or taking a boat into the Grado Lagoon to explore local trattorias serving the freshest fish and white wines known as Super-Whites.

A culinary tour of the up-and-coming region of Puglia is centered in the town of Lecce, where you'll explore everything from market shopping with a chef and grape picking to learning the intricacies of *cucina povera* (peasant cooking). www.deliciousitaly.com

What better way to learn to cook rustic Italian dishes than on an Italian farm? In the little-explored Marche region at the foothills of the Apennines Mountains, La Tavola Marche is an organic farm, inn, and cooking school housed in a 300-year-old stone farmhouse. In a daylong class, everything is made from scratch—no dishes of prechopped vegetables or dried pasta. The schedule varies based on the season. You might spend a morning picking olives, foraging for mushrooms, collecting eggs from free-range chickens, or jarring and preserving tomatoes. www.latavolamarche.com

It wouldn't be an experience in Italy without going to the market. Divina Cucina is run by Judy Witts Francini, an American chef and author who has made her home in Tuscany. A market-to-table class starts in the Friday market of Colle di Val d'Elsa, a medieval Tuscan hill town near San Gimignano and Siena. You'll pick up fresh fruits and vegetables from the local purveyors and then go into the kitchen to prepare a Tuscan meal. www.divinacucina.com

Canadian cooking doesn't get the attention it should, but when you're working with the fresh and diverse seafood of the Canadian coast, there's a lot to explore. We're talking all local seafood like salmon, swordfish, mussels, and six different types of tuna. Chefs at the **Nova Scotia** Seafood Cooking School source these ingredients from the nearby fisheries, and teach techniques like hot and cold smoking, making squid-ink pasta, and utilizing Creole cooking methods. You'll also go behind the scenes of the seafood industry, like an oyster farm where you'll eat oysters straight from the lake and a modern lobster storage facility to learn about some of the lobster in the world. www.acadianfarm.com/cookingschool.html

Ask food lovers about the cuisine of Oaxaca, **Mexico,** and they'll say one thing: mole! There are multiple types of this fabulously complex sauce, and not all of them involve chocolate. American expatriate Susana Trilling runs Seasons of My Heart, a kitchen and B&B

nestled in the palm fronds and desert cacti of the Etla Valley, just outside of Oaxaca City. If you opt to take her cooking lessons, your day will start with a trip to the Etla market to choose the ingredients for a five-course meal—which includes mole—that you'll be preparing for that night. While at the market, you can sample local items like Oaxacan cheeses, but you'll soon return to the kitchen for hours of hands-on lessons. Also on the menu is traditional Oaxacan chocolate pudding. www.seasonsofmyheart.com

It doesn't get much better than at Rancho La Puerta in Mexico's Baja California. Located in the town of Tecate, just south of the border (you can arrange free transportation from the San Diego airport), this 3,000-acre destination spa has all the elements for a foodie getaway. About 2 miles from the main property is a sprawling organic garden, Rancho Tres Estrellas, where more than 250 varieties of fruits, vegetables, and herbs are cultivated and harvested for daily meals. You can tour the gardens to learn about seasonality and organic growing methods—meaning minimal to no pesticides and a waste treatment facility to produce irrigation and fertilizer. Weekday hands-on cooking lessons mean you get to work side by side with the chef to make lunch or dinner. www.rancholapuerta.com

When someone says "Irish food," what comes to mind first? Potatoes, potatoes, or potatoes? Well, believe it or not, **Ireland**'s culinary scene is booming, and that's due in part to Darina Allen's Ballymaloe Cookery School. Based on a 100-acre organic farm, menus are focused almost entirely on what's in season and locally grown (they even source ingredients from neighbors). Seafood comes from boats that pull into the fishing village of Ballycotton, only a couple of miles away. You can participate in every aspect of farming: milking Jersey cows, feeding the free-range chickens, learning the basics of organic farming, and even pig butchering. Then, of course, there are the actual cooking classes. There is a longer-term, 12-week certification course, but shorter courses range from vegetarian dishes to one-pot meals. www.cookingisfun.ie

Located deep in a *hutong* (alley) off of Beijing, **China**'s bustling Nanluoguxiang Street is Black Sesame Kitchen. Founded by a

Chinese-American chef, this small school tends to cater to Western-ers looking for an authentic introduction into Chinese cooking. Led by Chef Zhang and a woman known as Chairman Wang, classes are both hands-on and demonstrative as you sit around a communal table that has everything from dumplings and noodles to braised meats and Chinese candied apples. www.blacksesamekitchen.com

With rich, slow-cooked *tajines*, colorful Moroccan salads, and the elaborate meat pie known as *b'stilla*, it's no wonder that **Morocco**'s cuisine is at the forefront of the culinary scene. With the Rhode School of Cuisine, you'll travel just outside of Marrakesh's city center to the luxury villa, Dar Liqama (the house of green mint). Your days will include tours of the souks (markets) and several cooking lessons to learn the basics of traditional Moroccan cuisine—paired with international and Moroccan wines. www.rhodeschoolofcuisine.com

Cooking Classes on Cruises

Sure, cruising is synonymous with eating—after all, those all-you-can-eat buffets aren't going anywhere. But these days, cruise lines are taking it to the next level and are offering a real culinary education on the high seas. You've heard of Le Cordon Bleu cooking school, right? Well, that institution has partnered with Regent Seven Seas Cruises (www.rssc.com) to offer both demonstrations and hands-on classes. The 3-day program ends with dinner at the school's only permanent restaurant aboard a cruise ship, called Signatures. The California-based Chefmakers Cooking Academy is no longer just for locals. It has teamed up with Royal Caribbean (www.rccl.com) to bring you the Chefmakers experience at sea. Hop aboard the *Liberty of the Seas* or the *Freedom of the Seas* for both adult classes and basic cooking classes for kids. Looking to pick up some local flavor and culture? SilverSea (www.silversea.com) has full cruises dedicated to the culinary arts through its partnership with Relais & Châteaux L'École des Chefs. Along with cooking demos and competi-tions, the cruise includes a local immersion experience called Market to Plate, where you pick up items from the local markets at the port followed by a chef-led class. After that kind of experience, you won't have room for that all-you-can-eat buffet. But you will come home with a new set of skills.

Have you ever heard of Karoo cuisine? If not, now is the time to learn. This African style of cooking originates from the Northern Cape of **South Africa.** It fuses South African, Middle Eastern, and Indian flavors, and relies on seasonal and local ingredients—most famously, the Karoo lambs that are raised in this region. African Relish offers daylong courses that include both lunch and dinner, where you can get hands-on experience learning the techniques and stories behind its culinary heritage. www.africanrelish.com

WALKING TOURS

Making your way through **New York**'s culinary scene is no easy task. What you really need is a local who can break down the history, the culture, and the flavor of each neighborhood. Foods of New York has multiple walking and tasting tours where you'll learn about the ethnic influences of the neighborhood—from the food to the architecture. Although there are several food-centered neighborhoods to choose from, my advice is to go with the original Greenwich tour. It's got Italian-American flavors, everything from Faicco's Italian Specialties to Joe's Pizza to Murray's Cheese Shop. www.foodsofny.com

Chicagoans love their food, and **Chicago** Food Planet can show you exactly why. There are three neighborhood tours, including the Near North which includes—and goes beyond—the expected deep-dish pizza. Browse through the enormous collection of spices and seasonings at the Spice House, explore an old-school Ashkenazi Jewish deli, and taste high-end olive oils from a specialty shop. That said, the Bucktown/Wicker Park tour has a very cool stop that you definitely want to check out—iCream, where you design your own ice-cream flavor (or frozen yogurt or milkshake) and they'll make it for you on the spot using a fast-freezing liquid nitrogen machine. www.chicagofoodplanet.com

It doesn't get more eclectic than **New Orleans**'s culinary landscape, with its French, African, Caribbean, Spanish, and Italian influences.

On the New Orleans Culinary History Tours, not only will you learn the difference between Creole and Cajun cuisine, but you'll also get samples from two of the oldest restaurants in the city, Antoine's and Tujague's. Also on the menu is the famed muffaletta from Central Grocery, with Italian meats piled high on circular bread and topped with a savory olive salad. www.noculinarytours.com

Mention **Los Angeles** and most people probably can't come up with a definitive cuisine. But Melting Pot Tours takes you behind the scenes of some of the oldest establishments in the city on its East LA Latin Flavors tour. Go into a family-owned tortilla factory where vats of masa (corn dough) are pressed and cooked, dine on *chilaquiles* at a cafe that's operated by former gang members, and make your way into the multilevel El Mercado de Los Angeles. For a less walking-intensive tasting, you can also tour the Original Farmers Market, where almost every ethnicity is represented in food stalls. www.meltingpottours.com

Thailand was practically tailor-made for foodies. Bangkok Food Tours combines street food and culture during its walking tour of the historic Bangrak neighborhood, where you'll explore samples like roasted duck, papaya salad, and custard buns. The cool thing about going on an organized tour, instead of doing it on your own, is that it focuses almost entirely on local establishments—no tourist traps. Plus it's a lot of bang for your buck, with eight to 10 tastings over the course of 3 hours, as well as some highlights of Thai temples, churches, and notable architecture. http://bangkokfoodtours.com

The heart of Kyoto, **Japan,** is its central covered market, Nishiki Ichiba, lined with vendors selling everything you can think of, from the freshest raw fish to roasted teas to bonito flakes. Wak Japan will guide you through the narrow lanes, visiting with the vendors and picking out ingredients for a traditional Japanese meal. You'll wander outside of the market to the city's more inaccessible lanes to see local craft makers and a former sake brewery for a tasting, followed by a hands-on cooking lesson inside a *machiya* (a wooden townhouse). www.wakjapan.com

Best Places to

LEARN TO MAKE CRAFTS

I'm a huge fan of learning something when I travel, and when I've had the chance to physically make something, it adds substantial value to the trip. You get to think and act outside the box—and sometimes you even get to make the box.

It's probably no surprise that a place called the Hotel Murano has an extensive glass art collection from as many as 40 artists (even the rooms have hand-blown glass lamps). But what's cool is this Tacoma, **Washington,** hotel also has an art-inspired package that starts off with a visit to the must-see Museum of Glass and ends with hands-on lessons at the Tacoma Glass Blowing Studio. You'll be able to choose your colors and twist, blow, or shape the molten, honeylike substance into your own paperweight, bowl, or other work of art. Or go on your own any weekend day and take a short, 30-minute class to make your own glass float—a hollow ball once used by fishermen to keep their nets submerged. You'll blow the glass into the right form and fill it with colorful shells and sand before sealing it shut. www.hotelmuranotacoma.com

In Louisville, **Kentucky,** the 21c Museum Hotel is known for its exceptional art collection. To further inspire art-loving guests, they've got a package that includes a glass-blowing lesson at the nearby Flame Run Gallery and Studio Hot Shop in the East Market District. You'll work with an artist to blow your own colorful glass ornaments any time of year. Or head to the studio on your own and spend the day in the 12,000-square-foot facility. You can make your own art, interact with the resident artists at work, and check out the display gallery with works from internationally renowned glassblowers. www.21chotel.com

In **New Orleans**'s artsy Warehouse District, the GlassWorks & Printmaking Studio has classes on everything from glassblowing and metalworking to printmaking and bookbinding. Most classes are longer term, but if you're only in town for a short stay, try a 2-hour course where the experts guide you through simple techniques to make your own glass beads or other take-home objects. www.neworleansglassworks.com

The renowned Thos. Moser wood furniture makers has a Customer in Residence program with the Harraseeket Inn in Freeport, **Maine.** You'll work alongside master cabinetmakers and learn the intricacies of joinery, how to shape and mold solid cherry, and how to bring out the natural luster of wood. This is a working vacation, which results in your own heirloom piece. www.thosmoser.com

Create your own handbag at M. Avery Designs in Hoboken, **New Jersey.** You can learn how to make one of six different handbag styles from designs provided in-house. During 2-hour workshops, you choose the fabric for the outside and lining of your bag, and you do most of the assembly legwork. The M. Avery staff then puts the finishing touches on and makes sure your bag is sturdy and professional looking. There is also a zipper bag workshop, which can be combined with the handbag workshop. http://maverydesigns.com/handbag_workshop.htm

Every summer, Purdue University in West Lafayette, **Indiana,** offers a 5-day guitar workshop where you can learn how to craft, engineer, and customize your own solid-body electric guitar. It is taught by Mark French, assistant professor of mechanical engineering at Purdue. Each attendee gets a complete kit containing all the necessary elements, which Mark teaches you how to put together, customize, and test. At the end of the week, you'll have a custom instrument to take home—and a deluxe Fender gig bag to haul it around in. Oh, and of course the workshop includes an evening jam session. http://metalsound.tech.purdue.edu/PGW.aspx

The world-renowned Bailey Guitars, based in Maybole, **Scotland,** offers courses in making and designing guitars. If you only have a day, take the Design Your Own Guitar class, which teaches the theory of guitar construction; introduces you to wood, materials, parts, and tools; walks you through the different building stages; and shows you how to create a drawing. You'll also get a tour of the Bailey workshop. You won't actually make a guitar, but you can take home your design drawing to use in the future. Weekend and 5-day courses go to the next level and instruct you in how to build an actual custom guitar from scratch. www.baileyguitars.co.uk/courses

The Vermont Teddy Bear Company in Shelburne, **Vermont,** has been making teddy bears for more than 20 years. While you're there, take a tour of the factory and see how the bears are made, from the cutting of the fabric to the sewing, stuffing, and stitching. (There's even a Bear Hospital, where you can send your bears should anything ever happen to them.) With the Friend for Life program, kids can make their very own teddy bear. Steps include selecting the "skin," choosing and inserting the stuffing, adding a heart, and sewing it up. You even get a specially designed travel case to take it home in. And what's more, every bear is unconditionally guaranteed for life, so it's a friend your kids will have and love forever. www.vermontteddybear.com/Static/Friend-For-Life.aspx

Seattle's Center for Wooden Boats offers a wide variety of workshops in all aspects of boatbuilding. Classes include half-model making, stitch and glue boatbuilding, Norwegian pram making, Ileut kayak making, canoe building, and oar making. There's even a BYOB (Bring Your Own Boat) program, where you can bring in that broken-down old boat that's been sitting around your backyard for years, and they'll advise you on how to begin restoration, make repairs, and move your project forward. Courses last from 1 to 8 days. Of course, one caution: Once you've built a boat from scratch, or restored an older one, there's that little detail of getting it back home. www.cwb.org

Take a step back in time at the Touchstone Center for Crafts in Farmington, **Pennsylvania,** which offers more than 100 weekend and weeklong courses that teach old-school crafts. For example, you can learn blacksmithing, stained-glass making, working with textiles, ceramic making, papermaking and printmaking, jewelry making, how to create your own cooking utensils, or how to forge steel knives. A 3-day class teaches basket-weaving techniques, accent coloring, and more, and leaves you with three handmade baskets at the end of the course. The 5-day Rings, Rings, Rings class is for beginner to intermediate metalsmiths and covers fabrication, stone setting, and assembling techniques for making your own custom rings. www.touchstonecrafts.org

The iconic Louisville Slugger bat can be yours when you travel to Louisville, **Kentucky,** to tour the museum and factory. While you can't actually carve the bat yourself, you can get the next best thing with your own personalized bat made inside the factory. www.slug germuseum.org

Few Westerners know this, but the town of Mashiko, **Japan,** is famous for pottery. Hundreds of artisans live and work there, and dozens of shops and galleries display and sell their wares. At Pottery Studio Fuwari, you can enjoy hands-on workshops in pottery making, including a 2-hour English-language course on the basics of shaping, firing, and glazing. http://kobofuwari.web.fc2.com/class_e.htm

Learn the ancient art of Maori bone carving in Nelson, **New Zealand,** the arts and crafts center of the country. Stephan Gilberg, known as "the Nelson Bone Carver," shows small groups of visitors how to take a slab of freshly cleaned bone and carve, sand, and polish it, and even inset *paua* stones. He also describes the historical and ritual significance of bone carvings to New Zealand's native Maori people. www.carvingbone.co.nz

Beekind, a honey shop and apiary in Sebastopol, **California,** brings guests closer to bees. In addition to selling honey, royal jelly, propolis, and beeswax, expert beekeeper Doug Vincent, Beekind's owner, offers a half-day Introduction to Beekeeping class. It covers acquiring hives, placement of bees, and extraction of honey for aspiring beekeepers. As a bonus, if you decide to start raising your own bees, Beekind can order packaged bees for you. A beeswax candle-making class is available, too. www.beekind.com

The folks at Creative Paper Wales are not ashamed to say that they make some of their unique handcrafted papers and paper products from . . . sheep poo. Yes, sheep poo. Turns out, the excrement of sheep contains a whole lot of cellulose fiber, which is great for making paper. You can tour the mill in remote Snowdonia (northern **Wales**) and see a demonstration of how the paper is made, and at the end you'll get instructions on how to make your own paper at home. www.creativepaperwales.co.uk

The Perfume Factory on **Grand Bahama Island** sells a variety of scents, but you can also mix your own custom perfume in their workshop! A mixologist shows you how to combine essential oils to achieve your preferred scent and how to use the special mixing apparatus to blend your oils with alcohol. You also get to choose a spray or splash bottle into which your perfume is decanted, pick a unique name for your creation, and create a label. www.perfumefactory.com

The Russian River Rose Company located in Healdsburg, **California,** is a specialty nursery and garden that grows 650 types of roses. They make rose water, eau de toilette, and rose oil from the petals of their flowers using ancient methods. On tours of the facility, you can participate in a mini-workshop where you'll help collect rose petals, stuff them into antique Prohibition-era copper distillation kettles, and watch the distillation process in real time. Workshops are only in spring, so book well in advance to make sure you don't miss one. www.russian-river-rose.com

Learn on Vacation

Vocation Vacations is a company that connects people with experiences that allow them to learn a new skill or try out a different job. Most participants are potential career changers seeking to test-drive a new profession, but those simply seeking a unique vacation are welcome, too. The list of experiences is endless; for example, you can learn alpaca ranching, chocolate making, jewelry design, oyster farming, or shoe design. These experiences are not workshops, but rather immersive one-on-one mentorships where you shadow someone who actually works in the field and learn firsthand what it's like to do their job. http://vocationvacations.com

DIGGING FOR FOSSILS

There's the study of archaeology, but then there's the hands-on Indiana Jones–style approach out in the field. I'm not talking professional-grade archaeological digs that require a master's degree or your own set of specialized tools. Instead, there are some truly accessible sites out there where all you need to bring is enthusiasm and a willingness to learn. Activities range from 1-day digs appropriate for all ages to multiday programs.

HANDS ON

The Museum of Western **Colorado** offers several dig experiences with experts as your guide. Head out to a quarry to assist paleontologists and learn excavating techniques. Or, for more serious enthusiasts, you can join a 5-day dig in Moab, Utah. Not only can you dig for bones, but you also help prospect for new sites and help track and log data. www.museumofwesternco.com

Follow the dinosaur trail in **Montana.** The Montana Dinosaur Trail (http://mtdinotrail.org) links 14 paleontology exhibits, museums, and field digs across the state. Along the way, Two Medicine Dinosaur Center has field activities led by expert paleontologist David Trexler, such as 3-hour fossil recognition programs, more intensive 2-day field collecting and preservation, and fully immersive 10-day programs. www.tmdinosaur.org

The "Jurassic Coast" of **England** is known for its sheer number and variety of fossils, which come loose easily from the limestone cliffs. The region is a World Heritage site on the English Channel and stretches 95 miles from Orcombe Point near Exmouth in East Devon to Swanage in East Dorset. Organizations like Fossil Walks, Lyme Regis Fossil Walks, and the Charmouth Heritage Coast Centre can take you on guided trips to the best spots, while giving you an overview of the history, geology, and biology of the region.

Volunteer vacation company Earthwatch Institute invites volunteers to join field experts on active digs worldwide. Whether it's collecting medieval artifacts in Tuscany's central coastal area, unearthing Roman ruins while overlooking the North Sea in South Shields, or mapping out an excavation site in an ancient Thai village, these programs incorporate hands-on experiences with cultural activities. A program fee is required, which also covers meals and accommodations. www.earthwatch.org

FAMILY FRIENDLY

Like its name suggests, U-Dig Fossils in Delta, **Utah,** is a dig site where visitors can roll up their sleeves and find their own Jurassic treasures. The private quarry contains one of the world's richest deposits of trilobites. The fossils are found in limestone shale, which splits easily into flat sheets with a basic hammer, so no special tools are required. The owners also offer an annual Geode Bonanza, a guided adventure that allows visitors to hunt for geodes on a private site in Dugway and bring home up to 150 pounds. www.u-digfossils.com

The **Wyoming** Dinosaur Center is more than just a museum about fossils. Visitors can see what happens behind the scenes in the lab and research facilities. Nearby is a 500-acre dig site, where families can take part in a daylong dig. www.wyodino.org

Unearth your kid's inner paleontologist with the Children's Museum of **Indianapolis,** which runs a family dig program at the Ruth Mason Quarry in South Dakota. The Dinosphere experience is led by a museum expert who teaches the basics of digging for fossils. Depending on what you find, the fossil can come home with you, or it may very well end up in the museum's collection. www.childrens museum.org

The Gobi Desert has a treasure trove of Cretaceous period dinosaur eggs and fossils, dating back to the early expeditions of Roy Chapman Andrews in the 1920s. Today, Destination Himalaya will take you to the desert's famous Flaming Cliffs to spend 3 to 4 hours a day assisting paleontologists with digs and research. The program was started by a man who wanted to incorporate his own children's love for dinosaurs into a family experience in **Mongolia,** so the Dinosaurs in the Summer program is designed to be a family-friendly adventure. www.destinationhimalaya.net

OBSERVATIONAL

If you want to simply look but not touch, then head to Mesa Verde National Park in **Colorado,** where you'll get a history lesson without getting your hands dirty. You can visit sandstone cliff dwellings inhabited by the Pueblo people for 700 years. Visitors can either take a 1-hour ranger-guided tour or sit back on a bus tour of the entire park. The nearby Chapin Mesa Archeological Museum will help you put everything into context. www.nps.gov/meve/index.htm

About 32 miles northeast of El Paso, **Texas,** is the Hueco Tanks State Park & Historic Site, where there are more than 2,000 rock paintings scattered over 860 acres. These pictographs have been made by ancient hunters and gatherers over thousands of years. The best way to see the site is with a guide, who can help you navigate the terrain and explain the significance of the symbols. www.tpwd. state.tx.us/spdest/findadest/parks/hueco_tanks

At the Mammoth Site research facility in Hot Springs, **South Dakota,** you can tour an active paleontological dig site and view the remains of these Ice Age creatures. The museum—and national natural landmark—formed around this site after housing developers accidentally discovered it in 1974. But what's really neat about this site is its in situ exhibit, meaning the bones are displayed within the bone bed, in the very location that they were found. www.mammothsite.com

Fossil Butte National Monument in southwestern **Wyoming** sits on a 50-million-year-old lake bed. It was established solely to protect the fossils found here, comprising 13 square miles. Of the two main formations here, the Green River Formation and the Wasatch Formation, you'll notice a variety of colors: pink, lavender, purple, and yellow. Well, guess what? You may be looking at fossils without realizing it, like teeth, bones, even fossils from early primates and horses. Don't miss the Aquarium in Stone program, which brings together small groups to close-up views and interact directly with the experts. www.nps.gov/fobu/index.htm

HUNT FOR GEMS AND GOLD

You don't have to be a scientist, Indiana Jones, or an heiress to enjoy prized stones. Rockhounding is fun, it's low impact, and it literally lets you dig for treasure, so get ready to unleash your inner geologist.

UNITED STATES

The Blue Ridge Mountains of **North Carolina** are prime mineral-hunting grounds. You can't go wrong at Little Pine Garnet Mine in Madison County, which is only open by appointment plus an entrance fee. You can dig just outside of the entrance in a creek bed, or head into the mine where garnet crystals are visible in the walls.

In Franklin County, North Carolina, rubies and sapphires abound, along with white moonstones and quartz crystals. In most cases, rather than digging in the mines, you'll get a bucket of "gem dirt" and go to the flume line to clean the gravel and pick out the promising stones. But if you want to get your hands even dirtier, Mason's Ruby and Sapphire Mine (www.masonsmine.com) actually lets you dig your own dirt to sort through and clean in the flume line. Once you've collected your stones, you can bring them to Ruby City Gems & Minerals (www.rubycity.com) to be cut, polished, and set, and browse its extensive private collection of gems, minerals, and fossils.

The aptly named Rockhound State Park in **New Mexico** is one of the best places in the country to hunt for rocks. Located in the Florida and Little Florida Mountains, it's one of the few state parks where you can actually take items with you—up to 15 pounds of rocks. The prized find here is "thunder eggs," also known as geodes. On the outside, they look like dirty rocks, but on the inside they reveal gorgeous crystals like amethyst, rose quartz, or hematite, or colored stone such as jasper and agate. Of course, you won't know what's on the inside until you break it open, so bring your own hammer and chisel to the site. www.emnrd.state.nm.us/prd/rockhound.htm

Northeast of Zion National Park are **Utah**'s west desert rock-hounding areas. Try the Dugway Geode Beds in Juab County, where you can dig up the coveted crystal spheres. While you're in Juab County, check out Topaz Mountain, where you might unearth crystals that formed in 6-million-year-old volcanic cavities. In Beaver County is the Mineral Mountain range, which is abundant in smoky quartz and feldspar. Just head to the Rock Corral Recreation Area on the west side of the mountains, where you can let loose with a hammer and chisel and bring home whatever you unearth. www.geology.utah.gov

You can actually dig for diamonds—and keep—them at Crater of Diamonds State Park in Murfreesboro, **Arkansas.** The entrance fee of $7 is not a bad deal if you strike it rich. Even better, a resident gem expert can tell you if your find is actually worth anything. And remember, rocks that are too small to be cut can still be mounted into a pendant. www.craterofdiamondsstatepark.com

The Oceanview Mine in Pala, **California** (near San Diego), allows you to do "screenings" several times throughout the year. Screening is where you take dirt that has been produced as a by-product from the mine-blasting process and filter it through a large screen to ferret out any hidden gems and minerals. Varieties of gems to be found include aquamarine, quartz, and mica (fool's gold). The day's activities also include a dune buggy tour of the historic Pala mining and gem district. www.digforgems.com

Maine's Mount Mica has an impressive quantity of colorful tourmaline, aquamarine, quartz, and much more. There are plenty of operations that will sell you buckets to pick through, but a better option is to get dirty with a hands-on dig in the nearby quarries, pits, and mine dumps with Maine Mineral Adventures (http://digmainegems.com) or Maine Mineralogy Expeditions (www.rocksme.biz). If you want to learn more about Maine's minerals and gems, stop by Mt. Mann Jewelers (www.mtmann.com) in the town of Bethel, where mineralogists can show you rough and finished products.

INTERNATIONAL

People from all over Europe come to the Juchem quarry (at Niederwörresbach) about 60 miles west of Frankfurt, **Germany.** During the week, it is a commercial mine site where andesite, dacite, and basalt are extracted, but on most spring and summer weekends, rock enthusiasts can hunt for agate, amethyst, calcite, and smoky quartz. There's nothing touristy about this site. There are few amenities (except a restaurant outside the quarry entrance), and you need to bring your own tools and hard hat. But once you get digging, you might be rewarded with intense red agates, glittering amethyst geodes, and striking quartz formations. The quarry limits visitors to 50 per day, so go to the Geracher restaurant outside the gate an hour before opening time to get tickets and permits. www.steinbruch-juchem.de/en/home

Rockhounding, aka fossicking or noodling, is a big sport in **Australia,** particularly in the opal-mining town of Andamooka. What's really cool about this place is that most locals live underground in dugouts. It's also the only town in Australia where none of the streets are named and the main thoroughfare is built in a creek bed. Casual mining is allowed, but make sure you're not on already claimed territory.

To get a broader rockhounding experience in South Australia, the US-based Geology Adventures can take you on a route that focuses on maximum collecting time. Explore Australia's gold rush country in Mooralla, Swan Hill, and Digby, and hunt calcite, selenite, smoky quartz, geodes, and even fossils at mining sites not normally accessible to visitors. Bring home as many specimens as you can fit in your

Rockhounding Resources

The US Department of the Interior's Bureau of Land Management (www. blm.gov) and individual state departments of natural resources are great places to contact for questions and concerns about legal rockhounding. Collecting can be illegal in areas such as national parks in order to protect resources, so check the local laws before you go.

Unless you are going to a rock-hunting spot that provides guides and gear, it is a good idea to plan ahead on these types of trips. Try contacting a local college, university, or museum, and ask them to direct you to specific sites at your destination, or to suggest a group that goes out on rockhounding expeditions. And remember, safety always comes first. Take a friend with you, and make sure you have access to the property you want to go to.

carry-on luggage, and the company will ship the rest home for you.

Geology Adventures can also take you to **Spain** to areas like Navajun, where you can find large, perfect cubes of pyrite; tour ancient salt mines; and visit with a collector who has arguably the world's finest collection of Berbes fluorite. www.geologyadventures.com

GOLD DIGGING

In **Alaska,** recreational prospectors can hunt for gold across several public parks, including Chugach National Forest and Chugach State Park. At Independence Mine State Historic Park, museum exhibits and hands-on activities show you what it was like to work at one of the state's biggest gold-mining camps. You can also prospect along Nome's famous "gold beach" and in other sites near Fairbanks and Anchorage, but remember to check out the rules with the Bureau of Land Management and other agencies first. Gold mining can be a serious business here, and you don't want to imperil yourself by venturing onto private property or use techniques that are harmful to the environment. www.dnr.alaska.gov

For an Alaskan gold excursion that's light on actual work and heavy on microbrews, head to the southeastern coastal community of Skagway and the Klondike Gold Fields. Here you can see the Dredge, a restored piece of heavy equipment from 1937; watch a gold-panning demonstration; and go next door to the Gold Rush Brewery for a pint of craft beer. www.klondikegolddredge.com

Roaring Camp Mining Company in Pine Grove, **California,** was a gold-mining camp during the California gold rush, but the site proved difficult to access in the days before paved roads. Hence, much of the gold remains. It is still an operating gold mine, in which you can do your own panning, sluicing, dredging, and dry-washing. Tours of the active mine and the Mining Artifacts Museum are also offered, as are lessons on how to pan for gold. www.roaringcampgold.com

In the other gold country, Yukon, **Canada,** check out a company called Goldbottom Mine Tours and Goldpanning. A half-day of panning costs only $20, and families can spend the night in an old-school log cabin. Cabin rates start at just $65 a night, which includes unlimited creek panning privileges. So even if you don't strike it rich, at least you come out ahead in experience. www.goldbottom.com

Back in the day, Kalgoorlie was to Western **Australia** what the Sierra Nevada was to California: pioneer gold-prospecting country. In modern times, this dusty outback region still reminds me of Dodge City, and it is mined for gold by commercial operators, but nuggets can also be found by amateur gold hunters. Kalgoorlie Tours & Charters offers a tour of the area's goldfields. You'll travel by off-road vehicle to prospecting territory with high-tech detectors to help uncover valuable nuggets. And of course you get to keep what you find. There's also a behind-the-scenes tour of the Super Pit, Australia's largest gold-producing mine, at 1 mile wide and 2½ miles long. You'll drive right into the mine, alongside the supersize pit trucks, where you'll see old 19th-century mine shafts next to modern mining machinery. www.kalgoorlietours.com.au

Become a Gem Expert

The Gemological Institute of America (GIA) has programs around the world where you can learn to be a gem expert. Long-term programs range from 7 to 26 weeks in Carlsbad (California), New York, Tokyo, Seoul, Osaka, Hong Kong, Taipei, Bangkok, Mumbai, Moscow, or London. If you just want a taste, GIA offers hands-on lab classes where you can learn to identify, grade, and design precious stones. If you take a class in the main Carlsbad campus, you have access to the impressive on-site museum, while New York students can work with experts in the diamond district.

And while the Gem and Mineral Hall at the Museum of Natural History is a can't-miss experience, there's another, well, hidden gem in Manhattan. Astro Gallery of Gems (www.astrogallery.com) contains what is probably the largest collection of gems, minerals, and fossils. With 10,000 square feet of space, you can see (and buy) everything from massive quartz crystals to garnets from Namibia to vanadinite crystals from Morocco. Although rock hounds will spend hundreds, if not thousands, of dollars here to add to their collections, the fun is just browsing through specimens on display.

Best Places to

LEARN A LANGUAGE

As the saying goes, "Those who can, do. Those who can't, teach." And, sure, maybe your sixth-grade Spanish class wasn't so inspiring. But those who can immerse themselves in a foreign language and apply those lessons on the road get to benefit from world-class experiences. Simply put, learning a language and then applying it overseas will make you the lifelong beneficiary of magical moments on a global scale.

And what better place to learn a foreign language than in the foreign country itself?

At Coeur de France Ecole de Langues (Heart of France School of Language) in Sancerre, families can enroll in total immersion courses set up to match their level of knowledge of the **French** language. This is a small private school that's owned by a local couple—as opposed to a more institutional program. In addition to group or private lessons, you also get access to daily excursions conducted entirely in French. Those excursions are their raison d'être and what really makes the difference between learning textbook versus practical French. You might attend wine or jazz festivals, tour a winery like Henri Bourgois, where you can see the cellars and barrel rooms, or visit family-run farms that produce the region's famous goat cheese known as Crottin de Chavignol. www.coeurdefrance.com

If you want to study **Spanish,** but you're not sure where, Spanish Abroad, Inc. coordinates Spanish-language vacations across Latin America and Spain. Although there are some fun programs like a

INSIDER'S TIP

You don't have to be in college to do a semester at sea. The Institute for Shipboard Education (www.semesteratsea.org) offers monthlong and semester-long courses where you can learn conversational Spanish, French, Japanese, and even Arabic, alongside academic subjects like biology and history. Or you can opt for Enrichment Voyages on the MV *Explorer* to destinations like the Amazon and the Galapagos Islands, which include language along with other expert-led courses.

language and surf camp in Tamarindo, Costa Rica, you're better off going for a more immersive program like the one in Madrid. It's in the center of Spain, both literally and culturally (the school is a stone's throw from the Madrid Opera House and Plaza Mayor), and it's where you can pick up Castellano Spanish (as opposed to more regional Catalan in Barcelona). The environment here is very close-knit, including daily lunches with the staff so you can practice your conversational skills outside of the classroom. www.spanishabroad.com

There are numerous **Italian**-language programs throughout Italy, and my advice is to combine language lessons with experiences that tie in with the region. Linguaviva has a program that combines language classes with programs in art, art history, photography, and design. And if you're planning a career in fashion, they even have a program in Milan that will teach you the vocabulary to work in the industry. www.linguaviva.it

At the Scuola Verde L'Olmo in Portico di Romagna, Italy, you can participate in courses designed to incorporate language skills with the Italian way of life. Best of all, it's extremely family friendly, with kid-appropriate classes and babysitting services. The school is located in a quiet little town between Tuscany and Emilia Romagna, where you can involve yourself with the local culture and head out on outdoor excursions like horseback riding, kayaking, and hiking. www.academyolmo.com

At the Language Immersion School in Veracruz, Mexico, you can take advantage of a combination **Spanish** language and cooking program. Along with conversational language lessons, you can also help the staff shop for ingredients at the central market and roadside stands, and help prepare that day's meals. The school organizes cultural excursions like visits to nearby ruins, snorkeling, or scuba diving. If you're really a beginner, they will even provide you with emergency flash cards to help you communicate in a sticky situation. www.veracruzspanish.com

Even families can learn Spanish together at Centro Lingüístico Internacional in Antigua, Guatemala. In the Learn Together program, parents and children, Monday through Friday, each receives

3 hours a day of individual study and at least 1 hour working with each other to better their Spanish. The program also includes extra-curricular activities such as soccer matches, bicycle excursions, and museum tours. The best part is, the activities are all included in the price. Families can choose from several different types of accommodations, including on-site apartments or living with a Guatemalan family, which includes most meals. www.spanishcontact.com

When Americans go to China, the best advice is to have someone at the hotel write down your destination in Chinese characters to show taxi drivers. But what if you could learn the art of conversational and written **Chinese** while you're there? Mandarin House, in both Beijing and Shanghai, is a great choice for a short, intensive Chinese-language course. There is a "standard course" of 20 hours of group lessons a week, but go for the more intensive course that includes group and private lessons. That's where you'll learn the art of conversation, like how to order food in a restaurant, take public transit, and express basic sentiments. You can also add on cultural excursions and courses in subjects like calligraphy and cooking. And here's a tip: Although the school can provide housing, you can usually find cheaper rates on your own. www.mandarinhouse.cn

Although there are plenty of **Japanese**-language programs in Tokyo, go to the more compact, relaxed city of Fukuoka in southern Japan. GenkiJACS is a small program run by a local couple that's geared toward Westerners. Along with daily language and cultural classes, you'll stay with a family to practice your conversational skills long after the lessons are over. www.genkijacs.com

If you absolutely can't go abroad to learn a new language, then a great alternative is taking a trip to . . . Minnesota. Concordia Language Villages is an unusual—and hands-on—language and cultural immersion school in Minnesota's North Woods. Part of Concordia College, the program is ideal for families on holiday, where you can learn a foreign language through cultural experiences, whether it's through dance, music, movies, or cooking lessons. The school offers everything from **Danish, Finnish,** and **Swedish** to **Chinese, Korean,** and **Arabic**. www.concordialanguagevillages.org

LEARN TO FIGHT

Whether you're looking for true, tough, street-survival-skills training or you simply want to be entertained (and not get hurt), you can learn to punch, jab, joust, or even be a matador.

In Warwickshire, **England,** you can learn to joust medieval-style in the shadow of the magnificent Warwick Castle. The Knights of Middle England offer both group and private lessons, where you'll get the full experience: Dress up in medieval costume and armor, and learn basic jousting skills on a horse using a lance, shield, and a flag. You'll learn how to strike the quintain (the target that spins when struck), collect rings off the tilt (the wooden fence that separates the two knights) with a lance, and test your skills by trying to unseat the Black Knight. They even provide you with a title and a coat of arms for the day—pretty much everything but the dragon. You can also learn sword fighting, archery, and medieval chivalry. Riding experience is an advantage but not essential. Since the Knights are based at the Warwick International School of Riding, you can take riding lessons there, if you wish. www.knightsofmiddleengland.com

Matador Dennis Borba is a native Californian who has fought bulls on foot and on horseback in Mexico, Peru, Spain, and Portugal since the 1970s. At the Dennis C. Borba Bullfighting School in **California**'s San Joaquin Valley, you can take a 3-day workshop on the art of *tauromaquia* (bullfighting). You'll learn the basic lances and passes, as well as how to wield the cape and stick. This is a bloodless version of the sport, where you actually mark the conquest with Velcro rather than a steel blade. Workshops also give you the chance to experience the day-to-day running of Borba's 700-acre, 200-animal *ganaderia* (livestock ranch) and tour the fields where the fighting bulls are bred. All levels of experience are welcome, and beginners get to practice with small, young bulls, so no danger is involved. Courses are held six times a year on weekends, from Friday to Sunday, and cost around $300. www.dennisborba.com

In Rome, **Italy,** a heritage group called Gruppo Storico Romano runs a full-on Roman gladiator training school called the Scuola Gladiatori Roma. Regular courses are months long, but if you're only in Rome for a short time, you can learn the basics in a 2-hour gladiator class. These English-language sessions are organized and led by members of Gruppo Storico, and cover techniques of gladiatorial sword fighting, gear, and history. You can take the class at Gruppo's facility in Via

Appia Antica, which includes a visit to the on-site Gladiator Museum; if you're staying at the Rome Cavalieri Hotel, the instructors will come to the hotel. At the Cavalieri, a gladiator "kit" is offered as part of the course, which includes a traditional tunic, Roman sandals, a belt, protective gloves, and a wooden training sword. www.romecavalieri.com

Japan is the home of many different styles of martial arts, including kendo, karate, judo, and aikido. Though most dojos (training centers) cater to those enrolled in long-term courses, there are some places around the country where short-term visitors can drop in and take a lesson or two. Kodokan Judo Institute (www.kodokan.org) in Tokyo is the headquarters of judo in Japan. If you have some experience with judo, you can drop in on a *randori* (freestyle) class and a women-only class. Or if you're looking for more intensive training, you can stay on the premises in dorm style accommodations.

The art of aikido unifies the principles of judo, karate, and kendo into a single form of noncontact self-defense. Hombu Dojo in Tokyo is the headquarters of the aikido community, and to take a class here requires membership in Aikikai Foundation. That gets you access to the five-story dojo with three training areas, where you can participate in classes ranging from 1 day to long-term apprenticeship programs. Tenshin Dojo (www.aitenshin.com) in Osaka is another prestigious option, where you can drop in on a class or remain for several weeks in a more intensive training program.

Muay Thai is a fierce form of kickboxing whose roots can be traced to the fighting style of ancient Siamese soldiers. It uses fists, elbows, knees, and feet and is an incredible workout for body and mind. Though Muay Thai schools are present all over **Thailand,** the popular resort Phuket (on the gorgeous Andaman Sea) happens to have a number of great gyms that welcome visitors from all over the world. At Tiger Muay Thai Training Camp, you can spend anywhere from a half day to 6 months in intensive training. Even beginners will work with a Muay Thai master, starting with morning yoga, followed by stamina and cardio training, plus one-on-one workshops and drills to learn the fundamentals. www.tigermuaythai.com

Best Places to

TANGO

It goes without saying that the best place in the world to enjoy tango and tango culture is in **Buenos Aires.** The trick is finding which places offer a truly authentic experience, not tourist traps or dinner theater.

At first glance, the Mansion Dandi Royal may not seem like a special place. The interior has a retro vibe and simple rooms. But this boutique San Telmo hotel is the place to completely immerse yourself in tango culture. The hotel incorporates group lessons and one-on-one instruction, professional tango shows, and every Wednesday, it transforms into *milonga*. Talk about an all-in-one experience. Longtime instructors Ernesto Balmaceda and Stella Báezcan work with dancers of all experience levels, so don't be shy if this is your first time. www.mansiondandiroyal.com

Confiteria Ideal is a classic salon with weekend performances, classes, and evening milongas where locals mingle with foreigners in the ballroom. The elegant interior is somewhat shabby but a throwback to turn-of-the-century dance halls of old-world Argentina. www.confiteriaideal.com

What El Niño Bien lacks in charm it more than makes up for in the local flavor. Couples old and young crowd the dance floor in the midst of dining tables, while the band plays on the stage. This is a traditional venue, so ladies, if you make eye contact with a man, he'll probably ask you to dance. (Or avert your eyes if you want to avoid someone else's prolonged stare.)

In the Villa Urquiza neighborhood of Buenos Aires, Sunderland Club is something of a local institution. Neither elegant nor trendy, it's more of the barrio style of a milonga, meaning the dance takes place in a building that serves another purpose during the week, not a dedicated hall or salon. This one? The dance floor is actually located in a gymnasium inside a sports club. www.sunderlandclub.com.ar

Or leave the traditional halls and tango under the stars. Barrancas de Belgrano is a large park in a residential neighborhood where locals gather in a big gazebo, called La Glorieta, to dance the night away. It tends to be a friendly bunch so get there early, before the crowds arrive, and get tips from the veterans.

San Telmo also has alfresco tango on Sundays during the popular Plaza Dorrego flea market. Browse for antiques and see the locals dance in the streets.

Then there are the places for tango that you would never expect . . . like **Finland**! That's right, the Finnish city of Seinäjoki (about 225 miles from Helsinki) celebrates the art of tango every July at the Tangomarkkinat festival. Established in 1985, this is a tradition that has to be seen to be believed. Street dancing, competitions, and tango singing are just a few of the festivities that take place over a 5-day period in this eagerly anticipated event. www.tangomarkkinat.fi

Turkey's tango scene may be new, but it's growing fast. Metin Yazir founded the world-class Baila Tango, and his dance schools can be found all over Turkey, even in the more traditional communities. Your best bet is the Istanbul location, where you can take daily classes from beginner to advanced. Every month, legendary Argentine dancers like Fabian Salas and Gustavo Naveira come in to hold workshops. www.bailatango.com

And in Shenzhen, **China,** Lianhua Mountain Park is a huge local gathering spot on the weekends. Crowds of men and women cluster for every activity you can think of—Bollywood and belly dancing, tai chi, group sing-alongs, and . . . tango! Go on a Sunday morning and prepare to be enchanted.

Tango Tours

Although **Argentina** (and other tango-loving locations) are easily explored on your own, you can get a real immersion course by going on an organized tour. Becka Tango Tours (www.beckatangotours.com) offers 8-day guided trips during which you stay at the elegant Tango House in Buenos Aires, visit several milongas, and have daily lessons. Argentine-born Nora Dinzelbacher (www.tangoweek.com), a professional dancer, teacher, and producer who has been credited with bringing the tango culture to the Bay Area, leads annual tango tours to Argentina. Her trips feature a mix of workshops with local tango masters, evening performances, and cultural immersion throughout the week. Or you can cruise with the masters with Tango at Sea (www.tangoatsea.com). Hop aboard a traditional cruise ship and your tango-centric group will also get access to workshops and lessons, milonga nights, and tango shows.

LITERARY TRAVEL/TOURS

If you really want to know about history, then follow the colorful trail of the writers who lived in a particular place. It's one of the best ways to see a city, better than being confined to a museum, and you get to immerse yourself in the neighborhoods that helped shape some of your literary heroes.

If I had to pick America's most literary city, it would have to be **Boston,** where countless authors, poets, scholars, and philosophers have been inspired over the centuries. An easy way to go about it is to follow Boston's Literary Trail, a 20-mile route that traces the lives of literary greats. It begins at the Omni Parker House, where Charles Dickens first read *A Christmas Carol,* and goes on to the homes of Louisa May Alcott, Henry Wadsworth Longfellow, and Henry David Thoreau. Other major stops include the acclaimed Boston Public Library; Mount Auburn Cemetery, where many of the literary greats are buried; and the Concord Museum (which has the desk on which Thoreau wrote *Civil Disobedience* and *Walden*). Or go with an organized tour group like Boston by Foot, which has literary-themed walking tours to explore the lives and works of a number of Victorian luminaries. www.bostonbyfoot.org

Don't overlook the small city of Hartford, **Connecticut,** as a literary travel spot. This is where Mark Twain chose to live and raise his family for nearly 20 years. It's also the site where he wrote some of his most notable works, including *The Adventures of Tom Sawyer,*

Literary Vacation Rentals

What if you could actually *live* like a renowned author? Naulakha (www.landmarktrustusa.org) is the name of the **Vermont** home that Rudyard Kipling designed for himself. Not only can you sit at the desk where he wrote *The Jungle Book*, but you and seven of your closest friends can actually rent the property. If you're a fan of Henry David Thoreau, head to his hometown of Concord, **Massachusetts.** Sure, you can visit his birth house, but what you really want to do is stay at the historic Colonial Inn (www.concordscolonialinn.com). Thoreau lived here as well, and today it's a bed-and-breakfast, complete with a suite dedicated to him. **Boston**'s Omni Parker House (www.omnihotels.com) is where the famed literary group, the Saturday Club, met every month. We're talking the likes of Emerson, Longfellow, and Hawthorne. And, of course, there's the grand dame of literary landmark hotels: The Algonquin (www.algonquinhotel.com) in **New York,** where the notoriously witty and caustic Round Table met for lunch daily.

The Adventures of Huckleberry Finn, and *A Connecticut Yankee in King Arthur's Court.* As an added bonus, the Mark Twain House & Museum (www.marktwainhouse.org) also shares a space with the Harriet Beecher Stowe Center (www.harrietbeecherstowecenter. org), which celebrates the legacy of the abolitionist author who lived in Hartford for the last two decades of her life.

Saratoga Springs, **New York,** is home to Yaddo (http://yaddo.org), a 400-acre estate founded in 1900 that functions as an artists and writers sanctuary. Former residents include Truman Capote, Flannery O'Conner, and Sylvia Plath. Nearby, in South Glens Falls, Cooper's Cave inspired some of the scenes from James Fenimore Cooper's *The Last of the Mohicans.*

In **Paris,** it's the cemeteries that are truly inspiring for literary types. In Cimetière de Montparnasse, visitors leave scraps of paper scribbled with Baudelaire's verse on his grave, while flowers cover Simone de Beauvoir and Jean-Paul Sartre's joint tomb. Oscar Wilde's massive white marble tomb in Père-Lachaise Cemetery is smudged top to bottom with red lipstick prints left by fans. Other must-see tombs include those of Guillaume Apollinaire, Honoré de Balzac, Tristan Tzara (founder of Dadaism), Paul Verlaine, Peret, and rock-and-roll poet Jim Morrison.

INSIDER'S TIP

Try to visit Dublin around June 16, which is known as Bloomsday, in honor of Joyce's most revered work, *Ulysses.* That's when the center holds a series of lectures, tours, plays, and exhibits in honor of the literary giant. Don't forget to take Leopold Bloom's lead and get a gorgonzola sandwich and a glass of Burgundy at Davy Byrne's in Duke Street. www.jamesjoyce.ie

Of course, following in the footsteps of Paris's great literary minds doesn't have to be so macabre. Instead, think like a local and . . . grab a cup of coffee! Café de Flore (www.cafedeflore.fr) and Les Deux Magots (www.lesdeuxmagots.fr) were the hangouts of some of France's greatest surrealist thinkers and still maintain their traditional decor. Here André Breton, Arthur Rimbaud, Apollinaire, and the Dadaists (Tzara and friends) sat and drank coffee and absinthe every day for hours.

Shakespeare and Company is located in the trendy area of the Saint-Michel metro stop, with Notre Dame and the Seine as a backdrop, and the best time to go is on Monday evening to hear readings from international writers. Want to brush up on your conversational French? The bookshop is where the Big Ben Club holds French-English conversation workshops. http://shakespeareandcompany.com

Few cities in the world have as much literary cache as **Dublin.** My favorite way to experience that is to combine the two things Dublin is best known for: literature and beer. Actors lead a pub crawl in the spirit of Dublin literary giants James Joyce, Samuel Beckett, Oscar Wilde, and Brendan Behan by quoting prose and verse and performing drama and song, while stopping in to four pubs throughout the city. www.dublinpubcrawl.com

Classical Pursuits is a Toronto-based company that designs literary trips around great works of literature and the destination(s) where the books were written or set. But be advised: There's homework involved. You're expected to read a book or two beforehand so that you can participate in discussions throughout the trip. You'll get to meet local experts or those connected to the literary world that revolve around these cities. Tours might include US cities like Savannah and Key West, or international spots like Paris, India, and Vietnam. My favorite: a "Lost Generation" tour of Paris that involves discussions on expat writers Ernest Hemingway, F. Scott Fitzgerald, and Gertrude Stein. Believe me, if literature is your passion, you're going to want to travel with these like-minded individuals. There have even been some marriages resulting from these trips! www.classicalpursuits.com

Organized Tours

For a more structured approach, the Sierra Club has a literary walking tour of **Dublin** and beyond. Not only do you get to attend Bloomsday festivities in the capital city, but you also visit Sandycove, home of the James Joyce Museum and the 40-foot pool from *Ulysses'* first chapter, and take a ferry to the Aran Islands where J. M. Synge wrote *Playboy of the Western World*. Explorations of Sligo, Iniskeen, and the ancient tombs at Newgrange round out the 12-day tour. www.sierraclub.org

Esotouric Tours cover several of **Los Angeles**'s literary personalities, from the well known to the obscure. We're talking hard-boiled noir writer Raymond Chandler, *The Postman Always Rings Twice* author James M. Cain, booze-addled poet Charles Bukowski, and Beatnik precursor John Fante. The tours are the exact opposite of most LA tours, taking you to unfashionable, off-the-beaten-path neighborhoods (like Skid Row), with funny, brainy guides who are passionate about and well versed in their subject matter. www.esotouric.com

Lynott Tours offers guided experiences that explore the literature and landscapes of such **British** and **Irish** greats as Beatrix Potter, the Brontë sisters, Jane Austen, George Bernard Shaw, Oscar Wilde, and William Wordsworth. You'll visit sites where great authors lived, died, worked, and worshipped; tour museums devoted to their works; see landscapes that inspired them; and sometimes attend annual festivals in their honor. Bonus tip: There's even a Harry Potter tour of London, where you'll visit platform $9\frac{3}{4}$ at King's Cross Station and see streets and buildings that appeared in key scenes in the movies. www.lynotttours.com

PHOTO TOURS/ LEARN TO TAKE PHOTOGRAPHS

We now live in the digital world of automatic cameras with cutting-edge stabilizing technology and the potential for instant gratification. But beyond just dumb luck, the real trick to great photography is in capturing—and sometimes waiting for—that perfect subject in the perfect light at the perfect moment. Taking an organized photography tour with an expert leader can often turn luck into a skill (not to mention being lucky enough to visit some of the most interesting places in the world). Here are some of the best places to practice the art of capturing truly striking images.

INDIA

It would take years of constant travel to capture the colors and contrasts of India. Each region has its own culture, language, and scenic beauty—from the urban chaos of Mumbai to the alpine beauty of the Himalayas to the majestic Taj Mahal in Agra. But if you have to choose a particularly photo-friendly region, it's the tropical wetlands of Kerala. In the capital city of Kochi (Cochin), you can photograph the cityscape with its heavy European influence and cultural performances like the ancient Kathakali dance. But the real photo ops are when you escape into the backwaters and sail along the network of canals, rivers, lakes, and lagoons to capture images of village life. The United Kingdom based Travelshooters offers several 2 week long Treasures of Kerala tours led by a professional travel photographer who lives in the region. You'll get a chance to photograph the expected tourist spots, but your guide also actively seeks out special experiences that take you into the local culture. You might encounter the weavers of Balaramapuram or see students training in the ancient martial art of Kalaripayattu. www.travelshooters.com

INSIDER'S TIP

National Geographic Expeditions also holds workshops for those with more photography experience in cities like New Orleans and Barcelona. These are more intensive trips, with daily photo assignments, critique sessions, and lessons in photo editing. www. nationalgeographicexpeditions.com

THAILAND

The landscape and climate of Thailand are so diverse it's like traveling to multiple destinations in one. In the north, Chiang Mai can be dry and cool in winter months, while in the south, the island of Phuket is tropical year-round. Although it's definitely worth spending a couple of days shooting the urban landscape of Bangkok, I'm always a fan of getting out of the city. New York–based Strabo Photo Tour Collection has a 2-week trip to Thailand and Cambodia, where you get instruction from an expert on photographing moments in Bangkok's marketplaces and the hill tribes of Chiang Mai. www.phototc.com

Outside the hustle and bustle of Bangkok, and away from the treasured temples, is the remote Koh Lanta Marine National Park, a less-populated archipelago of 15 protected isles about 45 miles from Krabi. Photograph the local fishermen in their traditional wooden boats capturing the catch of the day, or stroll through the gracious and well-kept wooden stilt houses and shop fronts in Ban Ko Lanta (Lanta Old Town), the island's original port.

Don't forget that there's plenty of cool stuff to photograph underwater, too. In Phuket, underwater photographer pro Adriano Trapani can teach you to effectively capture the beauty of the undersea world. Basic 2-day courses start with classroom instruction in topics such as composition rules, how to use a flash underwater, and how to get the best wide-angle shots. Then you proceed to a pool, where you practice the fundamentals of buoyancy. On day 2, you go out on the water and explore a local diving destination with your camera. Intermediate and advanced courses add computer editing skills, critique sessions, and instruction in advanced camera functions, plus 2 or more days of diving. Prerequisites for all courses include PADI basic or advanced Open Water Diver certification, but if you don't have it, you can take a combination diving/photo course. www.easydaythailand.com/adriano-trapani-underwater-photography-course.php

TANZANIA

I t's practically a no-brainer that visiting Tanzania requires a good camera and a steady hand. But to really get the most of your experience, a photography-intensive tour is the way to go. We're talking hands-on lessons to capture fast-moving images of wildlife migrations across the Serengeti, the grassy floodplains of Lake Manyara that boast incredible bird species, and the iconic Ngorongoro Crater and Ngorongoro Conservation Area. Photographer, author, and conservationist Boyd Norton leads his own photo safaris with Wilderness Photography where he has an intimate knowledge of the region and can explain how best to capture movement and light. Nothing is guaranteed, but you'll likely be able to drive right into the middle of a massive herd of migrating wildebeests for a full 360-degree view. In fact, sometimes lions and cheetahs will lie down in the shade of the safari vehicle (just don't get out!). www.wildernessphotography.com

---

INSIDER'S TIP

When booking a photography safari, make sure there are no more than four people in your vehicle for maximum viewing. Try to camp on-site in a park, which makes it easier to get spectacular sunrise photos. Use a telephoto lens of at least 300 millimeters, and instead of bringing a tripod, ask the camp or lodge to give you a bag of beans or rice to support the camera, as it's likely to be propped on uneven objects such as the car or on a rock.

ALASKA

Dazzling glaciers and icebergs, sparkling waterways, and majestic whales are the iconic images of Alaska's Inside Passage. In fact, it's practically impossible to take a bad photo here. But on a photography trip, you can learn how best to capture images of bald eagles soaring about, mountain goats scrambling on the cliffs, sea lions sprawled out on rock outcrops, or brown bears meandering along the shorelines feeding on salmon.

You can't lose on a National Geographic Expeditions photography trip, led by professionals who show you how to approach a scene as if it were a *National Geographic* assignment. The Inside Passage trip is led by one of the world's leading whale photographers who also happens to be a biologist. Don't worry about being intimidated. These expeditions are geared toward amateurs, and leaders break down the process—from choosing your subject and framing the image to capturing the best light. www.nationalgeographicexpeditions.com

GALAPAGOS

Expedition and wildlife photography require special techniques, and the Galapagos is the ideal place to hone those skills. This region is teeming with wildlife creatures that are ready for their close-up, from tortoises to iguanas to the famous booby birds. On a Lindblad Expedition cruise, a pro photographer is on board each ship to offer instruction on how to capture images of the brilliant color and life in the Galapagos. This program is designed for all levels, whether you're an amateur enthusiast or a professional building a portfolio. www.expeditions.com

BHUTAN

It may not be on your bucket list, but it should be. The Kingdom of Bhutan is a small, landlocked country bordered by the eastern Himalayas, Tibet, and several Indian states. From architecturally impressive *dzongs* (fortresses) to colorful religious festivals and astonishingly beautiful *lhakhangs* (temples), backed by the mighty Himalayan peaks, the country is rife with photo-worthy scenery. Because tourism in Bhutan is so regulated, you need to go with a guided tour operator. Destination Himalaya offers a series of photo-cultural tours through Bhutan and Himalayan countries where you can capture images at the best time of day. While a tourist might see Taksang Gompa (Tiger's Nest) in the cooler morning hours, your group would most likely be there in the afternoon when the light is more dramatic. www.destinationhimalaya.net

You can photograph in most Bhutan dzongs and lhakhangs, but not in the assembly halls or religious temples. People are generally friendly and open to being photographed, but it's always polite to ask first.

CANADA

Natural wonders are not always a continent away. Canada's Aurum Lodge is an ecoresort that overlooks Lake Abraham and is surrounded by forests and mountain peaks. It's adjacent to the stunning Banff National Park. The lodge hosts seasonal events for photographers, led by professional landscape shooters Leslie Degner, Darwin Wiggett, and Royce Howland. These hybrid work-shop/tours not only help out beginners, but can help lead pros to that idyllic shot of the Canadian Rockies. Excursions focus on out-of-the-way but still amazing spots that are overlooked by many guidebooks.

At least half of your photography subjects will be inside the national park itself, and other times will focus on the less-explored areas outside the park—whether it's nearby canyons, waterfalls, or subalpine forests. Depending on the season, you may explore areas known for fall foliage, wildlife sightings, or interesting ice formations. www.aurumlodge.com

COTSWOLDS, ENGLAND

In the scenic Cotswolds in England, try the beginner digital photography course at the Mayfield House Hotel in Wiltshire. These 3-day courses only require a point-and-shoot camera (though you're welcome to bring a digital SLR if you want). Professional photographer Terry Hewlett will walk you through the basic operation of your camera and help you explore all its capabilities, then take you to the Cotswolds countryside to capture some of the scenery. He'll give you tips on composition and lighting as you tour the Westonbirt National Arboretum, the Cotswold Water Park, the Bibury Saxon Church, and many quiet little towns and villages. At the end, you'll have a critique session where you'll get feedback on areas of improvement. One single price covers accommodation, most meals, and tuition. www.mayfieldhousehotel.co.uk

Shoot Like a Pro

When it comes to taking a photo, composition is everything. Don't just center your subject in the middle of the frame and hope for the best. Try dividing your field of vision into thirds, and arrange subjects either a third of the way from the top or bottom of the frame, or a third of the way from the left or right. Look for interesting shapes and textures, and experiment with lights and shadows. In fact, a great tip is to shoot the same picture at different times of day. Take pictures from every possible angle and play with the distance.

SHOPPING

SHOPPING MALLS, OUTLETS, AND DEPARTMENT STORES

If you were born to shop (or simply enjoy the fine art of buying), then you are always on the lookout for the best shopping malls. They do in fact exist—and, more often than not, size does matter.

MALLS

Dubai's Mall of the Emirates is 764,000 square feet of air-conditioned glory, where you'll find everything including the proverbial kitchen sink: 520 retail stores, four department stores, 85 restaurants and cafes, a 14-screen cinema, an arts center, a children's adventure and play area, and the famous indoor ski slope. The concourses are wide and uncrowded, and the architecture itself is lovely. There is a massive blue-glass domed skylight, overhead bridge walkways with intricate wrought-iron railings, plenty of seating for when you inevitably get tired, and even prayer rooms. The anchor stores include French gourmet grocery store Carrefour, the mid-range British department store Debenhams, and the UK-based Harvey Nichols (the latter two being the largest branches in the Middle East). Further cementing the mall's reputation as a destination unto itself are the two hotels attached to it, the five-star Kempinski and the Pullman Dubai, meaning you can stay overnight "in" the mall. www.mallofthecmirates.com

The Dubai Mall is bigger but not necessarily better than the Mall of the Emirates, though it has its own roster of superstar attractions. Located at the base of the Burj Khalifa, the tallest skyscraper in the world, this 12-million-square-foot megamall features a whopping 1,200 shops, an indoor amusement park, an aquarium and underwater zoo housing more than 33,000 marine animals, a 22-screen movie theater, an Olympic-size ice rink, and an indoor souk. Anchor stores include Bloomingdale's, Galeries Lafayette (the first in the Middle East), Debenhams, Marks & Spencer, and Paris Gallery. For kids, there's KidZania, an "edutainment" center where kids get to try being a doctor, firefighter, or news reporter for a day. Throughout the mall, musicians playing traditional Arab musical instruments and magicians, clowns, mimes, and other performers entertain shoppers. Outside is the largest dancing water and light fountain show in the world, designed by the same team that designed the water and light show at Bellagio in Las Vegas. www.the dubaimall.com

Sometimes, the concept of a megamall is so strong that a country will try to brand itself around it. Such is the case with the new Morocco Mall in **Casablanca,** one of the five largest in the world and the largest in Africa. Overlooking the Atlantic Ocean, this 250-acre complex opened with 600 shops and restaurants, as well as an aquarium with a million liters of water, an ice skating rink, and the first IMAX theater in Africa. Its first customer? Jennifer Lopez. Don't worry about crowds just yet . . . Ms. Lopez has left the building. www.moroccomall.com

Go to GUM in **Moscow** just to marvel, not necessarily to shop. There are several branches of department stores, but you want to go to the flagship mall, located right on Red Square opposite Lenin's mausoleum. Although the site dates back to 1890, the current structure was built in the 1890s in the style of a European train station, with a glass roof and steel frame. During the Soviet era, this multi-level emporium was a crumbling architectural gem that housed a series of decrepit, half-empty stalls where people queued up for hours for shoddy Bulgarian linens and ugly Chinese shoes. (Back in the day, the top floor boasted a secret clothing store for party officials.) Fast-forward two decades, and it's been transformed into a gleaming shopping powerhouse with luxury brands that reflect nouveau riche Russia. The prices are outrageous, and similar items can be bought for half as much in Paris or New York, but you can't go to Moscow without going to GUM.

Don't forget to jump across the street to Tsum, another shopping emporium of similar style and stature. The historic art nouveau building sits adjacent to the famed Bolshoi Theater, and the shops include luxury brands such as Dior, Gucci, and Prada, but also more affordable midrange brands. Even better, twice a year, in summer and winter, there are massive sales where you can save even more.

Milan's Galleria Vittorio Emanuele II may not be the biggest or have the most amenities of any mall, but it does have one thing going for it: It's jaw-dropping beautiful. This is one of the great buildings of the world and pioneered the covered mall concept in Europe, connecting il Duomo and La Scala. An ornate glass dome arches over an octagonal central square decorated with intricate mosaics. Bring your credit cards, or just plan to window-shop. After all, this is the fashion capital, and the mall is home to the highest of the high-end retailers like Prada, Gucci, and Louis Vuitton as well as exquisite jewelry shops. Stop by the historic Biffi cafe, which dates back to 1867, for a tiramisu and espresso. www.biffigalleria.it

Over the years, **Las Vegas** has reinvented itself as a shopping destination. It seems like every major resort casino has a shopping zone. But the one you don't want to miss is the Forum Shops at Caesar's Palace. This mall is seriously kitschy and campy, but fun. The ceiling is painted to look like the sky, the architecture is faux Roman, and the statues look like marble, but they actually speak and sing. Who doesn't love animatronic statues? For those with a sense of humor, the hourly "Fall of Atlantis" show is free. But the shopping is serious stuff—in fact, the mall boasts the highest sales per square foot in the United States, and nearly two-thirds of all

INSIDER'S TIP

The New South China Mall in the Guangdong Province opened in 2005 as the world's largest retail mall, with separate zones representing cities around the world— including a 75-foot-tall replica of the Arc de Triomphe, a canal complete with gondolas, and windmills. But a few short years later, it's become a veritable ghost town, with the majority of its retail space unleased and all the attractions empty of patrons. Is this a sign of the times, or an inevitable result of hubris when too big becomes too much?

visitors to Las Vegas shop here during their stay. What's cool about this mall is that it's usually the debut point of retailers new to Vegas. For example, in one year, they added H&M, Christian Louboutin, Sephora, and UGG Australia, among others. Three expansions over the last 20 years have added hundreds of thousands of square feet to the mall, which keeps outperforming its rivals, despite the recession. The latest expansion in 2004 added a reflecting pool, two exterior fountains (Trevi and Triton), and the first freestanding spiral escalator in the United States. Dining is also big business here, with most restaurants featuring legendary names like Guy Savoy, Raos, and Bobby Flay's Mesa Grill. www.caesarspalace.com

The Mall of America is a destination unto itself. In fact, more than 40 million visitors come to Bloomington, **Minnesota,** every year from all over just to visit the mall. With 520 shops, there is indeed plenty to buy, and as an added bonus, there's no sales tax on clothing and shoes. But people also come here to play, attend events, and even get married! There's the Nickelodeon-themed leisure park, with a roller coaster and dozens of other rides; the Chapel of Love, which has married more than 5,000 couples to date; the Lego Imagination Center, which features a 34-foot-tall Lego model; an underwater aquarium; and a flight simulator. Upcoming plans include a Radisson Blu hotel that will be connected by a sky bridge, a waterpark, and a 4,000-seat performing arts theater. www. mallofamerica.com

In **Bangkok,** Siam Paragon hits all the marks: It combines great architecture with a wide variety of shops, several "wow" attractions, and activities for kids. With seven stories, the mall includes a 21-screen cinema and IMAX 3-D screen, the largest aquarium in the Southern Hemisphere, a bowling alley, and a science institute for children. Definitely hit up Spice Story on the ground floor, which sells every kind of spice in the world divided into four sections: Chinese, Thai, Western, and prepared mixed seasonings for specific dishes. As a bonus, purchases from the mall are delivered to your hotel free of charge. Tip: Once in Bangkok, a good way to get to Siam

Paragon is to catch the BTS skytrain and stop at the Siam station, which connects to the mall. www.siamparagon.co.th

For the simple pleasure of people watching, go to one of the oldest malls in Bangkok, Siam Center, and its newer sister venue that focuses on household items, Siam Discovery. This is where Thai teenagers congregate daily after school and on weekends in the busy food court, shopping for the trendiest threads or listening to live music. Within the center, popular choices include Soda Pop, a famous Thai brand that features funky women's clothes, and its male counterpart, Guys' Soda. Another local favorite is Greyhound, one of the original Bangkok designers to hit the international scene. And don't miss the Good Mixer label from Chaichon Savantrat, one of the forerunners in Thailand's men's fashion design. www.siampiwat.com

With its ornate facade and towers on either side, Ngee Ann City has an imposing, regal presence in **Singapore.** This city within a city sprawls over 1.75 million square feet and is comprised of multiple squares and plazas. There are at least 130 stores in the mall, but the real reason to go here is to browse through the megasize Japanese bookstore, Kinokuniya, and Best Denki, a massive Japanese electronic shop. For locals, the main attraction here isn't necessarily the stores but the nearly 10,000 square-foot outdoor courtyard where there are events, competitions, and festivals throughout the year. www.ngeeanncity.com.sg

OUTLETS

Woodbury Common Premium Outlets in Central Valley, **New York,** is an amazingly comprehensive outlet center great for a day trip from New York City and the Catskills. It's also a huge attraction for international travelers—including Japanese tourists who head there straight from the airport with empty suitcases in hand. The 220 stores include some of fashion's top names such as

Versace, Saint Laurent, and Valentino, but also more moderately priced shops like DKNY and Lululemon. And don't forget the specialty stores that sell luggage, jewelry, and housewares. New shops are always opening, so it's possible to find something new on each trip. To avoid the crowds, visit on a Wednesday in the early afternoon. Throughout the year, temporary clearance stores pop up, offering even bigger discounts than you can already get, and every Labor Day there's a Sidewalk Sale that features super-deep price cuts. Tip: If you're age 50 or older, ask if you can get an additional 10 percent off. www.premiumoutlets.com

Chic Outlet Shopping is a collection of nine "villages" all around **Europe** where you can score some serious discounts on fashion and accessories, especially on collections from the previous season. These are geared toward international travelers, so you'll encounter multilingual staff and easy access by public transportation or shuttles. Ingolstadt Village is about an hour outside of Munich, with train service from Hauptbahnhof Central Station to Ingolstadt main station, where you can take a bus to the outlets. International and German brands abound here, with a special focus on skiwear, including names like Napapijri, Salomon, and Falke. Outside of Oxford, **England,** is Bicester Village, which is accessible from London via Chiltern Railways followed by a shuttle bus. Look for British names like Burberry and Thomas Pink alongside international designers, and start tracking down the deals. www.chicoutlet shopping.com

Located about a half hour from **Florence** in the Tuscan countryside, the Mall is known for its beautiful architecture as much as the discounts. It's laid out as a network of warehouse-style buildings in a bucolic setting with gardens and rolling hillside. You'll only find high-end brands here, like Armani and Balenciaga, along with its own VAT refund center and concierge service. Focus on Italian brands and you're likely to save anywhere from 25 to 65 percent, particularly on its large selection of accessories like handbags and sunglasses. It's easy to get to from Florence with daily buses and shuttles. www.themall.it

DEPARTMENT STORES

In the heart of **Berlin**'s Tauentzienstraße shopping district, Kaufhaus Des Westens—or simply, KaDeWe—is both a historical monument and a retail superstore. The store dates back to 1907, but in 1933 Nazi laws forced its Jewish owners to sell the building. In 1943 the store was destroyed when an American plane crashed into the building, which nearly burned to the ground. Its full restoration wasn't complete until the mid-1950s, but the massive structure quickly evolved into a cultural symbol of recovery, prosperity, and freedom. The building takes up an entire city block, and its crowning glory is its acre-long food hall with an astonishing amount of products. Basically, if you want it, they've got it: hundreds—if not thousands—of varieties of wine, beer, smoked meats, cheese, caviar, exotic fruits, pastries, and anything else you can imagine. www.kadewe.de

London's Harvey Nichols is a temple of high-fashion retail. Known by locals as "Harvey Nicks," the store contains a series of designer boutiques spread over eight floors in the heart of fashionable Knightsbridge. Though it is only a stone's throw from that other temple of retail, Harrods, Harvey Nicks attracts a hipper, more upmarket crowd and is more modern in its focus—not to mention it's smaller and more manageable. Highlights include the top-floor gourmet food shop and restaurant (which serves an excellent afternoon tea), the breathtaking (and often bizarre) window displays and mannequins, hard-to-find collections and items (like vintage handbags), and celebrity sightings. There are branches of Harvey Nicks all over the world, but the flagship store in London is the original and the best. www.harveynichols.com

The area around the Shinjuku train station in **Tokyo** is one of the largest shopping districts in the country, with six (yes, six) huge department stores and countless other types of retailers. Four of the department stores are actually within the station perimeter, and some are even associated with private train lines. Warning: This shopping area is not for the faint of heart. To say it's crowded is an understatement. Approximately 3 million people pass through Shinjuku station every day, so be prepared to be bumped, jostled, and generally overwhelmed by the sheer scale of it all. Here are four of the best places to focus your efforts:

Isetan: This 120-year-old store offers eight floors of shopping madness, including a tower just for men's goods. The top floor has multiple restaurants, and the basement has a massive food market packed with stalls hawking sushi, sandwiches, and a huge variety of pastries. As far as clothing and accessories go, you can find both European and local designer labels, plus a great selection of traditional kimonos. The striking art deco building is located on the east side of the train station. www.isetan.co.jp

Takashimaya: Part of the "Times Square" shopping complex just to the south of the station, this branch of the venerable Takashimaya is one of the largest in the country, consisting of 15 floors that are packed pretty much all the time. www.takashimaya.co.jp

Odakyu: Located on the west side of the station, Odakyu Department Store has 14 aboveground floors and two belowground—and features one of the largest cosmetics departments in the country. This store makes things easy for overseas shoppers, with store guides printed in several foreign languages and multilingual customer service reps at the tax-refund desk. It's owned by the Odakyu Group, which operates the suburban railway line from Shinjuku to Odawara. www.odakyu.jp

Keio: This department store belongs to the Keio Group, which also operates a suburban railway line from Shinjuku to western Tokyo. It sits on the west side of Shinjuku station, and the 11 floors include a food department in the basement, which is known for its outstanding candy counter, a Hello Kitty store on the seventh floor, and a fantastic stationery counter.

At Gump's in **San Francisco,** this one-of-a-kind store offers a sophisticated selection of furniture, stationery, flatware, crystal, antiques, jewelry, and objets d'art. In fact, people come to Gump's just to gawk at the beautifully curated collections, which range in price from reasonable to stratospheric. You'll often find odd creations such as lamps in the shape of birds, or 6-foot-tall ceramic flowers. Some liken it to a museum where you can buy all the art. During the winter holidays, they sell items like quirky tree ornaments and handmade wrapping paper. www.gumps.com

Move over, Barney's. Jeffrey, the "mini" department store in the Meatpacking District, is where well-off **Manhattan** fashionistas go to get their fix. The store is small but immaculately laid out, with collections of clothing, accessories, cosmetics, fragrances, and a fantastic shoe department. Buyers have an eye for the best pieces from the collections of both established and cutting-edge designers. This store is like one-stop shopping for top designers, because many of the items can only be found here or at the designer's own shop. The drawback is that they tend to have only one or two of each piece in each size. At the 75 percent off sale in July, prices do come down; otherwise, be prepared to shell out some serious cash. www.jeffrey-newyork.com

---

INSIDER'S TIP

Many of the larger stores in Japan that cater to foreign tourists offer tax-free purchasing, so hold on to your receipts. If you spend more than 10,001 yen on any given day in one shop, you are entitled to a refund of the 5 percent consumption tax (unless you're buying cosmetics, food, alcohol, cigarettes, medicine, film, and batteries). Go to the refund desk in the store before you leave, because unlike in some other countries, you can't get your refund at the airport.

SPECIALTY SHOPPING

Shopping for special, one-of-a-kind items is what makes travel an even more enriching experience—even long after you're home, you have mementos to remind you of your trip. But full credit goes to my childhood friend, Suzy Gershman, who literally wrote the book on this—or I should say books: the immensely successful "Born to Shop" series. Suzy knows all the backdoor stores, the hidden alley merchants, and not only where, but when to shop. So, with a lot of help from Suzy as well as my own world shopping experiences, here are our picks for the best inside shopping.

FASHION

You can't go wrong with a custom-made suit from WW Chan & Sons in Kowloon, **Hong Kong.** This unassuming little store on Nathan Road creates bespoke tailoring for men and women, using only high-quality European wool, Irish linen, and Italian cashmere. Each pattern is hand drawn, and every suit is made by hand. You can also find business attire for women at its sister store, Irene Fashions. www.wwchan.com

There's also a WW Chan outpost in **Shanghai,** but another local favorite for high-end custom suits is a man named Dave. Tailor Dave, to be exact. Like WW Chan, he uses the traditional Savile Row methods of tailoring, but for a fraction of London prices. Best of all, he can do a one-day turnaround, if necessary, although a typical waiting time is about 7 days for custom fitting, cutting, and sewing. www.tailordave.com

Then there's the best tailor for copying suits and other outfits you already know. Go to Trend Maker in **Bangkok** and ask for Mr. Lek. Bring your favorite outfit, and 24 hours later it's done. What I do is have a great tailored suit done in the United States, then take it to Bangkok. Mr. Lek then copies it exactly, in the fabric and color of my choice. But here's the best part: For every suit I give him to copy masterfully, he returns the new suit with one jacket and . . . three pairs of pants! How cool is that? The key here: Arrive, go to see Mr. Lek, and pick out your fabric and color for him to copy your garment. Then go see Bangkok. Two days later, your completed order is perfectly packed and delivered to your hotel. You can reach Trend Maker at tphirom@yahoo.com.

When visiting **Boston,** you know you can head straight to Newbury Street for high fashion. But savvy travelers go to the suburb of Hanover to visit Natale's Men's Clothier of Hanover, an unexpected home of high-end men's clothing. Owner Natale Agostino began his tailoring career as a 7-year-old boy in Reggio Calabra, Italy, where he was a tailor's apprentice. At Natale's, you'll find high-quality, custom-tailored items for mature men, designed by Natale himself, who creates on his own conception of what should be fashionable for the season. He claims he has never stepped foot in a retail store, but makes up his own mind on trends based on his travels to fashion shows in Europe and Brazil. www.natalesofhanover.com

J. Mendel of **New York** started out as a luxury furrier in 1870 but has since branched out in all directions and now makes a wide variety of items that blend fur and pelts with such fabrics as cashmere, silk, and leather. You can still buy the standard mink coat, but you can also get mink bikinis, fur-trimmed jeans and denim jackets, and sable-lined lace skirts with cashmere. www.jmendel.com

Corniche Furs has been selling furs, shearling, reversible raincoats, and cashmeres from its home on Seventh Avenue in New York City since 1991. But the great thing about this store is that it specializes in fur repairs, alterations, and "remodeling." Corniche will also refurbish and restyle your older, outdated garments into something fresh and fabulous. www.cornichefurs.com

Scotland is naturally the best place to buy kilts, but the place you want to go is Geoffrey Kiltmakers and Weavers (www.geoffreykilts. co.uk) in Edinburgh, for a traditional hand-sewn, made-to-measure tartan. It's worth a visit just to see the complete array of tartan waistcoats, trousers, blazers, and accessories such as buckles, sporrans, pins, and brooches. On the other end of the spectrum is 21st Century Kilts (www.21stcenturykilts.com), which specializes in cutting-edge kilts (yes, there is such a thing) made from modern materials and designs such as leather, denim, camouflage, and pinstripe.

It seems like there are a million places to buy saris in **India,** but Anokhi stands out because it combines bold, innovative designs with sustainable business practices. All saris are block-printed cotton and handmade by a team of 300 artisans in Jaipur. Its headquarters are also in Jaipur, along with the Anokhi Museum of Hand Printing. The proprietors have made it a point not to pay kickbacks, so don't let your driver or guide try to steer you to an alternate sari shop. www.anokhi.com

Muumuu Heaven in the town of Kailua, **Hawaii,** is a family-run shop that sells "repurposed" muumuus. That means vintage muumuus are deconstructed and refashioned into one-of-a-kind dresses and tops in modern silhouettes. As a bonus, you can also pick up pillows made from Hawaiian shirts. www.muumuuheaven.com

You can't go to **Bermuda** without coming back with a pair of Bermuda shorts. But don't just pick up a tacky pair at a souvenir shop. Get the real deal at Sampson's Too Tailoring in Hamilton, where you can get a custom-made pair or two—one in bright island colors, and one more subdued.

ACCESSORIES

On Rua do Carmo in **Lisbon,** behind an ornate façade is Luvaria Ulisses, a miniscule shop selling all kinds of exquisite leather and lambskin gloves. This shop has been around since 1925, and trust me, when you find the right pair, they'll fit you like . . . well, you get the picture. www.luvariaulisses.com/uk

The famed Panama hat actually originates in **Ecuador.** Homero Ortega P. & Hijos has been one of the top makers in Ecuador for more than 40 years. It carries not only the classic men's straw version, but also contemporary styles. You can buy an authentic hat in Quito, but the factory is located in the town of Cuenca, along with a museum dedicated to the process of the famous accessory. www.homeroortega.com

CA4LA (which is pronounced "Ka-shi-la" and means "head" in Japanese) is a major trendsetting hat designer in **Tokyo,** taking traditional styles and adding add a hip, youthful edge. At its flagship store you'll find trilby hats, bowler hats, pork pies, beanies, flat caps, berets, sailor hats, baseball caps, hair bands, and sun visors. There are about a dozen other branches around Japan and one in London. www.ca4la.com

For 87 years the Hat Store in Houston, **Texas,** has offered one-stop shopping for the best in custom cowboy hats. In addition to store-brand hats, it stocks and fits Bailey, Stetson, Milano, and Resistol hats. Employees will steam and hand-shape them to your exact specifications, ensuring a perfect fit. www.thehatstore.com

The area around Murillo Street in **Buenos Aires** is known worldwide as a mecca for leather goods. There are four solid blocks of at least 50 shops that sell everything from leather sofas to biker jackets. Murillo 666 is a favorite. They have an excellent selection of handbags, belts, furniture, and leather jackets (and can even custom make one for you). Unlike some other stores in the area, prices are the same whether you pay with credit or cash, and they don't give you the hard sell. www.murillo666.com.ar

Hester Van Eeghen in **Amsterdam** at 1 and 37 Haartenstraat sells stylish leather shoes, bags, wallets, gloves, and other accessories that are designed in Holland but made in Italy. The brightly colored, modern designs stand out in the damp, gray climate of the Netherlands. www.hestervaneeghen.com

At Beautiful Shoes in Phnom Penh, **Cambodia,** cobblers will whip you up a pair of sandals, boots, or pumps for as little as $12 and they can finish the job in about 3 days.

At the Lucchese outlet in El Paso, **Texas,** you can choose from among 4,500 pairs of the legendary cowboy boots. Starting at $190, they are not cheap, but they are a fraction of the price of the regular retail outlet. The outlet merchandise may have small imperfections such as tiny scuff marks or stitching irregularities, but hey, they're going to get scuffed anyway, right? www.lucchese.com

Blue Bag is a charming **Manhattan** boutique that sells two-of-a-kind handbags made by a stable of 28 nonfamous (but talented) designers. At any given time, there are 160 styles of clutches, purses, hobo bags, totes, and evening bags to suit all tastes and price ranges. www.bluebag.tumblr.com

In Florence, **Italy,** a tiny store called Venetzia sells the work of local artisans. Among them you'll find Birkin-style and Kelly-style handbags made of Venetian velvet trimmed with leather.

Perez Sanz on Calle Posadas in **Buenos Aires** offers true artistry in style. Its one-of-a-kind bags are made with handcrafted clasps and museum-quality creativity. www.perezsanz.com

Button Button is a quirky little shop on the edge of Gastown, in downtown **Vancouver,** carrying approximately one million modern and vintage buttons from all over the world. Of course there are standard plastic buttons in all shapes and sizes, but there are hundreds made of unusual materials like metal, recycled glass, tree bark, Bakelite, rhinestone, porcelain, and shell. www.buttonbutton.ca

Stefano Ricci exports its famous neckties worldwide, but they are made at the company's home base on via de Niccoli in **Florence.** Each tie is unique and handmade on antique looms using the finest Italian silk. In addition to ties, the store sells immaculately designed men's shirts, cufflinks, and luxury leather goods. www.stefanoricci.it

PERFUME

The best place to buy perfume is often at the source: the factory. Not only can you buy direct from the manufacturer and save money, but chances are you'll have a great behind-the-scenes experience, too. At the Fragonard perfume factory in Grasse, **France** (on the Mediterranean coast), you can take a tour on which you'll watch the entire creation process, from distillation to bottling. Even entering the factory is like walking through a garden, literally, since you walk through a collection of flowers and fragrant plants. And don't miss the museum, which contains artifacts and art that cover 3,000 years of perfume history. When you're done, go ahead and stock up on famous Fragonard scents like Belle de Nuit and Suivez-Moi, at factory prices. www.fragonard.com

That said, sometimes it's those tiny shops that have the best selection. You can't shop for perfume in Paris without checking out Salons du Palais Royal Shiseido, which showcases the creations of renowned perfumer Serge Lutens. The trick is choosing the right scent: Shiseido sells an export line, which you can purchase in high-end shops around the world; and an "exclusive" line, which can only be purchased in the shop (or online if you—or a friend—live in Europe). You'll know it from the distinctive 75 milliliter bell jar bottle and the exorbitant price tag.

Not all high-quality perfume has to come from Paris. In **Bermuda,** make sure to stop by Bermuda Perfumery at Stewart Hall. Not only can you shop for your signature perfume, but you can also actually see how master perfumer Isabelle Ramsay-Brackstone creates her one-of-a-kind scents the old-fashioned way, using Bermuda flowers and citrus trees for inspiration. www.bermuda-perfumery.com

JEWELRY

For good-quality gemstones and jewelry at reasonable prices, **Bangkok** is the place to be. But that comes with a caveat, since some vendors are more reliable than others. Here's a tip: If your driver or guide insists on taking you to a certain shop, you can assume they're getting a kickback. Make sure you're going to a place that's a member of the Thai Gems and Jewelry Traders Association. Johny's Gems (www.johnysgems.com) on Fueng Nakorn Road (near the Grand Palace), which focuses mainly on rubies and emeralds, is one of the more trusted shops. This 50-year-old family-owned store has necklaces, earrings, pendants, and rings at all price points. Hundreds of other reputable stores can be found in Bangkok's gem and jewelry district, which is spread out over Charoen Krung Road, Yaoworat Road, Silom Road, Mahesak Road, and Khaosan Road. Don't be afraid to negotiate if you see something you like.

There's no shortage of jewelry shops throughout **India,** but the can't-miss stop is Jaipur's Gem Palace. This unique and historic shop (which opened in 1852) has been run by the same family for eight generations and used to be the jewelry maker to maharajas. Today, it supplies high-end off-the-rack and custom-made baubles.

They also display (and sell) an unbelievable collection of antique Indian jewels and artifacts from the Mughal period. It's not the best place to find bargains, though you can haggle on price. But what's really fun is that you can watch jewelers create high-end pieces in the in-house workshop. Gem Palace also sells its jewels at Barneys in New York and Los Angeles. www.gempalacejaipur.com

For the best quality pearls, why not go to the original cultured pearl maker, Mikimoto? Its flagship store is in the Ginza district of **Tokyo** where you can get top-quality pearls at better prices than you can back in the United States. And the store itself is an amazing sight, with five floors of pearls in all sizes and arrangements. www.mikimoto.com

Another excellent, but surprising, place for cultured pearls is the Greenhills Shopping Center in **Manila.** This mall isn't a glam destination—in fact, it's an indoor upscale flea market venue with an entire section devoted to pearl and gem dealers. But great bargains can be found here on fresh water, cultured, South Sea, and man-made pearls in all sizes, shapes, and colors. There are bins of loose pearls, matched pairs waiting to become earrings, hundreds of hanging strands, and ready-to-wear pearl jewelry. www.greenhills.com.ph

In the area surrounding Passeig del Born in **Barcelona,** there are dozens of small lanes packed with trendy, creative boutiques offering local crafts, clothing, shoes, and accessories. One of the best streets is Carrer Argenteria (named for its resident silversmiths), with an array of stores offering unusual and often affordable gems and trinkets.

Most visitors to **Dubai** head straight to one of the many mega malls, but those who want a wide variety of bargain gold jewelry head to the gold souk (market) in the somewhat unfashionable Deira neighborhood. More than 300 vendors stock a total of 10 tons of gold jewelry, which can be literally blinding in its intensity at times. Haggling is expected, and the quality of the gold is regulated by the government, so you don't have to worry about buying something other than what you think you're getting. www.dubaigoldsouk.com

ART AND CRAFTS

Your memories of **Paris** may linger far longer if you pick up one of the dozens of music boxes at Boîtes à Musique Anna Joliet, a tiny shop that may have the exact style and tune that you didn't know you were looking for. www.boitesamusiqueannajoliet.com

The town of Stoke-on-Trent in **England** is known as "the Potteries" or the "world capital of ceramics" because it is home to more than 25 factory stores. You'll find famous brands such as Wedgwood, Royal Doulton, Portmeirion, Aynsley, Churchill, and Moorcroft. Then there's the Wedgwood Visitor Centre and Museum, the Potteries Museum and Art Gallery, and the Gladstone Pottery Museum where you can get behind-the-scenes tours and learn about the history and craftsmanship of fine ceramics. www.wedgwoodvisitorcen tre.com

Though it's got fewer stores than it used to, rue de Paradis in **Paris**'s 10th arrondissement is known for its shops that sell discount glass, crystal, and porcelain. The same pieces that can be found in Parisian department stores can be found here for less. Brands include Baccarat, Hermès, Lalique, and Rosenthal. A favorite is the Cristal-lerie de Paris, at 1, rue de Paradis. www.cristallerie-de-paris.fr

In **Vietnam,** Bát Tràng isn't just a store. It's an entire village dedicated to pottery and ceramics, including the coveted Bát Tràng porcelain. Located about 8 miles from the center of Hanoi, this village is chock-full of workshops and stores where you can purchase affordable and distinctive dishes, vases, jars, and more. www.gom subattrang.com

One of the more unusual artists' colonies in the world is just outside of Shenzhen, **China.** At Dafen Oil Painting Village, hundreds of artists have set up shop and can copy virtually any painting you desire, even from a photo, and ship it to you. Raphaelite cherubs? Chairman Mao? Alan Greenspan? Your grandchildren? It's all there. Dafen is also home to dozens of original painters producing top-quality—and a good amount of mediocre—art. Although the village has been remodeled over the years, it's a refreshing throwback with squat buildings and charming courtyards. www.dafenart.com

Commit to putting away your BlackBerry and write an old-fashioned letter. Cassegrain in **Paris** is the place to go to buy fine engraved paper products. Since 1919 everyone from diplomats to designers have been coming here to get elegant stationery and calling cards made to their custom specifications, but you can also buy items off the rack. They also sell glass-nib writing pens, office accessories, wallets, and other leather goods. There are two locations, but stick with the original at 422, rue Saint-Honoré. www.cassegrain.fr

There's a great paper district in Seoul, **South Korea,** of all places. The neighborhood of Insa-dong is rife with shops that carry traditional *hanji* (paper that's handmade from the bark of the paper mulberry tree), dyed woven rice paper, paper fans, cards, and other types of papercrafts. Notable shops to stop in at are the Myung Sin Dang Brush Store and Tong-In, which both carry paper plus an array of other traditional hand-crafted Korean items such as wooden masks and ceramics. www.tonginstore.com

The Chatuchak Market in **Bangkok** has numerous vendors who sell a bewildering array of writing paper, wrapping paper, gift bags, and just about any other paper product you can imagine.

Moser Glass in **Prague** is famous for its ecofriendly lead-free crystal stemware, which it has been making for 150 years. This high-end Bohemian glass is handblown, hand cut, hand engraved, and hand painted. It can be pricey though; consider visiting the factory outlet store in the town of Karlovy Vary. You can even see glass-blowing demonstrations there and visit the glass museum. www.moser-glass.com/en

Hoglund Art Glass offers one-of-a kind handmade blown-glass pieces made in the Hoglund family's workshop in **New Zealand**'s South Island town of Nelson. Swedish-born glass artists Ola and Marie Hogland started the business in 1982, and their artisans now produce a stunning array of award-winning designs that reflect the landscape and flavor of New Zealand, from their signature glass penguins to luminous abstract plates, vases, and wall pieces. www.hoglund.co.nz

The simple, yet innovative glass designs of Iittala (www.iittala

.com) in **Helsinki** really are one of a kind. Each piece has a distinctly Scandinavian flair and their creations include everything from vases and candlesticks to glass birds and glass-and-steel fireplaces. Although there are several stores throughout Europe, your best bet is to head to the outlet store at Hämeentie 135. Another Helsinki favorite is Vanhaa ja Kaunista, which sells vintage Finnish glassware and ceramics from the 1940s to the 1980s.

The **Kyoto** Handicraft Center is a seven-story craft emporium featuring hundreds of vendors selling traditional Japanese crafts made of clay, paper, wood, textiles, and more. You'll find everything from lacquer vases to samurai swords to kimonos to painted screens and calligraphy scrolls. Shoppers can buy, watch artisans at work, or try their hand at making items like wood-block painted fans or cloisonne jewelry. Instruction is in English. www.kyoto handicraftcenter.com

Viaduc des Arts is an arts center in the 12th arrondissement of **Paris** that was formerly a railway viaduct and now houses galleries and workshops of more than 50 artists and craftsmen who make and sell everything from picture frames to music boxes to bronze lamps. The galleries occupy the arched vaults beneath the former rail line, while a planted promenade occupies the top where the track used to run. www.viaducdesarts.fr

Phahurat Textile Market in the Little India section of **Bangkok** features hundreds of Indian retailers who sell fabrics in every color, shape, and pattern you could possibly imagine. You can find Indian

INSIDER'S TIP

In Paris, a shop window sign that says *soldes gros* **means wholesale only, so don't bother. Look for signs that say** *soldes détail,* **which means "retail."**

cottons, silk, batik, sarongs, children's clothes, and more. Since the fabric market is part of a large general merchandise market, finding it can be a bit difficult, so ask around when you get there.

The Montmartre area of **Paris** is clogged with dozens of fabric stores. The most famous one is the five-story Marché Saint-Pierre, which stocks thousands of bolts of leftovers from factories and designers. In addition to the basic cottons, silks, and linens, you can find hand-embroidered gauze, fake fur, and distressed velvet—but remember, the stock changes every day so if you see something you like, grab it while you can! www.marchesaintpierre.com

TOYS

Hakuhinkan Toy Park in **Tokyo**'s Ginza district offers four floors of nothing but fun. The first three floors display the latest dolls, board games, model kits, puzzles, stuffed animals, and more, while the top floor features a "radical" game arcade, complete with a life-size slot car racetrack. Oh, and they offer a small selection of toys from vending machines outside the front door—how very Japanese. www.hakuhinkan.co.jp/guide_en.html

For more than 250 years, Hamley's has been delighting the kids of England with their high-quality toys and enormous selection. The seven-story 54,000-square-foot flagship store in **London** has entire floors for boys' toys, girls' toys, soft toys, games and puzzles, and interactive toys. Don't miss the newer range of Hamley's-branded wooden toys, including a wood model of the famous red London double-decker bus. There are branches all over England, but you want to see the Regent Street store near Piccadilly Circus. www.hamleys.co.uk

No toy store list is complete without mentioning FAO Schwarz. Although it's on every traveler's radar, this is truly a remarkable store. The flagship store (though not the original location) is on Fifth Avenue, and it remains one of the best ways to spend a day in **New York City.** www.fao.com

FURNITURE

If some hotel beds can send you straight to dreamland, you may wonder where you can find your own feather nest. Turns out it's in Muscle Shoals, **Alabama.** The Pillow Factory and Outlet makes everything from feather beds to down comforters, pillows, and decorative throws. Chances are you've slept on the bedding, as it manages to supply major hotel chains while catering to individual customers with custom-designed items. Talk to owner Jim Crossno to determine if you want a feather-light 8-ounce pillow or a firm 10-ounce mattress pad. He'll make sure you're happy with your selection and will even make adjustments after you've slept on it for a night or two.

Jerome, **Arizona,** was once known as the Wickedest Town in the West during its days as a thriving copper mining town. By the 1950s, it was the Largest Ghost Town in America. Today, it's the unexpected spot to find high-end, custom-made furniture at Western Heritage Furniture. Its specialty is the Ghostwood Collection, made with reclaimed wood from old buildings, houses, and barns. (Owner Tim McClellan started the company after making a bed out of cedar trees that were left over from logging companies doing clear cuts.) The wood is processed and hand-carved into highly finished, refined rustic furniture such as coffee and dining tables, chairs, and armoires. www.westernheritagefurniture.com

Best Places to Find

STREET MARKETS

One of my favorite things to do in any destination is to check out the local market, whether it's a regular flea market for bargain-basement prices or a holiday market that rings in the season with artisan crafts and twinkling lights. It's a great way to mingle with the locals and immerse myself into the culture. And yes, I almost always end up filling an additional suitcase I didn't know I'd need.

UNITED STATES

The Rose Bowl in Pasadena, **California,** may be known to most for football, but Angelenos know that the Rose Bowl Flea Market is the best place to go to find all manner of pop culture artifacts and vintage knickknacks, from the unusual to the mundane. Open the second Sunday of every month, it features 2,500 vendors hawking everything from Star Wars action figures to antique birdcages to surfboards to lawn statues. The inside area caters to for-profit merchants, while the outside area caters to the garage-sale hawkers who are selling their personal stuff. This market is not free, and the price varies according to what time you arrive. Early birds pay more—but that's when you get the pick of the litter. Bring a rolling carry-on bag for your purchases, because this place is vast and can take a whole day to browse through. http://rgcshows.com/RoseBowl.aspx

Aloha Stadium in **Honolulu** is about 20 minutes from Waikiki Beach. There, a swap meet comes to life every Wednesday, Saturday, and Sunday, with more than 700 merchants to choose from. Items for sale include handmade crafts and artwork from local artisans,

---

INSIDER'S TIP

Antiquing can be a great travel activity, especially if you uncover a unique, authentic find for a dirt-cheap price. Try to get there as early as possible to find the best quality pieces. Don't invest in major pieces unless you have an expert on hand to determine whether the item is authentic. Always make sure you get a certificate of authenticity.

---

clothing, unique jewelry, home decor, ukuleles, fruits and vegetables, and tourist trinkets for half the price of chain stores. This isn't really the place to buy antiques or vintage gear, but it's a good spot to get Hawaiian souvenirs in a venue that's off the beaten tourist track. www.alohastadiumswapmeet.net

The Tesuque Pueblo Flea Market, outside of Santa Fe, **New Mexico,** is packed with artisans showcasing southwestern works. Though it's called a flea market, it's more of an art showcase, manned by locals who make a living selling their creations. Among the items you can find are one-of-a-kind pottery, sculpture, rugs, antiques, jewelry, and apparel for a fraction of the price you'd pay in downtown Santa Fe. The food stands are particularly fun to explore, with Native American and Mexican delicacies. This open-air bazaar is located off of Highway 84/285. www.pueblooftesuquefleamarket.com

While plenty of tourists head to Manhattan to shop, savvy travelers will head to the **Brooklyn** Flea Market. This is actually two markets, which feature hundreds of vendors of antique and repurposed furniture, vintage clothing, collectibles, and antiques, as well as a tightly curated selection of jewelry, art, and crafts by local artisans and designers. The Fort Greene location is open every weekend on Saturdays, and Williamsburg operates on Sundays. In addition, on Saturdays at the Williamsburg waterfront, the all-food market Smorgasburg features more than 100 food vendors and farmers. From April through Thanksgiving, the markets take place outdoors at the above locations; from late November through March, the markets move indoors to Skylight One Hanson at Atlantic and Flatbush Avenues. www.brooklynflea.com

INTERNATIONAL

Bermondsey market (also known as New Caledonian market), located in Southwark, **London,** sells items ranging from china dolls to jewelry and navigational apparatus. It is open from 5 a.m. to noon on Fridays. As usual, you have to get there early to get the quality pieces, but if you are looking for a deal on what the early birds miss, get there around 11 a.m. when vendors want to sell what's left of their stock. Fun fact: The market traditionally starts early because of *marché ouvert*, a medieval law that says that stolen goods can legally be sold between sunrise and sunset.

What about Portobello Road in Notting Hill, one of London's most well-known street markets? Yes, it's touristy and crowded, and not as "authentic" as it was in its '60s heyday, but it can still be a lot of fun if you take it with a grain of salt. Portobello is really several markets in one. The southern stretch of the road is lined with permanent antiques shops and arcades, plus antiques stalls are set up in the street; in the middle, north of Elgin Crescent, is where you'll find dozens of fruit and vegetable stands. The part under the Westway (the elevated highway) has the real flea market stalls, which stock vintage clothes and records. Near the northern end is where regular folks flog their used household goods. If you're not well-versed in antiques, don't try to buy anything pricey, because sometimes vendors have been known to exaggerate the age and value of their items. FYI: Saturday is the day the full market is open; other days, only a few food and flower stalls are open, along with the brick-and-mortar shops that line the street.

The Marché aux Puces de Clignancourt in Saint-Ouen, **France,** dates from 1885. With more than 3,000 stalls, you can find almost

INSIDER'S TIP

The easiest way to score a bargain on antiques in Europe is to ask for the "export price," which knocks off the VAT (almost 20 percent).

anything your mind dreams up, from rare postcards and fabrics, to jewelry, chandeliers, and vintage clothes. Although it's open on weekends, you're better off going to the Monday market that's less crowded.

For 10 days in the spring and fall, the National Fair of the Flea Market and Ham in Paris features more than 800 vendors from all over France. The antique collections here are astounding, and you can really score a deal if you know how to bargain. Fun fact: Why "ham"? The market began in the Middle Ages when pork butchers came to Paris to sell their wares. One enterprising butcher decided to sell equipment along with the pork products, and the market eventually evolved into arts and antiques. If you want lessons on how to negotiate a deal, consider going on an organized antiques tour: The Antiques Diva (www.antiquesdiva.com) is run by a professional bargain hunter and will take you to the biannual flea market, as well as the busy Paris flea market at Saint-Ouen and other vintage and attic sales.

The ancient town of Tongeren in southeastern **Belgium** (near the German and Dutch borders) has an enormous Sunday antiques and flea market with some of the best deals in northern Europe. It draws people from all three countries who come to browse and bargain. Here you'll find old books, silverware, glassware, jewelry, and lots and lots of furniture—from huge wooden armoires to delicate glass lamps.

Although every tourist goes to the Aalsmeer Flower Auction in the **Netherlands,** if you want to buy flowers rather than watch other people bid on them, stick to Amsterdam's Bloemenmarkt. Here you can buy Dutch bouquets and bulbs on row after row of permanently moored barges floating in the Singel canal. Other items available include plants, small trees, bulbs, seeds, and souvenir tchotchkes, for a few cents less than what you'd pay at flower stands elsewhere in town.

The San Telmo Flea Market in **Buenos Aires** is a two-part affair on Sunday: There is a small cluster of stands set up in the Plaza Dorrego, combined with a network of antiques stores on the streets bordering the plaza (especially Calle Defensa). The plaza stalls stock classic flea market fare such as old magazines, books, vintage clothing, old electronics, tango records, and colored seltzer bottles, along with gaucho paraphernalia such as lassos, bridles, spurs, and whips. The antique furniture shops on the side streets are renowned for their art deco and art nouveau furniture and accessories. A bonus with this market is that the atmosphere is always festive, with street performers and musicians entertaining shoppers, and impromptu tango performances erupting every so often.

The Chandni Chowk Bazaar in Old Delhi, **India,** is a vast, teeming complex of alleyways that each offer a different product: textiles,

The World's Longest Yard Sale

What's more uniquely American than supersizing and yard sales? Combine the two and you get the so-called World's Longest Yard Sale, a real-life phenomenon that started more than 20 years ago in the heartland of America. The sale consists of hundreds of mom-and-pop (and professional) vendors who set up makeshift stalls, tents, and shacks along a 654-mile stretch of America between Alabama and Ohio. You can find wares ranging from collectibles and antiques to used clothing, furniture, crafts, and original works of art. The event, also known as the Highway 127 yard sale, or 127 Corridor Sale, happens for three days in mid-August.

Of course, no one expects to visit the entire 654-mile expanse, so most people choose a town on the route and make a 3-day weekend of it. The yard sale kicks off from Noccalula Falls Park in Gadsden, **Alabama,** and travels 93 miles along the scenic Lookout Mountain Parkway. In **Georgia,** there's camping and small cottages for rent in the lovely Cloudland Canyon State Park. Once you cross into **Tennessee,** you'll likely spend the night in Crossville or Monterey. The trail doesn't quite hit Lexington, **Kentucky,** but there are several small towns along the way like Danville, Frankford, and Harrodsburg (home to the historic Beaumont Inn). Finally, it's the end of the road in **Ohio** . . . sort of. The yard sale has extended all the way up to West Unity, near the Michigan border! www.127sale.com

Some tips before you go:

- Book your hotel early because this is a huge event and rooms fill up fast.
- Bring cash. Not all vendors can accept credit cards or checks.
- Remember that shipping in rural towns can be a problem. If you think you may end up buying furniture or other bulky items, drive a bigger car.

electronic goods, watches, spices, figurines, saris, fabrics, jewelry, leather goods, and thousands more. It's not just limited to goods—there are plenty of services to be had, too. Astrologers, shoemakers, photographers, doctors, and barbers operate here all along the sidewalks and storefronts. Food also figures prominently at Chandni Chowk: Hundreds of food stalls, some centuries old, add a dimension of taste to this wild shopping experience. So take a deep breath, dive in, and be prepared to have a quintessentially chaotic but thrilling Indian experience.

If you want a more subdued Indian market experience, Janpath Market in New Delhi is a long stretch of roads filled with shops selling jewelry, crafts, saris, and Asian art. And for a really sanitized

Haggling at Markets

Many market vendors, especially in countries like China and India, up their prices in the assumption that they will be bargained down. So how to do it effectively? First, make sure you understand some language and currency basics. Be able to pay cash for an item and don't assume they take American dollars. Start off by offering a price much lower than you expect to get, then bargain up. If the price won't come down enough, try to have another item thrown in for free; this is always a possibility. Be clear on the amount that you will not go over. If the merchant won't come down to your maximum price, don't hesitate to walk away. Chances are, if you're anywhere in the ballpark of what the vendor wants for the item, the vendor won't let you—or your money—get away.

What if the market does accept credit cards? A growing number of markets are now accepting credit cards, but that doesn't mean merchants like plastic. The best way to haggle is to use two credit cards as weapons to actually get you a deeper discount for cash. Here's what you do. Negotiate the lowest price you can on an item. Then whip out an American Express card. Nine times out of 10, the merchant will freak out (because he or she doesn't want to pay the fee levied by American Express). Then take out your Visa or MasterCard, and ask for a lower price. Nine times out of ten, you'll get it. Then—and only then—ask what the vendor's final price would be if you pay cash. Ten times out of ten, you'll get a lower price!

market trip, Dilli Haat Market is an open-air bazaar with vendors and food stalls situated along clean, paved paths.

There's no better way to get to the heart of **Morocco** than by exploring its chaotic souks. Most images you see are of the Marrakesh shopping experience, but don't miss the ancient city of Fez, where the souk is a complicated labyrinth of narrow alleys crammed with shops, stalls, and places of worship. We're talking hundreds of acres of land (go with a guide) where vendors tend to cluster depend-

Holiday Markets

Few things ring in the holiday spirit better than the markets that light up European cities. In **Budapest,** the main holiday market on Vörösmarty Square has endless enchanting stalls selling intricately carved wooden ornaments, quirky crocheted hats, giant twists of strudel, roasted chestnuts, and, of course, Glühwein (hot mulled wine). All products are handmade by the Association of Hungarian Folk Artists. The lively music, folk dances, and puppet theaters serve as a cultural accompaniment.

In **Vienna,** the 700-year-old Christkindlmarkt, on the grounds of the Rathaus (city hall), offers a whopping 10 acres of wooden stalls to explore. Specialties include hand-painted Christmas ornaments and woolen hats. While you're there, don't forget to admire the Advent windows in the Rathaus, painted by local artists.

In **Dresden,** you'll find Germany's oldest Christmas market, called the Striezelmarkt, which has been running since 1434. Handcrafted wooden figurines from the Erzgebirge Mountains, handmade lace, hand-blown tree ornaments, and pottery from Lusatia are just some of the gifts available. You can also sample the spicy gingerbread, called Pulsnitz Pfefferkuchen, or the Christstollen, a Dresden specialty.

Between mid-November and December 23, **Düsseldorf**'s historic Old Town features seven separate Christmas themes and attractions, rather than one sprawling market. Each "village" has a unique flavor, like an Angel's Market, with thousands of lights flooding the area, and an artisan village where items are created before your eyes.

If you want to get the flavor of different city markets, both Uniworld Cruises and Grand Circle Travel offer winter Christmas market cruises on the Rhine and Danube Rivers.

ing on what they sell: carpets, textiles, leather, and food.

With more than 5,000 shops—that's right, 5,000—Chatuchak Market in Bangkok, **Thailand,** has pretty much anything you can think of. Pets, food, clothing, home decor, arts, crafts, beads, religious artifacts, plants, and flowers are there for the haggling. However, it's only open on weekends. This market is preferable to the more famous Patpong Night Market, which has become a tourist trap full of the same fake brand-name items and cheap clothes that you can get anywhere else in the city.

Tsukiji Central Fish Market in **Tokyo** is not so much a shopping experience as much as a viewing experience. More than 600,0000 tons of fish worth billions are sold here every year in the sprawling 54-acre site, which supplies 90 percent of the seafood consumed in Tokyo. The wholesale auction market is officially for fish vendors only, but the public can view the spectacle discreetly, staying out of the way of the merchants—if you're willing to get there at 5 a.m. Around 8 a.m., you can wander around the endless rows of wholesale fishmongers' stalls, where everything from octopus to *unagi* is sold by the boatload. The less busy "outer" market has a great lineup of top sushi bars and is a popular lunch spot.

A dirt market? Well, sort of. The Panjiayuan Secondhand Market in **Beijing** has thousands of stalls with every type of art, jewelry, and memorabilia (including vintage communist worker art). Both locals and out-of-towners crowd here 7 days a week, so it's a chaotic scene. While you probably won't score any authentic or valuable treasures, the selection is so varied and exotic that it's worth doing your souvenir shopping. And haggling is not just recommended—it's expected.

AND
EVERYTHING
ELSE . . .

Best Places to Go for

AMUSEMENT PARKS/ROLLER COASTERS

I'll admit it: I'm not one to jump on the longest, the fastest, or the scariest new roller coaster out there. But for those of you who are—or who are looking for one of those quirky, family-friendly adventures—this chapter is for you.

When you're searching for a post–water park burger or beer, look for the red "Classic **Wisconsin** Dells" signs. It means the business has been serving visitors for at least 40 years and has most likely always been in that very same location. The sign also means the business is staffed by the original owner's kin, so you're sure to get some deep-rooted local color when you visit these spots. The sheer volume of water parks makes Wisconsin Dells the country's best spot to cool off, get wet, and have a thrill. You'll find more than 21 indoor and outdoor water parks within almost 20 miles of one another, not to mention some of the country's longest, tallest, and fastest water coasters. Noah's Ark Waterpark is the largest in the country, with more than 80 indoor and outdoor attractions like the Black Anaconda, one of the country's longest water coasters at over a quarter mile long. The Point of No Return is another memorable one: It takes you up 10 stories high, only to shoot you back down the waterslide in 5 seconds flat. Mount Olympus, another Wisconsin Dells institution, combines 37 waterslides with drier options like go-cart tracks, batting cages, and wooden roller coasters. The water and theme park company also operates five resorts and several campgrounds that offer park tickets at no extra charge if you choose to stay in them. www.wisdells.com

Open since 1846, Lake Compounce in Bristol, **Connecticut,** is North America's oldest continuously operating amusement park. It's not the biggest or most thrilling amusement park out there, but there's something appealing about the old-school, retro feel here (kids can even get unlimited free fountain soda). The park still maintains some of its original rides, including a carousel dating back to 1911 and the Wildcat wooden roller coaster, which opened in 1927. www.lakecompounce.com

WACKY THEME PARKS

Suoi Tien Theme Park in Ho Chi Minh City, **Vietnam,** is devoted to the promotion of animism, an ancient spiritual belief system.

Sure, there is a roller coaster, a Ferris wheel, and pretty much everything else you would expect a full-scale amusement park to have, but there are also dragons, unicorns, tortoises, and phoenixes, the symbols of animism. And don't miss Tien Dong beach, an unusual "lazy river" sort of attraction where gigantic carved faces watch over beachgoers.

At Dickens World (www.dickensworld.co.uk) in Chatham, **England,** children can experience the harsh conditions of 19th-century London, just like those depicted in a Dickens novel. Hammy actors play the part of stern schoolteachers, pickpockets roam the period-decorated town square, and you can even take a boat ride through brown sludge that is meant to mimic the inside of a Victorian sewer.

If you like creepy fairy-tale scenes, appreciate a good bargain, and can handle a little kitsch, then the Enchanted Forest in Salem, **Oregon,** is for you. While kids can find plenty to do here, the Enchanted Forest also draws twentysomethings who want to walk down memory lane and see their favorite childhood fairy tales on the cheap. It's less than $10 for adults to get in, and buying four 90-cent tickets gets you a turn on one ride. www.enchantedforest.com

For fans of Hello Kitty, then Sanrio Puroland in **Tokyo** is right up your alley. The sickly sweet indoor theme park is bursting with Sanrio characters such as Hello Kitty, Cinnaroll, My Melody, and Little Twin Stars. www.puroland.co.jp/english

The first thing you might notice about Shenzhen, **China,** is the proliferation of oddball theme parks. After China opened itself to the world in the 1970s, Chinese officials were so impressed by Disney and Six Flags–type entertainment that they considered it a necessary part of development. The result? Splendid China, which showcases miniatures of China's famous sites and historical figures; the Chinese Folk Culture Park, featuring villages of cultural performances, parades, and artworks; Windows of the World, where visitors can check out replicas of the world's greatest attractions, from the Eiffel Tower to Angkor Wat to the Sydney Opera House; and mind-blowing theatrical spectacles that put Vegas to shame.

Anyone who grew up in **New York** has an affinity for Coney Island, even as it grew more and more ramshackle and dated. But these days, major investments are revitalizing the long-neglected theme park, where you can watch art films, eat old-fashioned taffy, see a minor-league baseball game, and ride a roller coaster all in the same day. Consisting of a string of loosely connected attractions spread across the shoreline at the southern tip of Brooklyn, Coney Island is the antithesis of impersonal, corporate-owned theme parks. Deno's Wonder Wheel Amusement Park features the can't-miss Wonder Wheel (www.wonderwheel.com). Dating back to 1920, this wheel has only stopped once, during the New York City blackout of 1977. (Riders got down safely because the owners hand-cranked them all to the ground.) Of course, Coney Island's Cyclone should be on every respectable roller coaster aficionado's bucket list. This 85-foot-high wooden ride debuted in 1927 and is now a New York City Landmark. www.coneyisland.com

Did you know that the Lego company is actually based in **Denmark**? Legoland park in Billund is the largest and oldest of the world's four Legoland parks and a best pick for families with young children. Since it opened in 1968, the park's heart has been Mini-land, where you can see famous buildings, capital cities, and villages built at 1:20 scale from nearly 20 million Lego bricks. My pick? The new Star Wars wing, which features nearly 2,000 models of distant

Skip the Line

Fewer things are more frustrating than waiting in long lines at theme parks, so here's how to avoid them—without getting in trouble for cutting. Buying special passes or staying in theme park–owned hotels can help your family avoid waiting in line at many amusement parks. At Walt Disney World in **Orlando,** guests staying at on-site Disney resorts can enter the park an hour earlier and stay up to 3 hours later than other guests. To avoid lines at Universal Studios **Hollywood,** go for the Front of the Line Pass. Available for $129 at UniversalStudios.com, the pass gets you park admission, priority access to rides, reserved seating at shows, and behind-the-scenes access. And at most Six Flags theme parks, ride reservations are available with the Flash Pass service. When your beeperlike device, called a Q-bot, goes off, it's time to ride.

planets, battle droids, clone troopers, and space stations, many of which are interactive. You can stay close to the action by checking in at Hotel Legoland, a family-oriented hotel that has themed rooms. If you can't make it all the way to Billund, Legoland parks are also located in Windsor, England; Gunzburg, Germany; Carlsbad, California; and Winter Haven, Florida (45 minutes from Orlando). www.legoland.dk/en

For a budget option, Holiday World & Splashin' Safari in Santa Claus, **Indiana,** is a well-rounded vacation destination for families. Where else can you find a Santa Claus willing to listen to kids' gift requests all year long? But what sets this park apart is that it's often cheaper than the other big players, plus you can get free sodas and sunscreen all day. It's also a good option for kids of all ages, with the speedy Wildebeest water coaster and the tamer Freedom Train ride through Mother Goose Land. www.holidayworld.com

Dubai has made a name for itself as the Middle Eastern entertainment capital, and Wild Wadi Water Park takes that image to the extreme. Imagine zipping down a cool waterslide in the heat of the desert with the ocean and the Burj al Arab looming on one side of you and the skyscrapers of Dubai on the other. Located next to the Jumeirah Beach Hotel, the park boasts 30 rides and attractions, 13 of which are interconnected, meaning you can go from ride to ride without getting out of the water—a great choice when temperatures can top 100 degrees. High-adrenaline rides include Tantrum Alley, Jumeirah Sceirah, and the Burj Surj, plus high-powered water jet rides and wave simulators. www.wildwadi.com

Some of the most-visited amusement parks in the world are in Asia, and **Japan** has some of the best. My pick? Nagashima Spaland near Nagoya. This complex has a full amusement park, a water park, and a children's park. We're talking nine roller coasters, including the Steel Dragon 2000, the world's tallest complete-circuit gigacoaster, and a massive wooden coaster called the White Cyclone, which has an amazing concentric-circle design. There's also a 295-foot-high Ferris wheel and a giant Frisbee ride. In summer, 10 swimming pools open up, including a massive saltwater pool. www.nagashima-onsen.co.jp

ULTIMATE ROLLER COASTERS

Every year, roller coasters get more and more extreme. The Kingda Ka at Six Flags Great Adventure in Jackson, **New Jersey,** is officially both the fastest and the tallest in the United States. It is 456 feet high, has a drop of 418 feet, and travels at 128 mph (in fact, it goes from 0 to 128 in 3.5 seconds).

The Sky Rocket, Kennywood, in West Mifflin, **Pennsylvania,** uses launch technology called Linear Synchronous Motor, which shoots riders from 0 to 50 in less than 3 seconds! The ride is launched up a 95-foot climb and hangs briefly before plummeting into a 90-degree drop. A second vertical free fall, a corkscrew turn, and the feeling of flying off your seat while upside down round out this 65-second thrill ride.

And don't forget the Steel Dragon 2000 at **Japan**'s Nagashima Spaland. This coaster has a 306-foot drop followed by two hills in excess of 20 stories each and goes more than 95 miles per hour. In 3 minutes, the ride covers 1½ miles (8,133 feet) of track.

Then there's my favorite coaster, which isn't an extreme ride compared to today's standards, but it is a nostalgic one. Jack Rabbit at Seabreeze Amusement Park, in Rochester, **New York,** was the fastest coaster in the world when it opened in 1920. Today, it's best known as the oldest continuously operating coaster in America. (There are two older coasters in the country, but neither has operated continuously since opening.) Although the ride is more than 90 years old, ongoing upgrades keep this coaster up to today's safety codes. The max vertical drop is 75 feet, and the speed is 42 mph, with a track length of 2,150 feet. Although it's not as thrilling as today's mega coasters, it is considered a rite of passage for generations of families across central New York. Even today, it's a milestone when kids are finally tall enough to enjoy the ride.

BOOKSTORE BROWSING

Getting lost in a great bookstore is almost as good as getting lost in a great book. Sometimes it's the quantity or selection of books that makes a bookstore special, and sometimes it's the architecture or just the hustle and bustle of the surrounding local community that gives these places their unique character.

INDEPENDENT BOOKSTORES

Powell's in Portland, **Oregon,** is the world's largest independent new and used book store—it occupies an entire city block in the Pearl District of downtown Portland and boasts more than 68,000 square feet of space on three glorious floors. Though the exterior of the building is nothing to look at, you'll be impressed by the vast rooms, each of which is the size of a lesser bookstore and where used books are shelved alongside new ones. To prevent visitors from getting lost, color-coded maps help navigate through the million-strong inventory, which includes rare books, fiction, nonfiction, and an outstanding children's selection. www.powells.com

In Denver, **Colorado,** Tattered Cover isn't just known for its extensive book collection, signings, and events. It's the best place to do book shopping because when you ship your purchases to an address outside of Colorado, you don't pay sales tax! In addition to books, the store also makes it a point to embrace electronic books and has Google eBook device tutorials on the Web. The newest location on Colfax Avenue in the historic Lowenstein Theater covers two floors and offers reading lamps and chairs that encourage you to

Best Building for Books

If there were an award for the best repurposed building, Selexyz Dominicanen in Maastricht, **Holland,** would be the winner. This bookstore is housed in a 13th-century Gothic cathedral that was refashioned into a bookstore in 2006, but still preserves the look and feel of the Dominican friary it once functioned as. You can climb to the uppermost stacks for a bird's-eye view of the ceiling frescoes and columns, and even order a glass of wine to make the experience more "spiritual." An excellent on-site coffee shop serves some of the best java in Holland, and there are regularly scheduled lectures, debates, and exhibitions. Genres run the gamut from literature to cookbooks to history to arts to computers, with a large English-language book section.

come, sit, and enjoy a book. www.tatteredcover.com

Opened in 1927, Strand Bookstore is the lone survivor of the 48 bookstores that once formed Book Row in **Manhattan.** Occupying more than 55,000 square feet of space plus kiosks in Central Park, it is still owned and run by the same family that founded it. To this day, it continues to sell new, used, rare, and pretty much any type of book you can think of. Although its tagline is "18 miles of books," Strand offers far more than that. In fact, there's even a Books by the Foot program where the store will put together a collection tailored just for you. My suggestion: Take the time to browse through the kiosks *and* outdoor bookshelves for some unexpected steals. www. strandbooks.com

Paris is known for a lot of things, but most people don't know that it is home to the first English-language bookstore on the European continent. The Librairie Galignani was founded in 1801 by a well regarded publishing family (in fact, their works date back to 1520). Today, the bookstore is a treasure trove with tens of thousands of books on art, architecture, design, and literature. But more than that, it's simply a beautiful place to wander around with old, mahogany bookcases from the 1930s and renowned window displays. www.galignani.com

For almost 100 years, Soor El Azbakia Book Market, a rambling used book market, has existed in various locations in **Cairo.** Currently it is located in front of the Puppet Theatre in Ataba Square and is a collection of shacks, stalls, and corridors. You can spend a whole day digging up out-of-print copies of foreign language novels, signed first editions, old issues of *National Geographic*, leather-bound copies of the Koran, and much more. Books are often piled messily and haphazardly, but half the fun is digging around these dusty stacks in search of treasures.

Tokyo doesn't do anything small, and Jimbocho Book Town is no exception. This massive emporium, centered around the Jimbocho Station—thought to have the highest concentration of bookstores in the world—consists of approximately 200 individual shops. Browsing through Jimbocho will give you a glimpse into a culture that is obsessed with both consumer goods and accumulating things. Books of all genres are piled up to the roof and spill from the narrow, bustling alleyways into the corridors onto the pavement.

RARE AND ANTIQUARIAN

Argosy Books is a **New York City** institution that specializes in antiquarian and out-of-print books. The 80-year-old institution has an atmosphere that harks back to the Gilded Age of New York; the high ceilings, old-fashioned elevator, and vaguely intellectual vibe are reminiscent of the days of the Rockefellers and Barrymores. All manner of Americana, modern first editions, autographs, art prints, antique maps, and books on the history of science and medicine fill the six museum-like floors in midtown Manhattan. Tip: If you want to see the rare First Editions room on the fifth floor, you have to ask for an escort. But it's worth it. www.argosybooks.com

The original Bauman Rare Books in **Philadelphia** is located on the 19th floor of the Sun Oil Building on Walnut Street. Open only by appointment, this is where the store's catalog of rare first-edition and antiquarian books are researched, documented, and photographed. The more well-known outpost is in New York, but here's the unexpected part: Bauman's newest location is in a city not exactly known for its literary clout—Las Vegas. Located in the Palazzo, the 2,300-square-foot gallery is a welcome respite from the usual Vegas shopping experience. www.baumanrarebooks.com

The Brattle Book Shop in Cambridge, **Massachusetts,** has been in the same place since 1825 and has had the same owners since 1949. Although the first two floors feature more general used and secondhand books, the third floor is where you'll find the rare and antiquarian items. There is no attitude in this old-school bookshop; just a friendly staff that welcomes visitors to look at the rare items and also offers free appraisals. www.brattlebookshop.com

In West Chester, **Pennsylvania,** in the Brandywine Valley, is a special place called Baldwin's Book Barn. Yes, it's literally housed in an old barn and, since 1946, has been a go-to place for the book obsessed. You can spend hours browsing among the five floors crammed with a 300,000-strong collection of used, rare, and anti-quarian books, maps, and manuscripts. Pore over your finds in a cozy nook, warmed by a wood-burning stove while the resident cats curl up underfoot. www.bookbarn.com

Located on **London**'s Kensington Church Street among a number of antiques dealers, Adrian Harrington Rare Books offers an impressive range. But what's really unusual about this place is the James Bond/Ian Fleming specialist on staff. Even if you aren't in the market to buy a rare book, the store offer a full bookbinding and restoration service. www.harringtonbooks.co.uk

TRAVEL GUIDES AND LITERATURE

Daunt Books in **London** is a mecca for travelers and those who want to explore the world via literature. Its unique layout—organized by geography, not subject or author—literally allows browsers to read their way around the globe. You'll find travel guides, phrase books, maps, memoirs, novels, an eclectic selection of children's books, poetry, history, field guides, cookbooks, biographies, crime stories, and short stories. There are also branches in Chelsea, Holland Park, Cheapside, Hampstead, and Belsize Park. Every month the stores offer readings, lectures, and book signings. www.dauntbooks.co.uk

Distant Lands in Pasadena, **California,** stocks nearly every brand of guidebook for nearly every place imaginable—from California's roadside monuments to sights in Chad. Stop by on Mondays at 7:30 p.m. for travel-related special events, like how to navigate Europe's rail system and how to plan an around-the-world trip. Beyond books, you'll also find luggage, maps, and other travel accessories. www.distantlands.com

GHOSTS AND GRAVES

There are two places I try to visit every time I travel somewhere. First, the local fire department. Why? Because firefighters have been everywhere in the city, usually more than once, and they absolutely know what's going on. The second place: the cemetery. That's where I discover what all the dead people did and the rich history of that community.

TOMBS, GRAVES, AND MAUSOLEUMS

f the line is too long at the Louvre in **Paris** (and it could be), then make your way to another museum of sorts—Père-Lachaise. This graveyard is huge, beautiful, profound, and a veritable who's who of deceased European glitterati and literati, from Marceau to Molière to Jim Morrison. The 109-acre grounds has plenty of less-frequented paths, and you can plot out a rough route before you start. Don't forget to head to the top of the hill and enjoy the view of the cemetery and parts of Paris. And don't worry if you miss Jim Morrison's grave—it's surprisingly small and usually covered in graffiti, dead flowers, and cigarette butts. www.pere-lachaise.com

St. Louis No. 1 is the oldest cemetery in **New Orleans,** famous for its 600 closely spaced, aboveground mausoleums adorned with ornate inscriptions, carvings, statuaries, and reliefs. Some allege that the tombs were built aboveground because the high water table made ground burials impossible, as bodies would eventually float to the surface. But experts now believe that funeral vaults were simply customary in the 18th-century French and Spanish traditions. Strolling through St. Louis No. 1 won't take you too long or treat you to views of green space, but you'll get a lesson on the history of the city. You'll see the tombs of Homer Plessy (of Plessy v. Ferguson fame), 19th-century voodoo priestess Marie Laveau, and former New Orleans mayor Ernest Morial (the first African American to hold the job). Anne Rice was inspired to create her famous vampire novels by this cemetery, and scenes from the movie *Easy Rider* were filmed here. The daily guided tours of the grounds are good for the history lessons, but you don't really need a tour to absorb the eerie vibe of this place. It's small enough to wander around and explore on your own, and admission is free. www.nps.gov/resources/site.htm?id=18953

When it comes to paying respects to our military, most people think of Arlington National Cemetery. But don't miss the opportunity to visit the final resting place of 9,387 American service members at the Normandy American Cemetery and Memorial in Normandy, **France.** Sitting on a cliff that overlooks Omaha Beach and the English Channel, about 170 miles west of Paris, this cemetery is reachable by train service to the town of Bayeux and then a short taxi or bus ride. Spanning nearly 173 acres, it's the first US cemetery on European soil during World War II, mostly comprised of service members who died in the D-Day landings or ensuing operations. Seemingly endless rows of white marble crosses and Stars of David mark the fallen. The Walls of the Missing are inscribed with the names of 1,557 service members whose remains were never recovered. Learn the stories of these fallen heroes through archival images, text, and interactive displays, and take a moment to stop by the chapel or reflection pool. www.abmc.gov/cemeteries/cemeteries/no.php

Beneath the Capuchin monastery in Palermo, **Italy,** is the Capuchin Catacombs, where thousands of centuries-old corpses have been placed upright in nooks, hung up on the walls, or set into chairs for public display. Talk about creepy: Some of the corpses still have their lips, hair, and eyelids intact. The oldest mummy, a friar, was entombed in 1599. One of the catacombs' most recent additions is the impeccably preserved Rosalia Lombardo, a toddler who looks as if she could just be taking a nap. Lovingly referred to by locals as "Sleeping Beauty," Lombardo was only 2 when she died in the early 1900s. The dead are dressed in their era's best finery, though much of the fabric has rotted away. Separate corridors are designated for professionals, women, and those who were part of religious orders. There is a separate chapel for women who died as virgins and another for infants.

In the **Czech Republic,** the Sedlec Ossuary sits beneath a Catholic church that's just a short day trip from Prague. This is an atypical example of an ossuary, or a repository for bones. When the church was constructed in the 15th century, the underground chapel was built to store bones that could not fit in the overcrowded town cemetery. Over the centuries, the heaps of human bones became disorganized, and in 1870 woodcarver František Rint was hired to arrange them. Rint accepted the challenge and transformed the remains of nearly 40,000 people into high art. The chapel's walls are covered with garlands of skulls, and he even signed his name using bones. Some of the more impressive pieces Rint made from the bones are a functional chandelier and a family coat of arms. www.kostnice.cz

The aptly named Capela dos Ossos (Chapel of Bones) in Évora, **Portugal,** is a 2-hour bus ride from Lisbon. Inside the chapel of the Church of St. Francis, the bones and skulls of more than 5,000 people cover the walls, arches, and ceiling beams. In the 16th century, several monks decided to open the chapel to remind their religious brothers of life's transience. A message from the monks to visitors warns: "We bones in here wait for yours to join us." Two desiccated bodies dangle from the ceiling on chains. After exploring the sobering chapel, take yourself to the public garden next door and reconvene with the living over a cool drink. Consider staying overnight to fully explore the city, which is a designated UNESCO World Heritage site for its Roman, Gothic, and Baroque architecture.

Famous Graves

Hang out with Hollywood's elite in their final resting places. In **Los Angeles,** head to the well-hidden Pierce Brothers Westwood Village Memorial Park and Mortuary (www.pbwvmortuary.com) to see old Hollywood's most famous names, including Marilyn Monroe, Burt Lancaster, Natalie Wood, and Dean Martin. And don't miss its more famous counterpart, Hollywood Forever Cemetery (www.hollywoodforever.com). This is where you can visit other celebrity residents, from silent screen stars like Rudolph Valentino and Douglas Fairbanks to punk rock legends Johnny and Dee Dee Ramone. In summer, you can sit among the ghostly graves as part of the Cinespia outdoor classic film series.

In Westchester County, **New York,** the place to see iconic Americans is Ferncliff Cemetery (www.ferncliffcemetery.com) where Judy Garland, Joan Crawford, Malcolm X, and Superman himself, Christopher Reeve, are buried.

Meanwhile, history buffs will want to go to the Granary Burying Ground (www.thefreedomtrail.org/visitor/granary.html). It's the third-oldest cemetery in **Boston** and the resting place of famous Revolutionary figures, from Paul Revere to John Hancock. In **Indianapolis,** Crown Hill Cemetery (www. crownhill.org) is home to legendary figures like bank robber John Dillinger.

Many people don't realize that Lenin's mausoleum in **Moscow**'s Red Square is not simply a memorial, but it contains his embalmed body under bulletproof glass. Since 1924 the revolutionary leader has lain in state in his eerie tomb, which literally millions of people have visited. He has remained perfectly preserved, thanks to regular maintenance by a staff of expert technicians who moisturize him every day and remove his body every 18 months to give him a special chemical "bath." The effect is astounding, as the body looks like that of a man who is merely asleep, rather than one who has been dead for more than 85 years. Since the fall of communism, various Russian governments have discussed whether to bury the body and close the mausoleum, but so far no action has been taken. However, it is still a live issue, so best to see this morbid spectacle while you still can. Also worth a look is the adjacent Kremlin Wall Necropolis, a burial ground for Bolshevik revolution victims, cosmonauts, and top Soviet-era officials and leaders.

Iran has a long tradition of poetry, reaching back more than 1,000 years, so it's no wonder one of the most unique mausoleums in the world is built over the graveyard holding the remains of some of Iran's most illustrious poets. Located in Tabriz (in the far northwest of Iran), Poets' Mausoleum (Maqbaratoshoara) is a dramatic stone edifice, designed in a geometric modernist style of the 1970s, and consists of a series of rising "arches" (which are actually rectangular in shape) that interlock at right angles to each other. The monument is particularly beautiful if viewed from the reflecting pool to the south. In addition to dozens of poets, the graveyard also holds famous Persian scholars, mystics, scientists, and other notable figures.

GHOSTLY TOURS

Did you know that ghosts haunt the Hawaiian Islands? The massive development in **Oahu** has desecrated ancient sacred sites and burial grounds, which many locals believe angers the spirits and results in supernatural activity. Oahu Ghost Tours lets you get up close and personal with the spirits during its walking and driving tours of some of the most sacred and haunted places on the island. You'll visit spots where sacrifices were made to ancient gods and goddesses, hospitals that housed sick children during World War II, and maybe even see the legendary Night Marchers (ancient warriors who march to the sounds of pounding drums). On the Honolulu City Haunts tour, you'll walk through downtown Honolulu and see the site of a modern-day murder, plus a former Hawaiian royal residence. On the Sacred Spirits driving tour, you'll visit the dwelling place of the Hawaiian Fire Goddess and see sites believed to have been built by the island's legendary "little people," the Menehune. www.oahughosttours.com

The Historic New Orleans Collection has a Historic Haunts tour that covers 10 allegedly haunted locations throughout the city. Every October, guides share hair-raising stories of notorious **New Orleans** residents such as the American socialite and serial killer Madame Lalaurie and voodoo queen Marie Laveau. The tours are a favorite among history buffs, as they reveal facts unearthed by the Williams Research Center and incorporate significant historic events, like the yellow-fever epidemic and pirate attacks. It's a two-part experience: The history lesson takes place within the galleries, and then you set out with a map for a self-guided walking tour. www.hnoc.org

Los Angeles has been the site of many notorious murders, such as "the Black Dahlia" and Nicole Brown Simpson. On Dearly Departed Tours' "Tragical History Tour," you'll visit almost 100 sites where stars drew their last breaths, from pop star Michael Jackson to actor River Phoenix. You'll see the houses where the Manson and Menendez murders occurred, and the spot where gangster "Bugsy" Siegel was gunned down. Tours last about 2½ hours and are conducted in a so-called Tomb Buggy. www.dearlydepartedtours.com

Or check out the city's more macabre history with Esotouric, which specializes in the offbeat, quirky side of Los Angeles. The True Crime tour tells the real story of the Black Dahlia murder, and brings to life the ghosts and ghouls of gritty downtown LA, including the Skid Row Slasher. www.esotouric.com

Malaysians believe in all types of spirits, from the eerie *ponti-anak* (female vampire-type demons) to *toyol* (goblins who steal money). In **Kuala Lumpur,** you can take a tour with Spooksters and view dozens of spots around the city where spirits are said to congregate or live. You'll walk through a Chinese cemetery in the middle of the night, visit an Indian religious shrine, and see an abandoned prison where many executions took place. Local guide Francis Nantha starts all his tours with dinner at a KL seafood restaurant to build group "protection" against the ghosts, and throughout the tour he explains the complicated Malaysian superstitions, taboos, and belief systems in great detail.

MACABRE MUSEUMS

The National Museum of Funeral History in **Houston** features a huge collection of funeral artifacts and exhibits on topics including historical embalming practices, mourning rituals from around the world, and Japanese funeral customs. The collection of caskets is a standout, including a casket built for three people, a glass-paneled coffin, and a casket made out of actual dollar bills and coins. In addition, the Fantasy Coffins exhibit features outlandish, one-of-a-kind coffins designed by Ghanaian sculptor Kane Quaye, carved in the shapes of animals, cars, and airplanes. There are also collections of historical hearses, presidential funeral memorabilia, and a full-scale replica of Pope John Paul II's crypt. www.nmfh.org

Commonly referred to as the "torture museum," the Medieval Crime Museum in Rothenburg, **Germany,** is actually a well-respected legal history museum in Europe. You can view old documents and illustrated legal guides, plus records of court proceedings, property transfers, and punishments. Of course, in medieval times, those who were found guilty of a crime received punishment of the most gruesome kind, and at the museum you can view all sorts of original torture devices, including finger screws and a "neck violin" that tethered together bickering women. www.kriminalmuseum.rothenburg.de

GHOST TOWNS

Bodie, **California,** was a thriving California mining town during the gold rush of the late 1800s. Nowadays it has a population of zero but is a state historic park where more than 100 of the original structures are still standing in what officials call a state of "arrested decay." There's a bank, a schoolhouse, a Methodist church, two hotels, a sawmill, a stamp mill, and about 65 saloons. The general store is still stocked with goods, and the old cemetery is marked by 80 headstones of former residents. Just remember, there are no facilities near Bodie, so stock up before you go. Since Bodie is located 8,000 feet up in the eastern Sierra, don't try to go in winter when the road is icy and treacherous, and bring a coat, even in summer. www.parks.ca.gov/?page_id=509

Curious tourists can now participate in government-sanctioned tours of the disaster zone around the **Chernobyl** nuclear plant, which melted down in 1986, killing hundreds and sickening thousands more. In January 2011, the Ukrainian government opened up the sealed 18-mile "exclusion zone" around the reactor and allowed tourists in for brief visits. They maintain that there is no risk to visitors who only intend to stay for a short time. Before participating, however, you have to sign a waiver that releases the tour operator from any potential radiation-related medical issues. Most tours depart from Kiev and include a visit to the actual nuclear plant— though you can't get closer than 650 feet from the reactor's sarcophagus—plus a trip through the abandoned village of Pripyat, where thousands of the plant's workers lived. The town is a snapshot of Soviet-era Russia, frozen in time. You'll also drive through the infamous "red forest," so called because the normally green pine trees turned reddish-orange from the effects of radiation.

HAUNTED HOTELS

If you have to pick one haunted hotel for a bone-chilling experience, it's the Stanley Hotel in Estes Park, **Colorado.** This hotel is so spooky it's believed to have inspired Stephen King's *The Shining.* It's named for Freelan O. Stanley, inventor of the Stanley Steamer automobile, and legend has it his ghost has visited the hotel's billiard room and bar; guests frequently complain about children roaming the hallways at night . . . even when none are checked in. www.stanleyhotel.com

Although doubters exist, there's an enduring legend that a ghost continues to haunt Hotel del Coronado, aka Hotel Del, in Coronado, **California.** In 1892, a pregnant guest named Kate Morgan checked into the hotel. Day after day, she waited for her husband to join her. Five days after checking in, her body was found on the outside staircase leading toward the beach, dead from a self-inflicted gunshot wound. To this day, guests and staff have reported flickering lights and cold breezes, and some have even claimed to see the tragic ghost herself. www.hoteldel.com

Anchorage Hotel in **Alaska** has had so many ghost sightings that it actually keeps a guest ghost log, in which many guests have shared their encounters. The ghost most often reported is the city's first chief of police, John J. Sturgus, who was shot in an alleyway behind the hotel in 1921. Also in the 1920s, a lady was supposed to wed her fiancé, but when he struck it rich in the gold rush, he jilted her on their wedding day. She was so distraught that she hanged herself while wearing her wedding dress. And, you guessed it, she allegedly appears in the dress and walks the halls. On the second floor, the curtains will sway and a picture over the mantelpiece has reportedly flown across the room. www.historicanchoragehotel.com

The Stone Lion Inn in Guthrie, **Oklahoma,** was built in 1907 by F. E. Houghton, the founder of Cotton Oil Company and owner of the first car dealership in Oklahoma. At one point in the 1920s, the house was leased to Smith's Funeral Home and was used as a mortuary. The Smiths lived upstairs, and the embalming occurred in what is now the kitchen of the inn. Today, the current owner uses the porcelain embalming table as a hallway buffet, where guests can enjoy refreshments. Guests have seen a ghost dressed in formal attire and derby hat, who trails the scent of cigar smoke. Besides the unknown gentleman, the Houghton daughter also haunts the inn. At the age of 8, she died of whooping cough; the family's maid supposedly overmedicated her with cough syrup, which contained then-common ingredients codeine and opium. Her ghost will creep into guest rooms around 2 a.m. and pat them on the cheek. She disappears soon after they awake. www.stonelioninn.com

Possessed Prisons

Eastern State Penitentiary in **Philadelphia** held notorious criminals such as Al Capone and bank robber Willie Sutton. It shut its doors in 1971 and is now a National Historic Landmark. Since the 1940s, there have been reports of supernatural occurrences within its walls. You can judge for yourself during the regular daytime tours or, even better, during the after-dark VIP tour (offered around Halloween). Who knows what you'll encounter during this hourlong flashlight-guided journey around the cell blocks, including Al Capone's cell, death row, and the underground punishment rooms. www.easternstate.org

The Ohio State Reformatory in Mansfield, **Ohio,** is where *The Shawshank Redemption* was filmed. Although a Morgan Freeman sighting is unlikely, a ghost sighting might be because the prison is allegedly a hotbed of paranormal activity and is haunted by spirits of the departed. Visitors can take a 2-hour nighttime walking tour that covers all the ghostly hot spots or go on one of the thrice-monthly ghost hunts. During these events, visitors are allowed to bring their own ghost-hunting equipment and explore the prison's nooks and crannies (reserve well in advance, as these book up fast). www.mrps.org

GO RETRO

I don't have an iPhone. I do have an iPad but am resisting using it. I still have an old Pentax 35mm SLR. And before you think I'm totally nuts, I own—use—about eight different rotary phones. It's not about the kitsch value—these phones actually work in a power outage! So the idea of going retro has always appealed to me, especially when substance can take precedence over style, when manual feels better than automatic, and when analog is more satisfying than digital.

SODA FOUNTAINS

Visit restored soda fountains to relive the days when the corner drugstore was the social hub of small-town America. Unlike cheesy retro diners, these feature authentic decor, classic American food, and antique fixtures.

Fair Oaks Pharmacy and Soda Fountain in South Pasadena, **California,** opened in 1915 and has since been a popular rest stop for hungry travelers who have made it to the far western end of Route 66. It was restored in the 1990s to its original turn-of-the-century decor, with authentic tin ceilings, honeycomb tile floors, and a complete set of antique pharmacy fixtures (as well as a state-of-the-art modern pharmacy, if you need a prescription filled while you're there). The trained soda jerks can whip up a hand-dipped shake or malt, old-fashioned phosphate, lime rickey, egg cream, or homemade ginger ale. If you've still got room, stay for a burger and finish it off with an enormous banana split. www.fairoakspharmacy.net

Known as the Double Gateway to the Rockies, the small mountain town of Lyons, **Colorado,** is a great spot for hikers, bikers, and other adventurers to fuel up—at the Lyons Soda Fountain. Opened in 1921, the fountain was originally part of Lyons Mercantile drugstore, a Prohibition-compliant place for neighbors to get together in a town that had previously housed more than 20 bars and saloons. In 1967 a fire destroyed the two-story Lyons Mercantile building, but firemen saved the almost century-old soda fountain and back bar, which are still used at the shop today. The soda jerks make dozens of vintage beverages ranging from root beer floats to phosphates. The lunch menu features hamburgers made from locally raised beef and other regionally sourced foods. www.lyonssodafountain.com

At the Franklin Fountain in **Philadelphia,** hipster-foodie local ingredients and novel combinations meet history and tradition—even though the shop is not technically "old." Brothers Ryan and Eric Berley opened the Franklin Fountain in a turn-of-the-century building in the heart of Philadelphia's Old City in 2004, using historically authentic equipment. The creative phosphate lineup includes the Japanese Thirst Killer, flavored with almond, grape juice, and Angostura bitters; and the Egyptienne Egg Shake, which combines rose and orange flavors and is topped with a sweet date. All of these ingredients are made in-house. Get an energy boost with the Lightening Rod sundae, one of the menu's many nods to Benjamin Franklin. It combines coffee ice cream with a dark chocolate brownie, shot of espresso, chocolate-covered espresso beans, white chocolate shavings, and a salty pretzel rod. www.franklinfountain.com

In Tallahassee, **Florida,** founder Gregory Cohen has combined a toy store with a full-service soda fountain, making Lofty Pursuits a paradise for kids with a sweet tooth or adults who are just kids at heart. "Fizzicians"—aka soda jerks with expertise in mixing flavors and textures—prepare handmade sodas in flavors like peach, vanilla, and cherry. Just like soda fountain purveyors did in the late 1800s, Lofty Pursuits makes its own cane sugar–sweetened cola base: no high-fructose corn syrup here.

The Yips, Freezes, and Double Awfuls are blends of ice cream or sorbet with seltzer instead of milk, resulting in a refreshing, slushy consistency. The staff encourages experimentation at the soda fountain and will help guide your unique creation. In a nod to modern preferences, the menu boasts more than 40 individually named sundaes, many of which can be converted to vegan or no-sugar-added styles. The "Spectaculars" menu section includes extreme concoctions like the Kitchen Sink, which combines 26 scoops (more than a gallon) with every topping in the shop, and serves it up in a bona fide stainless steel kitchen sink. Share it with friends or get on the Wall of Fame by downing it all in under 2 hours. www.loftypursuits.com

The James Pharmacy and Soda Fountain in Old Saybrook, **Connecticut,** was built in 1790 as a general store and has been a pharmacy and soda fountain since 1896. Back in the 19th century, Revolutionary War hero Marquis de Lafayette shopped here, and in more recent times Katharine Hepburn was a regular. From 1917 to

1967, the place was run by Anna Louise James, the first female African American pharmacist in the state of Connecticut. The pharmacy is now a Middle Eastern goods shop, but the soda fountain is still intact and retains the original cabinetry, tables, chairs (with heart-shaped backs), Vermont marble countertops, and milkshake maker from the 1940s. The menu is a combination of old-fashioned favorites, such as New York egg creams and ice-cream floats, and a modern selection of gourmet coffees. On the second floor is an old-fashioned bed-and-breakfast. www.pratthouse.net/jamesgallery.htm

Horton Bay General Store on Lake Charlevoix in Horton Bay, **Michigan,** dates back to 1876. Its most famous patron was Ernest Hemingway, who spent his youth and summers there and was a frequent visitor to the store. In fact, several of his "Nick Adams" stories drew inspiration from the store and the surrounding area. In homage to him, the store displays a collection of Hemingway memorabilia, plus antique artifacts such as an outboard boat motor and, of course, the period soda machine. A few years back, the store was

Vintage Trains

Before diesel engines took over in the 1950s, trains were powered by steam. As any rail enthusiast will tell you, this is the way to relive the golden age of train travel. **California**'s Niles Canyon Railway dates back to 1862, with the formation of the first Western Pacific Railroad Company. Its collection includes lumber and mining trains dating back to 1913. Plus, you can actually take a vintage General Motors coach to and from the railway. **Utah**'s Heber Valley Railroad runs through the original Denver & Rio Grande Western rail line along Highway 189 and through Provo Canyon. Both of its 1907 Baldwin steam locomotives have heated coaches, so these trains are even a great experience in Utah's winters. The Delaware River Railroad Excursions is the only operating steam locomotive in **New Jersey,** with themed rides all year long. Just be forewarned: Some of these companies operate both steam and diesel trains, so call to confirm which train will be used. After all, you may as well get the full vintage experience on your journey.

bought and renovated, but it still retains its historic character. The soda fountain serves up 1940s-era treats, but you can also buy contemporary deli items like gourmet meats, cheeses, homemade salsa, and whitefish pâté—and there's great tapas on the weekends. Make sure you plan ahead, as the store closes in late fall for the winter season. www.hortonbaygeneralstore.com

DRIVE-IN MOVIES

The days of the old drive-in theaters are long gone, thanks to multiplex cinemas, but there are still a few remnants. Why go? At drive-in theaters, you can wear pajamas, control the volume, use your cell phone, and even bring your own snacks instead of having to smuggle them in (although some discourage this). In warmer climates, some drive-ins are open year-round, while in places like Indi-

INSIDER'S TIP

To find a drive-in movie theater near you, visit www.drive-ins.com. The site features a database of 476 active drive-ins in the United States and 15 other countries, searchable by state or ZIP code. Driveinmovie.com offers a similar database, plus a lot more in terms of history and vintage photos of drive-ins from the 1920s to the present.

ana, Ohio, New York, and Pennsylvania, they are only open during the warmer seasons.

Mission Tiki Drive-In in Montclair, **California,** opened as a single-screen theater in 1956 and underwent a complete overhaul in 2006. It was revamped in classic 1950s tiki style, with ticket booths decked out like tiki huts and a concession stand that continues the theme. Special events nights are a big draw and include classic movie nights. The drive-in isn't just about movies: The swap meets that started here in the 1960s are still going strong four times a week, and more than 300 vendors come out to sell their antiques, housewares, and clothes. Swap meet admission costs an old-fashioned 50 or 75 cents (depending on the day of the week). General movie admission is just $7 for adults and $1 for kids ages 5 to 9, which is a bargain considering that all the shows are double features. www.missiontiki.com

In Orefield, **Pennsylvania,** Shankweiler's Drive-In was the second drive-in to be built in the United States, and it is still going strong today. A night at the theater is a real exercise in nostalgia—it

Vintage Cars

Listen up, car enthusiasts. Back in the early 20th century, Citroën became one of the first mass production car companies outside of the United States. Today you can still get the full experience on a Citroën 2CV tour of **Paris.** The convertible top and small size of the vehicle allow for up-close views that you could never get on a bus tour (http://en.parisauthentic.com). Sprintage Classic Cars Touring (www.sprintage.it) rents out classic cars like a 1950 MG "A" and a 1967 Alpha Romeo. You can opt for a personal guide or take advantage of a driving program to drive yourself through the region. Yosemite Model T-Tours (www.driveamodelt.com) near **Yosemite National Park** operates June through October and will let you drive a vintage Model T or Model A Roadster for the day. Trust me, when you roll the top down on the Model T 1922, it becomes a ride you won't soon forget.

feels just like it did when the theater opened in 1934. However, the technology is better now. The facility has a state-of-the-art FM radio sound system by which to hear the audio. This is a smaller theater, holding only 300 cars, so arrive early to ensure you get a spot. You can stay inside your car or, if you prefer, lay down a blanket and some beach chairs outside and make a picnic of it on a warm summer night. Even the food here is retro, with cotton candy and funnel cakes. And best of all, the popcorn is topped with real butter. www.shankweilers.com

Blue Starlite operates two locations in the artsy heart of Austin, **Texas,** that are modern, miniaturized versions of the historic tradition. Purists may balk at some of the features, but the hipster Austin customers love the vibes of what the company dubs "mini urban drive-ins." The speakers are real 1950s antique fixtures, and the grounds are decorated with antique children's cars and vintage movie posters. While many drive-ins discourage drinking your own beer, Blue Starlite is refreshingly BYOB. The theaters show a combination of classic and quirky contemporary films via high-definition digital projection on a 22-foot-by-12-foot-wide screen. Only a few cars can fit in each location (16 and 24, respectively), but pedestrians, bicyclists, and other nonvehicle-equipped folks can sit at one of the outside tables for $5. www.bluestarlite drivein.com

The United States is not the only place where drive-in theaters exist. **South Africa** used to have dozens in the 1950s heyday of drive-ins, and there are at least six left in the country today. Having said that, Menlyn Park is not one of the original ones—it was built on top of a modern-day shopping center in 1998—but it's the only one where you can watch movies from inside one of the theater's fleet of authentic '50s vehicles. You can book one of six restored automobiles, which include a 1957 Studebaker, a 1955 Chevy Bel Air, and a 1946 Chrysler. You can bring your own vehicle, of course, and as a bonus, every Tuesday is "cram-in" night, where you buy one admission ticket and squeeze as many people as you can into your car. www.menlynpark.co.za/drivein.htm

ICE-CREAM PARLORS

Nothing harkens back to the old days of lazy summers like an afternoon at the ice-cream parlor. But these days, ice-cream shops are using traditional artisan techniques to create modern, innovative flavors.

Il Laboratorio del Gelato is correctly named. The atmosphere in its two lower **Manhattan** locations is somewhat stark and laboratory-like, but as with true science, the 200-some flavors of gelato and sorbets actually taste the way they're advertised. Everything is handmade in small batches, with traditional flavors like maple walnut gelato and lemon sorbet, and more innovative items like chocolate Thai chili and an assortment of apple-flavored sorbets, from Fuji to Honeycrisp. www.laboratoriodelgelato.com

Who doesn't think back to the old ice-cream trucks with some fond-

---

INSIDER'S TIP

See how things used to be at the Americana Museum at Bird-in-Hand in Pennsylvania (www.bird-in-hand.com/americanamuseum). This complex showcases nostalgic items from yesteryear like an old apothecary and a fully stocked general store. In Lincoln, New Hampshire, the family-run Clark's Trading Post is better known for its menagerie of trained black bears, but it also has an Americana museum with old-timey items like phonographs and early telephones, an antique fire station, and a vintage gas station complete with a restored 1931 sedan.

ness? While Mister Softee trucks are still around, in **New York** the gourmet food truck craze lends itself beautifully to mobile ice-cream vendors. In fact, some have been so successful that they've parlayed their ice-cream trucks into brick-and-mortar storefronts. This is gourmet stuff, like Van Leeuwen Artisan Ice Cream (www.vanleeuweni cecream.com), which serves ice cream made from locally sourced milk and cream, fresh egg yolks, and sugar cane. Don't miss the Big Gay Ice Cream (www.biggayicecream.com) truck and East Village shop that serves old-school soft-serve ice cream with truly unexpected toppings, like olive oil and sea salt, fiery Sriracha, and Trix cereal.

Cajun and Creole flavors are a class of their own, but La Divina Gelateria is like having a slice of Italy in **New Orleans.** Artisan gelato is made daily with local and organic ingredients, including fruits and honey straight from nearby farms. The flavors change regularly, but if available, you can get a taste of the South with Peach Creole Cream Cheese or Moon Pie gelato. www.ladivinagelateria.com

San Francisco's Humphry Slocombe is known for its wildly inventive flavors of ice cream, sorbet, and sherbet. Bay Area locals will actually line up out the door for flavors like cayenne cantaloupe, peanut butter curry, prosciutto, and its real claim to fame, "secret breakfast," made with bourbon ice cream and cornflakes. www. humphryslocombe.com

Road Trip!

What's more retro Americana than a road trip? Make it an experience to remember by taking the slow route and stopping in the small towns and driving the "blue highways." RoadsideAmerica.com is a great resource for old-school Americana on your road trip. We're talking quirky sights like the old "shoe tree" at Hallelujah Junction, **California**—where locals and passersby have hung hundreds of shoes from the branches—and the decades-old A&W Root Beer statues in Tipton, **Iowa.** My best advice for any road trip is to skip the fast-food chains in favor of really local, off-the-map dining. Roadfood.com will guide you to the mom-and-pop barbecue joints, diners, and bakeries on your journey.

It doesn't get more old-fashioned than Little Man Ice Cream in the trendy Highland neighborhood of **Denver.** It isn't the small-batch, handmade ice cream with unexpected flavors like cupcake and Mexican chocolate (dark chocolate with cinnamon spice); it's the fact that it's located inside a 28-foot model of an old-school milk can. www.littlemanicecream.com

Ask anyone in **Boston** where the best ice cream is, and they'll point you to nearby Cambridge to Toscanini's. Located in Central Square near MIT, this shop has ice cream that's so rich and extra-creamy that the Dalai Lama even ordered a chocolate cone here. Along with classic favorites, owner Gus Rancatore will also churn out unusual options like bananas Foster and goat cheese brownie. www.tosci.com

Can a traditional Italian gelato shop make the grade even when it becomes an international chain? It sure can when you're talking about Grom. Originally opened in Turin, this gelateria has expanded all throughout **Italy** and into **Tokyo** and **New York.** But what really makes these guys stand out is their commitment to finding the best of the best ingredients. We're talking hazelnut chips from the Langhe region, lemons from the Amalfi Coast, and produce from their own farm, Mura Mura, in Costigliole d'Asti, Italy.

Natural, fresh, and uber-cool, the **Berlin** ice-cream shop Vanille & Marille creates some unusual pairings, like elderflower with mint, and dried apricot with candied pine nuts and white pepper. www.vanille-marille.de

On the road that leads to Magens Bay Beach, there's real grown-up fun to be had at Udder Delite Dairy Bar in St. Thomas, **US Virgin Islands,** which serves up ice-cream milkshakes with a dash of liqueur. Favorite flavors include Eskimo Sip (chocolate chip ice cream and creme de menthe) and Jamocho (chocolate and coffee ice creams with Kahlua).

La Casa Gelato in **Vancouver** makes more than 500 flavors and has more than 200 available at any given time, so you're likely to find something you like. If you're ever going to experiment, this is the time, with options like blue cheese, Guinness, and even one made

Retro from Above

The next time you want to go sightseeing, why not do it a few thousand feet above the ground in a vintage plane? It's a great throwback to the old days that airplane enthusiasts, like me, can appreciate. In **Atlanta,** BiPlane Adventures (www.biplaneride.com) will take you on a ride over the North Georgia Mountain foothills in a vintage N3N or WACO UPF-7. In **California** wine country, check out Vintage Aircraft Company (www.vintageaircraft.com). You can fly in an open-cockpit 1942 Boeing/Stearman used in World War II or a North American SNJ-4 over the vineyards of the Sonoma and Napa Valleys. Prefer to look, not fly? One of the best private vintage plane collections in the country is at Fantasy of Flight (www.fantasyofflight.com) in Polk City, **Florida,** about 20 miles from Disney World. Not only are there daily flight demos, but you can also take control of the cockpit for a few minutes while in the air on a New Standard D-25.

from the notoriously stinky durian fruit. www.lacasagelato.com

The town of Lares, about 1½ hours from San Juan, **Puerto Rico,** attracts visitors from all over the world who come to try the ice cream at Heladeria Lares. And since you're in the Caribbean, you may as well try flavors like sweet plantain or rice and beans.

Glacier Berthillon in **Paris** has been making high-quality, natural ice cream and sorbet since 1954—no preservatives or stabilizers here. There are usually at least 15 flavors to choose from, most notably the salted butter caramel. Although there are several outposts, your best bet is to go to the original shop, on Île Saint-Louis on the Seine. www.berthillon.fr

Believe it or not, the ice-cream shop that holds the most flavors isn't in Italy. Heladería Coromoto in Merida, **Venezuela,** holds the Guinness World Record for the most ice-cream flavors: 858 to be exact. Now, you're not going to see all of those flavors at once—more like 60. But there are some memorable ones to choose from: salmon, macaroni and cheese, and beer.

BEST VIEWS

I remember my first trip to the Empire State Building in **New York.** It was the first time I truly appreciated the size and majesty of the city. When I was older, some friends took me to the Top of the Rock observation deck at Rockefeller Center (www.topoftherocknyc.com), where I not only experienced the rush of Manhattan, but also got to see the Empire State Building from a completely different perspective. The key here is to go not once, but twice in the same day. Get the sunrise/sunset pass that gets you access to Top of the Rock twice. Go when it opens at 8 a.m. and again at 11 p.m., and witness two different worlds.

Here's another tip: Instead of going the tourist route, drink in the city skyline from a rooftop bar. 230 Fifth (www.230-fifth.com) features a 22,000-square-foot roof deck with unobstructed views of some of the most iconic structures, including the Empire State Building and the Met Life building.

The observation deck at Encounter restaurant at **Los Angeles** International Airport (www.encounterlax.com) was closed after 9/11. Now, after a multimillion-dollar, multiyear renovation, it has been recently reopened to the public. It's a great place for plane spotting and offers four free telescopes to get a close-up view of the jets as they take off and land. The deck offers free admission on Saturdays and Sundays and 360-degree views of the airport. Hungry for an alternative? You can also go plane spotting at LAX at the nearby In-N-Out Burger (www.in-n-out.com) at the corner of Sepulveda and Lincoln Boulevards. Grab one of their famous burgers (ask a local about the secret menu, like the "2x4" and "animal style"), sit back, and watch the planes take off and land.

The Willis Tower (www.willistower.com) in **Chicago** recently underwent a face-lift and got a series of four see-through glass balconies. When you stand on them, you get an unobstructed view of the city below, and you feel like you're walking on air. But if you want to skip the crowds, take Solidarity Drive to the Adler Planetarium where the Nichols Bridgeway offers views of Millennium Park, Lake Michigan, and the city skyline, while the rooftop Bluhm Family Terrace has a panoramic view that can't be beat.

In California's Marin Headlands, drive over the Golden Gate Bridge, then get off the highway immediately after and start heading up the hill. After a mile or two, stop, get out, and look back from whence you came: The view over the **San Francisco Bay** is astonishing, with the bridge and Alcatraz in the foreground, and the hilly, house-dotted city spread out behind. The best time to take a photo is when the low fog rolls in and shrouds the bridge.

Few views in the world rival the **Grand Canyon,** with its striated red cliffs and winding corridors. At 277 miles long and more than a mile deep, it's best seen from the air (either by helicopter or plane). But if you're earthbound, try Hopi Point or Mohave Point on the South Rim, which both jut out into the canyon and give unobstructed views. Or, for a more heart-stopping experience, set out onto the Grand Canyon Skywalk, a U-shaped, glass-bottomed ledge that juts out 70 feet from the edge of the Grand Canyon and sits a dizzying 4,000 feet above the Colorado River. www.hualapai tourism.com

Sydney Tower (www.sydneytowereye.com.au) in **Sydney,** Australia, is one of the best places in the Southern Hemisphere to get a view. The 880-foot tower looms high over the cityscape and lets you catch a glimpse of everything from the famous beaches to the distant Blue Mountains. The Skywalk on the top deck features a glass-floored viewing platform that is accessible via guided tour. And, of course, there's the Sydney Harbour Bridge with its postcard-perfect views. Climb the bridge for the most amazing views, but choose your time wisely. Instead of climbing in the glaring sunlight, do it at twilight when you can see the night sky darkening. Or—and this is my choice—do it at the break of dawn. For a classic nighttime experience, check out the equally rewarding Glenmore Hotel (www.glen morehotel.com.au) at the top of an area called the Rocks, which dates back to 1921 and is one of the few buildings with a rooftop view of Sydney Harbour.

Piazza Michelangelo, which rises high above **Florence,** offers an unobstructed view of this Renaissance city. You can see all the major monuments, such as the Duomo and the Uffizi Gallery, the Arno River, and thousands of the city's signature red-roofed houses sprinkled around. The rose garden on the premises and the replica of the statue of David are attractions in themselves. Go in low or shoulder season when there aren't so many tourists, and if you arrive in late afternoon, be sure to stick around for sunset. As an alternate option, the aptly named Golden View Open Bar (www.goldenviewopenbar. com) offers what is perhaps the best view of Ponte Vecchio in town.

For a real bragging-rights experience, you want to head to **Dubai.** That's quite a trip just for a view, but it's home to the highest observation deck in the world: the 124th floor of the Burj Khalifa sky-scraper. And here's a tip: The lines tend to get long, so buy your tickets in advance for a specific time. It's 75 percent cheaper than general admission. www.burjkhalifa.ae

The most over-the-top observation deck system may well be atop China's 1,968-foot-tall **Guangzhou** TV tower. There are several levels from which to walk, observe, and lounge, depending on your comfort level. There are outdoor viewing decks, an open-air skywalk that leads through the twisty latticework innards of the building, and at the very top—1,500 feet high—is a diagonally sloping deck with out-door bleachers with views of the old city center. www.gztvtower.info

Then there's the Sirocco restaurant high above **Bangkok.** Talk about a meal with a view. This is among the world's highest alfresco restaurants, towering 63 floors over the sparkling city. The wind can often pick up at night, so don't wear or bring anything that can become airborne. Still, the view makes it all worthwhile.

Table Mountain, the flat-topped centerpiece of **Cape Town,** offers 360-degree views of the town, ocean, and plains around it. Most people either hike up the front face (1½ hours) or take a revolving

Book a Great View

Want a hotel room with a great view? There are a couple ways to go about it. The Web site Room77.com uses Google Earth and other technology so you can actually see the real view from specific hotel rooms—so you can figure out which rooms actually have ocean views versus the ones that require you sticking your head out the window to catch a glimpse of the water. Then, the day before you check in, or even on the same day, call up the front desk and ask for one of those rooms. Or check out TheMostPerfectView.com, a collection that consists only of luxury hotels with great views. That includes the Empire Suite at the Standard, with a view of the Empire State Building; and Villa La Vedetta, located on a hilltop in Florence, where you get an unparalleled view of the Duomo, Palazzo Vecchio, and other iconic sights.

cable car (10 minutes). To the west, you'll see all the way out to Robben Island, where Nelson Mandela was held for more than 20 years; to the south, you'll see the Cape bushlands; and to the east, you'll see townships and plains that spread out toward the interior of the continent. But for an unforgettable experience, what you want to do is hike up the mountain and abseil (rappel) more than 350 feet down, as you look into the Atlantic Ocean and some of the most spectacular views in South Africa.

Best Places to Go for

MEDICAL TOURISM

What's the fastest-growing segment in tourism these days? It's not any particular destination. It's not a lifelong dream experience. Instead, it's all driven by special needs, money, and quality of care. Welcome to the brave new world of medical tourism.

This is not just about breast augmentation or liposuction. I'm also not talking about so-called healing springs or medicinal baths or special Botox clinics on the streets of Bangkok. This is about more serious forms of elective surgery and urgent care outside of America—at a fraction of the price here in the United States.

COSMETIC SURGERY

Cosmetic surgery was one of the first big trends in contemporary medical tourism, and doctors in Mexico, Costa Rica, and Brazil were treating travelers as early as the 1950s. Those first patients were well-heeled luxury travelers, but medical tourism today has put breast implants, tummy tucks, and face-lifts into the reach of the middle class. In addition to traditional stand-alone clinics, more and more hospitals are now offering cosmetic surgery. These can be a little more expensive, but hospitals give patients the added benefits of in-house emergency staff and 24-hour pharmacies.

In **Costa Rica,** the Rosenstock-Lieberman Center for Cosmetic Plastic Surgery can be a bit more expensive than other options, but its doctors have specialized in cosmetic surgery for decades. Patients prepare for surgery in hotel-like suites to encourage relaxation. The price varies by the type of room you choose, but all rates include 24-hour nursing care, laundry facilities, free calls to the United States and wireless Internet, and airport pickup and drop-off (with a minimum stay of 8 nights). www.cosmetic-cr.com

In **Mexico,** Hospital San José Tec in Monterrey is a mere 150 miles from the US border but light-years away in cost savings. They offer all sorts of cosmetic procedures, from breast augmentation and reduction, rhinoplasty, and Botox to gastric bypass and laser surgery. http://hsj.com.mx

A word of caution: The cosmetic surgery industry in Mexican cities like Tijuana, Juarez, and Cancún is particularly prone to disreputable clinics. Would-be patients should get a media reference plus at least two patient references, double-check the doctor's credentials, and make sure the facility staff speak English before proceeding with any surgery in these cities.

Those willing to travel a little farther for their cosmetic surgery should consider **Thailand.** Among many reputable providers is the Preecha Aesthetic Institute, which not only offers the full gamut of cosmetic procedures but is the world's preeminent center for gender-reassignment surgery. www.pai.co.th

DENTAL PROCEDURES

You can find good dental care in all the leading medical travel destinations, but the most popular places for US-based travelers to go are Mexico and Costa Rica—mainly due to their proximity to the States.

In **Mexico** the obvious choice is the town of Los Algodones, which is right across the border from Yuma, Arizona. It is nicknamed "the Town of Dentists" because there are around 300 dentists operating there, most of them trained in the United States. Every day between November and March, you will see hundreds, if not thousands, of Americans literally park their car at the border and walk across to get dental work done. In addition to the cost being a fraction of what it is in the United States, the dentists there are very efficient and generally have in-house labs, which means no waiting days for crowns or whatever else. www.losalgodones.com

If you want to go a little deeper into Mexico, the Imagen Dental network in Monterrey is a top choice, with English-speaking staff and an on-site point person who will help coordinate your stay and transport you to and from the clinic. www.imagendental.com

In San José you can get a whole new smile for a fraction of the price at Meza Dental Care, which offers implants, porcelain veneers, full mouth restoration, and more. Here, you can get a root canal for about $200 and veneers for about $500. www.mezadentalcare.com

Another San José favorite is Prisma Dental, which specializes in dental implants, dental restorations, full mouth reconstruction, and cosmetic dentistry. The highly trained dentists in this ultra-modern facility treat a client base that is 80 percent North American. www. prismadental.com

HEART PROCEDURES

In **Thailand,** the Bumrungrad International Hospital in Bangkok has a stellar international reputation, and the experience is akin to a four-star hotel. It was the first Asian hospital accredited by the Joint Commission International (JCI), and, in fact, at least 200 of its doctors are board certified in the United States! Covered costs include airport pickup and drop-off at your hotel, and access to a health concierge who will fill your prescriptions and escort you to your appointments. www.bumrungrad.com

In Singapore, **Malaysia,** a good option for affordable and high-quality cardiac care is the JCI-accredited Mount Elizabeth Hospital, which has made a name for itself in the high volume of cardiac surgeries in the private sector. This 345-bed private tertiary acute care hospital has Asia's highest concentration of cardiologists and cardiac surgeons, and performs the largest number of cardiac surgeries in the private sector in the region. In one year, as many as 33 percent of the cardiovascular procedures performed at Mount Elizabeth Hospital were on international patients. www.parkwayhealth.com/hospitals/mount_elizabeth_hospital

The Wockhardt Hospitals group is not only highly respected within **India,** but is also affiliated with the prestigious Harvard Medical International. There are eight hospitals throughout India, seven of which have full cardiac surgery facilities, but the 400-bed Wockhardt hospital in Bangalore is a leader among them all. www.wockhardthospitals.com

ORTHOPEDIC PROCEDURES

ndia, Malaysia, Thailand, and Mexico are among the best countries for hip surgery, but hospitals in a half dozen other countries also offer quality care, including those in Costa Rica, Panama, Argentina, Germany, and Turkey. India and Malaysia are among the most affordable, which can be an important factor for cash-strapped seniors needing back, knee, or other bone surgery to alleviate their pain.

Apollo Hospital in Chennai, **India,** is a top choice if you need hip resurfacing. It was here that a hip-resurfacing procedure was pioneered almost 10 years ago—a procedure that didn't take hold in the United States until much more recently. www.apollohospitals.com

Sime Darby Medical Centre in **Malaysia** is a favorite for orthopedic and other surgical procedures. In fact, the hospital has partnered with Malaysia Airlines's travel planning arm, MASholidays, to coordinate travel packages that include medical treatment. www.simedarbyhealthcare.com

In **Mexico,** the Christus Muguerza hospital group is one of the world's top providers of orthopedic care and has three facilities not far from the Texas border. www.christusmuguerza.com.mx

WOMEN'S HEALTH/FERTILITY TREATMENTS

hen it comes to helping couples make babies, **Barbados** takes the solid lead. The 20-bed Barbados Fertility Centre is a place for couples to undergo the fertility treatment process. Part of its success is credited to the tranquil Caribbean surroundings during this stressful experience. www.barbadosivf.org

Other good options include BNH Hospital in Bangkok, **Thailand** (www.bnhhospital.com/cn), which has a separate in-vitro fertilization (IVF) center, and the Anadolu Medical Centre in **Turkey** (www. anadolumedicalcentre.co.uk).

KK Women's and Children's Hospital in **Singapore** is also among the very best and is noted for producing the first in-vitro baby in Asia in the 1980s. www.kkh.com.sg

Fortis Healthcare in **India,** which operates the Fortis La Femme Centre for Women in New Delhi, is another standout for quality of service and cost. It's the leading facility in India for fertility treatments, including IVF, egg donation, and the growing business of surrogacy. www.fortishealthcare.com

For a full preventive health screening for women, Bumrungrad Hospital in **Bangkok** is the winner. The comprehensive "woman over 40" package includes a physical exam, Pap smear, digital mammogram, chest x-ray, abdominal ultrasound, blood tests, thyroid screen, and eye exam—and costs about $500.

COMPREHENSIVE HEALTH SCREENINGS

Preventive medicine is big overseas, and many hospitals offer thorough physical exams at discount prices, which is why some travelers choose to combine their vacation time with a comprehensive preventive checkup.

Seoul National University Hospital in **South Korea** is known for offering full health screenings—which combine costly procedures like hearing and visual exams for about $300, full bloodwork for about $200, and an MRI for about $1,000—a fraction of the US cost. www. snuh.org/english

At Sime Darby Medical Centre in **Kuala Lumpur,** the digestive tract screening package includes an endoscopy, gastroscopy, colonoscopy, ulcer assessment, and complete report, and totals less than $700.

WHAT YOU NEED TO KNOW

A few years ago, medical tourism was being marketed like a gimmick: Go to Buenos Aires to learn to tango and get a breast-lift; take a safari and get a face-lift. After all, if you were going to spend 3 weeks recovering, why not combine it with a legitimate vacation? (The reality was, most of the fun activities took place before the surgery. Who really wants to go dancing after undergoing an invasive procedure?)

The development of medical tourism as an industry has led to the development of accreditation and standards for both US and overseas entities, which is good news for patients. For example, an organization called the Joint Commission International (JCI) accredits foreign hospitals to ensure they meet Western medical standards.

To get good quality service, try to find a hospital or clinic that has been accredited by the JCI—there are about 300 around the world that meet its criteria. The American Medical Association also has its own guidelines on medical tourism, aimed at employers, insurance

INSIDER'S TIP

There are several companies that offer to facilitate your overseas procedure— but do your research. Check out www.patientsbeyondborders.com, one of the leading resources in international medical and health travel and advocacy. It has a list of reputable agencies, including MedRetreat (www.medretreat.com) and HealthGlobe (www.myhealthglobe.com).

THE COST OF MEDICINE AROUND THE WORLD

HEART BYPASS SURGERY

United States $144,000
Costa Rica $25,000
Thailand $15,121
Colombia $14,802
Malaysia $11,430
India $5,200

ANGIOPLASTY

United States $57,000
Thailand $13,000
Malaysia $11,200
Costa Rica $9,000
India $7,500
Colombia $4,500

HIP REPLACEMENT

United States $50,000
Mexico $13,000
Costa Rica $12,500
Thailand $7,879
Malaysia $7,500
India $7,000

HYSTERECTOMY

United States $15,000
South Korea $11,000
Costa Rica $5,700
Malaysia $5,250
Thailand $2,727
India $2,500

DENTAL IMPLANT

United States $2,800
Mexico $1,800
Colombia $1,750
India $1,000
Costa Rica $900

BREAST AUGMENTATION

United States $10,000
Nicaragua $4,400
Costa Rica $3,800
Mexico $3,500
Colombia $2,500

IN-VITRO FERTILIZATION

United States $14,500
Barbados $5,750
India $3,250
Costa Rica $2,800
Israel $2,800

GASTRIC BYPASS

United States $32,927
Costa Rica $12,500
Mexico $10,950
Columbia $9,900
India $5,000

All figures are estimates from the Medical Tourism Association 2010 Survey excerpted from the *International Medical Travel Journal*. Prices will vary based on ZIP code, region, provider, and other factors. Prices do not include airfare or hotel accommodations for the patient or a companion. Travel costs, including airfare and hotel, will vary, depending on the country and the length of stay for recovery.

companies, and medical facilitators in the United States. Their intention is to ensure that patients know their rights as far as the risks, costs, and logistics of medical tourism. Several foreign hospitals are even affiliated with prestigious programs like Johns Hopkins and Cleveland Clinic, and are subject to stringent standards and codes.

Now here's an important factor that not everyone considers: Having everything go right *after* the surgery—meaning no infections or complications—is key. Most of the hospitals that cater to medical tourists really take care of their patients. Not only are they more inpatient friendly—they're not trying to hustle you out of the room the day after your surgery—but most JCI-accredited hospitals also have partnerships with fine hotels where you can spend your outpatient recovery time. For example, the Apollo Hospital in Chennai sends patients to the posh Taj Connemara Hotel to recuperate. Overall, a good rule of thumb is to allow extra time for recovery when scheduling a medical vacation. Because once you leave the country, follow-up care is your responsibility.

Where you end up going for surgery should ultimately be an individual choice based on the type of procedure you need, the cost, distance, aftercare facilities, cultural familiarity, and recommendations and references from professionals and former patients (many hospitals that have long track records of catering to foreign patients offer American references). You have to look at the total experience; you can't only look at the procedure or country. A good place to start your research is by contacting the International Patient Services Centers of various hospitals overseas (most of the big ones have them) and inquiring about fees and services.

By the way, not everyone is a candidate for medical travel. Some experts recommend using the "$6,000 Rule," which says that if a procedure is going to cost you $6,000 or less in the United States, it is generally not worth the extra flight, hotel, and other costs associated with seeking treatment abroad. Others are not good candidates simply because their condition isn't conducive to the stress of international travel. Always, always talk to your physician before planning a trip overseas for a medical procedure.

Best Places to

RENT AN ISLAND

It sounds elitist and financially out of reach for most of us, but in reality, it's remarkably easy—and in many cases quite affordable—to rent your own island! You just need to know the best places and some basic arithmetic.

Renting your own private island becomes financially accessible if you play the numbers game and divide the total cost by the number of people you're bringing with you—whether it's family and friends (or both).

There are literally *hundreds* of islands available for rent all over the world, from postage stamp–size rocks off the US coast to tropical islands in the Caribbean.

AFFORDABLE

Getting away from it all doesn't have to involve a long overseas flight. The quiet, remote, and rustic Republic Island is a 2-acre getaway on the Michigamme River in **Michigan**'s beautiful Upper Peninsula. Starting at just $100 to $150 a night and sleeping up to 6 people, it's a year-round destination for hunting, cross-country skiing, snowshoeing, and boating. But the island is best known for its fishing in summer and miles of snowmobiling trails in winter. This island rental also comes with a pontoon, canoe, and paddleboat.

Nautilus Island in **Maine** is a hugely historic site, best known as the place that Paul Revere's troops captured from the British during the American Revolution. Sitting in the Penobscot Bay, this rugged island is home to an elegant Main House and several smaller buildings, including the Cape Cod Cottage that starts from $3,500 a week. Or, if you want to gather a group of friends or family, the entire island is available for rent for about $16,000 a week. We're not talking about rustic living: The property includes a housekeeper and chef, waitstaff, and even a boat captain. The island is a prime spot for duck hunting as well as typical New England activities like clamming, collecting mussels, and pulling lobster traps. www.nautilusislandmaine.com

The location of Melody Key means you can spend time in **Key West** and then go to this quiet private island. The main houses are fully equipped and connected, but the vibe here is quiet, laid back, and a world away from the more touristy Key islands. This spot is best suited for small groups of adults, as the minimum age is 16 and no guests under 21 are allowed without adult supervision. For about $15,000 a week, this property sleeps up to 6 people and includes the services of a caretaker who is on call 24/7. www.melodykey.com

MIDPRICE

You can unplug completely at Little Deadman's Cay off Long Island in the **Bahamas.** For one thing, to get here you really have to mean it. It requires flying on a propeller plane from Nassau (about 165 miles) to Long Island followed by a short boat ride, or taking a charter flight from Nassau (about $180 round-trip). There is only one three-bedroom beachfront home on the island, which is solar powered and supplemented with a windmill and a gravity shower. We're talking no TV and limited amenities like basic kitchen supplies and a CHF radio telephone. So why would you want to take over this remote island? It's downright beautiful, with nearly 10 acres of property, three entirely secluded beaches, natural swimming pools, snorkeling, and sunset views that you won't want to miss.

Although renting a Tahitian island may sound like a dream, it's entirely possible on **Dream Island.** Rates are only about $2,000 a week for access to three bungalows sitting on a private, 4-acre beach. I don't like to throw around the phrase "tropical paradise," but this is everything you can imagine about a South Pacific island: private, white-sand beaches, traditional bungalows, rich coral reefs with an array of tropical fish, and warm Pacific waters for surfing, swimming, and snorkeling. The good news is, if you need more structured activities or nightlife, Moorea is only 3 minutes away by boat. www.dream-island.com

LUXURY

Want to vacation like a rock star? Then you want to rent out a villa on the island of **Mustique,** one of the Grenadine islands in the Caribbean. In this case, you aren't renting the whole island but one of a handful of staffed villas (including Mick Jagger's six-bedroom mansion) or a room in the Cotton House Hotel. The vibe here is so upscale so that you can count on complete privacy and relaxation, but it's also got the feel of a small community without the attitude of a more populated Caribbean resort. That's why David Bowie, Princess Margaret, and Prince William and Kate Middleton can be counted among those who have frequented the island. Jagger's villa costs at least $11,000 a week, but with space for 10, it's not a completely outrageous price. www.mustique-island.com

Although a major fire destroyed much of the main house, Sir Richard Branson's private island is still a major destination for vacationers looking for a luxury escape in the middle of the Caribbean. **Necker Island** is comprised of 74 acres of land, with immaculately kept grounds and fully staffed accommodations. Rates aren't cheap, starting at about $56,000 a night for up to 28 guests (when the Great House is completely rebuilt). But the total bill for all this is surprisingly inclusive: all meals, drinks, at least 60 staff members, sailboats and speedboats, water sports equipment, and a whole lot more. Not included is the *Necker Nymph,* Branson's three-person aero submarine. www.neckerisland.com

The remote island of **Vamizi,** off the northern coast of Mozambique, is a dream vacation for nature lovers. Located within an

Rental Companies

Most people want sun, sand, and surf, but there are a surprising number of alternate options through brokers that handle regions throughout the world. How about a Croatian lighthouse on the tiny island of Dugi Otok or a private nature reserve in South Carolina's Low Country? Check out Private Islands Online (www.privateislandsonline.com) for some of the more offbeat and unusual. If the Caribbean is your dream destination, Island Hideaways (www.islandhideaways.com) specializes in this region. Whether you're looking to honeymoon on North Island like Will and Kate or rent an uninhabited island, Vladi Private Islands (www.vladi-private-islands.de/islandsforrent.html) offers anything and everything.

archipelago of tropical coral islands, Vamizi is part of the Maluane Conservation Project, so the landscape is pristine, with plenty of opportunities for whale watching, shore-based fishing, sea kayaking, and a whole lot more. But insiders know Vamizi as one of the top secluded diving spots in the world, with more than 400 species of tropical fish among the rich coral. Again, you're more likely to rent a villa rather than the entire island, but with only 10 beach houses, this is the kind of place where the wealthy go when they really want to get away. www.vamizi.com

There's only one private island off the coast Sri Lanka and only one villa on that island. The rocky, 2.5-acre island of **Taprobane** was built by a French count in the 1920s and has remained an exclusive destination ever since. What's truly unusual about this Weligama Bay island is that you don't need a private helicopter or boat to get there. During low tide, you can wade there, and staff members will transport your luggage with the help of elephants!

SCENIC DRIVES

So many of us drive so often that the "scenery" becomes one big blur. But there are still many places along highways and byways just begging for a real road trip, making time in the car feel leisurely and free. Here are a few of the best drives that have endured—some established, with a few surprises.

UNITED STATES

When you say **Hawaii,** most people think of two major drives: the Hana Highway, which features 600 curves and 54 one-lane bridges in a 52-mile stretch; and the 45-mile drive from Hilo to the Waipi'o Valley on the Big Island. But for an alternative to the usual tourist routes, check out the Mamalahoa Kona Heritage Highway on the Big Island, which runs between Kalaoa and Honalo, on the Kona Coast. This 12-mile stretch of CR 180, which is located slightly inland, offers sweeping views of the ocean on one side and the heights of Mount Hualalai on the other. What's really special about this route is that it offers a glimpse of old Hawaii as it passes by old coffee plantations, general stores, a disused sugar mill, over grown cemeteries, and historic buildings. Many of the old homes still look as they did back at the turn of the century: corrugated tin roofs, gingerbread trim, and crumbling lanais. A good place to stop is the artists' enclave of Holualoa, which is home to dozens of galleries and coffeehouses, or in Kainaliuhe, where you'll find the Aloha Theater

Motorcycle Tours

A guided tour can be a great option for those who want to see the country by motorcycle. You can maximize the fun and minimize the hassle by having someone else arrange lodging, plan routes, offer insight and advice, and even give instructions on how to navigate tougher roads. Most motorcycle tour companies also offer a backup van to carry your luggage and gear—or even your spouse, if he/she isn't the motorcycling type. EagleRider is the world's largest company specializing in Harley-Davidson tours. They offer guided trips throughout the United States, Mexico, and Europe. If you prefer the self-drive option, they'll provide a customized GPS route. Rentals range from $50 to $150 per day. Other reputable rental companies include Elite Motorcycle Tours, Ayres Adventures Motorcycle Tours, Ad-Mo Tours, and Southwest Adventure Tours.

and the Aloha Angel Cafe. Don't miss the Donkey Balls candy factory, and take a tour of Captain Cook Coffee's roasting house.

The North Fork Highway between Cody, **Wyoming,** and Yellowstone Park is the road that Teddy Roosevelt deemed "the most scenic 50 miles in America." Also known as the Buffalo Bill Cody Scenic Byway, this section of US 14 meanders between the cliffs and slopes of Shoshone Canyon in the Shoshone National Forest. Don't miss the rock formations at the turnout in an area near Wapiti called "Holy City." Watch, too, for the Buffalo Bill Reservoir and the 325-foot dam, which was the tallest in the world at the time it was completed in 1910. This drive is a wildlife lover's dream: mule deer, elk, moose, bighorn sheep, black bear, and grizzly bears all live along the route.

While most visitors to **California** tend to think of the trip up coastal Highway 1 as the ultimate overview of the state's natural beauty, an alternative route is the King's Canyon Scenic Byway. Located in central California's Sierra Nevada foothills, this short-but-sweet (50-mile) route goes through two lesser-known national

Drive in a Classic Car

Why not take a scenic drive in an even more scenic classic car? Near **Yosemite National Park,** you can rent restored original Model T or Model A Fords and cruise through the forest in retro style. Choose from a top-down 1915 Touring Car, a 1928 Model A, or a 1929 Model A Roadster, starting at $450 a day for four people (www.driveamodelt.com). In **France,** you can drive a classic Citroën 2CV or MGB Roadster through the countryside. The convertible top and small size of the vehicles allow for close-up views that you could never get on a bus tour (www.logisduparadis.com). Sprintage Classic Cars Touring offers classic car rentals throughout **Italy.** You can opt for a personal guide or take advantage of a driving program to drive yourself through the region in a '50s or '60s Alfa Spider, MG, Fiat, or Triumph (www.sprintage.it). If you want to explore the old **Berlin** behind the former Iron Curtain, take a Trabi-Safari tour in the tiny East German cars known as the Trabant. These were terrible cars, but it's a lot of fun. The hourlong tours take you well off the beaten path, through the eastern part of the city along the wall's remains and down Karl-Marx-Allee (www.trabi-safari.de).

parks. In Sequoia National Park, you'll pass by the largest contiguous grove of giant sequoia trees in the world, while in King's Canyon National Park you'll see a gorge that's thousands of feet deeper than the Grand Canyon. You can drive straight through in 1 hour, but a better option is to slow down, walk through Zumwalt Meadow, take short hikes to the base of Grizzly Falls and Roaring River Falls, and explore the bat-filled Boyden Caverns.

Shenandoah National Park in **Virginia** is one of the most scenic national parks in the country, and the 105-mile-long Skyline Drive runs right along its backbone. A designated National Scenic Byway, this road affords unparalleled views of the Shenandoah Valley to the west and the rolling hills to the east. There are 75 (yes, 75) lookout points along this north-south road. You're bound to see wildlife like deer, black bears, and wild turkeys, but the best times to go are in spring, when the route is flanked by millions of colorful wildflowers, or in autumn, to see the brilliant fall foliage.

Some places are more scenic at night, and the **Las Vegas** Strip, with its neon lights, is one of them. You'll see the illuminated pyramid at the Luxor hotel; the volcano at the Mirage; the skyscrapers of New York, New York; the Eiffel Tower at Paris Las Vegas; and the pirate ships at Treasure Island. Veer off the strip to Fremont Street in downtown Vegas, and be dazzled by the light show known as the Fremont Street Experience.

INTERNATIONAL

The **Netherlands**' 25-mile Haarlem to Leiden "Bloemen Route" traverses farmland with the densest concentration of flower fields in the country. To get the full effect, you must take this drive in April or May, when the crocuses, daffodils, hyacinths, irises, and tulips are blooming. Along the way, you'll be treated to the sight of country villages that look like paintings come to life and roadside vendors who sell garlands to decorate your car. At either end, you can explore by car or foot the beautiful canal-crossed cities of Haarlem and Leiden. Tip: Take this drive during a weekday, to avoid traffic and crowds.

The 2-hour Sea to Sky Highway in **British Columbia** encompasses both coastal and mountain vistas on its 83-mile journey between Vancouver and Whistler/Blackcomb. The scenery here is remarkable: Cliffs plunge to the sea at the same time as the road curves precariously through alpine forests, because it hugs Howe Sound—a fjord that juts into the coastal mountain range—for most of the journey. Highlights include Stawamus Chief, a granite monolith; the 1,100-foot Shannon Falls; the Cheakamus Canyon river rapids; the 8,800-foot Mount Garibaldi; and the pinnacle of lava rock known as the Black Tusk. Seven interpretive kiosks along the way give the history of the road and the surrounding towns. Tip: There are more than 300 road accidents here every year, so drive slowly and carefully, especially in bad weather.

Chapman's Peak Drive in **South Africa** is cut into the coastal cliffs just south of Cape Town. It's only a 5-mile route, but you will encounter 114 curves between Hout Bay (on the outskirts of Cape Town) and Noordhoek. On one side of the road is a sheer vertical drop to the churning ocean, and on the other are towering sandstone cliffs that lead to Chapman's Peak, the 900-foot mountain the road is named after. Note that the southern right whale is frequently spotted between July and October. Tip: This is a toll road, so be sure to bring some change. www.chapmanspeakdrive.co.za

Best Places to Find

SCENIC TRAINS

I love train trips and all kinds of trains. From China to Australia and South Africa to even right here in America, I'll do anything to hop a train. It's not just the journey, but the opportunity to spend time at a slower pace, to think, to reflect, and, yes, to sleep. To me, there's always been something soothing about a long train trip.

And every once in a while, if you're really lucky, you get to look out the window and be amazed by the ever-changing views. Herewith the best scenic train trips.

417

NORTH AMERICA

When it comes to scheduling and accessibility, America's railway system is nothing short of an embarrassment, especially when you compare it to the European model. But if you're someone who enjoys the journey as much as the destination (and don't care what time you get in), there's nothing like experiencing the country by rail.

One of my favorite routes is Amtrak's Crescent, between **New York and New Orleans.** Unlike the high-speed Acela train that connects the Northeast corridor, this is a leisurely trip that starts from the Big Apple in the afternoon and pulls into New Orleans the next evening, just as the city lights up for the night.

Amtrak's Coast Starlight between **Seattle, Portland, and Los Angeles** is one of the most scenic train rides in the country. What makes it so special is that it passes by the dramatic snow-covered peaks of the Cascade Range, does a full circle around Mount Shasta, and goes through forests, green valleys, and long stretches of Pacific Ocean shoreline.

The California Zephyr, which travels between **Chicago and San**

INSIDER'S TIP

Be sure to spend time in the Sightseeing Lounge on the California Zephyr, a glass-walled compartment on the upper level that gets you first-class access to the spectacular scenery. In spring and summer, the Trails and Rails lecture program takes place between Denver and Grand Junction, Colorado. www.amtrak.com

Francisco, is also a superb ride, offering a smattering of everything the United States has to offer. After leaving the West Coast, it crosses the stunning Sierra Nevada range, climbs through the heart of the Rockies, and chugs across the plains of Nebraska. Best of all, it's scheduled so you're traveling through the most scenic parts in the daytime and sleeping through the more mundane stretches.

The Lakeshore Limited travels 959 miles from **Chicago to Albany, New York** (and onward to New York City or Boston). It's a great way to view the Great Lakes, Finger Lakes, and other classic American attractions. From Chicago the train heads along the south shore of Lake Michigan, the Mohawk River, and the Erie Canal. When you get to New York State, you'll pass through the scenic Finger Lakes wine region before entering Albany. www.amtrak.com

The Alaska Railroad is one of the best ways to see the unforgettable scenery of **Alaska.** The railroad includes a variety of routes between Anchorage, Seward, and Fairbanks. For panoramas of Mount McKinley, glaciers, and moose, try the Denali Star Train, which starts in Anchorage and stops in Talkeetna and Denali before ending in Fairbanks. http://alaskarailroad.com

The Durango to Silverton Narrow Gauge train in **Colorado** is a one-day, 52-mile round-trip journey with canyon and cliff views of the 2-million-acre San Juan National Forest. It is called "narrow-gauge" because the track is narrower than a regular rail line, which makes it better able to navigate the mountainous terrain. www.durangotrain.com

Trail and Rails

Ask about the Trails and Rails program on the Coast Starlight, a partnership with the National Park Service, with lectures on certain stretches of the route. Between Santa Barbara and San Luis Obispo, California, the program is hosted by Juan Bautista de Anza National Historic Trail; between Seattle and Portland, it's hosted by the Klondike Gold Rush National Historical Park. www.amtrak.com

National Parks by Train

I'm a big fan of visiting our national parks as an affordable, family-friendly vacation. Add in train travel, and it's the all-American experience. You can certainly do it yourself, but there are several organized tour companies that will coordinate the experience so you can hop on and off, as well as arrange your hotel stays and meals. Vacations by Rail has a fully guided, 11-day tour of **Grand Teton, Yellowstone,** and **Glacier National Parks** that incorporates two iconic train trips: the California Zephyr from Chicago to Salt Lake City, and the northerly Empire Builder from East Glacier Park back down to Chicago. Not only do you get great photo ops in the Colorado Rockies, but you'll also get excursions to Grand Teton and Yellowstone and a motorcoach tour to Glacier. www.vacationsbyrail.com

The Hocking Valley Scenic Railway in southeastern **Ohio** features ample leg room and plenty of space to move around—which is always a good thing when you have fidgety kids! Kids also love the "themed" trips, like the 2-hour Robbery Train, where onboard staff pretend to be a sheriff and deputies who attempt to protect the train from robbers seeking to make off with a gold shipment. In the summer months, the train departs every Saturday and Sunday, twice a day, to the restored 1840s village of Robbins Crossing, and every Thursday and Friday in October is the scenic Fall Foliage Train. www. hockingvalleytrain.com

INTERNATIONAL

Not everyone associates **Canada** with rail travel, but it's actually one of the best ways to get around the country and catch a glimpse of some of the more remote, rugged areas. For anyone with the time, I recommend the transcontinental Toronto-Vancouver route on board the Canadian. But if you've got a more limited schedule, take the train from cosmopolitan Montreal to maritime Halifax.

This particular train ride is an exceptionally good option for couples and families: It's only 22 hours long and the scenery is always changing. Hop on in Montreal in the evening and settle in for dinner as you zip through the heart of Quebec. In the morning, you wake up to views of the Chaleur Bay coastline, and by early evening, the train arrives in Halifax. Go in fall, when Halifax is abuzz with autumn events and rates drop across the board. www.viarail.ca

If you think the Grand Canyon is dramatic, you haven't seen **Mexico**'s Copper Canyon. And the best way to see it? By train, of course. Located in the northern state of Chihuahua, Copper Canyon is the name used for a group of six unique canyons in the Sierra Tarahumara, part of the larger Sierra Madre Occidental. The overall group of canyons is actually larger than the Grand Canyon and, in some areas, even deeper. The Chihuahua al Pacífico, or Chepe, runs along the canyon between Chihuahua and Los Mochis, on the Gulf of California, comprised of more than 390 miles of rails with 39 bridges and 86 tunnels. The total trip takes approximately 15 hours and passes through traditional old villages, but the real attractions are the massive, towering cliffs and deep ravines that make this one of the most scenic rides out there. www.mexicoscoppercanyon.com/chepe.htm

The Qinghai-Tibet Railway stretches more than 600 miles through the **Himalayas.** It starts in Beijing and eventually rises to 16,640 feet above sea level, making it the highest railway in the world. The mountain scenery is really something, especially when you think about the fact that it's also some of the most inhospitable terrain in the world. Half the journey is over permafrost, passing by mountain peaks, saltwater lakes, and wildlife such as antelope, yak, and pheasant. And here's something unusual: To prevent passengers from getting altitude sickness, oxygen is pumped into the passenger compartments and breathing masks are available if needed. www. chinatibettrain.com

It's short but sweet, and one of the steepest in the world: The 12-mile Flam Railway in **Norway** travels from Myrdal, which is 2,838 feet above sea level, down to the fjords of Flam. You'll roll down a steep incline in fjordland to see some of the country's most magnificent scenery. We're talking snowy mountains with farmland along the slopes, deep ravines and rivers, and twisting tunnels that spiral in and out of the mountains. What I love about this train is that it slows down, or stops altogether, at the most scenic spots. At the bottom, you get a prime view of the majestic Aurlandfjord (a branch of Sognefjord, the world's longest fjord). www.flaamsbana.no/eng

The TranzAlpine train in **New Zealand**'s South Island takes you through four different ecosystems, 19 tunnels, four viaducts, and a mountain range as it travels from one coast to another in 4½ hours. The journey, which starts in Christchurch on the east coast and ends in Greymouth on the west coast, passes through the Canterbury Plains, the spectacular gorges and river valleys around the Waimakariri River, then climbs into the snowcapped Southern Alps before descending through beech rain forest. www.tranzscenic.co.nz/services/tranzalpine.aspx

The high-altitude Glacier Express travels through the Swiss Alps from **Zermatt to Davos,** allowing you to see the best of Switzerland in one trip. On the daylong journey, you'll pass by mountain landscapes, plunging gorges, and flower- (or snow-) filled valleys, plus 91 tunnels and 291 bridges. Notable highlights include the upscale ski town of St. Moritz and the sources of both the Rhone and Rhine Rivers. www.glacierexpress.ch

LUXURY TRAINS

The Great Southern Rail company operates several journeys throughout **Australia,** but if you have to choose, go for the legendary Ghan. First launched in 1929, the 3-day, 1,850-mile journey gives a broad, sweeping overview of the whole country—the green fields of the south; the barren, ocher-tinged desertscape of the Outback; the vast sheep and cattle ranches; the humid, mountainous jungles of the north. From the outside, the Great Southern trains look rather ordinary, but inside, the experience is not just comfortable—it's a throwback to the golden age of travel. www.gsr.com.au

Although you might think of the famous Blue Train when it comes

INSIDER'S TIP

The Man in Seat Sixty-One (www.seat61 .com) is the name of a Web site that features train and ship information, as well as schedules around the world. It even shows you pictures of the train interiors to help you decide if you can get by in economy class or should opt for first class. Then there's Railpass.com. It sells rail passes and has extensive timetables for trains across Europe. But unlike Eurail, Railpass actually includes British trains in its schedules.

to rail travel in **South Africa,** the one you really don't want to miss is Rovos Rail. My advice is to take the 48-hour journey from Cape Town to Pretoria. We're talking nearly 1,000 miles of mountain ranges and valleys and, of course, the renowned wineland. As part of the upscale experience, the wood-paneled train only accommodates 72 passengers. www.rovos.com

Canada's national rail system may put Amtrak to shame, but if you really want an upscale experience, go for the Royal Canadian Pacific. It traverses some of the most inaccessible parts of the Canadian Rockies in vintage 1940s cars. On a looping 6-day trip that starts and ends in Calgary, you'll pass by (or take excursions to) Waterton-Glacier International Peace Park, Crowsnest Pass, Yoho National Park, and Banff National Park. The train only holds 23 passengers, so you're assured of an intimate, relaxed experience, complete with gourmet meals, open bar, and wood-paneled staterooms. www.royalcanadianpacific.com

What about the Orient-Express? Legendary? Yes. But the best? Of all the iconic journeys, including the Royal Scotsman in Scotland and the Hiram Bingham to Machu Picchu in Peru, the real exotic winner is the Eastern & Oriental Express. A 7-day journey

INSIDER'S TIP

Attention train nerds! The New York City Transit Museum in Brooklyn is one of the cooler museums out there. It's located in a decommissioned subway station and offers experiences like riding vintage cars from Grand Central to the Bronx Zoo or visiting the Long Island Maintenance Shop for Commuter Trains.

through **Thailand** takes you to places that aren't normally accessible to visitors, like tiny villages to meet local handicrafters and visit ancient Khmer temples, through the rural landscape to the mountain kingdom of Chiang Mai and the city of Lampang. Best of all, you'll get to explore Thailand's oldest national park, Khao Yai, led by an expert naturalist, followed by a tour of a Thai vineyard. www.orient-express.com

Best Places to See

FIREWORKS

Those who think the best place to watch
fireworks is somewhere in the American
heartland might want to think again. And
many of us who grew up watching the July
Fourth extravaganza on the Hudson River
in New York or in Boston may not have the
best point of comparison. While the fireworks display on America's birthday is
impressive, the best places to see incredible
fireworks require a passport.

The world's top pyrotechnic techniques meet high art at the L'International des Feux Loto-Québec (also known as the Montreal International Fireworks Competition), a summer event series held Wednesday and Saturday nights at La Ronde amusement park in **Montreal.** Pyrotechnic firms from around the world compete at the annual contest, which takes place from late June through late July. Each country is given a half hour to present an original "pyromusical synchronization" program that pairs explosions with musical scores, where you can see as many as 5,000 pieces bursting into the sky. To get the best view, watch from La Ronde amusement park on Île Sainte-Hélène, the Jacques Cartier Bridge, or from either side of the St. Lawrence River.

Just a tiny dot on most maps of the mid-Atlantic, **Portugal**'s Madeira Island and the New Year's Eve festival in its capital city have won the Guinness Record for the world's largest fireworks display. We're talking 17 tons of fireworks causing about 8,000 explosions per minute, set off from nearly 50 spots around Funchal Harbor. Starting in mid-November and lasting until early January, the city's centuries-old streets are decorated with Christmas lights. Plan ahead, since January is the height of the island's tourist season.

The **Mexico City** suburb of Tultepec has a weeklong fireworks festival you definitely want to experience . . . from afar. On March 8, the festival honors San Juan de Dios, the town's patron saint, with the Burning of the Bulls. Life-size papier-mâché bulls are mounted onto towering scaffolds, stuffed with fireworks, and set aflame after dark. Locals dance alongside the fire-spewing bulls, dangerously close to the sparking mayhem. Be sure to arrive early, as public fireworks displays are often very crowded.

Every summer there are hundreds of fireworks (*hanabi*) festivals around **Japan.** One of the biggest is the Tondabayashi festival outside of Osaka, which draws up to 1 million spectators. Head to the Church of Perfect Liberty on August 1, when up to 120,000 are fired into the air, including a grand finale that can include up to 7,000 fireworks at once. For the best view, bring a blanket to the banks of the Yodo River, where you'll be surrounded by locals.

On the fifth of November, the **United Kingdom** celebrates the infamous Guy Fawkes Night. All around the country there are bonfires and fireworks, and replicas of Fawkes himself are burnt in effigy. But even though the plot to blow up Parliament took place in the capital city, London isn't the place you want to be on that night. Instead, you want to head to Lewes in East Sussex, which has arguably put on the biggest and best show since the 17th century. With tens of thousands of spectators flocking to this small village, the locals celebrate November 5 with massive bonfires, flaming torches, multiple parades throughout town, and, of course, several fireworks displays put on by the Bonfire Societies.

The annual Festa del Redentore in **Venice** is by no means the biggest or most spectacular of fireworks shows, but ask any Venetians and they'll likely tell you it's their favorite celebration of the year. On the third Saturday in July, the residents commemorate the end of the plague in 1577 with fireworks, food, and family. As soon as the sun sets, hundreds of small boats set sail in the middle of St. Mark's Bay, brightly decorated with balloons, garlands, and lanterns, while you picnic on the shores with the locals. Come nighttime, the spectacular fireworks are set off from a pontoon in the Giudecca Canal, reflecting

How to Take the Best Fireworks Photo

If your digital point-and-shoot has a "fireworks" setting, now is the perfect time to use it! If it doesn't, or if you are using a DSLR and want to customize the experience, try these steps: Use a slow shutter speed of 1 to 2 seconds. That's what it takes to catch a rocket's arc across the sky. Bring a tripod to keep your camera steady during the long exposure time. Stake out an unobstructed view and think carefully about composition before clicking the shutter. Add visual interest to your pictures by making sure the fireworks will frame a compelling subject—like a building, statue, or tree—that is in the foreground. For more tips, visit the New York Institute of Photography's guide at www.nyip.com/ezine/holidays/firewks.html.

over the waters and illuminating the city. www.redentorevenezia.it

And if you can't leave the United States . . .

Although **Disney World**'s Magic Kingdom nightly fireworks display may sound a little too touristy, I have to give them credit for a great show. And there's still a way to make it a special experience without the hassle. Sit on the sandy beach at Disney World's Polynesian Resort—just across the bay from the Magic Kingdom Park. My advice: Get there early and have dinner at the resort, then grab a couple of lounge chairs on the beach, and you can see the fireworks from the best seat in the house. Bonus: Kids can play in the sand or in the pool while the grown-ups have a cocktail on the beach!

There's a good reason to go to Dallas in July, and it's called Kaboom Town. Often overshadowed by more well-known fireworks displays on the East Coast, the event in Addison Circle Park is proof that everything is bigger in **Texas.** The day starts with an airshow spectacular and is followed by a 30-minute display with about 1,500 pounds of fireworks exploding into the skies.

THE SUNRISE/ SUNSET

Some of the most magical moments take place at the very beginning—or at the very end—of the day, when you can see your surroundings in the best light.

SUNRISE

To get the best view of the sun rising at dawn, of course you want to go east. West Quoddy Head in Lubec, **Maine,** is the easternmost spot in the continental United States and one of the first places in the country where the sun rises. The red-and-white striped lighthouse is an ideal spot to view the colors spilling over the horizon.

Bass Harbor Head Lighthouse in coastal Maine's Acadia National Park sits on a cliff on the southwest edge of Mount Desert Island. This is an offshore spot you can still reach by car. Short trails on either side of the lighthouse, which serves as a private residence for the local Coast Guard unit commander, provide spectacular sunrise views. Once you're in the park, you can ditch your car and take propane-powered buses around the island (bus service runs from late June to early October). Mount Desert Island also boasts an old carriage road system with stone-faced bridges that cross scenic waterfalls, streams, and rocky cliffs. www.nps.gov/acad

On **North Carolina**'s Outer Banks, Jockey's Ridge State Park in Nags Head is a unique place to see the sun rise or set. The 426-acre park features giant sand dunes that tower 80 to 90 feet above sea level. Climb to the top of one and watch the sun rise in the east over the Atlantic or set in the west over Albemarle Sound. Another great place in the Outer Banks is Hatteras Island. Though there are plenty of towns and homes on the narrow 50-mile island, there are also long stretches of pristine, unpopulated wild coastline. Get up before dawn, drive along highway NC 12, and find yourself a deserted spot on an east-facing beach. Then pull out a blanket or beach chair and witness the glorious, peaceful start of the day. www.outerbanks.org

On the slow-paced windward coast of Oahu, **Hawaii,** is Lanikai Beach, a hidden gem known for its outstanding sunrises. The turquoise waters are almost always calm with gentle trade winds, and the white sand is so soft it's like walking on powdered sugar. Best of all, it's uncrowded—just be prepared to forgo amenities like bathrooms and a parking lot (you have to park on the residential streets and walk in via a public footpath). Bonus: Just offshore—and within kayaking distance—are the twin island bird sanctuaries of Nā Mokulua.

Although it may sound touristy, the sun rising and setting over Angkor Wat in **Cambodia** is a magical experience. My advice is to get there predawn and stand in front of the lotus pond next to the temple. The sky will glow in shades of pink, blue, and purple before bursting into yellow. Come sunset, the nearby temple of Phnom Bakheng is the place to be: It sits on top of a hill for a 360-degree view of the sunset and horizon—and with Angkor Wat in the distance, the setting sun casts a golden orange hue over the whole area.

It is traditional to climb Mount Fuji in **Japan** in the predawn hours in order to watch the sun rise over the peak. Most sunrise seekers prefer to climb halfway up the mountain the evening before and spend the night at a mountain hut. About 3 hours before dawn, wake up and continue your ascent to the summit, where you should arrive just in time to see the sun peeking up from the horizon. The Yoshida trail is the most popular and places you at the correct angle to see the rising sun. On clear days, you'll see the Five Lakes region brilliantly illuminated by the early morning sun. On cloudy days, you'll have the satisfaction of knowing that Mount Fuji's peak rises above the cloud cover, and soon enough the sun will make its appearance in a display of pinks and reds. The best time to go is July and August when the sunrise starts between 4:30 and 5:00 a.m.

SUNSET

E very evening in Mallory Square, buskers, artists, acrobats, jugglers, food vendors, clairvoyants, and tourists gather to close out another day in Key West, **Florida.** Local legend says that Tennessee Williams started the custom of toasting the sunset with cocktails at Mallory Square, but the party really took off in the 1960s, when transcendence-seeking hippies took to the pier. The

Sunset Celebration gained the City of Key West's official approval in the mid-'80s, when the nonprofit Key West Cultural Preservation Society formed to manage the nightly event. Local institution Dominique LeFort—aka "The Catman"—and his team of highly trained house cats put on nightly shows in which the felines perform circus tricks. Juggler/tightrope walker/raconteur Will Soto is another Sunset Celebration regular. There's no charge to enter the open-air party, but tipping the musicians and other performers is appreciated. Food vendors serve up local favorites like conch fritters and Key lime tea. www.sunsetcelebration.org

Skip the pricey downstairs restaurant and head right for the rooftop bar at Bud and Alley's, a beachfront gem in the Gulf Coast town of Seaside, Florida (about 20 miles from Panama City). Every day as the sun dips below the horizon, staff members ring a cast-iron bell that came from a 19th century steam train to honor the moment. If you can predict the exact time the sun will set (no cheating online!), you get a free drink. www.budandalleys.com

It's a no-brainer that Sunrise Point in **Utah**'s Bryce Canyon is an ideal spot to see the sun rise. But don't miss the chance to watch the sun set over this majestic landscape. In most cases, the towering spires of rocks and sandstone cliffs don't face the sun, but locals know to go straight to Paria View. This is a point that is positioned perfectly to see the sun sink into the sky, lighting up one particularly massive hoodoo (rock spire) in a dazzling array of golds and reds. www.nps.gov/brca

Though it may sound counterintuitive, the airport is the best place to see the sunset in Sedona, **Arizona.** The airport is built on a high, flat mesa that overlooks the town and the red rocks that make Sedona famous. You can either drive to the top and watch from the Mesa Grill over a meal and drink, or watch from the 3.3-mile loop trail that circumnavigates the mesa. To get to the trailhead, drive a half mile up Airport Road and park where you see trailhead signs. Just be prepared for crowds around sunset and bring a flashlight if you think you'll still be out on the trail after dark.

Treasure Island, a barrier island on **Florida**'s west coast near

St. Petersburg, has 3 miles of uninterrupted beach from which to watch the sunset, including one that is aptly named Sunset Beach (at the south end of the stretch). There's no particular phenomenon that makes these sunsets so special, but the sky really does light up like it's on fire, turning the normally white clouds into a rainbow of pink, purple, and blue. The scene here is very communal, especially on weekend nights, when street performers, live bands, and drum circles convene.

While Rick's Cafe is a well-known hot spot in west-facing Negril, **Jamaica,** the nearby Rockhouse boutique hotel is a quieter option with several places to enjoy the memorable sunset. At the Rockhouse Restaurant, the hotel's more upscale option serving modern Jamaican dishes, you can sit on the outdoor balcony suspended over the cliffs of Pristine Cove. For a more casual evening, go to the Pushcart Restaurant and Rum Bar, where the menu is based on street foods from across the Caribbean. Or just bring your swimsuit and stay for sunset cocktails at the cliff-top Pool Grill. www.rock househotel.com

The Lofoten Islands, just north of the Arctic Circle in **Norway,** are a place where you can see the sun rise and set simultaneously in summer. From late May through mid-July, the "midnight sun" never completely sets—it just dips close to the horizon, then slowly begins to rise again. Stop at a west-facing village such as Eggum (on Vestvågøy island) and see the midnight sun over the sea from the beach, while the craggy mountains behind you turn various hues of purple. www.lofoten.info

Another great spot in Norway is the North Cape, the northernmost point in mainland Europe. You'll have a nearly 360-degree view of the sunrise or sunset (or both, depending on what time of year it is and which direction you are facing) as you stand on a plateau at the top of a 900-foot-high cliff. Here, you are literally at the edge of the world, with nothing but ocean between you and the North Pole. And if you prefer to watch the sun set somewhere farther south, go to the town of Bergen, on Norway's southwest coast. Take the funicular up to the top of Mount Fløyen (www.floibanen.com), and see the dramatic evening colors illuminate the sea and the old wooden houses that surround the harbor. Have a drink or a meal at the restaurant at the top as you watch the light fade and take in views.

Cap your day of seeing leopards, lions, cape buffaloes, and giraffes by watching the sun set over the Serengeti on **Kenya**'s Masai Mara Game Reserve. The sun's rays turn the desert sands into a kaleido-scope of reds and oranges and dramatically silhouette the herds of wildebeest and zebra crossing the vast reserve. If you're staying right in the reserve at the Fig Tree Camp, you can watch the sunset with other travelers in the camp's tree-top bar. Other options include seeing the sunset from the back of a safari Jeep, or from high above the horizon in a hot air balloon. www.madahotels.com

Clifton Beach in Karachi, **Pakistan,** is a great place for "sundown-ers," drinks you enjoy while watching the sun set. There are four west-facing beaches here, handily named First, Second, Third, and Fourth. All you have to do is arrive with a blanket and picnic basket to relax and unwind while watching the sun sink into the sea. Of course, the famous Table Mountain is also a prime spot for viewing the sun rising and setting where the Indian Ocean meets the Atlan-tic. Best of all, after 6 p.m., the cable car to the top is half price.

In Johannesburg, **South Africa,** you want to see the sun set from a lounge called Randlords, which is at the top of the 22-story South Point Towers. From here, there are 360-degree views of the city, making it an ideal location for a sunset view with a drink. www.randlords.co.za

The smoggy air in Cairo, **Egypt,** actually makes for glorious orange-streaked sunsets. Options include renting a felucca (tradi-tional Nile sailboat) and watching the sun set over the river, or find-ing a high-altitude spot from which to watch the show. The 40th-floor cocktail lounge at the Grand Hyatt is a prime viewing location, or if you prefer a more natural setting, go to the cliffs at Mokattam. The sky ranges from yellow to red, while the river takes on hues of pur-ple and pink as the city darkens. If you want to get away from the overcrowded city, head south to Aswan, where the setting sun pro-vides a dramatic backdrop to the ancient temples along the Nile.

VOLCANOES

Few things in nature are as awe-inspiring as volcanoes. Think about the destructive power that is unleashed from deep within these ancient craters! The burning question is, how close do you want to get?

For a low-danger encounter, try hiking up to the crater on the Greek island of **Santorini** (also known as Thira), in the Aegean Sea. This dormant volcano sits a short distance away from the inhabited main part of the island, across a narrow bay. These two parts of the island were once a single, enormous landmass, until a monumental eruption in 1600 BC caused the crater to collapse and wiped out the Minoan civilization on Santorini and nearby Crete. Only guided tours are allowed to hike right into the crater, where sulfuric gases hiss out of crevices. En route, you'll get one of the best views of the mainland.

Costa Rica's Arenal Volcano National Park features two volcanoes: the recently active Arenal Volcano and the long-extinct Chato Volcano, a collapsed crater that now contains a lagoon. Though Arenal has been quiet since October 2010, and has not been prone to showy displays of lava and ash, the park is still an excellent place to explore. Hiking trails crisscross the lush terrain, where you can walk through lava fields from previous eruptions, while rain forest hikes allow you to see the exotic native flora and fauna.

Iceland is one of the world's most active volcanic zones. With more than 130 volcanoes in various stages of activity, there is always something erupting somewhere. You can get a bird's-eye view from a small plane or helicopter, but my advice is to hop aboard a "super-jeep" to really get that immersive experience of the otherwordly

INSIDER'S TIP

Completely obsessed with volcanoes? Then the best option for you is Volcano Discovery's intensive 28-day World Volcano tour that takes you around the world to active volcanoes in Hawaii, Vanuatu, New Zealand, and Indonesia. Best of all, this is a totally upscale, easy trip that anyone can do, as long as you've got a spare $10,000.

terrain. A company like Iceland Rovers (www.icelandrovers.is) will take you in a 4x4 through the moonlike landscape of craters and lava, and to one of the best photo ops in the region: the geothermal springs and lakes of Krýsuvík. Remember the 2010 eruption of the Eyjafjallajökull volcano? The family that owns the nearby farm has built a visitors center, where you can see the progression of the massive eruption through photographs and video. And here's a fun fact: Iceland's Snæfellsjökull was the volcano that inspired Jules Verne's novel *Journey to the Center of the Earth.*

New Zealand sits on the Pacific Ring of Fire, the tectonic ridge that stretches from north to south and causes massive geological activity. Mount Ruapehu, Mount Tongariro, and Mount Ngauruhoe are part of the Tongariro National Park, a World Heritage site. The lunarlike volcanic landscape can be viewed from various vantage points on land and in the air, but the best way to see it is along the Tongariro Crossing, one of the world's top one-day hikes. It's an 8-hour trek through steaming fumaroles, jagged lava flows, the Red

INSIDER'S TIP

How about a drive-in volcano? On the Caribbean island of St. Lucia, you can literally drive right into the Qualibou caldera. This dormant volcano, which is located near the town of Soufriere, is not actively spewing lava, so you won't be in any danger. But you can park within feet of bubbling mud pools, boiling sulfur springs, and hissing steam vents. A visitors center shows videos about the volcano, and there's a small, pretty waterfall nearby. But beware—the whole crater smells of rotten eggs, thanks to the sulfuric gases that permeate the air.

See the Destruction of a Volcano

Mount St. Helens in **Washington State** erupted famously in 1980, wiping out much of the nearby vegetation, wildlife, and homes in the process. In 2004, the volcano semi-awoke again, and today more than 500,000 visitors per year come to see the ash, steam, and gases spewing from the crater. Much of the blast zone has been turned into the Mount St. Helens National Volcanic Monument, which can best be viewed from SR 504 (the Spirit Lake Memorial Highway) on the 51-mile corridor through the Toutle River Valley. The excellent Forest Learning Center has displays that tell the story of the eruption. Near the Coldwater visitors center is the 2.5-mile Hummocks Trail, a little-known gem where you can see terrain that has built itself back, as well as some that still looks how it did shortly after the blast. If you really want to immerse yourself in the experience, Mount St. Helens Institute has summer classes where you learn about geology, plants, and birds in and around the blast zone, and you can take a guided hike to the summit. www.fs.fed.us/gpnf/volcanocams/msh

The 1991 eruption of Mount Pinatubo in the **Philippines** was so bad it wiped out the nearby Clark Air Force Base and ashfall reached as far as Vietnam and Malaysa. Amazingly, there were no recorded eruptions before that cataclysmic event, which ravaged area villages and killed hundreds. Today, you can hike, drive a 4x4, or ride a helicopter to the crater lake, where the breathtaking scenery is still marked by heavy ash (known as lahar) that's a reminder of the sobering event.

Crater, and Emerald Lakes. Also in New Zealand, just offshore from Auckland, is Rangitoto Island, an extinct volcano where you can hike over rugged lava outcroppings on your way to see the view of Waitemata Harbor from the top.

You don't have to have a death wish to view two of the world's most active volcanoes: Kilauea and Mauna Loa, both part of the 330,000-acre **Hawaii** Volcanoes National Park on the Big Island. You do have to have a sense of adventure to tackle the Napau Trail, a 14-mile round-trip hike that takes you through rugged and rough terrain to view the spewing Pu'u 'O'o vent. Since the active vent actually collapsed recently, you can no longer camp overnight, but the trail is wide open for day hikes. For another challenge, try the Kilauea Iki Trail, which starts at the crater rim and drops 400 feet entirely through rain forest terrain to the steaming crater floor. www.nps.gov/havo

The volcanoes of **Ecuador** are more than impressive. Avenue of the Volcanoes is comprised of more than 200 miles of volcanoes stretching across a valley between the Cordillera ranges. Volcán Cotopaxi, one of the highest peaks in Ecuador, is manageable for nearly all levels of fitness, but it's definitely a challenge. Make sure you spend at least 2 days acclimatizing in Quito, and don't be afraid to hike at night, when the ground is firmer and you can ascend the peak at dawn when you can see the sun rising over the Andes. If you're feeling suicidal, try a 2-day hike up the mighty Antisana, where you'll cross lava and snowpacks, pass through a cloud forest, and climb a technically difficult glacier—and be rewarded with some of the most spectacular scenery in the world.

INSIDER'S TIP

Want an easy way to see a geothermal wonderland? Head to Rotorua on New Zealand's South Island, where the violent explosion of Mount Tarawera buried the Maori village of Te Wairoa in 1886. Whakarewarewa Thermal Village is a spectacular geothermal park, where you can walk, without fear, just inches from spewing geysers, bubbling mud pools, steaming vents, and mineral springs. Here, you can also meet descendants of the survivors of the Tarawera eruption. www.whakarewarewa.com

WATERFALLS

I grew up watching black-and-white news-reel footage of daredevils attempting to go over Niagara Falls in wooden barrels. Years later, I got up close and personal at Victoria Falls in Africa, at Iguazu in South America, and at some smaller but no less impressive falls in Hawaii, Alaska, and California. If you want to experience immense hydropower, just stop, look, and listen. The thundering sound is both jarring and soothing. It's an impressive moment no matter how many times you've seen one of these majesties of nature.

UNITED STATES

Most people associate Yosemite National Park in **California** with a handful of legendary, often-photographed waterfalls: Bridalveil, Yosemite, the Vernal, and Nevada Falls. But this park is filled with "hidden" waterfalls that are less accessible—and offer a rewarding experience without all the crowds. My picks? You can actually see an entire trail of falls starting from Tuolomne Meadows. You'll hike about 9 miles to get to Waterwheel Falls (which actually lives up to its name because of the winds that often blow the splashing water back into the falls). Along the way, you'll see Tuolumne, the White Cascade, and LeConte Falls. Start early in the morning so you can see the rainbows that emerge as the sun meets the misty waters.

Another option that most people don't know about is Illilouette Falls. It's hidden in a side canyon so you won't bump into many other hikers, and the reward is spectacular: a massive 370-foot drop that's best viewed if you can scramble up the rocks . . . carefully. Getting there requires a 2-mile hike downhill on the Panorama Trail from Glacier Point. Make time to stop so you can catch sight of Vernal Falls and Nevada Falls off in the distance and a back view of the famous Half Dome.

You can't talk about waterfalls without mentioning **Hawaii.** This is arguably the best place in America to see a huge variety of falls, from the Wailua Falls (which you might recognize from the opening scene of *Fantasy Island*) to a Big Island trail where you'll pass seven waterfalls in 1½ miles. But perhaps the most visually arresting of all is Akaka Falls on the Big Island. Akaka State Falls Park is an easy drive from Hilo (on the wet, leeward side of the island), and you'll pass by old sugarcane fields along the way. Once you enter the park, it's only about a half-mile hike through the jungle to reach the smaller Kahuna Falls, followed by the mighty Akaka Falls tumbling 442 feet through lush vegetation and into a crystal-clear pool.

Indoor Waterfalls

The International Center Building in downtown **Detroit** (next to the four-diamond Atheneum Suites Hotel) features restaurants, office space, conference facilities, a ballroom, and—in its eight-story atrium—the world's tallest indoor waterfall! The 114-foot-high geometric brown-marble structure has been certified by Guinness World Records. The **Dubai** Mall has an over-the-top indoor waterfall that's the height of the entire four-story building. It features dozens of fiberglass figures gracefully "swan diving" toward the bottom. At 75 feet high and 90 feet wide, it is surrounded by palm trees, giving it the feeling of a desert oasis. The White Swan Hotel in Guangzhou, **China,** has a three-story waterfall in its central atrium that's crowned by a pagoda and empties into a pond stocked with carp.

Prefer a more private experience? The island of Kauai is known as the Garden Isle, which should tip you off about how wet it gets in some parts (the top of Mount Waialeale is one of the wettest spots on earth!). But here's the catch. Many of its waterfalls are so far off the beaten path that it's actually too dangerous to get there by car or foot. Even the astonishingly beautiful Na Pali Coast on the North Shore is only accessible by boat or a tough 11-mile hike. And that's exactly when it's worth shelling out the money for a helicopter tour. Trust me, you'll be glad you did when you look down and catch your breath over the Na Pali Coast, with its waterfalls tumbling over the lush cliffs, the plummeting depths of Waimea Canyon, and the 350-foot Manawaiopuna Falls, which sits on private property.

When the snow starts to melt in the Mount Washington Valley of **New Hampshire,** the area comes alive with waterfalls. There are 12 in all, which you can explore over the course of a weekend. Jackson Falls is particularly accessible, with several pools and smaller falls that you can stand under and let the water pound over you. Arethusa Falls requires a short trail hike of about 1.3 miles to get there, and it's worth it: At 176 feet, it's one of the highest single falls in New Hampshire. Keep going another 0.7 mile and you'll be able to see Bemis Brook, Fawn Pool, and Coliseum Falls in one hike. If you want a romantic view, take a half-mile hike from the trailhead at West Side Road until you reach Diana's Baths. This series of small falls culminates in a set of pools that is just magical to see on a full moon night.

INTERNATIONAL

Iceland's waterfalls are world famous, particularly the spectacular Gullfoss (Golden Falls). But it's also one of the most crowded tourist attractions. That's why it pays to get off the beaten path a bit to see some of the other awesome, powerful falls throughout the country. The 300-foot-wide Dettifoss is among the most powerful falls in all of Europe, standing 150 feet high and falling at a flow rate 6,816 cubic feet per second. It's located inside Vatnajökull National Park, and a new paved road makes it easily accessible.

Svartifoss (Black Falls) in Skaftafell National Park is another worthwhile adventure. It stands only 60 feet tall, but it falls over a cliff made of hanging basalt columns (think pipes on an organ). Getting there isn't too challenging, involving a 1-mile hike uphill. But even better, you pass two other waterfalls along the way: Hundafoss and Magnúsarfoss. (There is also one other waterfall in the park, Pjófafoss.) Hike the path the other direction from the starting point to see the incredible Skaftafellsjökull glacier.

No trip to **Argentina** or **Brazil** is complete without seeing the Iguazu Falls. Located on the border of the two countries, this network of 275 falls is distributed between Argentina's Iguazú National Park and Brazil's Iguaçu National Park. Both sides afford incredible views from catwalks (and in Brazil, you can take a helicopter tour), but my advice is to get yourself to San Martin Island on the Argentina side. The falls are actually split by the island, which is only accessible by ferry and climbing a long staircase. From there, you can access a viewing point (locally known as "the window"), where you can get a panoramic view of the Devil's Throat chasm and the falls. If you want to see these falls at their best, brave the weather during the rainy season between November and March.

Venezuela's Angel Falls is superlative in many ways: It's the tallest waterfall in the world with the tallest single drop in the world. Its total height is 3,211 feet, 2,646 feet of which is an uninterrupted drop (that's 16 times higher than Niagara Falls). It is so high that the water actually atomizes during the dry season: The water disappears in a fine mist before it even reaches the ground. To get there is a bit of an ordeal, involving flying from Ciudad Bolivar to Canaima National Park, then taking a 4-hour riverboat to the Angel Falls trail, then hiking for 60 to 90 minutes on a soggy uphill jungle trail with a stream crossing.

Victoria Falls on the Zambezi River is arguably the most impressive cascade in the world, in addition to being one of the largest and most remote. With more than 1 million gallons of water tumbling over a 300-foot, mile-wide cliff, it's a spectacle you can't miss. Though getting to the **Zimbabwe-Zambia** border is a bit of a hassle (you either fly or take a bus tour from elsewhere in Africa), once you arrive, there are numerous ways to see and experience the falls. In addition to the hair-raising walk across the footbridge to the Knife Edge platform, you can go whitewater rafting in the Zambezi's rapids, abseil down the cliffs, ride a riverboat, go jet-boating, or bungee jump over the falls. My advice: Check the condition of the bungee cord hanging over the Zambezi. The last time I was there (and other travelers have confirmed this to me on recent visits), the cord seems frayed and frazzled.

The Plitvice Waterfalls in **Croatia** is really a network of many interconnected, cascading lakes, pools, and waterfalls within the 12,000-acre Plitvice Lakes National Park. The 16 stunning turquoise lakes are composed of mineral-rich waters that continually deposit travertine in unique underwater formations. The cascades are fairly easy to see on foot, as there are well-marked gravel paths and approximately 11 miles of boardwalks. Cars are not allowed in the park, but there is a park shuttle system that can take you from one side to the other.

Fiordland National Park is one of the must-see spots in **New Zealand**'s remote and rugged South Island. Inside, Browne Falls cascades about 2,000 feet down the walls of the Doubtful Sound. Get this: It's so off the beaten path that there is no path. It's only visible by water or air. But that's what makes this experience so special. Along with the magnificent falls, you'll also catch sight of the towering snowcapped peaks and rocky cliffs where dozens of other waterfalls flow. Take note: Boats sail here rain or shine, but flights are limited to favorable weather conditions.

Huangguoshu Waterfall in **China** is Asia's largest waterfall, but that's not what makes it stand out. It's one of the few in the world that can be viewed from almost every angle. Located 28 miles southwest of Anshun city in Guizhou Province, this 250-foot-wide rectangular fall is viewable from a looping trail that offers vantage points from the left, from directly opposite, from the right, and even from a cave that goes behind the waterfall. Translation? You can actually touch the water. The waterfall is part of a unique geological area that also features 17 other waterfalls, four subterranean rivers, and 100 caves. The flow is usually strongest during the rainy season between May and October.

Best Places for

SIGHTSEEING BY PUBLIC TRANSPORT

Why pay for a taxi or a tour bus when you can get around by public transportation and do some sightseeing along the way? **London** is one of the easiest cities to navigate by bus and get a view at the same time. Route 3 is a 9-mile, north-south route that connects Oxford Circus to Crystal Palace, traveling south on Regent Street.

Easy sights include the world-famous toy store Hamley's and the National Gallery and Nelson's Column at Trafalgar Square. Look to the right before the bus leaves the square, and you'll get a spectacular view of Buckingham Palace at the end of the Mall.

Meanwhile, the east-west route RV1 is one of the most scenic and historic in the whole city. It starts just north of the medieval Tower of London and travels south over the Tower Bridge, offering a perfect view of HMS *Belfast,* the London Eye, the Tate Modern museum, London Bridge, and Borough Market. www.tfl.gov.uk/buses

In **Paris,** line 69 is a roughly east-west route that passes some of the most famous landmarks in Paris. Board near the famous Père-Lachaise Cemetery. Nearer to the center of Paris, it allows views of the Place de la Bastille, the Marais district and Notre Dame, the Louvre, les Tuileries Garden, the Musée d'Orsay (off Gare d'Orsay stop), the Boulevard Saint-Germain, and, finally, the Eiffel Tower off the Champ de Mars stop.

Line 38 runs north to south through the city center and provides memorable views of the Latin Quarter and the Seine River. Get off at the massive Les Halles shopping center, and then hop back on to cross over the river where you can catch a glimpse of Notre Dame and Île Saint-Louis in the distance. Soon you will be in the thick of the trendy Latin Quarter. www.ratp.fr

Vancouver's TransLink routes gives a very budget-friendly ride through some of the city's best areas. The #5 Robson/Davie gives a tour of downtown via Robson Street, a trendy, stylish district that's ideal for people watching, and along English Bay and Davie Street.

The #250 Horseshoe Bay route from downtown travels along Marine Drive, offering views of Howe Sound, North America's southernmost fjord, and gets you to the ferry to Bowen Island. If you're up for doing a bit of hiking on your trip, Lighthouse Park is your stop on Marin Drive at Beacon Lane. Finally, Horseshoe Bay Terminal is a quaint little village to walk around and shop while waiting for the ferry. www.translink.ca

Los Angeles is so spread out that it's not the ideal city for public buses, but its Metro Rail system is surprisingly well organized.

Parts of the Metro Rail Gold Line travel aboveground, so you can take in the views as you go. It starts in the quaint Sierra Madre neighborhood east of Pasadena and hits Chinatown and the very walkable Little Tokyo/Arts District, as well as the fun Mariachi Plaza in East LA's historic Boyle Heights community.

The Metro Rail Red Line is best for visiting classic Tinseltown sights, starting from North Hollywood and ending in downtown. Start from Universal Studios and the Universal Citywalk and make your way to the busy Hollywood/Highland intersection, where you're just a short way from the Hollywood Bowl, the Hollywood Walk of Fame, Grauman's Chinese Theater, and much more. The Griffith Park Observatory is accessible on weekends at the Vermont/Sunset stop, if you connect to the LADOT observatory shuttle bus. www.metro.net

Route 30 in **San Francisco** starts in the trendy Marina district near the Presidio and the Palace of Fine Arts. As it heads east on Chestnut, it goes down Columbus diagonally and slices through the rollicking North Beach neighborhood. Look to your right as you cross Lombard Street and you may even catch a glimpse of the famous winding road. Next it heads down Stockton Street, right through the heart of Chinatown, before heading south to Union Square, the world-famous shopping and theater district.

Yes, San Francisco's cable cars are touristy, but they're fun and give great views of some iconic landmarks. The Powell-Hyde line passes Union Square, Nob Hill, Russian Hill, Grace Cathedral, and the top of Lombard Street and ends at the Aquatic Park near Ghirardelli Square. The Powell-Mason line also goes past Union Square, but then veers north past the edge of Chinatown, through North Beach (where you can see Lombard Street from the bottom) and ends about four blocks from Fisherman's Wharf.

The antique cars of the F train start in the heart of the Castro district and head east up Market Street before turning north to the Embarcadero along piers and wharves. About midway through your journey, you'll pass the San Francisco Civic Plaza, where you'll see City Hall, the courthouse, the Civic Auditorium, and the public library. After Market Street ends, the train turns north on Embarcadero and passes the Ferry Building on its way toward famous tourist landmarks like Pier 39 and Fisherman's Wharf. Get off at Pier 33 and you can continue your scenic trip on the ferry to Alcatraz island. www.sfmta.com

SIGHTSEEING BY FERRY

One of the best ways to cruise is by ferry. No, there won't be lavish buffets or Broadway revivals, Isaac from the *Love Boat* won't be your bartender, and you also won't be steered to buy unnecessary souvenirs on board. But the scenery will be priceless. In almost all cases, public ferries navigate shorter local or regional routes and they are much less expensive than taxis (or in some cases, they're free).

UNITED STATES

The **Staten Island** Ferry is officially for commuters, but here's a tip: It offers one of the best views of the Statue of Liberty . . . for free! On the way back, you get great vistas of the Manhattan skyline. And here's another tip: Jump on early in the morning to see the sun rise over the East River, or in the evening to watch the skyscrapers begin to light up at dusk. www.siferry.com

The **Alaska** Marine Highway System is made up of 11 ferries that traverse thousands of miles of waterways. The system is designed to service port communities, but parts of this marine highway are so beautiful that it's been designated an official National Scenic Byway. The one you don't want to miss is the 8-hour journey between Sitka and Juneau, which offers unbeatable—and reliable—views of seabirds and marine life such as killer whales and porpoises. But if you're feeling really adventurous, skip the luxury cruise ship and snag a ferry cabin from Bellingham, Washington, and ride all the way up to the town of Ketchikan, Alaska. It's a long way to go—almost 2 days—but it's all about the journey and the scenery along the way, and the price tag is significantly less than a cruise ship. www.dot.state.ak.us/amhs

Believe it or not, several other free public ferries in the country also offer great scenery. The Merrimac Ferry (www.dot.wisconsin. gov/travel/water/merrimac.htm) in **Wisconsin,** which dates back to 1844, crosses the picturesque Wisconsin River between Sauk and Columbia Counties.

The Galveston Island Ferry (www.galveston.com/galvestonferry) in **Texas** runs between Galveston and Port Bolivar. If you're lucky, you may spot dolphins on the way.

Four of the 21 ferries in **North Carolina** are also free. One of the coolest is the one that travels between Hatteras Island and Ocracoke Island (www.ncdot.org/ferry), which is part of the Outer Banks Scenic Byway and is only accessible by water. One piece of advice: Free ferries can get crowded with both commuters and sightseers, so go in off-peak hours and midweek.

INTERNATIONAL

One of the best ways to experience **Stockholm** is by ferry, since we're actually talking about an archipelago made up of more than 24,000 islands and rocks, connecting the capital city with the Baltic Sea. Although there are several private ferry and boat services, the main transportation company is Waxholmsbolaget. Looking for the freshest seafood meal? Ferry over to the island of Möja and head to the family-run Wikström fish market and restaurant,

INSIDER'S TIP

Once you get hooked on the Stockholm ferry experience—and you will—ask about the Båtluffarkortet, or ferry pass, which allows unlimited boat travel for 5 days. www.waxholmsbolaget.com

where the menu changes daily. In summer, take a late-night ferry and see the sunset from the Baltic Sea as late as 11 p.m.

Of course, **Sydney,** Australia's harbor is iconic, with the Harbour Bridge and Sydney Opera House dominating most postcards. But don't overlook the public ferries that transport commuters and students. For the best view, hop on at Circular Quay and ride all the way to Manly on the north side. On a clear day, this 30-minute ride offers great views of the bridge and the opera house, as well as beaches, skyscrapers, and upscale neighborhoods. Ask about the MyMulti day pass, which includes unlimited travel by public ferry, trains, light rail, and buses. www.sydneyferries.info

It's hard to envision the island of **Penang** without the colorful public ferries. Dating back to 1920, it is the best way to see Penang while traveling to and from the mainland. The 15-minute ride includes views of the Georgetown skyline, the prominent Komtar Tower, and the iconic Penang Bridge, making it a fast, easy way to access the island while surrounded by locals.

The Bosphorus Strait not only connects the two sides of **Istanbul,** but it actually also bridges two continents: Europe and Asia. Stretching about 20 miles from the Sea of Marmara to the Black Sea, the Bosphorus is accessible by several ferry lines, including a commuter ferry known as Sehir Hatlari. Crisscrossing between Europe and Asia, it is an efficient, cost-effective way to get stunning views of old fishing villages, hillside forests, and suspension bridges along the way. Or head all the way southeast to Princes' Islands, about 12 miles from Istanbul in the Sea of Marmara. This chain of nine islands (only four are accessible by ferry) are car-free getaways and a great place to escape city congestion. www.sehirhatlari.com.tr/en

WATER TAXI

Want to avoid traffic jams and cab fares? Try a water taxi as an alternative way to travel from point A to point B and see some great sights.

Boston's City Water Taxi fleet takes you between the Logan International Airport area and 20 major points in Boston. From any terminal at Logan, just hop on the #66 bus (it's free) to the water taxi stands. From the waterfront, it's only 7 minutes and $10 to get to downtown Boston, versus $20 for a cab. (Although it becomes less cost effective with 3 or 4 passengers, it's still a much better experience to travel by water than get stuck in a traffic jam!) The water taxi also stops at major points like the Children's Museum, Long Wharf near Faneuil Hall, the Charlestown Navy Yard where the USS *Constitution* resides, and historic South Station. www.citywater taxi.com

Florida's Water Taxi makes 13 stops in and around Fort Lauderdale, with connecting service to four stops in Hollywood, Florida. With the $20 adult all-day pass, it's an easy way to see the coastal areas of South Florida from a unique perspective. You'll pass megamansions and yachts, and stop at well-known spots like Las Olas Boulevard and Esplanade Park. Keep your eyes open for the Water Taxi pub crawl, which is offered periodically throughout the year. www.watertaxi.com

If you thought New Yorkers only travel by subway, think again. **New York** Water Taxi has 12 distinctive black-and-yellow checkered commuter boats going to neighborhoods that are worth exploring. You can travel up and down the East River, hopping on and off at stops like Wall Street, Fulton Ferry Landing by the Brooklyn Bridge, and Pier 84 in midtown Manhattan. The Ikea Express takes you from Pier 11 to the docks of Red Hook in Brooklyn. Yes, it's the site of an Ikea store, but Red Hook is a surprisingly hip neighborhood in the industrial waterfront. Or, if you're feeling really adventurous, try the Bike the Brooklyn Bridge/Water Taxi Back trip. As the name suggests, it involves renting a bike to ride across the bridge and a hop-on/hop-off pass to ride the water taxi back. Great views of Lady Liberty along the way. www.nywatertaxi.com

Shoreline Sightseeing of **Chicago** operates two water taxi routes on Lake Michigan and the Chicago River. The Lake Route connects the Navy Pier (Dock Street) with the Field Museum campus. This route allows you to take in the entire downtown Chicago skyline. At the Field Museum stop, you'll have access to not only the Museum of Natural History, but also the Adler Planetarium and the Shedd Aquarium. The River Route connects the Navy Pier, Willis Tower, and Union Station (or Erie Street) via the Chicago River. You'll pass Wacker Drive, the Chicago Sun-Times building, and the Lyric Opera. Take this route at dusk, when the buildings and bridges that criss-cross the river light up like Christmas trees, and you're in for a real treat. www.shorelinesightseeing.com

Some of the most scenic landmarks in **London** abut the river, so what better way to see them than via Thames Water Taxi? The service glides between Chelsea pier in west London to Greenwich in the east and passes sites like the historic Battersea Power Station, the Houses of Parliament, the Tate Modern, the Millennium Bridge, the Globe Theater, the London Eye, St. Paul's Cathedral, and Tower Bridge. This is also a fun way to get to Greenwich, one of the hidden gems of London, which features the maritime observatory, Prime Meridian, and weekend flea markets. www.thameswatertaxi.com

Best Places to See

FLOWERS

For many travelers, seeing great flowers is usually a coincidence or an accident. You chance upon a brilliant display in open fields or along your otherwise planned route. But even for dedicated flower lovers, the best places to see them are also often not part of the plan.

UNITED STATES

Volumes have been written about the wildflowers of **Yellowstone National Park,** so you're assured of seeing plenty if you go during the high season of June to July. In June you're likely to see yellow glacier lilies, while the pale blue phacelia peaks in July, and the pink monkeyflower hangs around until early August. Other varieties include the purplish lupine and the vivid red Indian paintbrush. Prime viewing spots include the Mount Washburn Trail, the Tower Roosevelt Area, the Lamar Valley, the Hayden Valley, and around Dunraven Pass, north of Canyon Village. If you're too tired to get out and hike, the flowers are so abundant that they can easily be seen from the Grand Loop Road by car. Schedules of ranger-led activities, some involving flowers, are available at visitor centers throughout the park. www.nps.gov/yell/naturescience/upload/286wildflowers.pdf

The exciting thing about the flowers in this desert landscape of **Joshua Tree National Park** (JTNP) is that they are unpredictable. Wildflowers are completely dependent on rainfall, and rain at JTNP is highly variable. In a good year, flowers can carpet the desert floor, but one species may bloom one year, and a different species the following year, depending on the timing of rain and amount. If there's a lot of rain in the winter, there will be flowers in March and April. But if there's also rain during the summer monsoon season, you'll get additional types of species blooming in spring. To get an up-to-the-minute snapshot of what's out there, check the park's Web site: There's a weekly wildflower report from February through April. Good places to hike are the Barker Dam Trail or Hidden Valley. Good viewing spots are Pine City and Covington Flats. To see flowering cactus, head to the Cholla Cactus Garden and Hidden Valley Nature Trails. www.nps.gov/jotr/planyourvisit/blooms.htm

More than 1,660 types of flowering plants blanket **Great Smoky Mountains National Park,** including showy orchids, violets, and the coveted rare pink and yellow ladyslippers. Mid-March to mid-April is the peak time, when wildflowers are off the charts. Where the best flowers are depends on the elevation and the time of year. Lower elevations bloom early in March, while higher ones, such as those up on the Appalachian Trail, bloom as late as early May. There are 900 miles of trails in the park, most of which provide good vantage points. But some of the best places include Grotto Falls, the Laurel Falls Trail, and the Chimney Tops picnic area. Don't miss the annual Spring Wildflower Pilgrimage, a weeklong festival that takes place in the park every April. Operated by the Great Smoky Mountains Association, the event highlights everything you would ever want to know about wildflowers, with more than 150 programs including guided hikes, lectures, and photography workshops. www.nps.gov/grsm/naturescience/wildflowers.htm and www.springwildflowerpilgrimage.org

There are three things you expect to see when you land in **Hawaii:** chocolate-covered macadamia nuts, pineapples, and leis. A much better travel experience is to hit the ground in the 50th state with the determination to look beyond the stereotypical fruit, nuts, and flowers. Skip the luau and check in with the Maui Flower Growers Association—it's a one-stop shop for flowers and offers tours of local

Flower Tours

Travel Dream West Tours offers nature tours in **California** during the height of flower blooming season. For example, the 13-day Desert Dream Trail tour includes guided tours of the wildflowers and scenery of Joshua Tree National Park, Anza-Borrego Desert State Park, and Death Valley National Park. www.traveldreamwest.com

Adventure tour company AlpineHikers offers 7-day guided and self-guided tours of the hills around the village of Mürren, **Switzerland.** These summer tours involve 5 to 7 hours a day of moderate hiking in the mountains, where wildflowers are abundant. www.alpinehikers.com

In August and September, **South Africa**'s west coast explodes with wildflowers. Antares Tours offers one-day flower tours to West Coast National Park, where in addition to millions of flowers, you'll see wildebeests, eland, and even southern right whales. www.antarestours.com

growers who produce everything from orchids to lavender. Maui Country Farm Tours also offers tours of various Upcountry farms, where you can picnic while surrounded by lush, tropical gardens and orchards. Or stop by the Maui Nui Botanical Garden, which works to protect Hawaii's native species. Guided tours are also available at Molokai Plumerias on the island of Molokai; Honolulu's Hui Kū Maoli Ola Native Hawaiian Plant Nursery; and monthly open houses at MAʻO Organic Farms.

INTERNATIONAL

While the Tuileries is perhaps the best-known garden in **Paris,** one of the best places to see flowers is actually the Jardin des Plantes. The 70-acre garden, on the Left Bank of the Seine, is part of the National Museum of Natural History, with dozens of displays: We're talking an alpine garden, an Australian hothouse with desert plants, and a rose garden. But what's really special about this place is that it's also got an educational component. There are four museums on the premises (the Evolution Gallery, the Mineralogy Museum, the Paleontology Museum, and the Entomology Museum) and a botanical school, which makes it an exceptionally family-friendly experience. In fact, there are also three playgrounds, a small zoo (which was originally founded by Napoleon), and organized programming such as treasure hunts and quizzes. www.jardindesplantes.net

Want a more laid-back experience? Jardin Atlantique is located on the rooftop of the Montparnasse train station in Paris. This garden feels as if it's a world away from the busy city, with sculptures, a sun-bathing deck, and plenty of greenery for a peaceful visit.

Provence is known around the world for its endless fields of lavender, which produce half the world's supply. June through August are the best months to see it, as that's when the bushes fully bloom and are harvested. Some distilleries allow you to visit and see how the flowers are turned into essential oil. Don't miss one of the many small-town festivals celebrating the flower, such as the Corso de la Lavande held every August in Digne-les-Bains, when the streets are sprayed with lavender water.

In **London,** just about every guidebook will report on the 326-acre Kew Gardens. It is, after all, the mother of all botanical gardens, holding one in eight of all known plant species in the world. But sometimes size doesn't matter. Instead, head to the 1.5-acre Roof Gardens—located 100 feet above Kensington High Street, including three themed gardens and an unbeatable view of the London skyline. The Spanish Garden, Tudor Garden, and English Woodland gardens are planted in just 5 feet of soil and include fully grown oaks, fruit trees, and a stream stocked with fish and flamingos. The gardens are only open on select dates, so check before visiting. www. roofgardens.virgin.com/en/the_roof_gardens/the_gardens

Springtime in **Japan** is synonymous with cherry blossoms, but where are the best places to spot them? Head directly to Ueno Park in Tokyo, where cherry trees line the walkway, and to the lone cherry tree in Kyoto's Maruyama Park. Both are great spots for cherry blossom viewing parties known as *hanami.* In Nara Prefecture, the slopes of Mount Yoshino are heavy with cherry blossoms. In fact, you can see a gradation of pale pinks as you look up the hillside, as the flowers blossom at a different pace depending on the altitude. Hirosaki Castle in Aomori Prefecture, on the northern tip of Honshu, is a 17th-century castle surrounded by cherry trees, while the 17th-century Kumamoto Castle on Kyushu Island, near Kagoshima, features an explosion of blossoms every year.

The **Portuguese** island of Madeira has a year-round warm climate, which means flowers can be seen every day of the year. On a hill overlooking the capital city of Funchal are two excellent botanical gardens nearly side by side: The municipal Botanical Garden boasts 2,500 plants, including orchids and rare flowers, while the Monte Palace Tropical Garden offers both native plants and those from around the world. My advice: Ascend the hill on the new cable car gondola, and return on the Monte toboggan. And in the first week of May, Funchal hosts its renowned Funchal Flower Festival, when the streets are decorated with carpets of flowers and the air is perfumed with thousands of blooms as locals compete against each other to see who has the most beautiful and elaborate display.

Then there are the famous Keukenhof Gardens in **Holland.** They are, after all, one of the most famous flower gardens in the world, with more than 7 million spring blooms like Dutch tulips, hyacinth, and daffodils. The second most popular floral experience is probably the Aalsmeer Flower Auction, the world's largest of its kind. But Holland actually plants more than 3 billion tulips every year, and you can catch sight of this spectacular riot of color every spring (March through May) beyond the gardens as well. My advice: Rent a bicycle to ride through the 20-mile Bulb District between Haarlem and Leiden.

INSIDER'S TIP

If you're a real flower buff, you want to experience London's Open Garden Squares Weekend. This annual event allows you to visit private gardens that sit in the middle of residential areas, many of which are normally closed to the public or off the tourists' radar. We're talking places like quiet Phoenix Garden, the last of the seven Covent Community Gardens that is planted on a former parking lot and entirely run by local volunteers; and the Battersea herb garden that is tended to by volunteers with physical or mental challenges as a part of their therapy. www.opensquares.org

Best Places to Do

SPIRITUAL TRAVEL

Whether you follow a particular religion or not, seeing a destination from a spiritual perspective can make the experience even more rewarding than a typical sightseeing tour. These are the places of the world where the essence of their culture and lifestyle have been shaped by religious history.

UNITED STATES

The Chassidic Discovery Welcome Center in Brooklyn, **New York,** aims to provide outsiders with a glimpse into the lives of the normally insular Chassidic Jews of the Crown Heights neighborhood. The 3-hour, $39 walking tours are led by various members of the community (including two rabbis) and include a visit to a synagogue, a Torah study center, a Chassidic library, a mikvah (ritual bathhouse), and a kosher deli. Guides use wit and humor to explain the religious traditions, dress styles, and daily lives of these ultradevout Jews, in an effort to demystify the community. They cover everything from kosher food to women's roles to history, and are popular with Jews and non-Jews alike. http://jewishtours.com

Welcome to the Holy Land . . . in **Orlando**? Move over, Mickey. The Holy Land Experience is a Biblical re-creation designed for faith-based travelers. Enter a replica of the Garden Tomb where Jesus was buried, visit a facsimile of the Qumran Dead Sea Cave, and grab some hummus or a turkey leg from the park's cafe. View several thousand Biblical manuscripts, scrolls, and artifacts at the Scriptorium; catch a live Passion play and check out the Wilderness Tabernacle, a replica of the mobile worship space that Israelites used during their 40 years in the desert. www.holylandexperience.com

The Zen Mountain Monastery, located on 230 forested acres in the Catskills of **New York,** is dedicated to teaching the principles of Zen Buddhism as practiced by the Mountains and Rivers Order. Every month, there is a 3-day Introduction to Zen Training retreat. Start on Friday with a strict monastic schedule that includes walking, meditation, chanting, and workshops. The retreat concludes on Sunday with a formal talk by one of the Zen teachers or senior students. You'll sleep on bunk beds in a dormitory-style room with 6 to 10 other people and eat mostly vegetarian fare. Leave your cell phone, musical instruments, and children at home, as they aren't allowed at this quiet retreat. www.mro.org/zmm

INTERNATIONAL

If there's one destination that receives a steady flow of religious pilgrims, it's **Israel.** In fact, Americans make up the second-largest group of tourists to Israel (58 million in 2009, according to the most recent statistics). Why? Set at the crossroads of Asia, Africa, and Europe, it's the holy land for Jews, Christians, and Muslims, and home to the world's most iconic religious sites: the Western Wall, the ancient fortress of Masada, the Old City of Jerusalem, the archaeological site of Temple Mount, and Nazareth, to name a few. Beyond that, Israel is coming into its own among adventure and nature travelers, whether it's scuba diving in the Red Sea, riding camels or mountain biking through the Negev desert, or off-roading in Galilee.

Israel is entirely accessible on your own, but with so many experiences out there, going with an organized tour company takes much of the planning out of your hands. The most popular tour for Globus (www.globusfaith.com), which specializes in religious travel, is the Journey through the Holy Land, in which you start in Tel Aviv and travel to ancient cities like Megiddo and Haifa, visit a kibbutz, sail along the Sea of Galilee, and spend five nights in Jerusalem. My advice: Opt for the Jordan add-on or a package that includes Israel, Jordan, and Egypt in one trip, for an even more complete Middle Eastern experience.

Turkey and **Greece** are fantastic Mediterranean destinations because you can see Christian, Judaic, and Islamic influences in one region. In Turkey, there's not just the famous Blue Mosque in Istanbul, but also Biblical sites like Tarsus, the birthplace of St. Paul; the churches carved into rock in Cappadocia; and historic Jewish quarters and synagogues in the city of Izmir. Pilgrims and scholars also travel to Greece for its rich religious heritage, including Byzantine monasteries in Thessaly, the city of Kavala (which was the first European city to convert to Christianity), centuries-old synagogues in Athens and Thessalonika, and more. Because these sites are spread out and not always in the guidebooks, an organized tour is a great idea for anyone who wants to focus primarily on religious sites. Aegean Tours (www.aegeantours.com) is a Maryland-based travel agency that arranges travel mostly in Turkey and Greece, and can arrange a personalized religious or heritage tour of the region.

When most people think of religious travel in Europe, the first place that comes to mind is **Italy,** particularly when you're talking about must-see Catholic sites (although there are Jewish quarters in Rome and Venice that should also be at the top of your list). But when following in the footstep of the Reformers, **Germany** is the place to go. Here, the Luther Trail connects the life and works of Martin Luther, including Eisleben, where he was born and died 63 years later; the town of Erfurt, where he studied and was ordained; and Lutherstadt-Wittenberg, the birthplace of the Reformation. With Reformation Tours (www.reformationtours.com), a tour called "Luther in a Nutshell (with a Bit of Bach and Bonhoeffer)" is led by a pastor who takes you on a 12-day tour to those major sites through-

Spiritual Travel

Tapping into your spiritual side doesn't necessarily mean a religious journey. Instead, it could mean taking a vortex tour in Sedona, **Arizona,** or tribal culture tours in areas like **South Dakota** or **Montana.** The Canadian company Sacred Earth Journeys (www.sacredearthjourneys.ca) arranges spiritual travel for transcendence seekers, including year-round yoga retreats in Baja, **Mexico,** in winter and in Torfino, **Vancouver Island,** in summer. You could also try tropical yoga and meditation in southern India, or a transformational yoga workshop in **Tahiti.** The Tree of Life Rejuvenation Center (www. gabrielcousens.com) in Patagonia, Arizona, has various programs that tackle healing and spiritual growth. Or you can find your own inner peace through spa treatments, organic vegetarian food, a labyrinth walk, yoga classes, or hikes in the mountains. Asia Transpacific Journeys (www.asiatranspacific.com) arranges specialty tours that explore retreats, monasteries, and spiritual sites of the **Himalayas.**

out Germany, with a stop in Leipzig to visit the Lutheran church where Bach spent years working as a choir master.

Or head to the **United Kingdom,** where major sites include London's Westminster Abbey, the magnificent Leeds Cathedral in northern England, and one of the only dedicated religious museums in the world, St. Mungo Museum of Religious Art and Life in Glasgow. You can easily create your own religious-themed tour, but Globus also has organized Protestant and Christian tours of the area.

Jewish Heritage Tours

■srael isn't the only destination for travelers looking to explore Jewish history and culture. ARZA World (www.arzaworld.com) leads Jewish heritage tours through **Europe, South America,** and **North Africa.** European stops include the Warsaw Ghetto Memorial, the Jewish Museum in Prague, and memorial services at Auschwitz and Birkenau. The 13-day Wonders of **Spain** tour explores ancient Jewish neighborhoods, offers lectures with scholars in residence, and visits synagogues and Jewish museums in Barcelona, Granada, Codova, and Seville. And if you're digging into your own family's history, the New Jersey–based Routes to Roots (www.routestoroots.com) offers personalized Jewish heritage tours in **Poland, Ukraine, Moldova,** and **Belarus.** They'll actually research your family name in public archives and arrange customized tours to your ancestral town.

THE NORTHERN LIGHTS

The aurora borealis, or northern lights, is created by electrically charged particles emitted from the sun that make the air light up like colored fluorescent lights. For the best chance of viewing them, go north. The thinner air around the magnetic poles is most conducive to the phenomenon, so you want to go to places above 65 degrees north latitude, such as Canada, Alaska, and northern Scandinavia, to catch a glimpse.

Winter is the best season, when nights are longer, but in some areas you can see them year-round. Remember, though, there is no guarantee you'll see the aurora borealis on any given night. Like any other natural phenomena, they are unpredictable and depend on a variety of atmospheric and terrestrial conditions.

UNITED STATES

In **Michigan,** the aurora borealis is sometimes visible on the Keweena Peninsula. Check out the northernmost town on the peninsula, Copper Harbor. Here, you can drive up to the top of Brockway Mountain, one of the best spots to see the lights when there is no moon. At 1,328 feet above sea level, it is the highest scenic roadway between the Rockies and the Alleghenies and has little interference from city lights. There is also excellent bird-watching, wildflowers, and views of Lake Superior from here.

Minnesota's Lake of the Woods separates the United States from Canada, and is about as far north as you can get and still be in the continental United States. Located north of the 48th parallel, it is far removed from urban light and air pollution, and as such is a great place to see the northern lights on a clear winter evening. State Highway 11, also known as the "Waters of the Dancing Sky" Scenic Byway, is a prime viewing spot.

INSIDER'S TIP

The Geophysical Institute at the University of Alaska in Fairbanks tracks aurora borealis updates with a forecast tool that rates the lights on a scale from 0 to 9. www.gi.alaska. edu/AuroraForecast

Fairbanks, **Alaska,** is located under the Auroral Oval, a ring-shaped region around the North Pole. Although the colors span the spectrum of green, red, and purple, the brightest and most common colors are yellow and green. The lights are so active here that you're almost guaranteed to spot them if you stay at least 3 nights and look out during the evening. In fact, the aurora is such an integral part of Fairbanks that a number of hotels offer wake-up calls based on a daily forecast in the local paper's weather section. The best times to catch them are between mid-August and April, particularly in the 2 weeks around the new moon in March. The Ester Dome mountain summit gets you an incredible view of the night sky from horizon to horizon. Getting to the 2,000-foot dome requires a 4-mile climb, or you can drive partway and hike a short distance up.

INTERNATIONAL

One of the best places in North America to experience the aurora borealis is Churchill, **Manitoba,** about 600 miles north of Winnipeg, on the Hudson Bay, which sits directly under an auroral zone. Although the prime viewing time is between January and March, it's thought that there's activity in this region at least 300 nights out of the year. A handful of companies can take you on guided tours along the frozen tundra in heated buggies to view the lights. Frontiers North Adventures (www.frontiersnorth.com) has a 7-day tour called "Northern Lights, Winter Nights," while Natural Habitat Adventures (www.nathab.com) has northern lights tours in February and March.

For an educational experience, Manitoba's Churchill Northern Studies Centre and Road Scholar (formerly Elderhostel) hosts a learning vacation program that focuses on astronomy and the northern lights. You'll learn from the experts in evening lectures followed by nighttime excursions, along with cultural activities and even dogsledding! www.churchillscience.ca

The auroral zone (which constantly shifts in size and location) often hangs over **Greenland,** making for some prime viewing there. Kangerlussuaq, on the west coast of Greenland, is one of the best places to see the northern lights because its mild weather means 300 clear days a year. Many of the tour companies operating in Greenland offer combination northern lights/whale-watching/dog-sledding trips, to take advantage of all the region's natural attractions. The United Kingdom–based Travelling Naturalist (www. naturalist.co.uk) has 11-day sailing expeditions to east Greenland (leaving from Iceland) in September, where you can take in the northern lights and see rare narwhal whales.

Another UK company, Exodus (www.exodus.co.uk), offers 8-day trips based at the settlement of Tasilaq on Ammassalik Island where you can go dogsledding, go ice fishing, build an igloo, and take trips out to icebergs—in addition to seeing the aurora borealis. Want a more DIY experience? Greenland-based WOGAC (World of Greenland Arctic Tours) offers a 1-night excursion to the remote countryside to see the lights, which includes a lecture on ancient aurora mythology (www.wogac.com).

One of the most enchanting ways to get a front row view of the dazzling light display is by taking a coastal cruise. Hurtigruten offers multiday aurora borealis cruises up the Norwegian coast, departing from Bergen, **Norway,** between December and March. You'll sail above the Arctic Circle—but don't worry about getting trapped in the ice. The water is ice free, thanks to the Gulf Stream. During the on-board lecture series, you'll learn about the aurora borealis and also about the city of Tromso, Norway, and the history of the Sami people. www.hurtigruten.us

The little town of Tromso, above the Arctic Circle, is considered one of the best places in the world to see the northern lights. There are literally dozens of tour companies that take visitors on guided tours. Haugens Naturinord offers a Northern Lights Bus that cruises through the tundra all night searching for the best place to see the lights (www.naturinord.no). Kjetil Skogli, a Norwegian photographer, offers popular nighttime "aurora chasing" trips, during

Seeing the northern lights can be a bone-chilling endeavor, but the Churchill Northern Studies Centre has a heated viewing dome. The Aurora Domes (www.tundrainn.com/aurora.html) is an indoor facility located on the tundra that was designed for maximum viewing without having to bundle up.

which he dispenses advice on how to best capture the phenomenon on film (www.kskogli.no). Other great viewing locations in Norway include Alta, Svalbard, and Finnmark.

In South **Iceland,** you don't even have to leave your hotel to get a great view. Hotel Ranga is remote enough that it's uncluttered by light pollution, so the northern night sky offers a spectacular vantage point. Best of all, since the hotel is located in the midst of the Ring of Fire, you can see the lights while relaxing in naturally heated geothermal pools. www.hotelranga.is

The Grand Hotel Reykjavik even invites guests to dine under the northern lights from its 14th-floor terrace, where the windows offer a 360-degree view of the phenomenon. www.grand.is

VOLUNTEER VACATIONS

Volunteering is one of the fastest-growing segments in the travel industry, and with good reason. In our expanding global village, more and more travelers want to get involved and to help others. Helping someone else is, arguably, the best present you can give yourself. And nothing builds better bridges of peace and understanding more than helping hands.

HUMANITARIAN

In the interest of full disclosure: I sit on the boards of two remarkable charitable organizations that also focus—as part of their mission statement—on volunteer vacations: Airline Ambassadors (www.airlineamb.org) and Operation USA (www.opusa.org).

Both organizations are at the forefront of often Herculean humanitarian efforts. Within hours of the earthquake that devastated **Haiti,** Airline Ambassadors had 17 airplanes to bring in medical assistance and 3 million pounds of aid. Founded by a former flight attendant, this not-for-profit organization is comprised primarily of travel industry professionals but is open to anyone. Today it coordinates regular missions to ongoing projects in Haiti, **Vietnam, Cambodia,** and **Mexico,** among many others. It is a leader in combating the ongoing tragedy of human trafficking, provides relief and aid to hard-hit nations, and has made enormous efforts in building sustainable programs so impoverished communities can get a leg up.

After the 2004 Indian Ocean tsunami, Operation USA mobilized

Voluntourism

Voluntourism is one of the fastest-growing areas of niche travel. And the good news is, it's easier than ever to give back to the local community. The Four Seasons has a program called 10 Million Trees, which invites guests to arrange a volunteer activity during their stay. Fairmont Hotels & Resorts has a program called Take Root, which is aimed at getting guests out into nature. At the Fairmont **San Francisco,** guests can volunteer with the Golden Gate National Parks Conservancy, doing everything from building trails to planting trees. The Ritz-Carlton **New Orleans** will help you coordinate a volunteer activity, whether it's rebuilding homes with Habitat for Humanity or working with the community through the St. Bernard Project. But you don't have to stay in a high-end hotel to get a similar experience. All it takes is a phone call to a community organization to arrange your own volunteer vacation no matter where you stay.

quickly to bring relief to countries like **Sri Lanka,** the southeast coast of **India,** and **Thailand.** On the island of Phuket, the program funded and implemented the addition of a building to an existing orphanage to accommodate newly orphaned children. Its small-group volunteer programs tend to be fund-raising trips to see projects in action, and you can arrange to get hands-on experience as well, whether it's distributing food to Japanese families still living in temporary housing or painting a school in **Haiti.**

Here are some of the other great organizations that offer amazing volunteer vacation experiences.

GlobeAware offers 1-week volunteer vacations that combine hands-on experiences with cultural activities. To get the most for your travel dollar, look for destinations like **Mexico, Laos,** and **Cambodia,** where you can get accommodations, meals, excursions, and volunteer activities for about $1,200 a week. Projects vary, but in Cambodia, you might teach English at a Buddhist school or get involved with a children's center in Luang Prabang. www.glo beaware.org

Roadmonkey was founded by a former *New York Times* war correspondent and offers adventure travel with a purpose. Its first expedition was to **Vietnam,** and volunteers continue with projects in the country, including building playhouses, greenhouses, and sustainable community gardens in impoverished local communities. www.roadmonkey.net

I-to-i Volunteering coordinates with more than 500 volunteer projects around the world, working with in-country coordinators

INSIDER'S TIP

Don't know what to do or where to go? Go to sites like VolunteerMatch.com and GoVoluntouring.com to see what opportunities are out there.

who support volunteers and liaise with local project leaders. Two of its longest-running projects have been in **Sri Lanka,** where you can do community work with local children, and in **Ecuador,** where there are opportunities with communities, conservation, and wildlife preservation. www.i-to-i.com

Formerly known as Elderhostel, Road Scholar focuses on learning programs, a handful of which include volunteer opportunities for the 50-plus crowd. That might include tutoring on a Navajo reservation in **Arizona** or in rural **Bolivia,** cultural and historical preservation, and marine conservation. www.roadscholar.org

United Planet brings volunteers to a variety of programs worldwide, including environmental and wildlife conservation, community development, and health care. There is also a significant cultural immersion aspect, with homestays and language classes during your program. www.unitedplanet.org

Habitat for Humanity's Global Village involves building homes and sightseeing everywhere from **New Orleans** to **Thailand.** www.habitat.org

Global Volunteers has programs worldwide, including several humanitarian projects right here in the United States. You can assist with community development and labor projects in **Montana**

Volunteer Locally

A volunteer vacation doesn't have to take place overseas. You've heard about working with elephants in India and Thailand. But did you know that there's also an elephant sanctuary in Hohenwald, **Tennessee**? Visitors are invited to participate in volunteer days to help at the facility. Turtle conservation is a common volunteer experience in Costa Rica, but if you prefer to stay closer to home, how about Barnegat Bay, **New Jersey**? This area is home to terrapin diamondback turtles, and there are ample opportunities to help out with Earth-watch Institute and other organizations. The Peace River Refuge and Ranch in **Florida** has a variety of exotic animals. Now, keep in mind, untrained volunteers are unlikely to interact with the animals, but there are plenty of ways to help out.

with the Blackfeet Tribal Nation, teach conversational English to immigrant families in **Minnesota,** or help transform former coal company houses in **West Virginia** into low-income housing. www. globalvolunteers.org

Projects Abroad Pro, a branch of Projects Abroad, is designed for professionals to use their skills in a volunteer capacity. That could involve doing social work in an orphanage, providing medical help in area hospitals, or practicing business development for impoverished communities. www.projects-abroad-pro.org

G Adventures and its nonprofit sustainable development arm, Planeterra, have projects around the world that rely on volunteer help. That includes working with Argentine youth to learn sustainable farming skills, animal conservation in the Peruvian **Amazon,** and joining community projects in **South Africa**'s Cape Peninsula. www.gadventures.com

ANIMALS AND WILDLIFE

African Impact has a multitude of volunteer programs throughout **Africa,** including lion rehabilitation programs on private game farms. You actually get hands-on interaction with the lions, whether it's feeding (or bottle-feeding the cubs), tracking and research, or on-site maintenance projects. www.african impact.com

On the Big Island, Three Ring Ranch is the only licensed exotic animal sanctuary in **Hawaii.** You can arrange a day or two of volunteering, where you might just end up working around animals like zebras, reptiles, and native Hawaiian birds. www.threeringranch.org

At the Best Friends Animal Society in southern **Utah,** one of the largest animal sanctuaries in the country, you can help out for a few hours or a few days by feeding, cleaning, and walking rescued animals like dogs, rabbits, horses, and potbellied pigs. You can't spend the night on the property, but they'll provide you with a list of nearby hotels and guest cottages. www.bestfriends.org

The Avocet Conservation Project in central Queensland, **Australia,** takes you deep into the bush to track, monitor, and analyze data to help protect the Flashjack wallaby population, along with other native creatures like gray kangaroos and wallaroos. www.wildmob.org

NATURE CONSERVANCY

The American Hiking Society relies on volunteers to help with trail maintenance and repair, from installing wildlife viewing platforms to pulling tree stumps and reconstructing drainages. College students can join short-term projects in the Alternative Spring Break program, while longer-term programs take place in environments like **Yosemite National Park, Valley Forge,** and **Flathead National Forest.** It's also one of the more affordable programs out there, about $250 for the week including meals and transportation. www.americanhiking.org

The Appalachian Mountain Club has volunteer trail clean-up programs in several places, from the White Mountains in **New Hampshire** to the **Virgin Islands.** www.outdoors.org

Based in France, La Sabranenque has been putting together historical restoration projects in rural **Mediterranean** locations for more than 40 years. Summer volunteer programs run from June to September and focus on preserving medieval villages. What's really neat about this program is that you can get a hands-on education with traditional building techniques used in rural architecture, like stone masonry, paving, and dry stone walling. Participating is as simple as paying the deposit and getting yourself to Avignon, Provence. www.sabranenque.com

Get involved with **New Zealand**'s Department of Conservation through Pacific Discovery. A monthlong voluntourism gig takes you from one end of New Zealand to the other, doing tasks like planting trees, controlling pests, building trails, and preserving forests. Of course, it's not all work, as you also have the opportunity to go cav-

State Parks Voluntourism

Even state parks offer short- and long-term volunteer opportunities. Several of **Arizona**'s state parks offer one-day opportunities, including trail restoration at Dead Horse Ranch in Cottonwood, or volunteer positions at park festivals and parades. Palo Duro Canyon in **Texas** has longer-term positions for camp hosts, which involves assisting guests and helping with park maintenance. In exchange, volunteers get free camping accommodations with water and electricity hookups. The same deal applies to many state parks in **North Carolina,** where campsite hosts get to stay for free. On the East Coast, the **New York** Restoration Project hosts clean-up and maintenance days at a state park in the South Bronx. At Minnewaska State Park Preserve in Kerhonkson, New York, volunteer hikers, bikers, and skiers help patrol the park. In many cases, finding volunteer gigs is as easy as contacting the state's office of parks and recreation or department of environmental conservation.

ing, rafting, rock climbing, mountain biking, and skiing. Other conservation programs take place in Australia and parts of Asia. www.pacificdiscovery.org

World Wide Opportunities on Organic Farms (WWOOF) connects travelers with farmers around the world. You work about 4 to 6 hours a day in exchange for free room and board. Most work consists of basic farm chores, like working with animals, cultivating vegetables, and repairing fences. Depending on the farm, you may also find unique activities like cheese making, helping out in a vineyard, or even working in environmental education and sustainable living centers or temples. There is no central agency but rather a different WWOOF branch for each country. In Romania, foreigners pay 10 euros to access a list of small-scale farmers who are seeking help in the fields and inside their homes. www.wwoof.org

'Ahahui Mālama I Ka Lōkahi on the island of **Oahu** is converting a 12-acre state park reserve area (Nā Pōhaku o Hauwahine) into a native dryland forest. Anyone is invited to volunteer for an afternoon or a short stint, which usually involves plenty of weeding and planting in a spectacularly beautiful environment. www.ahahui.net

Stay in a Lighthouse

If you plan properly, have a sense of adventure, and don't mind some of the best water views imaginable, then you can spend the night in a lighthouse. It is one of the more interesting hotel alternatives available, and you can even help preserve history in the process.

Many lighthouses are no longer considered officially functional by government authorities. Technology and modern navigational aids have replaced them. But that there are a growing number of trusts and nonprofit organizations dedicated to preserving these true beacons of light. Many of these groups are reopening lighthouses and keepers' cottages as bed-and-breakfasts.

To find a lighthouse near you (or near where you are going) that offers overnight accommodations, check out www.stayatalighthouse.com. It's weighted heavily toward New England but also includes lighthouses in places as far-flung as Ireland, Jamaica, Croatia, and Mauritius. Some allow you to actually stay in the lighthouse tower, while others allow you to stay in former keepers' cottages on the grounds.

UNITED STATES

Looking for a bit of history in your stay? The Lighthouse Bed & Breakfast, on Lake Superior in Two Harbors, **Minnesota** (25 miles north of Duluth), is the oldest operating lighthouse in the state. Dating back to 1892, it is on the National Register of Historic Places. Guests are treated to views of northern Lake Superior, with plenty of outdoor activities available. Local history buffs will appreciate the on-site museum, the restored Light Tower, the assistant keeper's building, and the Frontenac Pilot House, which contains displays about historical shipwrecks in the area. If you want a hands-on experience, you can perform light-keeper duties during your stay, like checking portholes, raising and lowering the flag, noting weather in a log, sweeping sidewalks, record keeping, and making sure the light is rotating properly. www.lighthousebb.org

In fact, hands-on experiences are a key factor in many lighthouse stays. At Browns Point Lighthouse in Tacoma, **Washington,** you can participate in the honorary keeper program, in which you track the weather conditions and prepare the cottage and museum for public tours. www.pointsnortheast.org

At the Rose Island Lighthouse in Newport, **Rhode Island,** you can take part in a weeklong training program in which you spend a few hours a day learning to raise and lower the flag at sunrise and sunset, take weather readings, do seasonal chores, and do light cleaning. www.roseislandlighthouse.org

If staying on a budget is your goal, head to the Pigeon Point Lighthouse in Pescadero, **California** (27 miles north of Santa Cruz). It's actually a low-cost youth hostel run by California State Parks. The 115-foot cliffside structure overlooking the Pacific Ocean has guided mariners since 1872. The tower has been closed to the public since 2002, but you can stay in the former Coast Guard family houses on the premises, which have been converted to dorm-style rooms; private, single, or double rooms; and private family rooms, all with shared bathrooms. The cost to stay next to one of the tallest lighthouses in America: as low as $25 per night. www.parks.ca.gov/?page_id=533

Talk about off the beaten path: At the Keeper's House Inn in Isle au Haut, **Maine,** they're not kidding about the "no electricity, no phone, no television" concept. It's their selling point. Innkeepers Jeff and Judi Burke equip you with oil lanterns and candles to lead you through the dark nights. The Burkes collect food from the sea and from their organic garden, make their own diesel fuel from vegetable oil, generate power from the wind, and even extract drinking water from the sea. This is an entirely undeveloped area, which means that to reach the lighthouse, you actually have to take a mail boat! It's worth it, though, because you'll be privy to a beautifully unobstructed view of the ocean and its marine life. www.keepershouse.com

INTERNATIONAL

The Lighthouse Capo-Spartivento in Cagliari, on the southernmost tip of Sardinia, **Italy,** was built in 1856 by the Italian navy. Now it's a small luxury guesthouse, with 550 rooms filled with Murano glass chandeliers and views all the way across the Mediterranean. Two of the apartment-style rooms have glass ceilings to allow guests to view the stars. The hotel is the epitome of luxury, with three in-house chefs, a huge wine cellar, and wild private beaches.

The Adriatic coast of **Croatia** is positively littered with lighthouses, which dot the many offshore islands. Veli Rat, built on the island of Dugi Otok in 1859, is a real standout. Legend has it that the lighthouse walls contain thousands of egg whites, which supposedly make them more resistant to the wind and the sea, and insulate them from the blazing sun in the summer. But the setting is what's really special about Veli Rat. Located on the southwestern cape of the island, it's surrounded by pine forests and beaches, and has spectacular views from the 130-foot tower. Summer vacationers use the lighthouse as a base for hiking, fishing, and exploring the island.

ACKNOWLEDGMENTS

The *Best Places for Everything* involved, of course, the best people. Stephen Perrine at Rodale believed in this book from day one and encouraged me to write it.

My research team worked tirelessly to investigate, source, and fact-check each item on my list. Led by Karen Elowitt from her base in St. Thomas and by my managing editor Sarika Chawla in Los Angeles, the team included Jessica Kate Soberman, Tatiana Rodriguez, Lily Kosner, Cully Hartfeld Schneider, Karen Hollish, Corinne DeWitt, Collette Torunyan, Steven Breazeale, and Gail Alexander. The overriding lesson: It's always 9 a.m. somewhere in the world, which means that for many months of hard work, sleep was either not an option or not easily scheduled.

This book would not have happened without invaluable support from my editor, Ursula Cary, and the design and production team at Rodale: Nancy Bailey, George Karabotsos, Mark Michaelson, and Wendy Gable.

Last, but certainly not least, thanks goes to Lyn Benjamin in New York, as well as my support staff in Los Angeles, Loretta Copeland and Andrea Pennywell, who were (and continue to be) instrumental in making sure I get from point A to point Z . . . and everywhere in between.

INDEX

Underscored page references indicate boxed text.

England. *See also* London, England
  amusement parks, 363
  educational travel, 296, 310
  fireworks, 428
  food and drink, 201, 207–8, 215,
    278–79
  literary travel/tours, 319
  outdoor activities, 22–23, 63, 191–92
  photo tours, 326
  shopping, 334, 346
  spiritual travel, 465
  wildlife viewing, 89
Equine tour companies, 68, 70. *See also*
  Horseback riding
Estancias, 25, 26, 29, 44
Ethiopia, 186
Eyre Peninsula, 91

F
Fabric, shopping for, 348–49
Fairbanks, Alaska, 408
Fall foliage, 30–39, 68, 74, 166, 415
Family friendly travel
  educational, 295–98
  facilities geared for, 60, 166, 171,
    362–66
  festivals, 74
  fireworks, 426–29
  food and drink, 219, 260–61
  outdoor activities, 26, 59, 82, 160,
    180–81
  shopping, 332–33
  trains, 420–21
  wildlife viewing, 89
Farallon Islands, 91
Farmers'/food markets
  Asia, 260–61, 359
  Canada, 275
  Europe, 257, 270, 279, 335
  US, 247–48, 265, 267, 276, 278, 279
Farm experiences, 283, 284, 285, 477
Fashion, 330–31, 339–41
Ferries, sightseeing by, 450–52
Fertility treatments, 402–3, 405
Festivals
  biking, 98–99, 199
  bird-watching/wildlife, 3, 7, 93
  boat races, 15

fireworks, 428
food and drink, 198, 207, 216, 225,
  253, 256, 257
hot air ballooning, 74
literary-themed, 317
skydiving, 170
Fez, Morocco, 358–59
Fighting, training for, 309–11
Fiji, 13, 111
Fiji, Mount, 432
Finger Lakes, 240
Finland, 313, 347–48
Fiordland National Park, 64
Fireworks, 426–29
Fish-and-chips, 278–79
Fishing, 40–51, 46, 261–62. *See also*
  Seafood
Flagstaff, Arizona, 122
Flea markets, 351–59. *See also* Markets
Florence, Italy, 343, 395
Florida
  amusement parks, 364
  fireworks, 429
  food and drink, 242, 259, 260, 277, 384
  outdoor activities
    boating, 17–18
    fishing, 45–46, 49
    golf, 54
    hang gliding, 166
    water sports, 79, 108, 110, 184
    ziplines, 190
  sightseeing, 392, 432–34, 453
  spiritual travel, 462
  wildlife viewing, 3, 7, 91, 92
Florida Keys, 46, 50
Flowers and wildflowers
  Asia, 459
  Australia, 162
  Europe, 23, 355, 416, 458–60
  US, 294, 415, 456–58
Fly-fishing, 43–45
"Flying foxes," 188
Foefie slides, 188
Food and drink. *See also* Farmers'/food
  markets; *specific foods*
  expensive cuisine, 267
  luggage restrictions and, 41
  outdoor activities and, 27–28, 49–51,
    181

New Zealand
  educational travel, 293
  food and drink, 215, 245, 278
  outdoor activities
    biking, 100–101
    boating, 12
    bungee jumping, 151
    fishing, 44–45, 49, 51
    golf, 56
    hiking, 64, 65
    horseback riding, 69
    skydiving, 169
    water sports, 84–85, 184, 185
    winter sports, 117
    zorbing, 191
  shopping, 347
  sightseeing, 438, 440, 446
  trains, 422
  volunteer vacations, 476–77
  wildlife viewing, 7, 90, 145
Ngee Ann City, Singapore, 333
Niagara Falls, 12
Nighttime activities
  ghostly adventures, 380–81, 381
  outdoor activities, 107, 189, 190–91
  sky-watching, 121–25, 158, 466–70
Normandy, 374
North Carolina
  educational travel, 300
  fall foliage, 34–36
  food and drink, 243
  outdoor activities
    fishing, 44
    hang gliding, 165
    rock climbing, 172
    water sports, 110, 127–28, 135,
      182, 183
  sightseeing, 431, 451
Northern Forest Canoe Trail, 80
Northern lights, 158, 466–70
Northern Neck, 79
  Norway, aurora borealis, 469–70
  Norway, food and drink, 261–62
Norway
  outdoor activities, 118–19, 157
  trains, 421–22
  views, 134–35
Nova Scotia, 35, 39, 51, 170, 254,
  284

O
Oahu
  outdoor activities, 83, 110, 127, 167,
    169
  themed tours, 376–77
  views, 431
  volunteer vacations, 477–78
OARS, 82, 179, 181
Oaxaca, 129, 212, 284–85
Observation decks, 393–97
Oceanic Society, 91
Oceano Dunes State Vehicular
  Recreation Area, 160
Ocoee River, 182
Odakyu, 336
Off-roading, 159–63, 162, 437–38
Offshore Sailing School, 17–18
Ohio, 356, 381, 420
Oklahoma, 7, 33–34, 175–77, 381
Old Saybrook, Connecticut, 384–85
Olive oil, 274
Olympic National Park, 144
Omo River, 186
Open Garden Squares Weekend, 460
Operation USA, 472–73
Oregon
  amusement parks, 363
  food and drink, 97, 197, 199, 256, 274
  outdoor activities, 12, 53, 97, 140,
    172, 181
  shopping, 368
  storm-watching, 175
  wildlife viewing, 146
Orlando, Florida, 166, 364, 462
Orthopedic procedures, 402, 405
Ossuaries, 374–75
Ouachita National Forest, 33–34
Outer Banks, 127–28, 135, 431
Outlet store shopping, 333–34
Oysters, 278

P
Pacific Yachting and Sailing, 18
Pacuare River, 185
Paddleboarding, 78–87, 126
PADI, 109
Paintings, shopping for, 346–47
Pakiri Beach, 69